PUSHING BOUNDARIES

In memory of my parents, Edward James Morrison (1917–2001) and Patricia Anne Morrison (née Crawley, 1928–2005): with immense gratitude for a household of books, for fostering a love of learning, and for a lifetime of unfailing support.

PUSHING BOUNDARIES

NEW ZEALAND PROTESTANTS AND OVERSEAS MISSIONS 1827–1939

Hugh Morrison

OTAGO
UNIVERSITY PRESS

BV
3665
. M67
2016

Published by Otago University Press
Level 1, 398 Cumberland Street
Dunedin, New Zealand
university.press@otago.ac.nz
www.otago.ac.nz/press

First published 2016
Copyright © Hugh Morrison

Editor: Paul Sorrell
Design/layout: Christine Buess
Index: Diane Lowther

Cover photograph: 'Mr. [George] and Mrs [Jane] McKenzie, New Zealand
[with Pandita Ramabai in India]', in Helen S. Dyer, *Pandita Ramabai: A great
life in Indian missions* (London: Pickering & Inglis, n.d.), facing p. 41. This
photograph was originally published in the *Otago Witness*, 20 January 1909.

Printed in New Zealand by Printstop Ltd, Wellington

Contents

Abbreviations

ASCU	Australasian Students Christian Union
BIM	Bolivian Indian Mission
BMS	Baptist Missionary Society
BWMU	Baptist Women's Missionary Union
CE	Christian Endeavour
CIM	China Inland Mission
CMS	Church Missionary Society
FMC	Foreign Missions Committee [Presbyterian Church of New Zealand]
LMS	London Missionary Society
MWMU	Methodist Women's Missionary Union
NCC	National Council of Churches
NZBMS	New Zealand Baptist Missionary Society
NZBTI	New Zealand Bible Training Institute
NZCMA/S	New Zealand Church Missionary Association/Society
NZJH	*New Zealand Journal of History*
PCNZ	Presbyterian Church of New Zealand
PIVM	Poona and Indian Village Mission
PRC	Presbyterian Research Centre (Archives)
PWMU	Presbyterian Women's Missionary Union
SCM	Student Christian Movement
SPG	Society for the Propagation of the Gospel
SVMFM	Student Volunteer Movement for Foreign Missions
WCTU	Women's Christian Temperance Union
WSCF	World Student Christian Fellowship

Preface

FOR THE LAST DECADE, New Zealand's historical involvement as a missionary-sending nation has been my constant research companion. It began initially as a doctoral thesis at Massey University (Albany Campus) under the careful and enthusiastic supervision of Professor Peter Lineham and the Revd Dr Allan Davidson (St John's College and University of Auckland), in whose collective debt I will always remain. Their ongoing collegiality and support is deeply appreciated. The initial thesis was supported by the award of a Massey University Doctoral Scholarship between 2001 and 2004. More recently, the project has moved in various directions as I have followed up emerging research questions. Further funding from the University of Otago (a University Research Grant, 2009–10; a Humanities Research Grant, 2011; and study leave in 2012) enabled me to conduct focused research on children and missions, and to complete the initial manuscript.

The chapters that follow are road-markers of this unfolding journey and indicate my wider concern to strategically situate the discussion of New Zealand religious history both historically and historiographically. In this book I am trying to model a helpful way of doing justice to the theological or religious elements of this topic – so easily missed or misunderstood, but so important for the participants under scrutiny here – while placing these elements in wider contexts of historical period, thought and practice. Religious history matters, but it does not exist in a vacuum, and I hope that this book will be a significant and timely contribution in this respect.

I am indebted to more people than I can mention here. However, I do want to acknowledge the following, while apologising to those not mentioned. Both John Roxborogh (Dunedin) and John Hitchen (Auckland) originally pointed me towards this research area, albeit unwittingly at times, and the resulting PhD thesis was indebted in no small part to their initial collective influence. In the postdoctoral phase, two years spent teaching courses on social and cultural history and on historiography, in the Department of History at the University of Waikato, were fundamentally important in reconfiguring my thinking with respect to themes and connections, and I especially want to thank ex-colleagues Giselle Byrnes, Catharine Coleborne, Peter Gibbons and Jeanine Graham. Then there are a host of other colleagues in a wide range of locations who have all contributed in ways big and small: Geoffrey Troughton (Victoria University of Wellington); Tony Ballantyne, Tom Brooking, Alison Clarke, Tim Cooper, Angela McCarthy, Helen May, Lachy Paterson, Murray Rae, John Stenhouse and Angela Wanhalla (University of Otago); Stuart Piggin, Malcolm Prentis and Ian Welch (Australia); Esther Breitenbach, Deborah Gaitskell, Elizabeth Koepping, Emily Manktelow, Mary Clare Martin, Cathy Ross, Brian Stanley, John Stuart, Andrew Walls and Emma Wild-Wood (UK); Jonathan Bonk (USA); Kristine Alexander and Rhonda Semple (Canada); and Felicity Jensz (Germany). Over the last eight years I have deeply appreciated the whanaungatanga of my many valued colleagues in the College of Education at the University of Otago. They have provided me with the stimulus and encouragement to explore further the myriad complex connections between religion, missions, children and education that mark my ongoing focus for teaching, research and writing. In particular, they note that I seem to enjoy what I am doing, which I do!

Of course, these acknowledgements would be incomplete without reference to the staff of the libraries and archives on which my research is based. Without them little could have been achieved. In particular, I value the sustained interest, support and collegiality (past and present) of Yvonne Wilkie, Anne Jackman, Eva Garbut, Andrew Smith and Myke Tymons (Presbyterian Research Centre, Dunedin); Judith Bright and Eddie Sun (John Kinder Theological Library, St John's Theological College, Auckland); Lesley Utting (formerly) and Liz Tisdall (Ayson Clifford Library, Carey Baptist College, Auckland); Martha Smalley and Joan Duffy (Special Collections, Yale Divinity School Library, Yale University, New Haven, US); and of both Bob and Marcia Arnold (formerly) and Tim Geysbeek (SIM International Resource Centre, Fort Mill, South Carolina, US). I also acknowledge invaluable help from the following institutions and access to their holdings: the Alexander Turnbull Library, Wellington; the Hocken Library, University of Otago; the Auckland War Memorial Museum Library; the Anglican Diocese of Auckland Archives; the Deane Memorial Library, Laidlaw College, Auckland (formerly the Bible College of New

Zealand); the Methodist Church of New Zealand Archives, Christchurch; the Salvation Army Heritage and Archives Centre, Upper Hutt; the J.W. Searle Library, Melbourne School of Theology, Australia (formerly the Bible College of Victoria); the Cambridge Centre for Christianity World-wide library (formerly the Henry Martyn Centre), Westminster College, Cambridge University, UK; and the Centre for the Study of World Chris-tianity, School of Divinity, University of Edinburgh, UK.

Permission has been kindly granted to cite or reproduce material held by the following institutions: the Hocken Library, University of Otago; the John Kinder Theological Library, St John's Theological College; the Ayson Clifford Library, Carey Baptist College; the Presbyterian Research Centre (Archives), Dunedin; and Special Collections, Yale Divinity School Library. Furthermore, permission has been granted to reproduce and adapt material of my own that was originally published as follows: 'Antipodeans abroad: Trends in the writing of New Zealand mission history', *Journal of Reli-gious History* 30, no. 1 (2006): 77–93 (part of the Introduction); 'It is our bounden duty: Theological contours of New Zealand's missionary move-ment, 1890–1930', *International Bulletin of Missionary Research* 29, no. 3 (2005): 123–28 (part of Chapter Two); '"A Great Australasian Scheme": Australian influences on New Zealand's emerging Protestant missionary movement, 1885–1922', *Fides et Historia* 38, no. 2 (2006): 87–102 (part of Chapter Three); '"We carry the joyous news that has made us free": New Zealand missionaries, the Bolivian Indian Mission and global engagement, 1908–1930', *New Zealand Journal of History* 39, no. 1 (2005): 39–56 (parts of Chapter Five); 'But we are concerned with a Greater Imperium: The New Zealand Protestant missionary movement and the British Empire, 1870–1930', *Social Sciences and Missions/Sciences Sociales et Missions* 21, no. 1 (2008): 97–127 (parts of Chapter Six); '"Little vessels" or "little soldiers": New Zealand Protestant children, foreign missions, religious pedagogy and empire, c. 1880s–1930s', *Paedagogica Historica*, 47, no. 3 (2011): 303–21 (Chapter Seven); and '"In seeking the welfare of others we are benefitted ourselves": The reflexive impact of overseas missions on churches in Aotearoa–New Zealand', *Stimulus* 16, no. 3 (2008): 30–37 (part of Chapter Eight).

Additional material relevant to this book's content and argument was also presented and trialled at the following venues: the 'Trans-Tasman Missions History' conference in Canberra (October 2004); the 'Empires of Religion' conference in Dublin (June 2006); conferences of the New

Zealand Historical Association in Wellington (November 2007) and Palmerston North (November 2009); the Spring Conference of the American Society of Church History, Montreal (April 2009); the 'Christian Missions and Global History' seminar group at the Institute of Historical Research, University of London (June 2010); the monthly seminar programme of the Cambridge Centre for Christianity Worldwide (formerly the Henry Martyn Centre), Westminster College, Cambridge University (June 2010); the annual 'Yale–Edinburgh History of Christian Missions and World Christianity Group' conference, Edinburgh (July 2010); and the weekly 'World Christianity' research seminar series held at the School of Divinity, University of Edinburgh (2012). I am grateful for the opportunities given to me by each of these groups.

In bringing this book to completion, I am in debt to the following wonderful people: the constructive critique and advice of the peer reviewer, which significantly enhanced my overall view of the book's broader significance; Rachel Scott's goodwill, generosity, enthusiasm and guidance as publisher at Otago University Press; my editor Paul Sorrell for his careful, interested and meticulous reading of the manuscript; and the valued expertise of Imogen Coxhead, Christine Buess and Diane Lowther. This book is dedicated to the memory of my parents, Edward and Patricia Morrison. They fostered a lifelong love of books and they valued education as both an intellectual and pragmatic pursuit. As Presbyterian children in Dunedin and Oamaru during the 1920s and 1930s, they also lived some of what I have written about here. While my father did not live to see me finish my doctorate, my mother did, and her attendance at my graduation day in 2005 on the sunny north shore of Auckland will be forever memorable for us all. My brother Stuart and sister Pamela and extended family members have all been generous in their personal support over more recent years. As always, however, it is my wife Anne who deserves my most heartfelt thanks. You support me, believe in me, listen to me, advise me, wave me off on yet another research or conference trip, and then carry on regardless. There are not enough words to express my gratitude. I am deeply and forever grateful.

Hugh Morrison, 2015

Putting Overseas Missions in Context

Saturday November 14 1896

I have been agreeably surprised with India thus far. The Sahara of my dream is more like a paradise in reality. The climate is agreeable. The foliage is very fine. The skies are pretty and the natives are far superior and more civilized than I had imagined … Coolies and bullock 'garis' were in great demand, particularly the latter, and the one I had to do with was a miserable affair. The luggage would not stay on. The bullocks would jib and when moved, would go dreadfully slow – terrible business. However, we are all arrived safely at the station, where we are to remain until the new house is built at Chandpur. And now we trust and pray that God will give us strength temporal and spiritual to learn the language successfully and in all our dealings with the people receive wisdom from on high – thus, 'under His shadow, we shall live among the heathen'. (Lam.4v20) … Pray ye the Lord of the Harvest to thrust forth more labourers.[1]

JOHN TAKLE, THE WRITER of these words, arrived in New Zealand from England as a teenager with his family in 1884. He was one of the thousands of British and European migrants who populated the colony in the last three decades of the nineteenth century. The family settled in Wellington, where John eventually worked as a clerk for Thomas Cook and Sons and where he joined the Vivian Street Baptist Church. In 1894, at age 24, he applied for missionary service in East Bengal with the recently formed New Zealand Baptist Missionary Society (NZBMS). He was duly accepted. Replete with two years' ministry training and an elaborate farewell certificate from Vivian Street Baptist Church, John set off, full of confidence, for India on 30 September 1896. On board ship, after his initial departure, John reflected in his diary on the differences between his own enthusiastic send-off and that of the English Baptist missionary William Carey a century earlier. In John's imagination, Carey and companions had left England 'silently and alone', yet with a strong sense that they were not alone. 'How different today!' remarked Takle. 'Thousands of sympathizers attended the farewell gatherings, including quite a number of ministers. … Truly, foreign missions are not a failure.' Two years later he married Maude Beavis, also of Wellington. Together they lived and worked in East Bengal until ill health finally forced them back to New Zealand in 1924. He returned as a well-respected figure within New Zealand Baptist circles and as a noted Western missionary thinker and writer on Islam.[2]

John Takle's somewhat inflated words of optimism, both at departure from New Zealand and on arrival in India, reflected the growing Protestant enthusiasm for 'foreign' or overseas[3] missions that emerged in colonial New Zealand from the late nineteenth century onwards, and which is the focus of this book. As it blossomed, this movement resounded with all the cultural brashness and confidence that marked the global advance of both Christianity and European civilisation during the nineteenth and early twentieth centuries. At the same time, it was underscored by a deeply seated sense of Christian obligation and sacrifice that thrust its participants out into the wider world. Here, cultural self-confidence was balanced by an essentially theological or religious world view. John and Maude together were among some 1000 Protestants who departed New Zealand as missionaries in the period up to 1939.[4] This was a modest figure when set against the larger numbers of British, European and North American missionaries in the same period, but it was significant given the relatively small size of the national population in those years.[5] In turn, these men and women were increasingly supported by the full spectrum of Christian denominations and a growing raft of missionary groups and organisations. Roman Catholic New Zealanders also went as missionaries or enthusiastically supported church missionary activity. The rhetoric was often similar, but structural and archival differences mean that the Catholic story needs to be told separately. While the sentiments and motivations varied, colonial Protestants were bound by a commonly held belief that Christianity's spiritual and physical benefits should be globally communicated and shared. Denominational statistics indicate that these initial decades formed a platform for even greater growth in numbers and budgets after World War II. Relatively high rates of missionary participation were sustained across the Protestant denominations until at least the 1980s. A recent statistical survey continues to rank New Zealand highly as a major supplier and recipient of Christian missionaries, both in regional and global terms.[6]

This book aims to promote a better understanding of the emergence and early development of this phenomenon, which was long held to be normative by most Protestant denominations and churches, but whose shape has undergone significant change in recent years. While I accept that what happened in New Zealand was intrinsically part of a larger movement among European, British and North American churches in the same period, I also argue that what emerged in New Zealand was as much home-grown as it was derivative. Therefore, in this book my brief is to examine aspects of the modern Protestant missionary phenomenon from the perspective of a small British colonial society at the physical margins of the world which, almost from its inception, was simultaneously a receiving and sending missionary nation. New Zealand, as a colonial and later national entity, emerged out of a negotiated treaty (Te Tiriti o Waitangi / The Treaty of Waitangi) signed between indigenous Māori and the British Crown in 1840. By this time, many Māori had adopted Protestant or Roman Catholic forms of Christianity introduced more formally by missionaries from 1814. Yet from 1840 onwards European settlement followed, further disrupting and complicating indigenous ways of life. As in other British settler colonies, cultural encounter and European settlement also served to transplant or to reshape the many familiar forms of mid-nineteenth-century British and European Christianity.[7] Within a generation, modest numbers of settlers and a handful of Māori began to move overseas as Protestant missionaries in their own right, especially to the South West Pacific and to South Asia. By the end of the nineteenth century this trickle had become a sustained flow.

Previously, this phenomenon has been studied and written about in a somewhat piecemeal and insular fashion. The overall New Zealand experience now needs a much broader interpretation. One of the underlying arguments of this book is that thinking about, support for and involvement in overseas missions was an integral facet of settler Protestant Christianity. Indeed, these concerns became an increasingly important marker of emerging settler Christian identity in the late nineteenth and early twentieth centuries. Scholarship in the field of New Zealand religious history is alive and well. It is practised by a significant bloc of specialist historians of religion and is increasingly integrated into the work of other academic and public historians. Lively historiographical debate and innovative research are both equally evident.[8] Until recently, however, this overseas missionary element has not always been integrated effectively into the writing of New Zealand's religious history,[9] and its theological dimensions have not been well understood. This gap potentially impoverishes our religious understanding of the past and obscures the important and dynamic ways in which settler religion was broadly and intricately connected to or shaped by international networks, thinking and practice. Therefore, this book sets the New Zealand context against the canvas of wider historical and historiographical issues and perspectives, through a series of linked essays that focus on representative denominational (Anglican, Baptist and Presbyterian) and non-denominational missions. The primary emphasis is not on the details of or information about New Zealand's overseas missionary involvement. That is another book. Rather, in this book I emphasise the ways in which colonial missionary support and involvement was historically linked, among other things, to issues of religious, cultural, national and global historiography; imperial expansion; cultural interchanges; global linkages; the reflex impact on domestic religion and society; religious, theological and attitudinal formation; religious identity; and gender roles in public religion. In these terms, it is a history of New Zealand and of New Zealanders, with particular regard to their place (both real and imagined) in the wider world. This story of global engagement throws further light on New Zealand's emergence as a nascent society doubly shaped by local and global influences.

Given this emphasis, the book offers a perspective that is significant for at least three reasons. While these will be explored more fully in the chapters that follow they are worth introducing here. In the first place, this study is one of only a few monographs that attempt to describe, explain or contextualise the modern missionary phenomenon from the perspective of either a single sending nation-state or of a colonial settler society. Second, the book presents the New Zealand case as an example of how the missionary movement was expressed and re-applied by a small colonial Australasian society with strong linkages to Britain and to North America. As a result, it attempts to contribute to a globalised interpretation of New Zealand's history. Third, it engages with the current scholarly interest in the relationship between religion, missions and empire, particularly with regard to the

British or Anglo world. Again, the perspective offered is that of an apparently peripheral society that was geographically distanced from, but culturally or mentally linked to, the British metropole.

The writing of New Zealand's mission history

In 1991 historian Allan Davidson sounded something of a lament when he drew attention to the dearth of serious historical reflection and analysis of New Zealand's involvement in overseas missions.[10] He contended that 'this neglect has been unfortunate, because missionaries have been on the frontiers of cultural interaction and there is much that can be learned from their experience. Negative stereotyping of missionary activity and uncritical adulation of missionary work, both miss out on what is a significant area of human encounter.' Therefore, he argued, there was a need for a 'critical, yet sympathetic, analysis of changing perceptions of mission'. In his article Davidson's lament turned into a programmatic statement identifying a number of areas worthy of further attention. These included an analysis of the differences and similarities between mission agencies with respect to theology, support and strategy; changes in theology and practice, and the influence of individual leaders on these; the role and place of women and of children; the contributions of missionaries to the places in which they worked; and the reflex impact of missionaries and missions on churches in New Zealand.

There is a substantial and rich body of literature on New Zealand missions that now needs to be further complemented and extended by critical, contextual and comparative studies. For convenience, the existing literature can be grouped into at least four categories.[11] The first encompasses denominational or organisational mission histories that were often written for centennials and anniversaries.[12] General denominational histories variously cover the missionary aspect of the Church, as do the few overviews of Christianity in Aotearoa New Zealand.[13] Historical overviews are more sporadic in their treatment of the various non- and interdenominational missionary organisations,[14] reflecting the extent to which New Zealand missionaries were component parts of international (especially Anglo-American) mission organisations and societies. These are all largely 'insider' narratives. They are thickly descriptive in content, often celebratory or didactic in tone and written with little regard for developments outside denominational or organisational boundaries. Their authors were often church or missionary participants as well as being male and European. In these respects, their works are based on an Anglo-American literary model pioneered by the Church Missionary Society (CMS) historian-cum-activist Eugene Stock.[15] They are valuable for the historical reconstruction of events, personnel, methodologies and issues encountered. While they include details of both the home and field-based aspects of mission work, the treatment of indigenous cultures varies. Older histories often had a particular pedagogical or theological aim: to contrast 'heathen' peoples with Western Christianity, or to show either how much had been achieved or was yet to be achieved by the missionaries. More recent works give space to the development of indigenous churches and the notion of New Zealand organisations as 'partners in mission'. Three histories – of Associated Churches of Christ, Brethren and Presbyterian missionary work – further break the mould.[16] They outline discernible patterns, attempt a more contextual explanation and offer missiological assessments based on reflective hindsight. At the same time, they also embody hagiographic, esoteric, Western and paternalistic elements and are written with little regard for wider historical contexts. For all these reasons, these kinds of histories have been little regarded by mainstream historians, secular or religious.

A second category of mission literature encompasses a wide variety of autobiographies, biographies, personal narratives and recollections dating from the early twentieth century onwards.[17] These works include a blend of biography and narrative designed to provide information or devotional inspiration. Again, as with their counterparts in the wider literature of the Western missionary movement, they do not always help readers to engage critically with the issues. Denominational publishing houses served to raise the profiles of such works. Missionaries from the non- or interdenominational groups in this period often published their own accounts in later life.[18] Some of the more recent biographies have attempted to place their subjects' individual stories within their wider domestic and international contexts.[19] Despite their analytical shortcomings, these works are rich in detail, useful in terms of understanding both missionary mentality and motivation, and are significant in profiling the important role of women as missionary participants and supporters. In particular, New Zealand women were authors of this kind of literature from at least the very early 1900s. They did not produce a systematic set of missionary books equivalent to the extensive series published by the American Central Committee on the United Study of Foreign Missions.[20] Yet they did produce one-off missionary study books, inspirational titles and biographies. Baptist, Methodist and Presbyterian evidence suggests that these books were published in sizeable numbers and were widely read, educating and inspiring readers and underscoring the notion that women's involvement in overseas missions was normative. These writers, especially in the period up to World War II, reflected wider international trends in that they tended to reinforce, rather than subvert, prevailing Western stereotypes of the non-Western world (including Christian views of non-Christian religions) and to accentuate notions of racial superiority.[21] At the same time, women's literature also highlighted the needs of women and children in other parts of the globe, and brought the colour and vivacity of the inaccessible and exotic 'other' into many New Zealand homes.

The third category encompasses unpublished university theses. Because these will be drawn upon extensively throughout this book, it is worth noting the chronological progression of their concerns. A number of narrative-based theses appeared from the 1940s, including a study of the New Zealand Baptist Missionary Society (which is still a concise and useful measuring stick for other interpretations of Baptist missionary work) and another on early missionary work in the New Hebrides.[22] Here the emphasis was on a chronological treatment of origins, developments and structures. In the 1960s and 1970s a handful of thematically based research essays tackled such topics as the origins and development of interdenominational missionary groups and the home-based policies and structure of Presbyterian work in the New Hebrides.[23] Roberts' thesis on interdenominational organisations usefully borrowed from both sociology and theology, and indicated key areas that still required in-depth research and reflection. Since 1990 a number of theses have reflected more recent historiographical concerns – particularly women's history, Pacific history and culture contact, and the interface between European settlers and twentieth-century nationalist movements. Using the conceptual and analytical language of feminist, gender and postcolonial studies, they have engaged extensively and thoughtfully with existing New Zealand missionary archives, usefully locating the missionary phenomenon within a wider set of historical and historiographical contexts.

The fourth category encompasses published works that have reflected more widely, and sometimes academically, on New Zealand's missionary involvement. Early attempts at this were represented by two small volumes written in the 1930s and 1940s. One, by the Revd Alan Brash (who was also intimately involved in the emerging post-1945 ecumenical movement), assessed the activity of a range of New Zealand Protestant missionary organisations. The other, by long-term Presbyterian missionary Alice Henderson, sought to account for the origins and growth of the influential Presbyterian Women's Missionary Union.[24] Yet, as Davidson noted, such works have been few and far between. It is only more recently that these concerns have begun to reappear – previewed in three wide-ranging essays by Allan Davidson and Peter Lineham – raising many of the questions still to be answered in the New Zealand context.[25] This book is one such attempt to broaden that discussion further and in a more substantive fashion.

Mission history as a sub-discipline is not new – it has its precedents in the writing of such histories from at least the late nineteenth century, if not earlier – and it is a field of international scholarly inquiry that has many participants and supporting structures such as dedicated associations, conferences and journals. In the New Zealand context, as we have seen, it is a less-well developed sub-discipline. Perhaps now is a timely moment for that to change. A growing proliferation of conferences and related publications exhibiting a keen interest in the modern missionary phenomenon indicate a wider climate of interest among historians.[26] Over the last two decades, international scholarship on mission history has been greatly energised by a more synthesised approach, in which missions and religion are considered more deliberately and holistically in relation to a host of other contextual factors. This observation was made in the context of Protestant American mission history as early as 1994 by Dana Robert, outlining how emerging academic interest in women's history, race and gender, for example, could potentially enrich the history of missions.[27] With respect to missions and empire, John Stuart more recently noted that it is now 'increasingly the case that historians take mission (and Christianity more generally) into account when researching and writing about empire', and Tony Ballantyne has trenchantly signalled the ways in which the new imperial history should take greater cognisance of the religious and missionary factor.[28] In the British context, Jeffrey Cox tolls out a similar message by asserting that

Now is a good time for a new overview of the history of British missions. The barriers between three distinct fields of history – imperial history, ecclesiastical history, and mission studies – have been breaking down in the last twenty years. Within these fields the self-confident certainties about the historical role of missionaries are receiving critical scrutiny, and historians have begun to pay attention to anthropologists, who have been interested in missionaries for decades … [The] British missionary movement has always operated between worlds, in spaces between the colonizer and the colonized that are difficult to place within recognized traditions of interpretation.[29]

For New Zealand, as in other British settler society colonial settings like Canada and Australia, mission history is also being enriched by this same open dialogue between multiple historical discourses.[30]

At the same time, an interest in mission history coincides with two specific developments in historical scholarship that further accentuate its place and potential, relevant to the New Zealand setting. On the one hand, there is lively debate over how to write the history of settler societies. In the New Zealand context, for example, hitherto prevailing emphases on the nation, nation-building and the formation of exceptional national identity are being forced to at least give consideration, if not totally yield, to other ways of historical thinking. In particular, questions are being posed about the relationship between indigenous and Western historiographies, the efficacy of having the 'nation' at the centre of historical narratives and explanation, and the extent to which 'colonialism' was historically definitive or remains an ongoing experience. This historiographical 'turn' is linked to the prevailing influence of bodies of scholarship that are variously identified as postcolonial or transnational and which, in turn, intersect with the new imperial history and with world or global history. Furthermore, as represented in two recent collections of essays – in the *New Zealand Journal of History* and the *New Oxford History of New Zealand*[31] – this unpicking or 'de-centring' or 'unsettling' of the nation is by no means a one-off occurrence; it is represented now by a considerable body of scholarship.[32] It needs to be taken seriously.

On the other hand, there has emerged a stronger lobby that argues for a more effective integration of religion into settler society historical narratives – but perhaps not always in ways that are immediately recognisable in terms of how religious history has been traditionally conceived. This was signalled, for example, in an essay by John Stenhouse in the *New Oxford History* in which he suggested, among other things, that if we are to 'understand the churches' place in settler society' then it is 'crucial to disaggregate them by denomination and reconnect them with the Old World'.[33] Stenhouse has led the charge in arguing for a more transnational and inclusive approach to New Zealand's religious history and in modelling a robust critique of secular–nationalist paradigms of historical thinking that have tended to exclude or marginalise the religious factor.[34] This exclusion or marginalisation – intentional or not – is somewhat ironic given the extent to which religion has been an important cultural element for tangata whenua (indigenous Māori) and tauiwi (subsequent immigrants) alike. Furthermore, as I show in Chapter Five, religion emerges as an important factor that helps to disrupt an exclusively national focus within our view of history, especially when the missionary element is considered. When we examine the relationship between Asia and New Zealand, for example, missionary linkages help us to understand better the ways in which emerging settler nations like New Zealand were 'dynamic and diverse communities constantly being remade by the migration, trade and international conflict born out of British imperialism'.[35] For all these reasons, religion is an integral and dynamic part of the historical landscape to be considered.

Of course, all categories of historical analysis are fraught and problematic, and perhaps none more so than those of 'religion' and 'nation'.[36] Nevertheless, a theme running throughout this book is that factoring the overseas missionary component more deliberately into New Zealand historical writing and thinking is legitimate, important and long overdue given the conceptual and historiographical contexts sketched out above. Among other things, such a focus stands to enrich our understanding of how colonial societies developed, both as integral components of wider global systems and as quasi-unique societies in their own right, cultures that were equally shaped at the national and the local level. It adds the missionary (and thus religious) dimension, partly as a corrective to previous scholarly lacunae, but more so because an emphasis on this dimension of our history helps to emphasise the fuzzy edges of the concept of the nation and the porous nature of the boundaries between what we consider to be local, national, regional and global.

Centre or periphery? Complementary perspectives

Thus, in order to render the subject problematic, and to signpost possibilities for further consideration, the ambiguous notions of 'centre' and 'periphery' are deliberately invoked here, both in response to the gaps or trends in scholarship outlined above and as an alternative entry point into the subject of New Zealand's mission history. As already indicated, it is possible to argue long and hard whether or not the mission history of a society like New Zealand should be treated on its own terms or simply as a subset of the wider Euro-American movements of the late nineteenth and early- to mid-twentieth centuries. This book argues that the subject can be usefully approached from both angles.

On the one hand, the New Zealand missionary story was intimately related to those of the wider Euro-American family of Protestant nations and societies to which it belonged, especially the British and increasingly the North American worlds. The lack of comparable national studies or statistical surveys makes that comparison difficult, but not impossible. Cox's British study includes useful appendices of statistics that, while not easily comparable in terms of their format, do provide indicative evidence of similar patterns.[37] The problem is that, until recently, no one has really attempted a truly national history of a missionary movement in terms of its origins, motivations, structure, dynamics or impact. Most studies tend to focus on a denomination or a destination. Ruth Brouwer's excellent book on Canadian Presbyterian women in India is a typical case in point, as is Stephen Maughan's more recent in-depth treatment of the Church of England and foreign missions.[38] There are exceptions, such as Daniel Bays and Grant Wacker's cultural history of North America as a missionary home base, and Mark Hutchinson and Greg Treloar's engaging compilation on Australian overseas missionary involvement.[39] Yet even these works are mostly collections of multi-authored essays rather than coherent surveys, whether in collected essay or monograph form. In the British literature, three exceptions are Esther Breitenbach's study of the ways in which missionary and imperial involvement helped to shape Scottish national identity and civil society; Alison Twells' examination of middle-class England's focus on domestic and foreign 'civilising mission' in the early nineteenth century; and Susan Thorne's analysis of how Congregational missions contributed to the formation of nineteenth-century middle-class English cultural attitudes and values.[40] Admittedly, the task is huge and the data are not always easily found. Enough secondary and primary evidence exists, however, by which to make valid comparisons between metropole and non-metropole missionary-sending societies. In these terms, the history of a society like New Zealand can be thought of as a case study or as the wider movement writ small. Both scale and population size makes it an easier option for a more systematic and comprehensive analysis.

On the other hand, societies like New Zealand, Australia and Canada offer interesting contexts within which mission can be analysed more closely. This is so in at least two respects. First, they were different from so-called metropole societies in terms of both culture and history. This point could be examined from any number of angles, but especially with regard to the coexistence of both indigenous and settler communities and, indeed, to the increasing demographic and ethnic complexities that emerged within settler populations. In the New Zealand religious context, however, it seems particularly apposite to consider further the relationship between denominational formation and missionary activity.

National denominationalism became a major feature of New Zealand Protestant Christianity from the mid-nineteenth century. It was a significant means by which hitherto different groups might forge a common identity. This was the case, for example, for the Presbyterian Church, which by the early 1900s incorporated both Māori and Pākehā (albeit often in separate spheres)[41] and which welded together people of ethnic English, Welsh, Scottish and northern Irish origin or descent. It was also an important means by which various migrant groups self-identified, especially those groups that perceived a threat from quasi-establishment Anglicanism, or that sensed a need to keep intact their theological distinctiveness as minority groups. There was also a strong seam of anti-Roman Catholic sentiment involved. Denominations were also one, but by no means exclusive, means by which settler Protestant piety was institutionalised in its colonial context.[42] Mission both to Māori and overseas became a major vehicle for this. All denominations developed their own distinctive geographical sites of missionary activity that served to bolster this sense of denominational identity and belonging; for example, Methodists in Tonga and the Solomons, Presbyterians in South China, Baptists in East Bengal and Anglicans also in the Solomons. Missionary involvement was also important for such minority denominations as the Baptists (never more than 2 per cent of the population) and the Open Brethren (never more than 1 per cent).[43]

Both in total numbers and per head of population these two denominations punched well above their weight, sending almost 50 per cent of all Protestant missionaries abroad between them by the 1930s. At the same time defensiveness on the part of the larger denominations, as much as theological disagreement, explains some of the antipathy between denominational and non-denominational missionary organisations. The expansion of Presbyterian and Anglican overseas missions around 1900 can be explained partially by the perceived threat presented by the recruiting abilities of such popular and influential early faith missions as the China Inland Mission and the Poona and Indian Village Mission. These non-denominational missions were internationally popular by the late nineteenth century with their primary focus on evangelism and premillennial theology, their policy of 'quiet faith in God to meet financial needs' and an ability to recruit broadly from among 'poorly educated but highly committed missionaries'.[44] In the New Zealand context the attraction of such groups, and their potential to hobble fledgling denominational missionary ventures, was accentuated by the relatively small size of the colony at the turn of the nineteenth and twentieth centuries.

Second, colonial societies were also different collectively in that they were simultaneously recipients and progenitors of mission. The frontiers of missionary involvement were both within and beyond their physical borders. For the New Zealand context, Allan Davidson offers the useful metaphor of two 'streams' of Christianity that emerged in the nineteenth century.[45] It is an image that makes most sense to those New Zealanders who live near the great braided riverbeds of the eastern South Island plains. One stream, the 'Māori missionary' stream, owed its origins to the early energies of the modern British and European missionary movements. The other, the 'colonial settler' stream, owed its origins to the mass migrations of the nineteenth century to the 'new world'. For this and a host of other emergent reasons, they often existed apart from one another. Certainly at the local level, Māori and settler Christians interacted on a week-by-week basis. Sometimes the overlap came in the form of singular individuals – people like Eunice Preece, a missionary nurse in China with the Society for the Propagation of the Gospel (SPG) in the 1920s, who was descended from both CMS missionaries and North Island Māori. Her maternal grandmother was most likely the daughter of Te-Tuhi-o-te-rangi, of Ngāti Mahuta, a hapū of Tainui, and therefore also related to the Māori King, Tawhiao.[46] Eunice's story, however, was not typical; structurally, functionally, culturally and mentally the two streams largely remained apart.

The great 'promise' of Māori Christianity was dealt a severe blow by the series of wars, racial conflicts and land confiscations that persisted from the 1850s through to about World War I. These issues only began to be definitively addressed, in both society and church, in the 1960s and 1970s. In the process many Māori, although not all, became alienated from the missions and denominations with which they were previously involved. The abiding identification of Ngāti Porou with the Anglican Church is one of the main exceptions.[47] A variety of Māori religious movements, Christian and other, co-existed uneasily alongside traditional church structures. By the end of the nineteenth century, a prevailing notion that Māori were a dying race re-ignited Māori Mission work among most of the major denominations. In Protestant churches, Māori existed for many decades into the 1900s as 'missionary subjects', as 'other', and as a body of people still perceived to be in need of rescue. Perhaps it is for these fundamental reasons that we do not find many Māori as missionaries for the mainstream denominations beyond the shores of New Zealand after the 1850s. Mission to the 'regions beyond' for settler Christians meant both mission to the colony's own peoples and mission to the wider world. In effect, overseas missions were a predominantly settler priority or activity. That is why, rightly or wrongly, the New Zealand settler church and Pākehā Protestants are the focus of this book.

Structure of this book

Informed by this introductory discussion, the chapters that follow fall into two groups. The four chapters grouped in Part One map the local contours of the movement by providing a chronological, theological and thematic overview of New Zealand Protestant missionary participation and support. Chapter One explores how church engagement in overseas missions emerged and evolved up to World War II. It identifies key points of growth and change, and indicates representative ways in which churches were mobilised and organised with respect to their perceived missionary obligations. In Chapter Two I put pre-World War II theological constructions of mission under the microscope. I argue that both missionaries and their supporters articulated a wide-ranging and slowly changing theology of mission. This was broadly evangelical in definition, across the denominational spectrum, and was not restricted to any one philosophy or methodology. Chapter Three extends this discussion by considering selected local and international influences that shaped the theology, spirituality and ethos of the movement. In particular, it focuses on the religious relationships between New Zealand, Australia and the United States of America. In Chapter Four I tackle the more problematic issue of missionary motivation. Drawing on both New Zealand data and international literature, I argue that motivation can be best understood by considering the intersection of personal, theologically framed missionary narratives with their wider historical, gendered, socio-religious and mental contexts.

The four chapters grouped together in Part Two address the intersection of local mission history and broader historical and historiographical themes. In Chapter Five I create a platform for what follows by arguing that an alternative approach to the history of a colonial or settler society like New Zealand can be found in wider themes drawn from world or global history, and that mission history provides one useful angle by which to achieve this. I thus provide a case study of the Bolivian Indian Mission, which had its origins in early twentieth-century New Zealand and which was both representative and indicative of broader patterns. In the next two chapters, I proceed to interrogate the intersections between colonial missionary engagement and British imperialism in particular. In Chapter Six I argue that New Zealand missionaries and their supporters held a range of positive and more ambivalent positions towards the British Empire. However, I also argue that patterns of geographical involvement and organisational affiliation both supported and confounded this thinking. I use the example of New Zealand's missionary involvement with India to argue that the mission–empire relationship is best teased out in the context of specific missionary sites. Chapter Seven then explores this relationship more closely with respect to New Zealand Protestant children and their engagements with mission. First, I outline what it meant for colonial children to be missionary supporters. Second, I indicate the ways in which notions of imperial citizenship were entwined in the religious pedagogy and rhetoric associated with the missionary movement. Chapter Eight returns to the issue of gender, and I seek to assess the reflex impact of overseas missions on domestic church life. It takes as a specific case study the Edinburgh 1910 world missionary conference and its local impact at home. I argue that the impact of the Edinburgh conference was felt most prominently among

New Zealand's Presbyterians, certainly with respect to women's groups and education. It fed directly into a growing missionary study movement which, in turn, evolved into a significant site of global education for women and those that they influenced. The book concludes by considering the significance of New Zealand's Protestant overseas missionary engagement from both historical and historiographical perspectives.

PART ONE

LOCAL CONTOURS

CHAPTER 1

Protestant Churches and Missionary Involvement to 1939

A question of origins

The Scottish mission historian Andrew Walls argues that Christian mission is now 'from anywhere to anywhere'. He notes that Christianity 'has not one but many centres; new Christian impulses and initiatives may now be expected from any quarter of the globe. Christian mission may start from any point, and be directed to any point.' In like manner, American religious historian Mark Noll suggests that 'once-fixed notions of "sending country" and "receiving country" have been tossed into the air'.[1] As I argued in the Introduction, New Zealand's historical experience also confounds the extent to which such terms as 'centre' and 'periphery' can be used in thinking historically about Christian mission, even earlier than the modern period commented on here by Walls and Noll. Such distinctions were quickly blurred or rendered problematic by the emergence of parallel missionary and settler streams of Christianity within the young colony, and by simultaneous missionary ventures within and beyond its shores.

This blurring of conceptual boundaries is also relevant for dating the beginnings of New Zealand's involvement in the international missionary movement. New Zealand's image, as conjured up by British immigration agents in the 1870s, was that of an 'alternative promised land in the virgin countryside beyond the seas'.[2] The 1860s and 1870s were pivotal decades for British immigration to New Zealand, with unprecedented numbers of settlers arriving and remaining.[3] It was from this 'promised land' and from among this particular generation of colonists that the Protestant interest in overseas missions bloomed, in terms of long-term support and involvement. One might conceivably argue that this period should form a logical starting point for assessing origins. The starting date, however, needs to be shifted back several decades to the first half of the nineteenth century, where the issue of origins emerges as a much more complex issue.

In 2014 churches and communities commemorated and reflected upon 200 years of Christianity's formal presence in Aotearoa New Zealand. In December 1814 Samuel Marsden and a handful of English Anglican artisan missionaries, more or less completely dependent on local Māori goodwill, established a Church Missionary Society (CMS) venture in northern New Zealand. Their arrival came a good two decades after the first European sealers, whalers, flax-cutters and adventurers who had among their numbers men and women of varied Christian faith. These Anglican missionaries were eventually followed by the Wesleyan Methodist Missionary Society in 1823 and by the French Roman Catholic Marist Mission under Bishop Pompallier in 1838. These missions were early expressions of the wider evangelisation and Christianisation of the Pacific basin from the late eighteenth century. The Pacific was an early focus of the great missionary energy that emanated from Britain and Europe in the decades following the French Revolution, and had become a missionary showcase for northern hemisphere Protestants and Roman Catholics alike by the mid-nineteenth century. To many of these early arrivals, replete with a full set of European lenses through which to interpret what they saw, Māori were a people of 'simple habits' (to quote Methodist observers) whose religion appeared to be a 'long round of absurdities'.[4] The reality, of course was vastly different as the missionaries learnt soon enough. They encountered a long-established and culturally sophisticated society with a well-formed and reasoned cosmology.[5] Māori quickly became adept at co-opting Western cultural accoutrements and values for their own ends. Moreover, the arrival of early British and French missionaries coincided with a period of significant change and upheaval within Māori society, marked especially by inter-tribal warfare exacerbated by the musket trade.[6] Christianity, education, literacy and the Bible became potent elements when introduced into this mix.[7]

Christianity gradually spread among Māori in both main islands in the decades surrounding the signing of the Treaty of Waitangi in 1840 and prior to the disastrous wars of the 1860s and 1870s, which continued to disrupt race relations. The transmission of the new faith was by both Māori and missionaries. In particular, many slaves released by the dominant northern iwi (tribe) Ngāpuhi in the 1830s carried both the Gospel message and literacy to their home tribes, thus setting off a chain reaction of religious transmission that often preceded the arrival of British or French missionaries, or then necessitated their formal presence. This mirrored a similar pattern of indigenous agency and transmission that occurred across the Polynesian and Melanesian regions throughout the nineteenth century.[8] As a result, missionary identity quickly became ambiguous in this early period of colonisation. Raeburn Lange argues convincingly that the ongoing leadership of Māori evangelists and teachers was as critical as that of European missionaries with respect to the process of both evangelising and Christianising other Māori, particularly in the CMS and Wesleyan Methodist spheres of missionary influence.[9] Critical indigenous leadership was less obvious for the Roman Catholic Marist Mission in the early decades, although Māori catechists were certainly utilised and active, as were lay teachers and preachers for the Presbyterian Māori Mission from the end of the nineteenth century.[10]

At the same time, there is some evidence that Māori were also actively involved as missionaries beyond the shores of New Zealand, albeit sometimes as a by-product of other activities. They had already proved to be intrepid travellers in these early years of European contact, working on whaling boats or in other parts of the southwest Pacific, or travelling to Sydney and further to Britain or Europe. The northern rangatira (chief) Ruatara was one such traveller who, among a number of other Ngāpuhi rangatira, was instrumental in ensuring that Marsden's early CMS venture in the Bay of Islands became established. Therefore it is not surprising to find Māori among those counted as missionaries, particularly in Polynesia and Melanesia. The details are patchy, but we know that the Methodist missionaries Revd Nathaniel and Mrs Turner took three or four young Māori with them to Tonga in 1827. This was arguably the first overseas missionary venture from New Zealand, and it predated formal European settlement. Other individuals were named in connection with the Methodist work of the Revd Walter Lawry, also in Tonga, and the LMS missionary John Williams on Rotuma.[11] In the 1840s and 1850s a number of Māori accompanied Melanesian Mission Bishop Selwyn on trips from New Zealand to the Solomon Islands. In 1852 Henare Taratoa worked with William Nihill on the island of Mare in the Solomons; later, in 1910, another man with the surname of 'Popoata' accompanied the Revd Durrad to Tikopia. Some Anglican Māori were also financially supporting the Melanesian Mission by the 1850s. Wider missionary support by Anglican Māori endured into the early twentieth century.[12]

In 1908 Archdeacon Hector Hawkins and the Revd Papahia scoped out the possibilities for future evangelisation by Māori of Polynesian-speaking islands in Melanesia, on behalf of the New Zealand Anglican Māori Mission. Their report was positive, but did not lead to further action. One source suggests that the potential cultural and geographic isolation of Māori missionaries from New Zealand proved to be too great a barrier.[13] Charles Fox commented somewhat controversially, and with an apparent lack of understanding of the wider historical role of Māori evangelists in New Zealand, that the 'Maori [Anglican] Church has never been missionary. How different might have been the history of the Polynesian-speaking islands if this recommendation had been acted on, and what fresh life have been infused into the Maori Church itself! for a Church that is not missionary cannot be strong.'[14] Nevertheless, the fact that these admittedly modest numbers of early Māori missionaries were not replicated in later decades, in any of the missions emanating from New Zealand, is an issue that needs further research and reflection.

Between the 1840s and the 1860s, the early notion of New Zealand as a missionary-receiving land at the geographic and religious margins of the globe was further shaken by concerted European settlement. With settlement came a host of Christian denominations that developed their own priorities and agendas; colonisation was as much religious as it was economic and cultural.[15] By the 1870s the numerically and historically dominant groups were Church of England (40 per cent), Presbyterians (25 per cent), Roman Catholics (14 per cent), Wesleyan Methodists (8 per cent), Baptists (2 per cent) and Congregational Independents (1.5 per cent).[16] These proportions remained relatively constant through to the mid-twentieth century. By the end of the nineteenth century, Plymouth Brethren, the Salvation Army, the Society of Friends and Seventh Day Adventists were further significant religious minorities, and the Latter Day Saints had also established significant mission work among Māori in the North Island.[17] While the colony opted out of a formalised 'established church' arrangement, Protestant settler Christians did form themselves along diocesan, parochial, congregational and assembly lines that replicated familiar British patterns. They demanded clerical or lay leadership and, in the longer term, buildings and infrastructure. It was inevitable that the energies (and budgets) of churches and church leaders would become focused on these priorities for much of the nineteenth century and beyond.

Yet while this was the case, there is very early evidence of settler churches expressing missionary interest beyond the colony itself. In part, this was influenced by prevailing structures. The Wesleyan Methodist Missionary Society's Australasian Conference, centred on New South Wales, naturally combined mission to Māori, New Zealand settlers and to Tonga from the late 1820s. The lines of demarcation between early Methodist missionaries and ministers were often hard to distinguish in the colony. As an example, Lydia Brown (née Wallis), possibly the first New Zealand-born settler missionary when she left with her new husband George for Samoa in 1860, was herself the daughter of an early Wesleyan missionary to New Zealand's north.[18] One legacy of this fluidity was that the names of individual missionaries and missionary families became equally revered among Australian, New Zealand and Tongan Methodists. In the case of other denominations, individuals effortlessly shifted between categories. For instance, the Revd John Inglis, a Scottish Reformed Presbyterian, originally arrived in the colony in 1844 as a missionary to Māori in the lower North Island. Over the next eight years he also officiated as a Presbyterian minister to settlers in Otago, Southland and Auckland. In 1852 he moved on to join the Nova Scotian Presbyterian missionary John Geddie in the New Hebrides [Vanuatu], where he worked for the next 24 years.[19] In turn, Inglis's presence, both in the New Hebrides and New Zealand, served to galvanise Australasian Presbyterian missionary awareness and action through the 1860s and 1870s.

This same blurring of the boundaries between mission to, from and within colonial New Zealand was also evident in the early life of the Anglican Church's Melanesian Mission, whose energies were directed primarily to the Solomon Islands and northern New Hebrides from 1848. In this instance, as David Hilliard so aptly puts it, 'Victorian Anglicanism entered Melanesia not as the result of an upsurge in missionary interest within the Church of England, but through the imagination and restless energy of one man: George Augustus Selwyn, first [Anglican] Bishop of New Zealand.'[20] Although criticised from many angles, Selwyn unapologetically combined the tasks of missionary and of colonial bishop.[21] In forming the Pacific Diocese and the Melanesian Mission in particular, he placed a high value on both the missionary task of the Church and on New Zealand's unique geographical location in the southwest Pacific. He argued that the colonial Church had a special obligation to pass on the Christian Gospel to its geographic neighbours irrespective of its youth or lack of resources.[22] From 1848 to 1866 Loyalty Island and Melanesian young men, brought back to St John's College in Auckland by Selwyn and others, rubbed shoulders with Anglican Māori and settler students. It was not until the formation of a Melanesian missionary diocese in 1857 and the consecration of its first proper bishop, John Patteson, in 1861, that the Mission's work was more clearly separated from that of the Anglican Church in New Zealand. While recruits and financial support came primarily from England for much of the nineteenth century, the Mission remained connected to and was closely identified with selected New Zealand dioceses and supported by many individual Anglicans.

That settler and missionary Christianity were interwoven in New Zealand through the first half of the nineteenth century is significant and yet unsurprising. Early Scottish and other British Presbyterians, English Baptists and Methodists, and English or Irish Anglicans came as migrants with a heightened awareness of missions. They were, for instance, barely one generation removed from the formation of influential British missionary societies in the 1790s (Baptist Missionary Society, Church Missionary Society, Glasgow Society for Foreign Missions, London Missionary Society and Scottish Missionary Society), the formation of the Church of Scotland's own mission society in 1824, or from the ardent missionary zeal of the 1843 Scottish Disruption. In the Scottish case missionary enthusiasm, if not organisation, predated all of these and had wider roots than just evangelicalism or post-Disruption zeal.[23] Many of the settlers, both adults and children, came to New Zealand having been shaped by or directly involved in these movements.

While colonial missionary projects only emerged slowly over the succeeding decades up to 1900, New Zealand churches and denominations fed off this inheritance. In the 1870s, a handful of touring missionary speakers, the support of colonial clergy who had themselves been missionaries in other parts of the empire, and a growing diversity of imported and locally produced literature all served to further nurture this consciousness. Missionary awareness was further raised by events closer to home; these included Presbyterian agitation for British intervention in the New Hebrides (to control the Melanesian labour trade and to counter French annexation) and the martyrdom of Bishop Patteson with two other Melanesian Mission men in 1871. The later nineteenth century was also marked by further missionary projects at home. From 1882, Anglican dioceses gradually took over Māori missionary work under an agreement with the CMS. This process was completed by 1902. Presbyterians, Baptists and the Salvation Army each initiated their own Māori mission work in the 1880s and 1890s. All denominations made 'home mission' projects a priority among remote rural settlers well into the early twentieth century. Thus even by 1900, mission 'to', 'from', and 'within' were all categories of colonial church activity that continued to confound notions of centre and periphery. The 'regions beyond' were both domestic and international.

Institutional development: The example of the Presbyterian Church

In another sense, however, the early overseas missionary focus of Wesleyan Methodists and Anglicans in the first half of the nineteenth century was atypical for the New Zealand context. It was linked more to structures or traditions unique to those particular denominations, as well as replicating the established priorities of British home churches. The second half of the nineteenth century was marked by the slow awakening of settler Protestants and churches to their perceived missionary obligations – what Christchurch Anglican Bishop Churchill Julius later referred to as 'our bounden duty'.[24] Again, this mirrored what was happening among Protestant churches across Britain, Europe and North America. In his magisterial history of Christianity's expansion, American historian Kenneth Scott Latourette famously called the long nineteenth century the 'great century'. While the rhetoric is now somewhat dated, he sums this up well:

> Not so many continents or major countries were entered for the first time as in the preceding three centuries. That would have been impossible, for on all the larger land masses of the earth except Australia and among all the more numerous peoples and in all the areas of high civilization Christianity had been introduced before A.D. 1800. What now occurred was the acquisition of fresh footholds in regions and among peoples already touched, an expansion of unprecedented extent from both the newer bases and the older ones, and the entrance of Christianity into the large majority of such countries, islands, peoples, and tribes as had previously not been touched ... [In the nineteenth

century] Christianity was now taken to more peoples than ever before and entered as a transforming agency into more cultures than in all the preceding centuries.[25]

These obligations were acknowledged relatively early on in the settlement process, but more in principle than in practice. The experience of the fledgling Presbyterian Church is instructive in this regard. At its first meeting in 1856, the Auckland Presbytery publicly affirmed that Christian mission was a 'duty', an act both of 'obedience' and 'gratitude to God', and a task that was intrinsic to the Church's 'spiritual welfare'.[26] This statement anticipated later Presbyterian missionary involvement in the New Hebrides/Vanuatu (1868), in southern China (1901), and in northern India (1910). It was a sign of the limited nature of Presbyterian time and energies, however, that this ideal was not turned into reality overnight. A year later the Presbytery corresponded with other parts of the colonial church to test interest and to canvass ideas. It then took another two years for the New Hebrides to be nominated as a suitable location. This venture was premised on existing Nova Scotian and Scottish missionary work (the New Hebrides Mission), personal contacts through the Revd John Inglis, and a plea by the New Hebrides Mission for New Zealand and Australian support.[27] By 1863 the Church had agreed to be involved in the New Hebrides and approved a process for selecting a missionary. A lack of local applicants and the division of the Church into two autonomous branches in 1866 meant that it was another five years before missionaries were finally appointed and placed in the New Hebrides. The inaugural missionaries were specially co-opted Scottish Presbyterians. In 1869 William and Agnes Watt settled on the island of Tanna (on behalf of the northern Presbyterian Church), while Peter and Mary Milne settled on the island of Nguna (on behalf of the Synod of Southland and Otago).[28] It had taken 13 years to activate the initial Auckland resolution of 1856. At this stage, preferred missionaries were male, ordained and married, which meant recruiting from Britain or adopting British missionaries already in the New Hebrides. This policy certainly contributed to slow growth; just three more couples were added as missionaries over the next 20 years. Lay and single missionaries were not considered until the late 1880s. Following the Church's national re-unification in 1901, the vision rapidly expanded as new geographical locations and more missionaries were sought.

The late nineteenth-century experience of the Presbyterian Church also indicates the extent to which an effective missionary infrastructure was important for future growth and consolidation. The development of such infrastructure was costly, time-consuming and resource-dependent, which further explains the slow growth of colonial church missionary endeavours. What the Presbyterian Church achieved in this respect by the early 1900s, however, eventually became normative across all denominations and organisations. Both branches of the Church quickly established missions committees that were accountable to church governance, but which had executive responsibility for foreign, Māori and domestic Chinese ministry. In the case of the northern Church, 'Foreign' and 'Māori' functions were separated out into two committees from 1867. In 1901 there was a seamless transition into one national Foreign Missions Committee (FMC) for the united Church. Business revolved around missionary recruitment, appointment and fundraising; keeping contact with missionaries; and raising the profile of missionary life, issues and needs among the Presbyterian constituency. Committee convenorship was demanding, clergy-led, and often the preserve of enthusiasts. The Revd William Bannerman, for instance, convened the southern Synod's committee from 1872 until church union in 1901.

Over several decades a number of other structures accrued around these committees so that, by the early 1900s, committee work was supplemented and sustained by a range of other institutions that reached out into many different aspects of Presbyterian life. Together, these fed into an increasingly sophisticated and comprehensive mechanism for raising and sustaining annual missionary revenue. Individual missionary associations were fostered at the congregational level. From the beginning, the inclusion of missionary news and information in denominational literature was important – both from Britain and locally, in the form of various regional and national church newspapers. Presbyterian children had their own magazine in the early to mid-1880s in the form of the *New Zealand Missionary Record*. As I show in Chapter Seven, juvenile sympathies and pennies were widely sought from an early stage. This interest was often focused around specific projects like maintaining the mission ship *Dayspring*[29] – a well-established tradition for British and colonial children's missionary support – but it was more than just financial in motivation. Over the longer term, the critical issue was character formation and fostering a lifelong interest in the work of missions. By the early 1900s, Presbyterian children had their own missionary magazine (*The Break of Day*), their own groups (the Busy Bees), and a raft of other mission-orientated projects through Sunday schools, Bible classes and

Christian Endeavour groups. Women too had their own missionary magazine by the early 1900s, in the form of the *PWMU Harvest Field*. It quickly
became apparent during these decades that women's support for missions
was critical (outlined further in Chapters Two, Four and Eight). The idea
of a Church-wide 'Ladies' Missionary Society' was broached as early as
1883, but the momentum for this venture really came in the early 1890s.[30]
A 'Ladies' Mission Aid Association' was formed in 1891 to attend to the
welfare of missionary children from the New Hebrides being schooled in
New Zealand. By 1897 a network of regional women's missionary unions
had been established, all of which were ultimately organised into a national
Presbyterian Women's Missionary Union in 1905. Similar national organisations also emerged in Baptist and Methodist circles in the early 1900s.
Together, these voluntary unions became enduring powerhouses of spiritual, practical and financial missionary support.

In reflecting on the Church's 25th jubilee in 1926, the Foreign
Missions Committee noted the increase of missionaries from 17 in 1901
to 32 in 1926, with a consequent rise in annual income from £427-1-10
to £15,888-13-0 over that period.[31] This growth had been further enabled
through close attention to structures and strategies. In 1913 the Revd
Alexander Don was appointed the first full-time and fully paid foreign
missions secretary; this position took pressure off ex officio FMC members
and ensured a more sustained profile for missions. Similar appointments
were made in other denominations in this same decade. Don's Dunedin-
based position was transferred to Auckland, as a more strategic location,
in 1929.[32] Also in 1913, the FMC published its first list of 'own missionaries' – that is, missionaries adopted and wholly supported by individual
parishes or organisations. Churches like St Andrew's in Dunedin, Trinity
in Timaru and St John's in Wellington undertook to provide salaries for
individual missionaries in addition to their regular missionary giving, as
did groups like the Young Men's and Young Women's Bible Class Unions.
This somewhat informal strategy had become well established by the 1920s
with, for example, 20 such parishes or organisations involved in 1923,
sometimes supporting several missionaries.[33] At the same time, Presbyterian missionary finances were vulnerable. In 1920 a nationwide appeal
to avert a financial crisis resulted in churches contributing over £20,000
for overseas missions, but with a consequent decrease in giving for other
branches of denominational work. A year later, the national church for the

first time set annual budgets for its various departments so that such inequities might be avoided and greater financial prudence would prevail. While overseas missions continued to have a 'special power to draw out generous and sacrificial giving', it was also obvious that such enthusiasm could not be unbounded and that the Church's 'capacity to keep on increasing its commitments had begun to diminish'.[34] The years of Depression and of war that followed certainly tested Presbyterian resolve over missions. While missionary redundancies were avoided, there was a noticeable slowing of recruitment. Further special appeals to rebuild finances became ever more common and missionaries accepted reduced salaries for a time. As war darkened the future in 1940, however, the FMC commented:

> [P]erhaps never before have there been such alternations of feeling between fear and hope, between a sense of frustration and thankfulness. The year began with the fear of possible retrenchment … and it has witnessed also the outbreak of the greatest war in history and one in which we are vitally involved. But at the same time the year has also revealed national traits of character in our people which give us courage and hope, and an unprecedented willingness so to subscribe to the missionary work of the Church that withdrawal from any part of it for financial reasons, is unthinkable.[35]

Institutional development on a broader scale

New Zealanders began to apply for missionary service in ever-increasing numbers by the late nineteenth century. As Table 1.1 (overleaf) indicates, however, the establishment of New Zealand-based missionary structures was a much slower process.

Perhaps the slowest of all was the Methodist Church – somewhat ironically, given its early presence as a missionary influence. It took almost 100 years for New Zealand Methodists to take on their very own missionary 'field'. Local overseas missionary support had been overseen by a New Zealand-based auxiliary established in 1903. However, Wesleyan Methodists remained within the Australasian General Conference until 1913 when they finally became autonomous, thus ending decades of trans-Tasman debate and indecision. At that point, the various Methodist groups united into one New Zealand Methodist Church. Finally in 1922, in a related move to rationalise trans-Tasman Methodist missionary work in the Pacific, the New Zealand Church was given the Solomon Islands as its own responsibility.[37]

TABLE 1.1. New Zealand-based Missionary Organisations and Committees, 1827–1939[36]

1827?	Wesleyan Methodist Missionary Society
1852	Melanesian Mission
1869	Presbyterian Church of New Zealand
1886	New Zealand Baptist Missionary Society
1891	New Zealand China Inland Mission
1893	New Zealand Church Missionary Association
1896?	Poona and Indian Village Mission
1896	New Zealand Open Brethren
1898	Associated Churches of Christ
1899	Zenana Bible and Medical Mission
1899	South American Evangelical Mission
1900	Australasian South American Mission
1900	South African Compounds Mission
1903	Ramabai Mukti Mission
1903	NZ Methodist Missionary Auxiliary
1903	Baptist Women's Missionary Union
1905	Presbyterian Women's Missionary Union
1905	Methodist Women's Missionary Union
1906	Salvation Army (New Zealand)
1908	Bolivian Indian Mission
1911	South Sea Evangelical Mission
1912	Sudan United Mission
1916	New Zealand Church Missionary Society
1920	New Zealand Student Christian Movement
1921	Sudan Interior Mission (SIM)
1922	New Zealand Anglican Board of Missions
1924	Anglican Diocese of Polynesia
1926	Pentecostal Church of New Zealand
1926	New Zealand National Missionary Council
1932	Unevangelized Fields Mission
1933	Oriental Missionary Society
1935	World Evangelization Crusade

As Table 1.1 also indicates, institutional support grew noticeably by the early 1900s. This mirrored the great expansion of missionary numbers and support structures that occurred across the Anglo-American world between the 1880s and World War I, at least.[38] Growth at this stage also intersected with a range of local and international factors: local religious and revivalist enthusiasm; the influence of Australian and American activist evangelicalism; overseas political events; increasing professionalism; new economic growth; the political enfranchisement of women; and the increasingly critical roles of women as moral reformers and in the educational and medical professions. Correspondingly, the 1890s were the first of two pivotal decades for missionary development in which annual numbers of departing missionaries increased dramatically (indicated in Figure 1.1), followed more slowly by an increase in structural support.

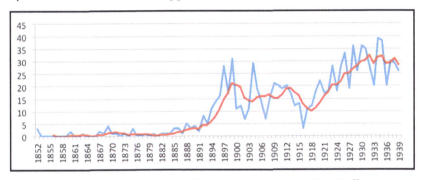

FIGURE 1.1. New Zealand Annual Missionary Departures, 1852–1939[39]

By 1900 Dunedin, Otago–Southland and, to a lesser extent, Canterbury served as the important geographical loci of influence, places in which many committees were established and from which much of the country's missionary energy emanated. Committees also emerged as local organising centres for the increasingly popular non-denominational and faith missions, notably for the China Inland Mission and the Poona and Indian Village Mission. Increasing numbers of missionaries were also channelled through a range of lay training institutes, particularly in Sydney, Melbourne and Adelaide. These provided an alternative for men who were not seeking ordination prior to their departure, and were the only training option for women. In New Zealand, the first – and for many years the only – such institute was the Missionary Training Home for women established in Dunedin by the ex-Baptist missionary Annie Driver (née Newcombe) in 1899. In

1903 this centre was handed over to the Presbyterian Church to become the long-lived Presbyterian Women's Training Institute for missionaries and deaconesses.[40] During the 1890s a growing number and variety of overseas missionary speakers toured New Zealand, setting a pattern for decades to come. For some of these, such as American missionary statesman John R. Mott on his first visit in 1896, raising missionary awareness was just one of the aims of speaking engagements. For others, such as Charles Reeve, the Australian founder and leader of the Poona and Indian Village Mission, his annual visits between 1896 and 1899 explicitly focused on enlisting more missionary recruits and building support. The combined effect was a heightened expectancy that many local congregations would interact with international missionaries.

During the 1900s and 1910s these patterns became more established as missionary enthusiasm was sustained. There were obvious signs of growth within denominations. Anglican missionaries, for example, now served with at least six different Anglican mission groups: the CMS, the NZCMA, the Australian Anglican Papua Mission, the Church of England Zenana Missionary Society, and the Society for the Propagation of the Gospel. In 1922 the New Zealand Anglican Board of Missions was finally established, linking these various ventures together for more systematic diocesan and parish missionary support.[41] Baptists increasingly paid for large capital projects as well as missionary personnel. The now united Presbyterian Church of New Zealand embarked on new mission ventures in southern China and in northern India. New Zealand continued to be drawn in and influenced by overseas developments. A second visit by John R. Mott in 1903, combined with the students' missionary conference of the same year and visits by others involved in student work, contributed strategically to student missionary enthusiasm until at least World War I. Other movements like the American Laymen's Missionary Movement had a brief but pointed impact. The 1910 World Missionary Conference in Edinburgh also had a downstream impact on New Zealand missionary thinking and support (see Chapter Eight). Overall, mission incomes grew, reflecting a more consistent commitment to missionary support throughout this period.

The 1920s was the second pivotal decade of growth in missionary support and involvement up to World War II. While many of the old certainties had gone, and denominational groups invariably struggled to increase annual income over expenditure, the annual numbers of departing missionaries were twice as high as for any previous decade and were largely sustained through the 1930s. This was partly a function of myriad localised developments that, when added together, made for significant growth. Yet there were more profound dynamics at work in this era. World War I had curtailed the hitherto prevailing sense of optimism about human progress, and had begun to unleash forces of liberation in non-European societies that would culminate in post-1945 independence for many. For varying reasons Christian people perceived, in starker reality than previously, a world in need of physical, moral and spiritual rescue. This explains some of what Latourette calls the 'brave surge'[42] in missionary numbers in the years following 1918, both from countries like New Zealand and from other Western nations. At the same time, missionary growth from the mid-1920s was partially a function of the growing conservative evangelical Protestant sense of discomfort with liberalising tendencies in both society and church.[43] Conservative evangelical missions and missionary numbers were not halted by the Depression years, unlike the budget cuts experienced by many denominational missions, mainly because of their attachment to faith mission principles.

In the New Zealand context, growth occurred chiefly among the nondenominational organisations and fledgling Pentecostal churches. Pivotal to this growth was the newly established New Zealand Bible Training Institute (NZBTI) in Auckland (1922), which contributed a significantly large number of new Protestant missionaries in these decades,[44] and the high commitment of Baptist and Brethren churches to the missionary imperative. Auckland, now New Zealand's largest city, emerged as the new geographical focus for missionary interest and support. The presence of Anglican and Methodist theological institutions, the NZBTI and the Baptist Theological College all served to raise the profile of the city as a focus for training and resources. Auckland's growing size demanded a more sophisticated response, symbolised in the formation in the mid-1920s of the Auckland Baptist Foreign Missionary Committee and the Auckland Missionary Association. It also became a centre for national administration, with the relocation to Auckland of the Presbyterian FMC secretary and executive in 1929. While theological differences remained, there was also a growing desire to act ecumenically across organisational boundaries. Many leaders and participants perceived that understanding and cooperation were at least ideals to be worked towards. John R. Mott visited for a third time

in 1926 as the keynote speaker at a nationally convened missionary conference in Dunedin. The National Missionary Council that evolved from this
meeting indicated that, in a small country like New Zealand, there was little
room for separatism. Although the council did not ultimately achieve much
in practice, it marked a significant step along the way towards a broader
ecumenism.

Patterns of missionary involvement

So who were these missionaries who were increasingly sought and supported
by New Zealand's Protestant churches, and where did they go? Over the
following chapters we will encounter these people either singly or collectively, so it is useful here to at least outline some broad descriptive features
by way of background. For a small country, with a population that only
reached one million by about 1908,[45] 1000 Protestant missionaries was not
an insignificant number. At the same time, this figure reflected a period
of rapid population growth and sustained transience. The movement of
missionaries should be set against a larger canvas of continual internal and
external population movement. Table 1.2 is an attempt to describe these
1000 missionaries in broad brushstrokes.[46]

Clearly, missionary trends mirrored wider population and social trends;
for instance, the increases in New Zealand-born missionaries over time and
the growth of Auckland's demographic importance are hardly surprising.
There are a number of features, however, that require brief comment. The
participation of women across the decades is perhaps the most obvious. In
the early period, women missionaries were married missionaries, but no less
involved in missionary work. Some, like Presbyterian Agnes Watt in the
New Hebrides, remained childless and worked in complementary spheres
alongside their husbands. More typically, married women combined the
roles of mother and missionary in often challenging circumstances. Until
the early 1900s at least, children were often the invisible, but perhaps
taken-for-granted element, in how missionary activity was reported. The
departures of Rosalie Macgeorge, Annie Newcombe and Hopestill Pillow
(NZBMS) for East Bengal, between 1886 and 1889, heralded the dominant place of single women missionaries well into the twentieth century.
This was an emerging feature of the Western missionary workforce from
the 1890s onwards, accompanying the contemporary trend to employ more

TABLE 1.2. Selected Features of New Zealand's Missionary Workforce, 1852–1939[47]

	1852–84		1885–99		1900–18		1919–39	
	M	F	M	F	M	F	M	F
Proportions	53%	47%	46%	54%	38%	62%	37%	63%
Median Age	26.5	26	26.5	28	29	28	27	28
Unmarried	50%	27%	79%	76%	68%	70%	71%	77%
New Zealand-born	47%	58%	85%	81%	86%	88%	89%	86%
Main Regional Origin	Otago	Otago	Otago	Otago	Otago	Otago	Auckld	Auckld
Main Denomination	Presb.	Presb.	Baptist	Presb.	Presb.	Presb.	Baptist	Presb.
Median Service (Years)	12.5	5.5	10	7.5	11	14	14	14
Service Ended by:	Illness	Death	Illness	Illness	Illness/ Death	Retired	Retired	Retired
Highest Educational Background	Other tertiary	?	Other tertiary	Other tertiary	Other tertiary	Other tertiary	Other tertiary	Other tertiary
Main Occupational Background[48]	Petty Officials	?	Skilled worker	Semi-prof	Semi-prof	Semi-prof	Semi-prof	Semi-prof

single missionaries. While married missionaries remained important, and many single men and women married once they were in mission contexts, the undivided energies of the young were valued. Women's involvement was also facilitated by the increasing specialisation of missionary work. Teachers, doctors, nurses and administrators were all needed alongside those in more general evangelistic or pastoral roles. Men and women together were affected by disease and death. Mortality was higher in the earlier decades, especially for those in Melanesia and India, and illness frequently curtailed missionary careers across the whole period. Children were susceptible too, and the experiences of some missionary families make distressing reading. However, the sustained service of New Zealand women Grace Paterson, Amy Evans, Mary Moore, Miss E. Smith, Kate Fraser and Catherine Colley (all Church of Scotland missionaries), and of couples like Dr Norman and Reta Hamilton (Brethren) and the Revd George and Margaret McNeur (Presbyterian), became the norm by the early 1900s.

Denominational and geographical origins were often interrelated. Presbyterian and Baptist missionaries from Otago–Southland were prominent until at least World War I, as were Anglicans from Auckland, Nelson–Marlborough and Christchurch, and Methodists from Auckland. Yet, as we have already noted, Baptist and Brethren missionaries, by the early 1900s, were numerically dominant nationwide. Furthermore, these two denominations had by far the highest ratio of missionaries to church members or affiliates. Missionary involvement quickly became an important marker of being 'Baptist' or 'Brethren' in colonial religious society. While involved in their own denominational ventures, their participation in myriad other missionary organisations was also enthusiastically supported by church members. The role of the NZBTI in sustaining this pattern, from the early 1920s, was important, as were a range of other evangelical institutions, from the production of literature to annual conventions that complemented the NZBTI.

Geographically, at least two further patterns were apparent. One was the increasingly urban origins of missionaries – not surprising given the increasingly urbanised nature of the population and the numerical growth of boroughs. By the 1930s missionaries came from a great variety of localities, indicating that a missionary consciousness was now embedded in a very wide cross-section of regions, towns and cities. The other pattern was the link between geography, families and missionary enthusiasm. There were discrete geographical pockets that provided proportionally more missionaries than other places – the areas surrounding Gore, Blenheim, and Nelson, for example. While many families contributed two siblings, others were even more prominent: five sisters from the Shirtliff family in Nelson, three from the Opie family in Christchurch, and four children of pioneer Presbyterian missionaries Peter and Mary Milne departed New Zealand as missionaries in this period. Families were often linked by the marriages of missionaries and, as time progressed, siblings and children also became missionaries across several generations. Families also helped to link together particular denominations, churches, localities and organisations. In the process, parents became missionary organisers because of their children's involvement. It was to be expected, perhaps, that with a relatively small population and many dispersed or discrete communities, such linkages would have a considerable emotional and financial impact.

Despite reflecting the wider settler population in many respects, over this period missionaries stood out as atypical with respect to education and occupational background. The introduction of compulsory primary schooling from 1877, along with the growing provision of and expectations for a high school education, meant that missionaries came to their task with ever-improved qualifications by the early 1900s. More specifically, however, missionaries with post-school qualifications quickly became the norm. There were more missionary university graduates than in the wider population. By the 1910s, more women missionaries than ever before held university degrees, although the missionary occupations they moved into often still reflected the pattern of women's occupations at home. Teaching or missionary work, for example, was the main employment goal of early women graduates from Otago University College.[49] While missionary applicants came from a broad range of occupational backgrounds, those who became missionaries were predominantly semi-professionals such as ordained ministers, teachers, nurses and doctors. The provision of lay ministry training through the various institutes also meant that growing numbers of people from diverse occupational backgrounds received a higher level of education than might otherwise have been the case. For younger Protestant folk in the 1900s and 1910s, a missionary occupation had clearly become a valid career option to consider, even if the possibilities for employment were not inexhaustible. On the reverse side, missionary organisations increasingly looked for well-qualified applicants to meet the growing professional needs of mission contexts, or for those who would be appropriately trained within an acceptable age range. By World War I, among the recorded reasons for rejection of applicants, 'too old' and 'a lack of qualifications' were frequently cited. New Zealand missionaries of the 1920s and 1930s came from a more diverse range of backgrounds, and the faith missions opened up educational and work opportunities previously beyond the reach of many churchgoers. At the same time, this was a distinctive and well-qualified workforce that reflected middle-class religious aspirations while facing the ever more specialised demands of missionary work.

Finally, missionary work took these 1000 people to a diverse range of global locations. Figure 1.2 depicts both the main points of destination and the changes that took place up to 1939.

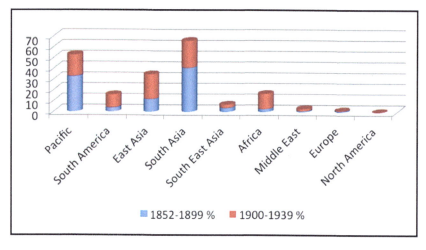

FIGURE 1.2. Regional Destinations of New Zealand Missionaries, 1852–1939

The relationship between these destinations and denominational priorities will be explored further in Chapter Six. From the very beginning, however, New Zealand Protestants were linked to various parts of the Pacific – particularly Polynesia and Melanesia – albeit often in paternalist ways up to World War II. As early as the 1870s and 1880s, the opinion was expressed that the 'Churches in Australia and New Zealand' should have major responsibility for this region.[50] Pacific locations and communities became forever linked with the identities and concerns of most New Zealand Protestant denominations. Yet at that very same time, and to the chagrin of some, the heavily populated areas of East Asia and the South

Asian subcontinent opened up to missionary attention. Thus began a great love affair between New Zealand Protestants, China and India. The subcontinent took almost a third of all departing missionaries up to 1939, and remained an important focus in the years after World War II. South America and, increasingly, Africa also became important destinations from the early twentieth century. In the cases of India and many African territories this was often, but not always, linked to the interests of and opportunities afforded by British imperial administration.

These, then, are the bare facts. What New Zealand's missionaries and their supporters thought about their task, how they were influenced in their thinking, and what motivated them are the subjects of the following three chapters.

CHAPTER 2

Theological Contours and Trends

IN SEPTEMBER 1890 Annie Bacon was farewelled from the Hanover Street Baptist Church in Dunedin as a New Zealand Baptist Missionary Society (NZBMS) nursing missionary to East Bengal. In his farewell address, the Revd Alfred North made a very telling statement. He observed that Annie, 'in the Zenanas and among the low-caste women, will be able to alleviate bodily sufferings, and to preserve imperilled life, as well as carry the good tidings of the Great Healer, whose loving care embraces our nature in its entirety, and who Himself set the example of the combination of these ministries'.[1] This was a surprisingly broad formulation that was firmly rooted in a Christ-centred rationale for missions. Yet barely a generation later, George Allan, the New Zealand founder of the Bolivian Indian Mission (BIM), commented critically that '[t]here was a time when it could be taken for granted that missions existed for the purpose of carrying to the heathen an accepted standard of saving evangelical truth which was known as THE GOSPEL [his emphasis]. That is no longer the case … For while [the larger missions] have in the ranks of their workers very many who are true to that Gospel standard, they also have those who have embraced that which is subversive of the whole truth of the Gospel, and which is destructive of faith in God's Word.'[2] By 1916 George Allan's thinking about missions appeared to be much more tightly circumscribed, much less expansive and much more defensive than Alfred North's statement of 1890. Both were southern New Zealanders steeped in evangelical Protestant Christianity, in many ways cut from the same religious and cultural cloth, but separated by time and circumstances.

Archival evidence provides many clues as to how overseas missions were theologically constructed and perceived throughout this period, both by early New Zealand missionaries themselves and by those who supported them. This evidence, derived from across the Protestant denominations, indicates that missionary theology was initially fluid and variegated in how it was defined and conceived. Until the 1920s, this fluidity existed within the boundaries of a broadly evangelical conception of both task and context. In the 1920s, as a result of World War I and the conservative evangelical reaction to theological modernism, these patterns began to change. In this chapter, I outline this shift with reference to the language and imagery employed by a wide range of men and women from both denominational and non-denominational backgrounds. There is a focus on clusters of images that emerged, the nuances within them and how these changed.

An overview of the theological construction of overseas mission

Protestant New Zealanders employed an astonishingly wide range of terms, images and concepts to articulate their understanding of and rationale for overseas missionary involvement. While the evidence for the period prior to the 1890s is relatively fragmentary, two broad observations can be made for this earlier period. First, there was a considerable degree of consensus with respect to how the missionary venture was theologically understood within the international missionary movement of the later nineteenth century. The emerging New Zealand movement was largely evangelical, with particular roots in British evangelicalism. By the late 1880s there seemed to be a 'generic evangelical comity' within the wider international movement and a considerable degree of optimism that the conversion of the world was possible.[3] The theological sentiments emanating from New Zealand reflected that same confidence in what the Revd Peter Milne earlier called the 'certainty of the world's conversion'.[4] Mid- to late nineteenth-century British and New Zealand evangelicalism, and the missionary movement in particular, also reflected Enlightenment-inspired optimism in the ultimate progress of European civilisation.[5] Second, the early New Zealand movement was theologically nuanced, albeit to a limited extent, reflecting the wider contemporary British movement; that is, not all Protestants adhered to exactly the same tenets. For example, Anglicans tended not to refer to the so-called 'Great Commission' of Matthew 28:19–20 that was so central to other Protestant constructions of missions, placing a greater emphasis on the more abstract imagery of prophetic and apocalyptic biblical literature.

Again, the early Presbyterian appeal to generic notions of 'duty', and 'obedience to her Master's Command', differed to some extent from the Baptist emphasis on the perceived spiritual and social needs of the Indian people.[6] Presbyterian statements also tended to emphasise the notion of Christianity as a leavening influence in society, more so than Anglicans or Baptists.

Table 2.1 is an attempt to outline the ways in which missionary thinking was predominantly phrased from 1890 onwards, using categories that arose out of the data collected for this study. In what follows, I go on to consider these more fully. These categories of thought were by no means discrete or mutually exclusive. Some categories waxed and waned or oscillated, others consistently grew in importance and some, initially non-existent in the data, appeared only later. One category – establishing indigenous churches in mission territories as the goal of missions – did not in fact appear in missionary rhetoric until after World War I.

Mission as	Overall Rank	1890–1918	1919–1930
Salvation/Conversion	1	1	1
Response to Great Need	2	3	2
Going/Taking the Gospel	3	2	4
Duty/Obligation	4	4	7
Preaching/Teaching	5	5	8
Warfare	6	9	6
Extending God's Kingdom	7	6	10=
Christian Leavening	8	7	12
Enlightenment	9	8	9
Response to God's Command	10	10	5
Service/Sacrifice	11	11	3
Representing Christ	12	13	10=
Reaping a Harvest	13	12	13
Liberation	14	15	14
Premillennial Urgency	15	14	16
Biblical Fulfilment	16	16	17
Establishing Indigenous Church	17	–	15

TABLE 2.1. Ranked Descriptions of Mission by New Zealanders, 1890–1930[7]

As Table 2.2 further indicates, these descriptors can be reworked to yield a wide range of antithetical word pairs, concepts that were defining images in the theological construction of missions.

Christendom	Non-Christendom	Christendom	Non-Christendom
Light	Darkness	Happy	Wretched
Sight	Blind	Pure	Degraded
Freedom	Slavery	Blessed	Cursed
Knowledge	Ignorance	Wealth	Poverty
Saved	Unsaved	Whole	Incomplete
Nourished	Starving	Hopeful	Hopeless
Life	Death	Culture	Uncultured

TABLE 2.2. Dualistic Images of Mission, 1890–1930[8]

Underlying these polarities was a dualistic view of the world that differentiated between non-heathen Christendom and heathen non-Christendom, creating a kind of global mental geography defined in religious terms. Many of these contrasting pairs reflected a growing awareness of the gap in material welfare between settler society in New Zealand and many other parts of the world – an awareness influenced, for example, by such disasters as the terrible famine that devastated India in 1900 and that was publicised throughout the British Empire. These images referred primarily to the perceived spiritual condition of those outside Christendom. Vivid imagery of this kind was intended to act as a spur to further missionary action and support on the part of the New Zealand churches.

The data also indicate that a relatively wide range of biblical texts were appealed to in missionary sermons and addresses. In the pre-1890 period we find few references to the more prophetic and apocalyptic literature of the Old Testament. While the use of Psalms and Isaiah was most noticeable from 1890 onward, in the mission context biblical texts were almost exclusively drawn from the New Testament, particularly from the Gospels. Most popular were Matthew 28:19–20 and Mark 16:15, the so-called Great Commission texts. By the 1920s these two sets of verses were commonly conflated into a single broad command from God to go and preach the gospel worldwide; for the international Protestant movement, they persisted as defining texts well into the 1900s.[9]

Mission as conversion, salvation and evangelisation

Overseas missions were theologically understood, throughout this period, in predominantly conversionist terms. Eugene Stock, visiting New Zealand in 1892 on behalf of the Church Missionary Society, told those gathered in the Christchurch Cathedral that 'after nineteen centuries there was yet more than half the population of the globe who had not heard of the word of God ... the world had to be converted'. In 1902 an article in the China Inland Mission (CIM) magazine *China's Millions* suggested that if 'there were only one Christian in the world, and he worked for a year and won a friend to Christ, and those two continued to win each year another ... in thirty-one years every person in the world would be won for Christ'.[10] These sentiments mirrored those to be found in the colony itself and were prevalent in the literature read by colonial Protestants. 'Conversion' was a broadly defined concept. Underlying the whole missionary discourse was a fundamental concern for both the spiritual state of those not Christian and for the moral and societal transformation of non-European and non-Christian societies. This agenda was consistent throughout the period, and across lines of gender and denomination. Thus conversion was understood to be an act of enlightenment, liberation, and of spiritual and social transformation. It was also perceived to be a metaphysical transplanting of individuals and societies from the sphere of heathenism to the new progressive sphere of Christendom. As the period progressed, it was obvious that some groups, like the CIM and BIM, emphasised the personal aspects of this task more than others. It was also obvious that the denominational societies ultimately sought to establish communities of believers, among a range of other priorities, and that a few aimed at a limited enculturation of their message. As a result, both the philosophy and the methods of 'conversion' – preaching and teaching, medical work, women's work, education – were necessarily broadly defined and conceived. 'Conversion' was co-equally the conversion of souls, bodies and minds, and of geographic, cultural and social space.

The commonly used term 'evangelisation' encapsulated this breadth and fluidity. This was a slippery term, the meaning of which is best understood within its immediate historical and textual locations in the 1890s and early 1900s. Historically, the use of the word in the New Zealand context was most directly affected by both the rise of the American Student Volunteer Movement for Foreign Missions, established in Australasia in 1896 and discussed further in Chapter Three, and by the movement's watchword, 'the evangelisation of the world in this generation'. This slogan was vigorously debated and eventually accepted by the New Zealand branches of the Australasian Students' Christian Union in 1899.[11] Early international formulations of the slogan were pre-millennial in tone. If all means possible were used to hasten the return of Christ, then the complete evangelisation of the world, in the lifetime of those alive at the end of the nineteenth century, was of paramount importance. Within this formulation 'evangelisation' was defined primarily as the proclamation of Christianity, rather than the conversion of the world.[12] From around 1900, the American missionary statesman John R. Mott helped to shift the focus away from these pre-millennial associations, arguing that 'the evangelization of the world in this generation ... means the preaching of the Gospel to those who are now living'.[13] The emphasis, however, still lay on evangelisation as proclamation rather than conversion.

When the textual uses of 'evangelisation' in the New Zealand literature are examined, it seems reasonable to reach similar conclusions about the way the term was locally understood and used. Again, its use was influenced by exposure to the Student Volunteer Movement and the changes in thinking that had occurred by 1900. Yet it was still a very ambiguous term. On the one hand, it seemed to refer to missionary proclamation rather than to conversion. The CMS Gleaners' Union, for example, sought to unite 'all who are interested in the cause [the CMS] represents, viz. the Evangelisation of the world'.[14] On the other hand, the word was occasionally used almost as a synonym for the act of conversion. George Allan (BIM) explicitly used 'evangelisation' in the late 1890s in the context of observing that the people of South America were ready for Christian conversion.[15]

Two formulations of the term after 1900 helped to define it further for New Zealand audiences. In his presidential speech before the Baptist Union in 1903, the Revd R.S. Gray argued that 'the purpose of God' found its 'best, and indeed only adequate expression, in [the phrase] the Evangelisation of the World', and that the 'place of the Church in this purpose of God is that of the divinely constituted agent'. He went on to press the need for the Church to be primarily 'missionary' in its focus and activity.

'Evangelisation' was the all-encompassing activity of 'going with and communicating the gospel'.[16] In this sense, 'evangelisation' incorporated both the means by which the Christian message could be communicated and its intended outcome of conversion. Similarly, the Revd Herbert Davies, a Presbyterian missionary in southern China, suggested that 'a country is evangelised when every man, woman and child has had an adequate opportunity of hearing carefully and fully expounded the Gospel of Jesus Christ'.[17] In most cases then, 'evangelisation' was used as a form of shorthand for conveying the message of Jesus Christ that the vast majority of the world's population still had not heard. Some New Zealanders may have understood the term in pre-millennial terms. For most people, however, 'the signs of the times' (for example, open access to previously inaccessible parts of the world and increasingly sophisticated communication and media technologies) indicated that the time was ripe for a concerted response to the great needs of the world. Against this background, the methods and strategies to be adopted by missionaries and missionary organisations could be broadly and imaginatively defined.

Mission as a response to great need

Before 1890 the notion of mission as a 'response to great need' was predominantly a distinctively Baptist concern. From the 1890s, however, this category became an increasingly prominent feature of all colonial Protestant groups. In the contemporary literature of the wider international movement, there was a growing tendency to emphasise statistics relating, for example, to Asian populations and the numbers adhering to religions other than Christianity. Statistics were often deployed to help define the – mostly deplorable – religious state of the world and to rally the Church to the missionary cause. One typical graphical diagram, published in 1889, was accompanied by the observation that 'of every three persons walking on the vast globe, two have never heard of the Saviour, have never seen a Bible, know nothing of heaven and nothing of hell'.[18] New Zealanders were ready consumers of such representations, whether locally or internationally produced.

At the same time, there were indications that the 'great need of the heathen world' was also to be understood in humanitarian terms, particularly with respect to the perceived plight of Asian women and children and the reports of widespread famines in India and China. In addition, there were often references to specific cultural practices, such as foot binding in China and child brides and widow-burnings in India, or to systemic issues concerning public health or the Indian caste system. New Zealand missionaries often wrote accounts in missionary publications that reinforced these stereotypical images for the churchgoing public – a phenomenon that was also common throughout the broader international missionary movement.[19]

Yet missionary writers and speakers also articulated a more sophisticated sense of the needs of others that reflected their everyday realities. Dr John Kirk, a medical missionary in China, remonstrated with the Presbyterian General Assembly in 1910 that 'the name of our hospital [Ko T'ong] stands for "Universal Love", and if this is to have any meaning at all in the hearts of the people – aye, if the Gospel of Jesus Christ is to have any meaning at all – we cannot afford to turn poor, pain-burdened, weary souls from our door'.[20] Various publications by the non-denominational BIM also argued that the social amelioration of Bolivia's Quechua Indians, and the righting of their socio-political injustices, was just as important as evangelism per se. There were clearly those who saw specialist activities, such as medical and educational missions, as inherently valid and important, and not just as precursors to overt evangelism. These attitudes must also have filtered back to the New Zealand public. Later application records across denominations indicate that, from 1910 onwards, a growing number of people were applying specifically to be medical or educational missionaries.

Obligation, duty, service and sacrifice

From the early 1900s this strong theme of 'responding to great need' was linked with a distinctive cluster of theological categories that included the divine commandment to incarnate the gospel worldwide; a strong undercurrent of spirituality that emphasised service and sacrifice; and the duty, obligation or responsibility attendant upon both individuals and churches. The latter was most often based on St Paul's sense of obligation to both 'Greeks and non-Greeks' (Romans 1:14; NIV). When she applied to the New Zealand Church Missionary Association (NZCMA) in 1911, Doris Wilks suggested that 'we who know the joy of His salvation should be keenly anxious to pass on the same privilege ... to lift them up from the darkness of ignorance and sin into the glorious light of Christ's gospel'.[21] Here, she was reflecting specifically upon Christ's missionary commandment found in Matthew 28:19. In a similar, if somewhat balder vein, one Presbyterian commentator suggested that 'it is the duty of happy people to thrust their happiness upon others less happy'.[22]

A variety of factors contributed to this aspect of missions including youth movements like Christian Endeavour, the Student Christian Unions and the Bible class movement; women's groups like the Presbyterian, Methodist and Baptist Women's Missionary Unions; missionary literature, mission study circles and visiting missionary speakers; and Christian conventions. As a result of all these influences, the motivation for overseas missions was increasingly as much humanitarian as it was theological; this again mirrored international trends both before and after the Edinburgh World Missionary Conference of 1910. This situation was epitomised in a drawing included in a 1905 Australasian Baptist Prayer Calendar, reproduced in Figure 2.1. The caption read: 'The touch of Christ upon India is one of compassionate longing and beseeching appeal.' The call of Christ to sacrificial service, the perceived needs of India, and the obligation of the Church (all elements present in the drawing) became co-equal elements in the consciousness of the New Zealand churchgoing public.

The focus on service and sacrifice was evident right throughout the period up to 1939. Mixed up in this were notions of personal usefulness, of service motivated by love, of the need for personal surrender to the call of God, and the view that the urgent task would not be completed without human agency or availability. This emphasis became particularly obvious in the documentary evidence after 1918. The impact of World War I on New Zealand society was unprecedented – of the 100,000 men sent to fight, around 58,000 died or were wounded, comprising some 25 per cent of males of military age. While the years quickly passed, the traumatic memories did not. During the 1920s the erection of public memorials and the annual ritual of Anzac Day reflected how close to the collective surface the trauma of war remained, and gave New Zealand the closest thing the nation had to civil religious observance. James Belich muses that a 'cult of 18,000 Kiwi Christs emerged, whose sacrifice simply had to have been for a noble cause'.[24]

It was hardly surprising then that the potent language of warfare, and of sacrificial service and duty, was co-opted for the missionary cause.

FIGURE 2.1. India's Need
and Christ's Call, 1905[23]

The New Zealand experience of war, especially the Gallipoli campaign, provided many of the anecdotes and much of the imagery used to stir people up in the cause of missions. A classic example of this was in the 1915 NZBMS report, where the secretary included the following annotated anecdote about the Gallipoli campaign: 'When our boys landed at the Dardanelles, a group of them, occupying an advanced position, had its officer shot dead. Another officer, somewhere in the rear, thereupon signalled for the members of that group to retire. Instead of obeying, they flashed back the words, "New Zealanders never retire." Into the work of the Kingdom let us put the same spirit as these men are putting into the fight for the Empire.'[25] Missionary publicists and speakers exhorted young people to emulate the spirit of sacrifice shown by soldiers and other wartime volunteers. Furthermore, they did so because they had a keen sense that while wartime service had been of great importance, so also was the cause of taking the gospel to a world in heightened spiritual and humanitarian need. This was promoted as a high and worthy cause, and the language of patriotic service, heard so often between 1914 and 1918, fitted readily into the missionary rhetoric of the postwar years. The Revd William Hinton, newly installed as Baptist Union President in 1921 and a past missionary with the Poona and Indian Village Mission, captured the spirit of the times when he reminded young people that 'the call is to sacrifice ... the Master and His service are abundantly worthy of it. No greater honour to a home or a church can be conceived than that they should have a representative on the Mission Field.'[26] Indeed, the subtext of his message may have been that the missionary cause was ultimately more important than the cause that had so recently left such a terrible scar on the national psyche.

By the 1920s and 1930s the general call to responsibility and sacrificial service had been intensely personalised. Dorothy Mathew's comment to the Presbyterian FMC, that 'God commanded "Go". I heard and, in consequence am offering my services', was a common refrain in applicant records.[27] In the light of the above discussion, her response suggests that the post-World War I rhetoric did indeed have an impact on individuals. It further indicates that many people interpreted the biblical texts on mission as being personally addressed to them. The notion of mission as a response to God's command, embodied in Matthew 28:19–20 and Mark 16:15, was of crucial importance. The original Greek rendering of both texts indicates that the task of mission was originally entrusted to a community of believers. Yet a generation or more of Protestant evangelical theology and spirituality, which increasingly emphasised individual conversion, private devotional practices, and personal accountability before God, had resulted in a general commandment to the whole Church being subconsciously internalised as a personally addressed imperative. Missionary publicists thus wielded a very potent tool in their repertoire of publicity and recruitment methods.

Expansion and a changing world

The final cluster of terms or images to be considered here emphasised the expansionist nature of Christianity, in particular the acts of going with, carrying, or taking the gospel; of conquest; and of extending the Kingdom of God. At colonial centennial celebrations for the Baptist Missionary Society in 1892, Auckland Baptists sang:

Let the Indian, let the Negro,
Let the rude barbarian see
That divine and glorious conquest
Once obtained on Calvary:
Let the gospel
Loud resound from pole to pole.

Fly abroad, thou mighty gospel,
Win and conquer, never cease;
May thy lasting, wide dominion
Multiply and still increase:
Sway thy sceptre,
Saviour, all the world around.[28]

This was a period of optimism, and of confidence in the belief that Christianity would 'win and conquer', 'multiply and still increase', and finally 'loud resound from pole to pole'. In this, the local missionary movement mirrored the expansionist sentiments of the era of 'high imperialism', in which it was embedded, and celebrated its continuity with the past at the same time as it anticipated a bright future. As I explore further in Chapter Three, the notion of expansion embraced by New Zealanders may also have been increasingly influenced from the 1890s by the American factor.[29] There were strong resonances between the two societies with respect to 'pioneering' and frontier expansion.

On the surface, it seems fair to argue that such thinking was not easily disentangled, by the participants, from language that more particularly extolled the virtues of the British Empire. This is the further focus of Chapter Six. In the colonial context, such sentiments emerged out of historical, cultural and familial proximity to British roots and remained strong up until at least the late 1920s. The two decades following World War I, however, also marked a change in this perspective. Although New Zealand was still intensely proud and supportive of the British Empire, at the same time, in both the local and international missionary rhetoric, there were at least indications that significant changes lay ahead. The war itself had exposed a disturbing human heart of darkness, raising serious questions about human progress. Many people now understood that world peace was a fragile commodity and that, rightly or wrongly, the new forces of liberation emerging around the globe were a potential threat to that peace.

On the one hand, nationalist movements and sentiments, particularly in India and China, were having a ripple effect among indigenous Christian communities. It became increasingly obvious to missionary societies across the spectrum that a key task in this period would be the establishment of independent churches and structures. Dr J.J. Kitchen, chairman of the Australasian branches of the CIM, declared in 1922 that 'the most important feature of missionary work in China to-day is the preparation of the Chinese Church to undertake its responsibilities ... a self-supporting, self-propagating, and self-governing [Church] should surely be the ultimate aim of all Foreign Missionary effort'.[30] There was a noticeable maturing of attitudes. Some had the hindsight to realise that European domination was a 'historic accident'.[31] They at least acknowledged the inevitable democratisation of colonial societies, even if they were unsure about it, and they affirmed the principle of equality between European and non-European Christians. After visiting Presbyterian missionaries in 1921, the Revd H.H. Barton argued that 'most of all, perhaps, are we called upon to take our place alongside the Chinese and of the Indians as our brothers, not as lords over God's heritage, and to do what in us lies to help them to develop along lines that shall be natural to them and free from all suspicion of being a foreign importation imposed upon them from without'.[32]

On the other hand, fears increased that these rapidly modernising societies would be swamped by the non-religious and materialist elements of Western civilisation, and that local churches would not be mature or strong enough to stop or reverse this process. Yet there was something more than just this fear evident in the post-1918 era; New Zealand and international commentators of the early 1920s repeatedly used the phrase 'race problem' when referring to the ferment of nationalist feelings in Asia. In 1924 J.H. Oldham, secretary of the newly formed International Missionary Council, devoted a book to the relationship of Christianity to the race problem, in particular the 'ethical problems which arise from the contact of races and which constitute a grave menace to the peace of the world and to the co-operation and progress of its peoples'.[33] John Mott picked up on this theme at the 1926 New Zealand National Missionary Conference in Dunedin, and his comments make interesting reading:

The shrinkage of the world ... has set the races to acting and re-acting upon each other with startling directness, power, and virulence ... A serious aspect of the matter is that wherever two or more races are brought into close contact, without the restraining influence of a power greater than human, demoralisation all too often follows. Something takes place which tends to draw out the worst in each race ... There are in races, as in individuals, not only heights which reach up to highest heaven, but also depths which lay hold on deepest hell. The deepest hell into which I have ever gazed has been in places where the races have been thrown against each other without adequate restraint.[34]

Undoubtedly, the missionary rhetoric on this issue sought to apply a Christian voice to complex global issues. Many would have argued that this was basically a theological problem, that 'individual regeneration afford[ed] the only solid basis for social betterment', and that 'only in Christianity do we find the higher synthesis in which mankind can thus be lastingly reconciled'.[35] Yet perhaps what Mott, Oldham and other New Zealand commentators were also expressing was a fundamental fear of change and of global disharmony, a situation in which the West might come off second best and through which its progress, of which Christianity was the perceived apex, might be nullified. The 'problem' of Bolshevism, in the wake of the Russian Revolutions of 1917, must have added to this mix of fear and confusion. Thus while Christianity was the 'restraining influence' that Mott alluded to, the question may have remained as to what needed restraining. This fear found its most extreme expression in the words of an Australian Baptist, who openly argued that the evangelisation of the 'dark races' neighbouring Australia was the only certain way by which the nation might be spiritually and morally protected.[36] While this was clearly an Australian opinion, it was carefully reported verbatim in the *New Zealand Baptist*. Similar fears were perhaps not so far below the surface in New Zealand. Tom Brooking notes that successive New Zealand governments, at least up until 1945, maintained an implicit and 'less honest version' of Australia's 'white policy', a point of view that must have had its share of supporters scattered throughout the New Zealand population.[37] Thus the rationale for colonial overseas missions may have been partly construed, after World War I, as a restraining, civilising influence on what were perceived to be potentially uncontrollable and anarchic forces.

An evaluation of the theological contours of mission

In light of the major role played by women as missionary supporters and participants, it is first of all pertinent to ask to what extent New Zealand mission theology in this period was gendered. On the surface, at least from analysis of the data displayed in Tables 2.1 and 2.2, there appeared to be little differentiation between statements made by men and women about their reasons for choosing missionary work. Women, after 1900, possibly placed a greater emphasis on mission as a response to human need and as service or sacrifice. Men perhaps placed more emphasis on the socially ameliorative aspects of mission, or on duty and obligation. There may be a case here for arguing that men, as the decision-makers and arbiters of denominational or organisational power, saw mission differently from the women, who were more involved at the grassroots level of missionary support. For example, was it significant that many of the statements on mission that emphasised duty and obligation were found in annual reports written and delivered by men, or were uttered by men in various leadership positions?

There were some indications, however, that women did have an ongoing and important role in shaping missionary thinking. Women's missionary support groups drew attention to the fundamentally theological and spiritual nature of the missionary project through their devotion to and emphasis on prayer. For the Baptist Women's Missionary Union (BWMU), overseas missions were conceived of as a four-way partnership between God, missionaries, indigenous Christians and supporters at home, and, as Figure 2.2 indicates, prayer was the essential glue that held this relationship together. The BWMU members' card portrayed this relationship as a three-stranded rope strung between New Zealand and East Bengal, held tight in the middle by a brightly blazing sun and accompanied by the legend, 'Keep the Ropes Taut'.

Women's groups, along with the student unions, were also important initiators and organisers of the formal study of mission especially following the 1910 Edinburgh conference. In this role, they helped to shape a core of supporters who were quite well informed in terms of international awareness and understanding. Further, through writings and publications, women in particular accentuated the motif of 'need' by highlighting the perceived plight of women and children in places like India and China. As a consequence, they also contributed to the prevailing dualistic view of a world divided between Christendom and non-Christendom and reinforced

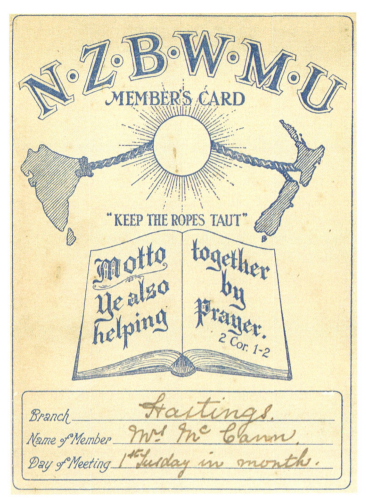

FIGURE 2.2. A Sample Baptist Women's Missionary Union Membership Card[38]

popular stereotypes of non-Western peoples and societies. Finally, women developed a strong sense of connection between New Zealand missionary supporters and their international sisters. For example, a formal association existed between the PWMU and a North American Presbyterian women's missionary alliance that, in turn, had links with the American-based World's Missionary Committee of Christian Women formed in 1888. This kind of relationship was essentially viewed as a partnership of equals. By philosophically and theologically identifying with their international 'sisters', Presbyterian women understood that they were doing so in the company of the incarnational Christ, and saw themselves as forming part of a great feminine 'girdle around the earth', albeit one that was predominantly white and Prot-estant.[39] These connections will be picked up again in Chapter Eight.

As a second major question, it is also appropriate to ask to what extent early mission theology in New Zealand was framed or packaged in distinc-tively local forms. In other words, was there a discernible body of New Zealand mission theology emerging by 1939? The evidence for this is rela-tively thin. Prior to the 1890s, the local movement was largely the product of a missionary worldview imported and fed from Great Britain. As it devel-oped, from the 1890s onwards, a variety of contributory and contextual factors served to further shape and entrench this movement as an essentially integral and inextricably linked component of the wider Anglo-American missionary movement. Even though, from the early 1900s onwards, Prot-estant New Zealanders consumed increasing amounts of locally produced missionary literature and heard returned New Zealand missionaries speaking in their churches, the content was substantially no different from what was written, read or heard in Australia, North America and Great Britain. Furthermore, it would appear that what was expressed theologi-cally in New Zealand reflected wider international trends. David Bosch argues that in the course of the nineteenth century there was a fundamental change in the formative theological motifs underlying the missionary move-ment. As an example, he cites the general shift in understanding mission from being a response to the 'glory of God' to missionary outreach being a response to both the love of God and to the perceived plight of non-Chris-tian peoples (summed up, in both cases, by the same phrase 'constrained by Jesus' love'). He further argues that different periods were marked by an appeal to different biblical texts. As we have seen, the main text appealed to was Matthew 28:19–20. Bosch argues that although this was a defining text for the wider movement, it became the dominant text for the emerging conservative evangelical elements of the missionary movement in partic-ular.[40] These features were all evident in the New Zealand context.

Having said this, however, there is some evidence that suggests that the question of independent domestic trends may be worth further reflection. In the BIM, for instance, it is possible to detect the influence of an earlier pioneering mentality that spurred on its initial pre-World War I workers, and a self-effacing attitude that tended to direct any honours away from the mission and its personnel.[41] Among New Zealand Baptists, there was a curious blend of colonial independence, self-congratulation and a sense of imperial obligation with respect to mission work in East Bengal. NZBMS reports repeatedly carried the refrain that the several millions of people in that region were New Zealand's special responsibility, entirely dependent on a handful of colonial Baptists for their eternal salvation and wellbeing. By inference, there would be dire spiritual consequences if New Zealand Baptists did not live up to that responsibility.[42] Anglican, Methodist and Presbyterian missionary applicants often expressed a strong feeling of responsibility that issued from a sense of dual privilege. On the one hand, the fact of being a Christian, and of living in a Christian society, was seen as a great privilege. On the other hand, there was an emerging perception that to live in New Zealand was itself a great privilege. This had its roots in an older notion held by European settlers that New Zealand was an intrinsically healthy and unsullied place in which to live, with no endemic diseases and very few Old World scourges like smallpox or cholera.[43] In the context of the early twentieth century, however, such attitudes must also have reflected the growing awareness of perceived developmental gaps between European and non-European societies. This sense of privilege, born out of a specific environment, was part of the motivational mix for many New Zealand missionaries.

Finally, it is also pertinent to ask to what extent significant differences in mission theology were emerging by the 1930s. Late nineteenth-century and early twentieth-century theological developments, added to the horrors, ethical issues and geopolitical changes thrown up by World War I, helped precipitate a general crisis for Western Protestantism. As Timothy Yates observes, it was inevitable that missionary work in the interwar decades, 'along with many other aspects of Western life and culture, should have been subjected to extreme and searching scrutiny'.[44] New Zealand was not untouched by these concerns. As early as 1912, the Revd John Takle noted with some concern that

[i]nnumerable articles and bewildering proposals have been thrown off the printing presses of the world, and they have exercised the minds of many a faithful soul as to where they stand in regard to faith in Christ. The criticism of the Bible, Evolution, Socialism, and the findings of certain scientists ... [a]ll this religious unrest at Home, affecting both laymen and ministers, has a tremendous influence on the conception and work of missions ... For example the 'New Theology' with its higher pantheism can never help missions. Such views undermine

the missionary imperative … On the Mission Field the pendulum of thought has been swinging in the direction of liberalism at a very rapid rate for some time, and one wonders when it will stop.[45]

Changing views about how the missionary task was to be conducted and about the very rationale for missions, plus the formation of various theological camps as a response, were simply a reflection of wider debates and developments. In New Zealand, however, it seems fair to argue that, at least up to 1939, the impact of these debates was limited to certain groups and contexts.

One example will suffice to illustrate this. World War I had a particular impact on the emerging missionary thinking of the various Western student movements. The New Zealand Student Christian Movement (NZSCM) debated missionary policy in the mid-1920s, and produced at least one reformulated policy statement as a result. This statement placed a new emphasis on intelligent engagement with world issues, and on identification with other peoples under the twin rubric of the 'Fatherhood of God' and the 'Brotherhood of Man'. Mission was essentially viewed as a co-operative exercise with indigenous peoples and churches.[46] At the same time, student missionary thinking became a major site of ideological conflict. In response to this report, one commentator critical of its contents sought to delineate the 'dangers of the present position' that it adopted. It is possible that the anonymous author of these comments was Dr William Pettit, who had been a medical missionary in India with the NZBMS up to 1915. By the 1920s he had become increasingly strident in his criticisms of the direction taken by the NZSCM. His opposition centred primarily on a perceived overemphasis on the terms 'fatherhood of God' and 'brotherhood of man', which in his view served to blur distinctions between 'the saved and the unsaved', and on an alleged misunderstanding of the concept of the 'Kingdom of God'. The writer concluded that such rhetoric would weaken overseas missions, warning that 'it is at our peril that we turn aside from our divinely appointed task to some fascinating programme of social betterment and internationalism'.[47]

Differences in opinion over the content and direction of overseas missions served to demarcate those willing to embrace new modes of thought from those seeking to defend what they understood to be old and non-negotiable orthodoxies. In the New Zealand case, a more irenic, pietistic and denominationally entrenched conservative evangelicalism in the post-1918 years meant that this dividing line had a minimal impact. At the same time, the various faith-based missions, like their international counterparts, partially cast themselves as the true defenders of biblical and evangelical faith, and as the true dispensers of the Christian gospel overseas. As a result of these tensions, the underlying theological rationale for, and the potential ecumenicity of, the missionary movement was well under threat by the mid- to late 1920s.

Conclusion

In this chapter I have deliberately steered away from any reference to a fixed or finite entity called 'New Zealand mission theology' for the period up to 1939. Rather, I have preferred the concept of 'theological contours', which more fairly reflects the breadth, fluidity and variegated nature of the landscape of missionary theology throughout this period. It would be fair to say that most groups or denominations accepted a number of core theological components with regard to mission: God as Creator and Redeemer (of both individuals and societies); the comprehensive sinfulness of humanity (regardless of geographical location, race or ethnicity); the overarching, grace-filled love of God; the responsibilities and duty of God's redeemed people (the Church) to be agents of global salvation, liberation and enlightenment; and the eventual eschatological consummation of the Kingdom of God. At the same time, however, acceptance of these common truths did not restrict missionaries and mission organisations to any one philosophy or approach. Rather the fluidity – and, indeed, ambiguity – that marked the period served to locate missionary work at varying points on a scale of oppositional terms. Thus mission as defined by a particular group ranged between conversion and social amelioration, proclamation and Christianisation, and incarnation and religious or social activism. Only as the debates and conservative defensiveness of the post-1918 period emerged did this underlying fluidity or cohesiveness begin to dissipate.

Yet it was obvious late in the period that there was still an overall mood of optimism concerning the place of missionary organisations in the wider global context. The Revd John McKenzie, a Presbyterian missionary in China, asserted optimistically in 1928 that 'to-day in China we face the symbolic challenge of the Open Road'.[48] Cataclysmic world events, and the prospect of future changes, were mostly viewed as a stimulus for greater effort. Furthermore, it is probable that what missionaries were doing – and what the public perceived them as doing – was essentially not so different from previous decades. Nor were the two all that different with respect to how they were portrayed in the media, as a children's cartoon in an Anglican publication from 1932 illustrates (Figure 2.3).

FIGURE 2.3. Children's Cartoon: The Adventures of Inky and Nugget, 1932[49]

While the comic strip series from which this frame is taken will be considered further in Chapter Seven, we note here that the cartoon was clearly aimed at a younger audience and may not have been given much attention by the magazine's adult readers. Yet it was the product of an adult artist. It suggests that the missionary discourse of the 1920s and 1930s, just as much as in earlier years, still contained a certain degree of paternalism, some deprecation of non-Christian religions, and an emphasis on Western cultural accoutrements right down to the deckchair and the missionary's cigarette. Furthermore, in a period in which missionary women outnumbered men two to one, it was curious (and telling) that the missionary in the cartoon was still depicted as male.

Some comment is appropriate, here, as to the theological trends that emerged from 1939 onwards. My first observation is that as the post-1918 gaps within New Zealand Protestantism widened, at least two missiological streams emerged. These could be labelled broadly as 'conservative' and 'ecumenical', and were local manifestations of international trends. In the 1930s and 1940s this was most evident in the establishment of a National Missionary Council as a precursor to the ecumenical National Council of Churches; the rapid growth of interdenominational missions; the increasing dominance of the Auckland-based NZBTI among Protestant conservatives; and the creation of two divergent Christian movements among secondary school and university students. From the 1950s this dividing of the ways was also a feature of much denominational thinking, as church assemblies and synods wrestled with the postcolonial era of indigenous political and ecclesiastical independence. Many of the mainline denominations moved away from a conversionist or expansionist mode of thought, to embrace instead the notion of partnership and a commitment to wider socio-economic aid and development.

My second observation, however, is that the growing theological divide between so-called evangelical and ecumenical missionary thinking was often more rhetorical than real. There continued to be a great emphasis placed on the ameliorative aspects of mission, regardless of where organisations or denominations lay along the theological spectrum. This trend became more pronounced from the 1980s onwards, as evangelicals in particular embraced a more holistic approach to mission. Thus mission was still predominantly defined as a response to the physical, socio-economic and spiritual needs of others. In other words, the ambiguous and variegated nature of mission remained. Innovative organisations such as Servants to Asia's Urban Poor (which originated in New Zealand),[50] and wide public support for both interchurch aid ventures and organisations like World Vision and Tear Fund, underscored an essentially pragmatic Antipodean approach to the wider world and its needs. In these respects, then, late twentieth and early twenty-first-century formulations of mission show that the original words of the Revd Alfred North in 1890 still have strong resonances for the present.

CHAPTER 3

Transnational Influences

THREE BAPTIST MISSIONARY departures provide a framework for this chapter. The first was that of a Christchurch woman who went by the delightful name of Hopestill Pillow. Probably English-born, she sailed to East Bengal in 1889 to work as a missionary for the NZBMS. This society had been formed in 1885 specifically to supplement the work of the parent English Baptist Missionary Society (BMS) in East Bengal. While it was a New Zealand initiative begun with South Australian assistance, the NZBMS was deliberately 'English' in its inspiration and values. The ghost of William Carey, the English founder of the original BMS, stood resolutely behind the Antipodean endeavour. Hopestill was the third of three women who made up the society's workforce by 1890. Tragically, in 1895, she was also the second to die from illness.[1] She was preceded to India by a second Baptist missionary – Annie Newcombe – in 1887. Annie was born and raised in Melbourne, Australia. Originally a Congregationalist, she joined the Baptists as a young adult after graduating from art school, and initially offered her services to the Victoria BMS. Ill health forced her early return from India in 1889. Annie remained in New Zealand, married the Revd Harry Driver, established a women's missionary training home in Dunedin (1899–1903) that later became the Presbyterian Women's Training Institute, and became one of the key leaders of the BWMU. Her brother Dr Fred Newcombe also worked briefly with the NZBMS as a medical missionary in India before succumbing to illness in 1905.[2] The third Baptist departure involved Alfred Roke and Christina (Tina) McLennan, who departed respectively in 1929 and 1930. Tina married Alfred in Addis Ababa in 1932. They had met while attending a church in Auckland, and were both students at the New Zealand Bible Training Institute (NZBTI). Unlike Hopestill and Annie, however, they went to Ethiopia (and later Anglo-Egyptian Sudan) with the

Sudan Interior Mission (SIM), whose origins lay in the pioneering work of Canadian Rowland Bingham in the Niger during the early 1890s. By the 1920s SIM had become identified with American conservative evangelicalism, and found a niche with like-minded people in New Zealand. Alf and Tina finally returned home in 1947 to take up further Baptist ministry, after a difference of opinion with the mission had led to their resignation.[3]

While in the previous chapter I outlined a general set of theological influences on New Zealand's emerging missionary movement, in this chapter I focus on the ways in which New Zealand's missionary involvement was more particularly shaped by Australian and American influences. Hopestill Pillow's ministry issued from wider, pre-existing missionary ties with Britain – families, marriages, organisations, theology, training, education and recruitment – which were enduring and significant. The rhetoric of imperial citizenship was important and bound the colony and British metropole together until at least the late 1920s. These connections are further developed in Chapters Six and Seven. Historiographically, New Zealand's links with Britain have also been important, theorised most notably in the recent scholarship of James Belich with respect to such concepts as 'recolonisation' and 'better Britonism'. These studies, in turn, are located within a wider arena of Anglo-world scholarship.[4]

Yet, as the other two missionary vignettes indicate, the British connection was not the whole story. New Zealand's fortunes have also been intimately linked to both Australia and America in myriad cultural and economic ways. Miles Fairburn has used the examples of Australian and American influences on New Zealand's cultural history to further challenge the notion of New Zealand exceptionality, and to balance the focus on British ties emphasised in the writings of Belich. He contends that settler New Zealand was increasingly characterised by a 'pastiche culture' that was a product of combined British, Australian and American influences.[5] While religion and mission were not in his purview, they do provide additional social and cultural categories of analysis by which to better understand this process. Of the two the link with Australia is the least surprising, given the proximity, shared histories and cultural commonalities of the two nations. The influence of the United States of America, however, is perhaps the more neglected element. In this chapter I examine some of the ways in which Australian and American Christianity influenced the early development of New Zealand's missionary movement. I explore the dynamics of this relationship through some representative examples, and focus on the historiographical issues that emerge.

New Zealand and Australia

While the fortunes of New Zealand and Australia have been historically intertwined since the late eighteenth century, this interconnection has not always been apparent in historical narratives and analysis. James Bennett notes that 'there remain many significant gaps in our understanding of the historical relationship between these two companion societies'; there has been a long history of 'reciprocal amnesia' and 'benign neglect'.[6] His concerns have been taken up by other historians keen to advance a more dynamic and interconnected view of trans-Tasman histories.[7] There is a new consensus that this historiographical elision should be addressed by more rounded transnational and comparative approaches. Over the last decade or so, these have been well represented by the Blackwell history of Australia, New Zealand and the Pacific, and by the 'Anzac Neighbours: 100 Years of multiple ties between New Zealand and Australia' project.[8] The 'Anzac Neighbours' project includes the stated intent to examine the 'links between Australasian religious, state, academic, business and other elites'.

While the writing of both New Zealand and Australian religious history has become more reflective and nuanced over the last three decades, it has also often been pursued within discrete national parameters. Comparative histories are more recent and limited in number. Hugh Jackson's thematic approach to Australian and New Zealand Christian history indicates the potential of studies framed within defined regional parameters.[9] Ian Breward's comparative history encompassing the South Pacific as well as New Zealand and Australia is more ambitious in scope.[10] In the same vein, and in keeping with the 'Anzac Neighbours' project, Australian historian Malcolm Prentis provides a helpful overview of trans-Tasman interchanges of religious ideas, culture and personalities with respect to the major denominations.[11] Despite these advances, there is much more that needs to be understood, both in terms of historical and contemporary religious patterns.

Overseas mission is one area that needs further attention. Prentis notes, for example, the potential for further research on 'cooperation in missionary service', especially with respect to the South West Pacific.[12] Such coopera-tion was certainly important, particularly but not exclusively for Australasian

Methodists, but the links were much broader. Australian-based missionary organisations employed the services of many New Zealand missionaries throughout the period. Conversely, a handful of Australians served with New Zealand organisations. In many respects, it is difficult to distinguish many of these organisations as being either New Zealand or Australian up to at least World War I. With respect to home-based missionary support, some of the early impetus for the women's missionary unions among Baptists, Methodists and Presbyterians came from Sydney and Melbourne in particular. The three examples discussed below indicate the ways in which Australian church and missionary leaders, public speakers and training institutions all gave an impetus to the development of New Zealand missionary involvement around the turn of the nineteenth and twentieth centuries.

(a) Australians and the origins of the New Zealand Baptist Missionary Society
In October 1885 the NZBMS was officially constituted by the New Zealand Baptist Union. The impetus for its establishment had come directly from Baptist missionary enthusiasts in South Australia. Baptists had been in New Zealand from the beginnings of formal European settlement in the 1840s. By the early 1860s there were Baptist churches in most of the main and provincial centres and, by 1881, Baptists made up 2 per cent of the population.[13] In 1882 the New Zealand Baptist Union was formed. While there had been no New Zealand Baptist missionaries up to this point, there was a measure of missionary awareness. In 1883 the Revd Charles Carter, a former English BMS missionary, suggested that one of the fledgling Union's objectives should be to accomplish 'our part in fulfilling the last commission of our Lord to go into all the world and preach the Gospel to the whole creation'.[14] The formation of the Baptist Union was an essential prerequisite for any future missionary initiatives, bringing together individual churches that were often geographically isolated and administratively autonomous.

Into this mix, late in 1884, was introduced a letter and proposal from the Revd Silas Mead, minister of the Flinders Street Baptist Church in Adelaide. As a missionary enthusiast, Mead had been instrumental in forming the South Australian BMS in 1864. In 1882 the first two Australian Baptist missionaries (both single women) went to work in East Bengal, as zenana workers – women working with women – employed by the South Australian Baptist Missionary Society.[15] Mead outlined a 'great Australasian scheme' that he envisaged would incorporate all of the Australasian Baptist Unions, including New Zealand.[16] It was a co-operative plan for Baptist missionary work in East Bengal, encompassing a number of contiguous districts centred on present-day Dacca with a combined population of around nine million. Mead's scheme envisaged a federation of Australasian Baptist missionary societies, working together but each taking responsibility for a specific district. The plan introduced a theme that would recur in Antipodean Baptist missionary rhetoric. In short, if India was an English Baptist responsibility in general, stemming from the pioneering work of William Carey, then East Bengal should be a specifically Australasian Baptist responsibility. In part, this proposal was driven by Mead's concern to create a more cohesive federal union of Australian Baptists.[17] It also underlined a concern for an economy of effort in terms of how colonial missionary resources and finances might be deployed. Ultimately, however, the plan reflected a clear theological imperative that colonial Baptists should assume their wider spiritual responsibilities.

Although it did not go ahead, Mead's plan served to push New Zealand Baptists towards the idea of a New Zealand-based missionary society. When it was published in the *New Zealand Baptist* in January 1885, Mead's letter struck a chord with similar-minded Baptist leaders. The editor opined that it was 'needless to say that our churches must deeply sympathise with mission-work in India, and that we should all be glad to take our place and part in the great and glorious work'.[18] The *New Zealand Baptist* continued to give Mead's ideas a high profile throughout 1885, and in particular it introduced a regular missionary news column. New Zealand Baptists now had regular access to English BMS news updates and reports, interesting stories and news from other mission organisations, biographical sketches of 'native' converts, topical issues, and missionary exhortations.[19]

The drive for a missionary society gathered further momentum with Ellen Arnold's visit to New Zealand in March and April of 1885. One of the two original Australian Baptist missionaries in India, Ellen was on furlough for health reasons and had been asked by Mead to do a grand tour of the Australasian colonies in support of his scheme.[20] Her tour covered at least all the main centres in New Zealand, addressing audiences of adults and children, and was the first time that many Baptists had heard firsthand from a missionary speaker. She came primarily to foster public support for a Baptist Missionary Society in New Zealand. The editor of the *New Zealand Baptist,* the Revd Alfred North, hoped that 'our Churches will be so healthfully influenced by [her] addresses that when they send their representatives to the Union meetings in October next, they will send them under instructions to support the formation of the NZBMS'.[21] In her farewell to the New Zealand Baptist public, Ellen Arnold echoed these same words, suggesting that, ultimately, the responsibility lay with the people 'to make it a success'.[22] When North gave public notice of the two resolutions he intended to table at the Union meetings, there could have been few Baptist readers who were unaware of what was to transpire. On Thursday 15 October 1885 the New Zealand Baptist Union unanimously agreed to the formation of a New Zealand Baptist Missionary Society, for missionary work in India.[23] By 1900 the NZBMS had placed 19 missionaries in East Bengal and gained wide support from the colony's Baptists (see Chapter Six for further details).

(b) The Poona and Indian Village Mission

My second example was more short-lived than the first, but more dramatic. Stuart Piggin argues that the period from about 1870 up to World War I was the 'high noon of Australian Protestantism', with relatively high figures for church attendance (up to 40 per cent) and a strong commitment to social transformation and engagement.[24] Australian revivalism, while not denominationally or geographically uniform, served to generally heighten religious enthusiasm, a pattern Australia shared with New Zealand. The Revd Silas Mead, for instance, was influenced by early 'holiness' sentiments prior to the establishment of the English Keswick movement in 1875.[25] The Keswick movement itself had its greatest impact in Australia from the early 1890s, with the establishment of such evangelical institutions as the annual Geelong Convention. Similar developments took place in New Zealand from the mid- to late 1890s. Piggin further notes that, as a result of these developments, 'the most prestigious institutions of the evangelical movement and the accepted thermometer of its spiritual temperature were overseas missions'.[26] Several Australian-based missionary ventures can be dated to this period; they include the Queensland Kanaka Mission (later the South Sea Evangelical Mission), the Australasian branch of the CIM, various Australasian Church Missionary Society associations, and the Australasian South American Mission (a predecessor of the BIM). Each of these organisations developed strong and long-lasting New Zealand links.

Perhaps the most curious development in this period, however, was the emergence of the Poona and Indian Village Mission (PIVM) in 1893. While details of its origins are hazy, the mission's seemingly dynamic and somewhat enigmatic founding figure Charles Reeve was central to its initiation and early growth. While there is no entry for him, for example, in the *Australasian Dictionary of Evangelical Biography*, bare biographical details are hinted at in other sources.[27] According to one unpublished account of his life Reeve was a Tasmanian farmer who was also a Baptist evangelist and, later, an ordained Baptist minister.[28] Different accounts of the mission's beginnings exist. According to the SIM official account, his Christian faith was enlivened by revivalist influences during the late 1870s, leading him to form the mission in collaboration with others in response to a visit to Australia by an Indian Christian seeking missionary help for the town of Poona (now Pune, just southeast of Mumbai).[29] Ian Welch, however, notes that the initial visitors who successively sparked Australian interest in 1892–93 were Europeans, not Indians.[30] Whatever the details, an exploratory group, including Reeve, must have departed for India shortly after.

By 1896 there were up to 10 Australian missionaries in Poona. In that same year, Reeve probably made his first visit to New Zealand, encouraged by local supporters to speak on behalf of the mission. He remained for several months. Reports of his meetings and lists of those involved as local supporters suggest that he quickly gained a profile in a range of denominations.[31] Reeve continued to be welcomed to church pulpits and town hall platforms in New Zealand over the next decade. More spectacular than Reeve's personal progress, however, was the surge of recruits in the late 1890s. At least 42 New Zealanders went to India with the PIVM, and 38 of these were sent between 1897 and 1899.[32] This was an unprecedented level of recruitment, in such a short time span, by any missionary organisation up to 1939. While New Zealanders continued to work with the mission in later decades, they never did so again in the same concentrated numbers. The details of the PIVM's story remain sketchy at best. It seems safe to assume, however, that the large number of recruits were the direct result of the sustained public profile and somewhat charismatic presence of Reeve in these years. While a core of recruits hailed from the southern provinces of Otago and Southland, the balance came from a broad range of localities outside the South. They were drawn mostly from Anglican, Baptist and Brethren churches, with smaller numbers of Presbyterians and Methodists. At the same time the PIVM, and other missions like the CIM, regularly became recipients of fundraising efforts by Presbyterian and other denominational youth groups.

This development reflected the confluence of external missionary agency or initiative and local evangelical religious enthusiasm. Support and enthusiasm for missionary work was a latent but potent force in 1890s New Zealand, which only needed an external spark to set it alight. In this respect, it may have been purely coincidental that the catalyst was of Australian origin. Yet it also illustrated that geographic proximity was advantageous for ongoing contact, support and recruitment. At the same time, there were tensions in this relationship. In Presbyterian circles, for example, there were serious misgivings about the impact of the PIVM on denominational missionary finances.[33] Further criticism turned on such issues as theology and strategy. One Presbyterian commentator referred to the Poona mission as a 'Plymouthistic Mission' (referring to the Plymouth or Open Brethren), from which 'we shall soon see considerable departures from the faith'.[34] Again, it was simply coincidental that this was a problem with Australian origins.

The emerging faith missions more generally were perceived as a threat by the larger denominations, as noted earlier. New Zealand Anglican and Presbyterian missionary growth and innovation between 1890 and 1910, for example, were partially a reaction to this threat. Interest in forming Australasian branches of the Church Missionary Society, in 1892, can be partially understood in the context of Anglican concerns over faith missions. Eugene Stock notes that some New Zealand bishops 'felt that similar facilities [to the CIM] ought to be provided for members of the Church of England going out [to the mission field] in connexion with a Church Society'.[35] Similar concerns were included among the reasons given by the Revd Alexander Don in 1898 for launching Presbyterian missionary work in the vicinity of Canton (now Guangzhou). He argued that 'a channel would thus be provided within our own church and our own denomination for the sympathy, prayer, and gifts of our people. These at present flow through other channels, and will continue to do so. This may be well, but the increase of such to the extent of alienation will not be so. Surely we shall do well to take steps to share in such increase, so that it may not reach the point of alienation.'[36] George McNeur, the first Presbyterian missionary to Canton, was one such 'gift'; previous to Don's enlistment of his services, he had been about to apply to the CIM for service in China.[37]

(c) The influence of Australian missionary training institutions

Perhaps the most discernible and enduring influence in this period came from the growing number of Australian-based missionary training institutions. For most New Zealand denominations there were options for ministry training for male missionary candidates seeking ordination, but lay training was virtually non-existent. By 1900 there was only Annie Driver's general training home in Dunedin for women which, in 1903, was handed over to the Presbyterian Church as a deaconess training institute.[38] Similar attempts came to nothing, until the establishment of the NZBTI (1922) and the Baptist Theological College (1926) made lay training locally and more broadly available.

By way of contrast, in Australia there was a growing array of lay training options from the early 1890s, and it was to these that many New Zealanders turned in preparation for a missionary vocation. The move across the Tasman typically preceded a longer-term move overseas for many prospective missionaries from the 1890s. These institutions were intensely practical in their training focus. One such 'home', founded in Melbourne in 1892 for women missionary candidates and run by Dr William and Mrs Warren, was typical. Training centred on core biblical, doctrinal and historical subjects, basic medicine and first aid, 'Gospel Work' and other practical evangelistic and pastoral activities.[39] The Warrens' home was established in the wake of the 1891–92 tours of Australia and New Zealand by an English Anglican evangelist, the Revd George C. Grubb. By 1900 New Zealanders were to be found in a variety of such homes in Sydney, Melbourne and Adelaide. For non-denominational missionaries, the most influential of these were a network of Adelaide institutions for men and women, founded in 1893 by the Presbyterian missionary enthusiast the Revd Lockhart Morton.[40] His original intention had been to establish a men's training home, following the model provided by the Warrens' institution in Melbourne.

Two such institutions were particularly important for the training of New Zealand Anglican women working with the New Zealand Church Missionary Association (NZCMA), renamed the New Zealand Church Missionary Society (NZCMS) in 1916. The NZCMA was formed in late 1892 following the influential Australasian tour by the Revd Robert Stewart (a CMS missionary in China), and the CMS editorial secretary, Eugene Stock.[41] From its inception, women made up the majority of candidates, yet they lacked a suitable local training venue. By 1894 the NZCMA executive had reached an agreement with the Marsden Training Home in Sydney over the training of its women missionaries. This was a distinctively Anglican institution that sought to foster 'spiritual evangelical Christians' who would be 'staunch members of the Church of England'.[42] A further agreement, in 1903, also saw New Zealand women being trained at St Hilda's Missionary Training Home in Melbourne, an institution that was also used by the CIM.[43] Both of these institutions had high expectations of their students. Courses were invariably two to three years in length, with a balance of biblical, doctrinal and practical training. An undated curriculum document for the Sydney Home indicates that the lay training offered to women was no less sophisticated than that for men. Courses in apologetics, comparative religion and pedagogy complemented the core courses.[44] Higher academic expectations for both Anglican men and women were further entrenched in the wake of the 1910 Edinburgh conference. In 1912 the NZCMA executive acted on the recommendations of Commission V of the conference, regarding missionary training, by setting more formal standards.[45] A university education was recommended for all men and women candidates, except for nurses. There was also a mandatory phase of theological training required which, for women, continued to be provided by the Australian lay training institutions. The relationship envisaged was akin to that between universities and teacher training colleges of the same period.

Although the relationship between New Zealand mission agencies and their Australian educational providers was relatively harmonious, there were some inherent tensions, particularly for women. In the first instance, there were tensions over where authority lay. While NZCMA candidates were under the overall authority of their executive, as students, they were also under the authority of their respective training institutions. New Zealand women at Sydney's Marsden Training Home, for example, were to be 'subject to the control' of both the home's committee and 'the Lady Superintendent'.[46] There was a late-Victorian girls' high school feel about these institutions, where the strict rule of the 'Lady Superintendent' was not unlike that of a school headmistress. Some adult students struggled with this regime.[47]

The tensions over authority were exacerbated by the problems posed by the geographical distance between New Zealand and Australia. A handful of New Zealand Anglican women had attended St Hilda's in Melbourne between 1903 and 1907, which on the surface seemed an amicable arrangement. However, late in 1907 Ethel Baker returned to New Zealand for the summer, highly critical of the expectations and operation of St Hilda's which, she argued, left students exhausted and unfit for immediate departure for the mission field.[48] This came as news to the New Zealand-based executive, which was clearly embarrassed and acutely aware of the relational delicacies involved. Ethel's criticisms were not isolated to one person and prompted a full investigation by the NZCMA. Their conclusion was that the 'constant grind from morning to night' was a cause for concern.[49] The correspondence that ensued indicated that St Hilda's at least listened to the concerns emanating from New Zealand, although the nature of any action taken was less clear.[50]

The Australia–New Zealand relationship may have been a derivative problem in this case: the real issue may well have been the gendered nature of missionary training and the extent to which women candidates were under more pressure than their male counterparts. Ethel Baker's criticisms highlighted the fact that women students at St Hilda's were expected to run many of the domestic functions of the Home, as well as do their studies and participate in practical church or community work outside the home.[51] It is unclear whether the same demands were incumbent upon men in their equivalent institutions. Men may have seen this situation differently, as hinted at by an Australian doctor in his report on the systems in operation at St Hilda's: 'It seems to us that if a young woman cannot stand the strain inseparably and necessarily connected with a Training Home she would be unfit for the arduous work of the Mission field … Concerning house work we think it might be even beneficial if they did somewhat more, say one hour daily!'[52]

New Zealand and the United States of America

Interactions between New Zealanders and Australians took place within an accessible, if not exactly contiguous, geographic space. The Tasman Sea was an oft-travelled maritime highway. With the opening up of the Suez Canal, Australian ports also became regular stopping points for colonials travelling to various parts of Asia and on to Europe and Great Britain. The distances across the Pacific were much greater, and the connections with America initially less accessible. This changed significantly from the mid-1870s, when steamships began to ply the Pacific between eastern Australia and the West Coast of America via Honolulu and Auckland. From this time onwards, New Zealand became consciously linked with its American 'neighbour', and both cultural and economic exchanges became more regular and sustainable.

Historians have been inclined to focus on American influences in the post-World War II era, rather than on earlier decades. In part, this emphasis was a result of the American 'invasions' of the 1940s and 1950s – one military (New Zealand was a key staging-post for American operations in the Pacific theatre of war), and the other cultural (music, magazines and movies).[53] American influences on modern New Zealand's economy, culture and society have been undeniable and abiding – earlier influences are still to receive a fuller and more satisfying treatment. Cultural historian Chris Hilliard perceptively comments that 'a settler society's cultural "inputs" do not cease with its "first ships", and they emanate from other places as well as the imperial metropolis. "Americanisation" is a conspicuous example, though it would be interesting for New Zealand historians to reach back past World War II.' He goes on to note that American 'cultural imperialism' was increasingly influential in early- to mid-twentieth-century New Zealand.[54]

Religious interaction between the two societies is a useful marker of such influences, and indicates that 'Americanisation' did indeed reach back into the nineteenth century. American influences on the development of New Zealand Christianity can be found, for example, in the formation of an Anglican constitution in the 1850s, in Protestant and Roman Catholic revivalism from the 1860s, and in adaptations of American conservative evangelicalism from the 1920s.[55] By the 1880s and 1890s international speakers and promoters of various causes saw New Zealand and Australia as a convenient package deal. This was especially the case for the Gospel Temperance movement and the formation of the Women's Christian Temperance Union.[56] Similarly, in 1896, the American missionary statesman John R. Mott made the first of three visits (returning again in 1903 and 1926), touring all the main university centres in New Zealand, Victoria, New South Wales and Queensland. As a result, student Christian organisations were established on all campuses and missionary support was given a distinctive boost.[57]

American influences on religious behaviour and attitudes can be most readily discerned with reference to the missionary movement. Mott exemplified the impact of individual speakers who occupied the platforms of a host of denominational churches and town halls. Other influences were more organic. Women's groups had sustained links with sister groups in North America. Sunday school and Bible class youngsters were increasingly taught with American pedagogical resources, and news from American sources was given space in denominational and missionary literature. Between 1910 and 1914 the Laymen's Missionary Movement had a brief but concerted impact on Presbyterian and Baptist men. From the 1920s American missionary organisations took on increasing numbers of New Zealand recruits, or received enthusiastic missionary support. None of this was surprising, if it is accepted that the New Zealand missionary movement was integral to the wider movement; yet it was a significant shift for a culture hitherto linked more comprehensively to Britain. By this period American missionaries and organisations had become more numerically dominant than their European and British counterparts across the globe. This was the beginning of the 'American century' with respect to global mission.[58] When contemplating options for missionary service, people like Alfred and Tina Roke increasingly turned their gaze towards America.

There does seem to have been a significant mental reorientation underlying these dynamics, and it is likely that what happened in the 1920s was the logical extension of a longer-term trend. American influences seem to have been as much about the exchange of ideas and mentalities as anything else. The following two examples focus on the period up to World War I: both Christian Endeavour and the Student Volunteer Movement helped to shape domestic religion and the missionary impetus that emerged in this period.

(a) Christian Endeavour

Christian Endeavour (CE) was founded in 1881 by American Congregationalists the Revd Francis and Harriet Clark. By the early 1890s it had become a successful transnational youth movement and its worldwide growth continued unabated for at least another decade.[59] In a range of Western contexts, the movement sought to mitigate the impact of modernisation on adolescents and young adults, addressing such perceived social issues as juvenile delinquency, poverty and alcohol abuse. By the early 1900s it had also taken on the characteristics of a well-oiled machine, rather than just an idea or movement, complete with its own manuals, literature and music.[60] New Zealand's first group was established at Auckland's Ponsonby Baptist Church in 1891, with a Christian Endeavour Union (that transcended denominational boundaries) being formed in 1896.[61] Within three years, there were an estimated 115 CE societies nationwide with 3888 members. By 1907 there were 257 societies, with 8396 members; growth peaked around World War I. The greatest involvement appeared to be within Wesleyan Methodist, Baptist, Presbyterian and Congregational churches. Regional CE 'unions' blurred existing denominational boundaries by bringing children, young people and their leaders together on a regular basis. Local or regional conventions were being held as early as 1894 and national conventions by at least 1897.[62] The one exception to this widespread participation was the Anglican Church because, in the words of one Anglican commentator, 'churchmen have no need to join a Society smaller than the Church, in order to be Christian Endeavourers of the truest character'.[63] From 1893 there was a regular CE column in the *New Zealand Baptist*, and the Otago–Southland Presbyterian Synod anticipated a positive impact on southern churches.

Local congregational or parish activity was at the heart of Christian Endeavour's existence. However, a rigorous statistical assessment of the organisation's impact on the shape and growth of the missionary movement is problematic, due to the dispersed nature of local church records. Anecdotal information in missionary application records, published missionary testimonies and reports of valedictory meetings indicates that it had a relatively broad impact on the missionary movement. There were ex-CE male and female members in most denominational and non-denominational missionary organisations, apart from Anglicans. The overall impact on missionary awareness, enthusiasm, participation and support was probably greatest in the period up to 1914; after this time the New Zealand Bible class movement became more influential among Protestant young people.

Christian Endeavour was primarily a devotional or spiritual movement, which accounts for its impact on missionary supporters and aspirants. Constitutionally, 'the object of this Society shall be to promote an earnest Christian life among its members, increase their mutual acquaintance and make them more useful in the service of God'.[64] The movement tapped into prevailing revivalist sentiments and accentuated the increasingly privatised view of faith emerging within late nineteenth-century evangelicalism. Personal salvation was foundational. Janet McKinnon told members of her Presbyterian CE group that 'Jesus is always ready to save anyone who comes to Him, pleading his promise. No other way of salvation, but God's, will be of any avail, and all who do not accept His way will be eternally lost.'[65] Yet salvation was simply the entrance point. In the overall CE scheme, young people were also encouraged to devote or 'consecrate' themselves both to God and to Christian service.[66] Central to the movement's spirituality was a consecrated life of usefulness; 'useful service' proved the genuineness of an individual's faith, irrespective of gender or socio-economic status, and signified ongoing personal spiritual growth. It was also cast as a practical way of repaying what was seen as the unwarranted love of God. 'Life is a gift from God', Presbyterian Endeavourers were told, and it should be 'used in His Service and for His glory'.[67] This notion of usefulness loomed large as a motivational factor, because missionary work was readily perceived as a possible future avenue or outlet for service.

The core activity reinforcing these sentiments was the monthly prayer or 'consecration' meeting. Members regularly restated their commitment to the society's pledge, worshipped and prayed together and listened to topical addresses. These typically focused on subjects like 'Kept for the Master's use', 'Giving our best to God', 'Privileges and responsibilities', 'Gratitude and service', 'Be ye doers of the Word and not hearers only' and 'Blessed be drudgery'. Biblical exemplars were Christ the servant and the Good Samaritan (Luke 10:25–37).[68] Participation in meetings and on committees also reinforced another dimension of popular spirituality, that of whole-hearted commitment. Greatest pressure was placed on 'active' members to attend every consecration meeting, to systematically pursue the devotional practices of Bible-reading and prayer, and generally to 'lead a Christian life'.[69] This was a period in which institutional commitment was both expected and accepted. The notions of consecration and commitment were common in the statements of prospective missionaries, and were qualities demanded by the circumstances they would face in cross-cultural missionary life and work. A poem by a young New Zealand Endeavourer in 1897 ended with a declaration of personal commitment to a life of consecrated service, because 'so few willing hands are helping, and but once I will pass this way'.[70]

At the same time, Endeavour spirituality emphasised an expansive vision. The constitution stated that 'the ultimate aim of Christian Endeavour is the evangelization of the world for Christ', and that as an organisation 'intensely evangelistic and missionary in spirit, [it] desires to do all it may … for missionary extension the world around'. In the same vein, Endeavourers attending a united Dunedin convention in 1896 were told that they would be a 'mighty force for good'.[71] Missionary committees were integral to the CE committee structure. At the congregational level, these committees sought to educate members, promote the missionary cause and fundraise for specific projects. Missionary topics and hymns were a regular component of consecration meetings. Financial generosity was encouraged, and many groups supported missionary personnel and projects.

Ultimately, the CE movement sought to harness youthful energy and potential for a perceived greater good by accentuating notions of heroism.[72] The ultimate act of heroism was to become a missionary. This was an ennobling act because it called for absolute commitment and the highest qualities of character and fortitude. Such sentiments were not without precedent – missionary heroes and heroines were a firm feature of the popular mental landscape of the late nineteenth century.[73] Events like the deaths of Bishop Patteson, the CMS martyrs at Ku-Cheng, the Boxer martyrs and of James Chalmers all had an impact on New Zealand audiences, and added to this semi-romanticising of the missionary project. The notion of missionaries as heroes or heroines was a particularly prevalent trope in children's missionary literature. Endeavour members heard about these paragons in their meetings and, occasionally, met them at larger public events. At the same time, CE set such aspirations within an intensely practical framework, with members encouraged to contribute in simple but effective ways: committee membership, topical addresses, visiting the sick, fundraising and organising missionary exhibitions. These activities taught valuable organisational and communication skills, built self-confidence and shaped a personal spirituality that had tangible dimensions. Presbyterian missionary Winifred Stubbs noted that as a Christian Endeavourer, 'I first learnt to pray aloud and speak [publicly] … I began to grow a new conception of the possibilities of the Christian life, the power of Jesus Christ in our daily lives, and the call to service for Him.'[74] In these terms Christian Endeavour, as an imported idea, was an incubator for future missionaries that did not discriminate between the genders and that made missionary service and support accessible to a wide social grouping of younger New Zealanders.

(b) The Student Volunteer Movement for Foreign Missions

The Student Volunteer Movement for Foreign Missions (SVMFM or SVM for short) was initially an American movement that arose in the same period as Christian Endeavour. On a global scale, suggests Dana Robert, it was the 'most important example of the fusion of Christian youth culture with foreign missions'.[75] It was sparked by a mixture of pre-millennial enthusiasm and evangelical piety among college and university students in 1886.[76] This enthusiasm was then channelled through the SVM and became more organised under the influential leadership of people like John Mott and Robert Speer, with a decreasing emphasis on its pre-millennial focus. In 1892 a similarly inspired movement, the Student Volunteer Missionary Union, was established in Great Britain with links to the Inter-University Christian Union. Both these groups became affiliated to the World's Student Christian Federation, founded in 1895. By the time that Mott first visited New Zealand in 1896, as the international representative of all these groups, there were an estimated 5000 student volunteers worldwide, with 1000 of those going into direct overseas service.[77]

Mott's first visit was the catalyst for the formation in Australia and New Zealand of both the Australasian Student Christian Union (ASCU) and the SVM.[78] ASCU branches were initially established in each of the university colleges, and the SVM established as an integral part of ASCU structures.[79] By Mott's second visit in 1903 the movement had found a niche in New Zealand. A newly appointed Australian travelling secretary and other international visitors then linked branches and members to the wider movement. In 1913 the ASCU became the Australasian Student Christian Movement, with the New Zealand SCM becoming autonomous in 1921.[80]

The missionary impact of the student movement is somewhat easier to quantify than Christian Endeavour, although this must be taken with some caution as statistics are patchy and apparently non-existent after 1918. Between about 1896 and 1918, around 410 Australian and New Zealand students signed the Volunteer declaration: 'It is my purpose, if God permit, to become a foreign missionary.'[81] At least 157 of these were New Zealand students – around 38 per cent of all Australasian signatories. While relatively balanced in gender terms, greatest interest came from Presbyterian, Anglican and Methodist students at Otago and Canterbury University Colleges. Although this reflected wider population patterns, it was not so representative of overall missionary cohort patterns in this period. Furthermore, the 53 known volunteers who went on to missionary service, mainly with denominational missions, only made up 12 per cent of total New Zealand missionaries by 1918.

Mott asserted that 'one of the strongest contingents of the Student

Volunteer Movement is coming from these Colonies'.[82] This confidence was possibly misplaced, as the above statistics indicate. Yet acknowledging this fails to do justice to some of the particularities thrown up by the evidence. For example, in the late 1890s early New Zealand student volunteers were quick to leave the country as missionaries. Of the 13 who signed up to 1900, seven had departed by 1897, and New Zealanders made up the majority of all Australasian volunteers departing as missionaries up to 1906. Even if, as Renate Howe suggests, students were 'reluctant missionaries', it seems fair to argue that the movement's impact accounts for some of the significant increase in missionary numbers at the turn of the nineteenth and twentieth centuries.[83] Furthermore, while the numbers were small, those who did become missionaries often became influential leaders or respected figures in the movement. Their longer-term impact was felt in terms of literature, deputations, recruitment, education, missionary leadership, and the shaping of domestic missionary thinking. The SVM was a significant factor in these men and women becoming missionaries and missionary or denominational leaders, and in their longer-term contributions.

Any assessment of the SVM's impact also has to take into account a range of other, more indirect factors. The SVM was viewed primarily as a religious or spiritual movement whose contours were not dissimilar to CE. The ASCU constitution placed an equal emphasis on personal conversion, ongoing discipleship and the expansive vision of 'extending the Kingdom of Christ throughout the whole world'.[84] Members had to affirm that they acknowledged 'the Lord Jesus as my only Saviour' and promised to 'abide by the Constitution of this Union, and to unite with it earnestly in Christian work'.[85] Meeting topics covered the spectrum of devotional practices, character formation, biblical and historical exemplars and missionary topics, as well as other themes more pertinent to the intellectual life of the university.[86] Similarly, SVM spirituality placed great importance on personal vitality and usefulness; self-sacrificing service that was both heroic and humanitarian; communal and institutional commitment; and a practical, public-minded Christian faith.

In other ways, however, SVM and CE spirituality were different. Students were challenged to develop a more informed and 'educated' spirituality. One of the complaints levelled against Christian Endeavour was that it had too easily settled for a trite and superficial personal spirituality that was informed more by 'chorus singing' and 'brief, bright and brotherly meetings' than by 'Bible study of a more thorough and systematic order'.[87] By contrast, students were prompted to develop a robust spirituality through a broad mix of prayer, personal and group Bible study, regular meetings, and both academic and reflective reading about contemporary events and issues.[88] It was further argued that students formed by an educated and mentally robust spirituality were strategically important both to New Zealand and the wider world. In 1896 Mott argued that a voluntary student movement active in New Zealand's universities was a key strategy in attempting to reverse what he perceived to be a largely secularised colonial society. Students were also important because of Australasia's geographic proximity to the Pacific Basin and the 'gates of the three greatest mission fields of the world; Africa, India and China'.[89] It was a mark of Mott's eternal optimism that no obstacle was too large. By his second visit in 1903 he was convinced that real progress had been made along these lines.[90] Ultimately, the numbers of student volunteers within the overall missionary movement may not have been large. In these graduates, however, the movement had supporters and participants who possessed a deep and keen spiritual sense of the strategic importance of home and overseas missions.

Given SVM's academic context, there was a willingness to critically examine some of the existing shibboleths, including the student volunteer slogan: 'the evangelisation of the world in this generation'. The adoption of this motto was debated before being accepted by British and European students in 1896.[91] New Zealand students further debated the issue in 1899. Those in favour emphasised the slogan's potential to capture a wide measure of attention and energy, and its fundamental congruity with the Great Commission. Its detractors highlighted the ambiguity and essential meaninglessness of the phrase 'in this generation', the intemperateness of the concept, and its potential for bringing the movement into disrepute.[92] This propensity to give an intellectual edge to missionary thinking was further highlighted in the postwar era. The war itself, along with the deepening theological rifts discussed above, undermined student missionary enthusiasm, at least in the ways that it had been expressed earlier. Both internationally and locally, it presaged the divisions that would occur from the mid-1920s. As we saw in Chapter Two, the New Zealand student movement responded to this changing climate by a readiness to revisit and revise its missionary thinking. By the 1930s this exercise resulted in the creation of an evangelical counterresponse to the perceived threats posed by modernism.[93]

At the same time the movement harnessed student energies in eminently practical directions. In 1903 the first-ever national missionary conference was held, bringing together school and university students along with lecturers and church leaders.[94] One of the initiatives that resulted from this conference was the formation of summer student missionary deputations. Students visited a great range of Protestant churches, raising the profile of mission, seeking to initiate support groups or prompt further recruitment, and to boost missionary giving.[95] Yet these student deputations were more than vehicles for fundraising. On the one hand, students helped to raise the profile of missionary claims, and of informed missionary awareness, among both rural and urban congregations. On the other hand, through their reports, the students helped denominational missionary leaders to form a much more realistic picture of the relative depth and breadth of congregational missionary awareness. In this way, two otherwise quite separate elements of the missionary movement came together for their mutual benefit; town, country and gown sought ways of working together for the cause of world evangelisation.

Conclusion

American historian Mark Noll argues that '[t]he impression that Christianity in its essence is either European or American is … simply false. Christianity began as Jewish; before it was European, it was North African, Syrian, Egyptian and Indian. While in recent history it has indeed been American, it has also been Chilean, Albanian, Fijian and Chinese. [Christianity] belongs to every one in every culture; it belongs to no one in any one culture in particular.'[96] Noll's emphasis on both the particularity and universality of Christianity is pertinent for the New Zealand case under discussion here. Colonial missionary and denominational leaders readily absorbed, co-opted or adapted imported ideas, strategies and structures from a range of sources. In this respect, New Zealand settler Protestant Christianity, like its underlying geology, was shaped by intersecting and constantly moving tectonic forces that were both national and transnational in nature. Cablegrams, steamships and locomotives enabled the interchange of people and ideas at an ever-increasing pace. In these respects, Australian and American influences highlight the degree to which New Zealand was both regionally and globally positioned, as much outward-looking as it was introspective.

As a result it seems more accurate, for example, to think regionally about Australia and New Zealand as a single unit, rather than to discretely analyse the two nations' respective missionary movements. Likewise, in the future fruitful discussion is more likely to be centred on the notion of multilateral cultural interchanges, rather than on the idea that New Zealand unilaterally imported or exported missionary personnel, concepts and values. An interesting research angle, for example, would be to ask how the Bolivian Indian Mission (considered further in Chapter Five) might have changed over the longer term if it had lacked Australasian origins. To what extent did its small colonial beginnings determine the way that it took shape under more explicitly American influences from the 1920s onwards, perhaps differentiating it from other American missions with a conservative evangelical bent?

The Australian case is indicative of two interrelated issues that cohere around the idea of regionalism in mission history. The first issue has already been signalled in the Introduction and is considered further in Chapter Five: that is, how far is it accurate to frame mission and, indeed, religious history in discrete national terms? Missionary links and initiatives over the period considered here suggest that it may be more appropriate to conceive of a more broadly linked and interrelated Australasian Protestantism. In many ways, trans-Tasman missionary ventures were ambiguous in character, and it becomes difficult to categorically state which were New Zealand or Australian. This was particularly the case for the many interdenominational groups or faith missions. With their executive functions variously located on both sides of the Tasman Sea, intricate transnational familial links, and missionaries drawn with little distinction from both countries, it might be more accurate to consider these organisations in wholly trans-Tasman terms. Such links go far in explaining the geographically seamless popularity among, rapid uptake of and significant support from Anglican, Methodist and Presbyterian denominations (at least in early decades) and organisations like the PIVM and the South Sea Evangelical Mission in both New Zealand and Australia. This phenomenon was by no means limited to religious or missionary interchanges. By way of further example, such trans-Tasman movements and careers were also typical of the education sector and of the teaching profession.[97]

The second issue concerns the construction of the trans-Tasman relationship in terms of older and younger siblings. This has been an enduring historical theme in the political, economic and cultural histories of the two countries. Australia's political federation in 1901 was the occasion for an outpouring of national diatribe and angst among New Zealanders, reflected by the rhetoric of politicians and the content of the popular press. In reality New Zealand's non-involvement in federation stemmed doubly from a renewed sense of British imperial and economic connections, and from an emerging self-constructed national narrative of cultural and racial superiority.[98] New Zealanders were exemplary Britons and Māori were exemplary indigenous peoples, reversing the notion of being the younger sibling and thus rendering ambiguous the relationship between the two.

Protestant missionary data for the trans-Tasman world emphasises further this ambiguity. While there was a growing missionary consciousness among churchgoers and leaders in New Zealand by the late 1880s and 1890s, it was evident that much of the early initiative and drive had come from Australian enthusiasts. In a sense, New Zealanders rode on the ebullient coat-tails of an Australian evangelical religious enthusiasm that was so influential from the 1880s and 1890s onwards. Over the longer term, however, this argument is less sustainable. Early Australian missionary enthusiasm was just as fragile as in New Zealand, and there was a considerable flow of missionary energy, finances, personnel and leadership in both directions up to World War II and beyond.

In this mix, the American side of the equation elicts a question that deserves further discussion beyond this book. It is this: to what extent is it accurate to talk of an influence being Australian or American? Japanese Christian leader Kanzo Uchimura asserted in 1926 that 'Americans themselves know too well that their genius is not in religion' and the fact that 'they serve as teachers of religion ... is an anomaly. [Indeed] it is no special fault of Americans to be this-worldly; it is their national characteristic.' Andrew Walls notes that, from Uchimura's perspective, the American Christian influence was to be found in things like 'immense energy, resourcefulness, and inventiveness', in 'first-rate technology', democratic structures, 'an uninhibited approach to money', and 'materiality'.[99] In a more recent discussion, Noll affirms these American traits as well as adding others: a belief in authority residing in the Bible and 'personal conscience', pragmatism and commonsense, entrepreneurial or middle-class leadership, and an 'elective affinity with free-market initiatives'.[100]

While this analysis fits the New Zealand case in part, if it is accepted that both Christian Endeavour and the SVM were spiritual movements then the fit is not altogether an easy one. There is certainly a case for arguing that the American influence was also to be found in the ways that religious expression and culture were systematised, structured, commodified and channelled in directions that had definable outcomes. There was also a pragmatic and 'no-nonsense' element to American Protestantism that clearly resonated in some New Zealand circles. Yet this in itself raises a further question: can these factors be counted as discrete or imported influences, or rather as indicators of intersecting values and ideals shared by these two Pacific Rim settler societies? The notion of a distinctive American influence per se, at the turn of the nineteenth and twentieth centuries, is itself problematic, especially with respect to the notion of national exceptionality. This is as true of American historiography as it is of such colonial derivative societies as New Zealand.[101] With respect to overseas missions it is questionable, for example, to what extent North American and British spirituality can be usefully differentiated and in what direction such influences ran. More recent scholarship rightly traces out the interrelatedness of transatlantic Protestantism, especially in its evangelical forms; 'insofar as America stands for the West, America is the West writ large, Western characteristics exemplified to the fullest extent'.[102]

Whatever the degree of influence, and to whatever extent American, Australian or British influences can be differentiated, this discussion is worthwhile having for at least one reason. New Zealand Protestants, whether supporting or involved in mission overseas, represented a slippery category with respect to national or exceptional identity. If nothing else, the American example points again to a sector of the population whose allegiances were progressively focused outwards from the late nineteenth century, and who were enmeshed in emerging semi-global networks that were shaping or reshaping identity, meaning, ethical world views and life trajectories.

CHAPTER 4

Personal Motivation

THUS FAR WE HAVE LOCATED early New Zealand Protestant missionary endeavour and enthusiasm in terms of changing historical context(s), theological thinking and transnational influences. These extrinsic factors are, perhaps, somewhat easier to account for than the more intrinsic and complex issue of what motivated missionaries, supporters and churches. In this chapter, I first focus briefly on underlying motives and then, in more detail, on individual missionaries and how they understood their task at the time of application or commencement of missionary service. The language used in their narratives was primarily theological and spiritual. Yet, as Irish historian Myrtle Hill correctly observes, in reality it is 'virtually impossible to disentangle the religious and secular motivations' involved.[1] As a result, the links between wider motivation and imperial sentiments, for example, will be treated further in Chapter Six – these go beyond personal narratives and into the territory of broader motives and prevailing modes of thought.

By way of introduction, the case of a young Napier Anglican woman illustrates the complexities involved in seeking to understand individual missionary motivation. In April 1913 Mona Dean wrote a letter of enquiry to the NZCMA. Having just finished high school, her interest in missionary work had been aroused at a student conference the previous summer. She wanted to become a music teacher in China. Mona wrote:

> This has been puzzling me … whether it is God's Will that I should go. I am only nineteen, and how can I tell whether it will be His Will at say 23 or four? In many ways my idea is of duty … But when at Rangiora Conference … it came to me suddenly that here was something I could do for Christ, and it seems now as if all my life has been working up to this point … There is only one place in all the world where your life can obtain the maximum of usefulness and blessedness and that is

the one place where God would have you be … There is this thought also in my mind if Christ did so much for me such [sic] I can give up my life, to help those in [the] mission field who are trying to extend his Kingdom.[2]

In reply the NZCMA organising secretary, the Revd Oliver Kimberley, reassured Mona with some sensible advice about training and preparation. Later, because a music teaching opportunity had not arisen, he suggested that she qualify for missionary work 'in the ordinary way'. This meant going to university or completing a professional course such as nursing or teaching.[3] In response, Mona complained that gaining matriculation and professional qualifications would delay her departure interminably. Further, she argued that her first love of music would be lost: 'Would it be right to give up the talent God has given you on which you have spent all your time and energy and money, in trying to develop, for something quite strange? Music draws me, so, it would be a big thing to give up, but I hope I should do so if God willed it. But at present I can't see daylight … My father will object to my giving up the music I am afraid.'[4]

Three years later, with the possibility of a music teaching position in Ceylon being raised, the correspondence came to an end without resolution. Mona did not end up going overseas as a missionary. Her final letter to the Revd Kimberley contained a mixed set of sentiments:

> But there are these reasons in the way, my father has been very ill … Don't you think it is my place to work hard and earn as much as possible, for the only other earning member of the family is my brother and he is at the war. [Further] I am sure Dad will object on account of my health … The last reason is you know how unfit I am to take up a position in the Mission Field. I don't know my Bible nearly well enough and I have not even touched the subjects in connection with my 1st Grade [Theology] exam.[5]

From the perspective of historical enquiry, this correspondence raises a number of intriguing questions. What was the source of such a confident conviction in a young woman just leaving school? Was there anything especially significant in the apparently confused mix of theological, spiritual and personal sentiments expressed here? Was Mona Dean's desire to serve a misguided notion, or was it indicative of a deeper and more tenacious set of expectations, sentiments and values? To what extent does the correspondence reveal the interplay of individual personality and compulsion and of wider socio-religious influences? What was the role of age and gender? Was there a fundamental disconnection between the populist religious context from which such thinking emerged and the realities of missionary training and work? In essence, using Hill's terms, where does the 'secular' end and the 'religious' begin when we try to disentangle the factors involved in personal missionary motivation?

Robert Glen's observation that 'in missionary service there were various layers of motivation which might come into play together or at varying stages in a missionary's life' is a sensible caution against seeking simplistic or categorical answers to this issue.[6] Yet it is also an obvious and ultimately unsatisfying observation, if only because a more nuanced excavation of the interplay of the personal and contextual factors at work in any given period is required.[7] Earlier general studies of Anglo-European missionary motivation, notably by R. Pierce Beaver and Johannes van den Berg,[8] have been subsequently supplemented by scholarship that is focused on factors specific to particular periods, types of organisations and national contexts.[9] This quest has been complemented and informed by the more recent academic discourses of social, cultural, feminist, gender and postcolonial history.[10] New Zealand research thus far has tended to locate missionary motivation within the latter two discourses.[11]

While this more recent research has provided necessary correctives, there are at least two inherent difficulties. On the one hand, for a variety of reasons, the underlying theological factors that would have been important to aspiring missionaries of the period often tend to become obscured or minimised. The net result is a potentially myopic or emasculated understanding of missionary motivation. On the other hand, any attempt to draw on this increasing array of interpretative perspectives, while necessary, ends up becoming unwieldy and piecemeal. In reality, as Myrtle Hill has more recently argued for Irish Protestant women, 'a combination of religious, cultural and educational influences, strength of personality and lack of challenges on the home front made missionary work an attractive option'[12] for many settler Protestants in late nineteenth and early twentieth-century New Zealand. Individual motivation issued out of this complex matrix of factors.

Motive and motivation

In reality, individual motivation was intrinsically linked to an under-lying and often communally agreed upon understanding of missionary motive, outlined more fully in Chapter Two, which was further shaped by a range of changing domestic and international influences. There was an implicit difference, not always clearly articulated, between 'motive' and 'motivation'. While this chapter emphasises individual motivation, the interplay between the two needs to be kept in sharp focus. This is particularly pertinent because of the way in which generally understood motives were increasingly translated into a more personalised perception of missionary responsibility and calling. Beaver notes, for example, that 'a highly individualized and personalized sense of missionary obligation or duty, combined with the conviction that God in His providence had now prepared all things for success' was the driving force behind the SVM slogan, 'the evangelization of the world in this generation'.[13] This change of emphasis, in an American setting, was indicative of similar changes that were being articulated through New Zealand missionary applicant narra-tives by the early 1900s.

Perhaps the earliest programmatic statement of missionary motive in the New Zealand context was that offered by Presbyterian members of the Auckland Presbytery in 1856 (noted in Chapter One):

> That the Presbytery believing that it is the duty of the Church of Christ, in obedience to her Master's Command, – in harmony with her design, – in gratitude to God for all the unspeakable benefits she enjoys, – and out of respect to her own Spiritual welfare, to endeavour to extend the knowledge of Salvation throughout the world, feel called on thus early to acknowledge the obligations that rest upon them, while seeking to advance and maintain the interests of the true religion at home, to enter on the work of Missions, in general, so soon as in God's Providence they shall be in circumstances to [do so].[14]

'Duty', 'obedience' and 'obligations' remained as overarching motives for the entire period and were echoed in the broader theological motifs that we have already considered. Similarly, the 'Master's Command', embodied in the so-called Great Commission texts in Matthew's and Mark's Gospels, provided the commonly accepted biblical mandate for missionary involve-ment. For some, this command was the only true motive. A PIVM writer exhorted would-be applicants not to 'listen to any other voice: don't admit any other motive, don't advance any other reason. Let your going be only on the lines of Matthew 28, 18–19.'[15] These texts were more usually understood to constitute a divinely authoritative, universal, sustaining and binding motive.[16] Other commentators went one step further back, locating the missionary motive in the person of Jesus Christ. German theologian Gustav Warneck argued that the life, teaching and incarnational presence of Jesus formed the deepest basis for mission, from which the Great Commission was simply the logical extension.[17] Closer to home, the Revd Frank Oldrieve told the dominion's Baptists that 'it is devotion to the King which prompts self-sacrificing labours … With Paul we say, "The love of Christ constraineth us".'[18]

WSCF travelling secretary Ruth Rouse argued in 1917 that love, once dominant as a universal missionary motive, had been largely replaced by duty in the early twentieth century.[19] While duty was a dominant motivational theme, Christ's love and a responsive love for Christ remained a very important motive in the New Zealand context. This was influenced by a prevailing evangelical emphasis on personal piety and responsiveness. Auckland Baptist Endeavourers were reminded in 1894 that 'it is in the union our hearts have with [Christ] that gives whatever reality or strength our profession of Christianity may have. Religion has its seat in loyalty of heart, and devotion to the Saviour.'[20] Once loved, the Christian was then exhorted to return that love, primarily through a life of service to others. The Revd Herbert Davies (Presbyterian) captured this notion when he wrote that 'the man who knows God in Christ becomes imbued with a restless love that can never be satisfied until it sees the whole world sharing its own joys and privileges'.[21] PWMU women read in the *Harvest Field* in 1913 that 'if we are to be really helpful we must be filled with Christian compassion. Love must determine our attitude, love for Christ must be our prime motive. Our love for Christ impels us to take up the same attitude that He took up.'[22] The perceived spiritual and humanitarian plight of non-Christian peoples, coupled with a call to duty and responsibility, were increasingly linked with this underlying motive of love. Other motives were also stressed at different times. One Presbyterian commentator proposed seven motives that fleshed out the phrases 'love of God' and 'love of neighbour'. No less than 12 different motives were suggested for recruiting student volunteers.[23] Against prevailing trends, the CIM continued to stress the 'thousands dying daily in darkness' as a key motive for missionary work.[24] These were the driving religious sentiments that underlay the more individualised expressions of motivation encountered throughout this chapter.

Approach, methods and general patterns

The approach taken in this book is to begin with the narratives (stories) and details of individual missionaries and applicants, in order to identify the extrinsic factors that broke into their otherwise ordinary lives, and then to work outwards to consider the interplay and influence of contextual factors. This approach is not without precedents. In her study of British women missionaries in the same period, Rhonda Semple notes the 'importance of the individual to the missionary encounter', whereby 'a complex interplay existed among [individual missionaries] both created by and acting in reply to the many constituents of British society at the time'.[25] In the New Zealand context two questions implicitly shape the analysis of the motivational material: what were the elements that made up an individual's personal narrative and context, and what factors catalysed or impelled individuals to contemplate moving from the familiar to the unfamiliar? More broadly, we also need to ask to what extent personal context interacted with wider historical and social contexts to motivate individuals towards missionary service.

For the New Zealand setting, the sources for assessing individual motivation are twofold in character. Presbyterian and Anglican application records make up the core of the narratives considered here, because they exist in a much more complete and systematic form than other denominations' holdings. These records consist of letters of enquiry, completed application forms (which included questions on motivation), correspondence and, in the Presbyterian case, appended freehand accounts of personal Christian experience. These sources are complemented by motivational data for other denominations and organisations gleaned from sporadic application material, missionary periodicals, and both published and unpublished biographical accounts. Overall, the most comprehensive material dates from the 1890s.

While interpretation based on these types of sources must remain somewhat tentative, there are good grounds for assuming the essential veracity of the motivational comments in application papers and published testimonies. Diane Langmore notes that the motives of British and Australasian missionaries to Papua were carefully scrutinised by all organisations involved. Stuart Piggin argues that the essential veracity of missionary motives documented in early to mid-nineteenth-century British sources can be accepted because of the influence of personal piety and the accepted practice of intense spiritual self-examination during this period. For New Zealand Presbyterians, Brooke Whitelaw draws attention to the rigorous process through which candidates were put to prove their eligibility.[26] Of course, the surviving data are not wholly representative; the extant sources are largely Presbyterian and Anglican, and indeed the NZCMA/S material represents only a part of the Anglican constituency. While motivational statements were obviously formulated with a particular purpose or audience in mind, two factors mitigate this. For Presbyterian applicants, a substantial quantity of unsolicited motivational data survive in the appended freehand accounts of their spiritual experience. When these statements are compared with answers to a similar question in NZCMA/S papers, and with the more formulaic testimonies of BIM and CIM missionaries, there is a surprising degree of congruity. This suggests that there was a commonly conceived mental narrative structure regarding missionary motivation that ran across Protestant denominational or confessional boundaries throughout this period, and more especially among evangelicals.

For convenience, motivational statements are broken down into two sets of data. The first set, represented in Table 4.1, contains the identifiable factors that catalysed or precipitated the act of enquiring about or applying for missionary service. This aspect has received little systematic attention, and there are no existing guidelines on how to categorise the data.[27] As a result, the categories adopted here are those that emerged from the data. Because individuals often referred to more than one motivating factor, the data are presented here in ranked form (with '1' representing the most frequently given category).

TABLE 4.1. Factors Catalysing Enquiry or Application for Missionary Service, 1890–1939 (Ranked)[28]

Category	1890–99	1900–18	1919–39	Overall	
				No.	Rank
Life-stage transition	6	1	3	88	1
Personal contact	2	2=	1	83	2=
Visiting speaker	1	2=	4	83	2=
Advertised position	4	6	2	62	4
Divine guidance	3	4	5	52	5
Life-stage dissatisfaction	7=	5	7=	24	6
Missionary literature	5	8	9	18	7
Other	–	9=	6	16	8
Student volunteer	7=	7	–	14	9
Bible study / prayer group	–	11	7=	9	10
International events	–	9=	10	4	11

In most cases, the applicants or missionaries explicitly cited these reasons. 'Life-stage' reasons were sometimes also inferred from wider comments made in the correspondence.[29] 'Divine guidance' was often bracketed with other information that indicated how that guidance had been discerned. The 'other' category contained a range of miscellaneous reasons, with wives often citing their husband's application as the catalyst. The main factors set out in Table 4.1 were relatively consistent across the whole period, with 'advertised position' discernibly more important for Presbyterians by the 1920s.

Similarly, there was little difference in the data with respect to gender and organisation. 'Personal contact' and 'visiting speaker' were cited marginally more frequently by women, and 'life-stage transition' by men. The latter category was also higher for denominational applicants (reflecting the fuller nature of the Presbyterian and Anglican sources), and 'visiting speaker' and explicit statements about 'divine guidance' appeared more frequently for non-denominational applicants.

The second set of data contains the identifiable motivational factors for missionary service (Table 4.2 overleaf). These categories are based on two earlier Anglo-European studies,[30] with 'life-stage transition' the only additional category created for the New Zealand context. The data have again been ranked because of the multiple motivational comments offered by individuals. With the exception of a 'sense of usefulness', the main factors were relatively consistent across time, and again displayed little difference with respect to gender or organisation. Women more often cited 'obedience' as a motivational factor. Denominational applicants tended to more frequently stress the notion of being 'useful'.

Personal narratives of motivation

New Zealand's missionaries came from varied personal, socio-economic, geographical, denominational and even theological backgrounds. Yet despite these differences, their personal narratives were essentially couched in common religious, theological or spiritual terms, through which they primarily understood and described their own experience of missionary interest and calling. Without paying attention to these concepts, it is difficult to make sense of the ways in which the various extrinsic factors broke into individual lives and circumstances, propelling people towards missionary service. In other words these factors, and their implications, had to be intelligible to the participants. They penetrated a mental world that was already prepared for their reception. Most applicants came from overtly Christian homes or at least had been brought up attending church, Sunday school, Christian Endeavour or Bible class.[32] So at the very least, their perception of the world, and how they should relate to it, was increasingly shaped by regular exposure to missionary publicity and calls for financial support.

A commonly shared narrative of religious experience emerged among this group that helps to explain the impact of the extrinsic factors. This

TABLE 4.2. Motivational Factors for Missionary Service, 1890–1939 (Ranked)[31]

Category	1890–99	1900–18	1919–39	Overall	
				No.	Rank
Obeying God's command	1	1	3	90	1
Sense of usefulness	9	3	1	86	2
Response to need	3	2	2	83	3
Sense of personal calling	2	4	4	71	4
Sense of pity	5	5	5	54	5
Sense of duty	4	6	6	48	6
Love for God	6=	7=	7	30	7
Life-stage transition	6=	9	10	20	8
Heavenly reward	10=	7=	–	13	9
Personal aptitude	10=	12	8	12	10
Other	–	10=	9	11	11
Civilising / imperial impulse	–	10=	12	5	12
Eschatological	6=	13=	–	4	13=
God's glory	–	13=	11	4	13=
Sense of adventure	–	13=	13	2	15

narrative followed a basic trajectory of Christian upbringing, childhood and adolescent faith development, and an increasing ownership of personal faith from late adolescence onwards. It had at least four conceptual permutations. The first and least recorded version, more common among women, was the notion of Christianity as an organic and relatively untroubled life-long process. Elsie Goodson (Presbyterian) was 'taught from the tiniest tot to love and serve God and to follow in the footsteps of my Lord Jesus Christ', while Nellie MacDuff (CIM) noted that she could 'never remember the time' when she 'did not love the Lord Jesus'.[33] A second version identified a moment or phase of religious 'conversion'. This experience was variously described as 'being converted', acknowledging 'Christ as Saviour', making a 'stand to follow Christ', 'accepting' or 'appropriating Jesus Christ as personal saviour', and being 'brought to a personal knowledge of Christ'.[34] Conversion was both the fulfilment of a Christian upbringing and the springboard into a life of useful service. For Presbyterians and Anglicans, it was often bracketed with baptismal confirmation and church membership.

A third version identified significant crisis points that, once resolved, often led to a deeper sense of faith and a greater desire to serve God. These crises were typically an expression of adolescent individuation, or involved traumatic events that impacted on family life. Katherine Ensor (Anglican) related how she was 'led astray ... by the allurements of Theosophy', until a missionary friend later 'disabused my mind of many illusions ... and gradually turned my thoughts more and more to the meek and lowly Jesus'.[35] George McNeur (Presbyterian) credited the untimely death of his brother James as the means by which God 'brought me into a closer union with Christ' and 'led me to look with more of the traveller's eye on the things of this world, and to lay up treasure in Heaven'.[36] Such crises could also be precipitated by experiences that cast doubt on the content and confidence of childhood faith, or by perceived (and often prolonged) struggles with sin. They could also be external crises that impacted on otherwise disengaged individuals. The reported death of Baptist missionary Hopestill Pillow in 1895, and the nagging internalised question 'who will go in her place', set Presbyterian missionary Alice Henderson on the road to lifelong work in northern India.[37] The fourth and final version, again often found among women, involved individuals arriving at a significant new understanding of Christian faith. These experiences included a new apprehension of God's perceived loving nature through Christ, a spiritual 'awakening', or a personal awareness of the role of the Holy Spirit. Such paradigm shifts often occurred during evangelistic campaigns, conventions and camps.

There are at least two equally valid ways of interpreting such narratives. On the one hand, following the developmental theory of James Fowler, they indicate the natural stages through which religious faith may progress.[38] Whatever the individual's circumstances, the transition between stages often involved moments of personal decision, crisis and revelation. On the other hand, these narratives employed common rhetorical devices that reflected how Christian faith was popularly and emotionally constructed within the increasingly privatised schema of late nineteenth-century evangelicalism. These devices typically included the struggle with human sinfulness, the need for personal encounter with Christ as Saviour and personal submission to Christ as Lord, and the notion of sacrificial service as an outworking of such encounters.[39] Local churches generally formed the context within which this interpretation of faith was shaped and explicated, allied with the impact of specific groups on denominational life.

A narrative provided by an early NZCMA missionary applicant further illustrates the interplay of these experiences. Although from a strong Anglican family, she wrote in 1893:

> My first remembrance is rebellion against any authority – God or man's … Then a conversion which took the form of many many [sic] 'comings' to Christ before I was sure he had accepted me. From seventeen to twenty-eight I was known as a Christian: taught, wrote etc as such: but was a slave hand to foot, to one special besetting sin. Early in 1890 it came to this: first three or four days temptation to most awful thoughts, downright blasphemy: with no desire to escape from them: a coming to myself, which made me desperate over my helplessness: and in bewilderment as to what the Bible could mean practically by its glorious description of the life of Christ's redeemed: for I knew I was saved from death – yet they did not describe my life. Mr Grubb's mission in 1890, and the teaching of the Holy Spirit's work: I came to Christ in faith to keep me from my sin, against which twenty years of struggling had done nothing: and He has kept me from that day to this, for I am well assured I am not keeping myself. [Then, when asked specifically what led her 'to engage in Foreign Missionary work' she went on to say] … Ever since the mission in 1890 I have cared that Christ should love those for Whom He died: but waited, not knowing if He would have me [as] one of those who went abroad.[40]

There is a mysterious element here, for it is not immediately clear why these particular individuals should be especially moved when this was obviously not the experience of all churchgoers, even within the same religious milieu. Religious or spiritual experience was apparently more intense for some, and less so for others; more cerebral for some, and much more explicitly emotional for others. The narratives highlight individuals for whom faith was so enlivened that they sought to respond in like manner, reflecting a mix of unique personality and general context.

The narratives reflect a common sense of spiritual experience or progression that led individuals to significant points of self-understanding, heightened spiritual awareness or perceived divine revelation. These interpretative categories are unfamiliar in a more secularised age, and sit uncomfortably within a reasoned approach to historical explanation. Yet this was how the participants understood their own experiences. Considered overall, their narratives reveal that they viewed their relationship with God to be the primary expression of personal Christian faith. They variously felt loved, accepted, forgiven and empowered by God. Furthermore, they perceived that they belonged to God in a way that was hitherto not understood. Their narratives commonly displayed a developing awareness that to be Christian meant more than regular involvement in the rituals and activities of denominational and local church life, and that it entailed certain obligations. Movements like Christian Endeavour and the Bible classes served to reinforce such sentiments. The unnamed Anglican woman quoted above used the phrase 'He has kept me' to describe her perception of how God related to her. The corollary was that she 'cared that Christ should love those for Whom He died'. This sense of 'Belonging to God' also carried the sense that there were others, the 'heathen', who did not yet belong, and hinted at the Christian's duty to rectify that imbalance. With empowerment came a desire to live a life of meaningful and useful service on behalf of others. This sentiment was explicit in the correspondence of Mona Dean cited earlier in the chapter. Most important of all, in gratitude for receiving the gift of God's love, many missionary applicants stated their desire for consecrated service. Annie Hancock (Presbyterian) most eloquently observed that

> I have found that the greatest, grandest, and best things are open to those only whose lives are illuminated by the Christian faith; that there is possible to men and women, love so great as to make tremendous

sacrifices for their fellow-men ... When we think that the love of God was so great as to send His Son to bring about this happier state, we begin to appreciate the value which God himself places on humanity, and perhaps to have an inkling that we ourselves ought to set a higher value on the lives of our fellow-men.[41]

Motivation and personal context

These then were the ways in which the various extrinsic factors encouraging missionary endeavour made a personal impact on people's lives. The words spoken by a friend or a known person over the meal table, or by visiting speakers recruiting both sentiments and bodies for the missionary cause, or penned in a published advertisement – all made perfect sense to those primed to respond. The specific images, geographic contexts and organisations involved may have been new to many hearers or readers, but the underlying appeal was not. An activist spirituality mixed with colonial settler pragmatism meant that individuals perceived the apparent socio-economic and religious disparities of their world with surprising clarity. For those whose life's journey had been arrested by this perception, there was a logical inevitability about their response. John Olley (Brethren) captured this best in a letter to a close friend when he wrote that 'there is no other way possible for me. I am a bond-servant. I must go.'[42] Any interpretation of missionary motivation, then, must take seriously the personalised and overtly spiritual or religious content of these narratives, and the theological construction of the world to which they led.

At the same time, the data displayed in Tables 4.1 and 4.2 indicate that there were other factors in the motivational mix. Their significance may be assessed by a closer examination of two important motivational categories, 'life-stage transition' and 'a sense of usefulness'. Mona Dean's propulsion towards missionary service apparently came at a significant transition point in her life. This was a common experience for many of the missionary applicants and enquirers. It was clearly the most important catalytic factor for men and, for women, was grouped equally with 'personal contact' and 'visiting speakers'. Further analysis of this category, represented in Table 4.3 in ranked form, reveals some significant patterns.

TABLE 4.3. Breakdown of Life-stage Transition, 1890–1939 (Ranked)[43]

Category	Male	Female	Overall	
			No.	Rank
End of study	1	3	26	1
Older and single	2=	1	19	2
End of family commitments	5=	2	17	3
Career transition	5=	4	6	4=
Job dissatisfaction	2=	5	6	4=
Death of spouse or fiancé(e)	2=	6=	5	6
Seeking new opportunities	7	8	3	7
Divorce/broken engagement	–	6=	2	8
Family problems	–	9=	–	9=
Illness	–	9=	1	9=

A key transition point was the change from study to a career, particularly for men but also increasingly important for women. For men, this experience was further differentiated by age. Many student applicants were older men, in their late twenties and thirties, who were moving from secular occupations to ordination and ministry. Missionary application or enquiry came in the midst of their theological training, and thus within a phase of personal transition. The death of a spouse was also more likely to be a motivating factor for men. Conversely, for women life-stage transition was most often linked with two factors: the cessation of family support roles – caring for parents or siblings – or a combination of being older and single.

Mona Dean also expressed a desire to put her personal abilities to beneficial use. Again, this was a commonly cited motivational category for many people, and was often linked with a heightened perception of global needs. Both men and women readily emphasised notions of service and stressed their desire to put experience, aptitude, qualifications and privileged lifestyles to good use. It was also linked with a perceived aptitude for a particular vocation, especially education or medicine. Annie Astbury (Presbyterian) encapsulated much of this in her application:

> I feel it is my duty, not only as a Christian, but also as a citizen of a nation that has enjoyed all the benefits, advantages and privileges of Christianity, to teach and tell other people of heathen religions, of my religion, and what it has meant for myself and my people … [At the Hawera Bible Class Conference c. 1920] I was faced with the question as to whether or not I was making the most use of my life … [The speakers] asked us very direct, very personal and very searching questions. Were we in the place God intended us to be in? Were we quite sure that God did not want us for some special service? … The result was that I came home absolutely dissatisfied with my daily occupation. As a matter of fact I have never really been satisfied with my work [as a stenographer].[44]

Annie's theological language, here, was intertwined with elements of socio-geographic context and a sense of vocational dissatisfaction and opportunity.

Motivation was inextricably linked to significant moments of personal development and change. Such circumstances were highly variable. Leaving school and still full of adolescent optimism, Patrick Lane (Anglican) asserted that 'it has been my one desire … to carry out the Gospel in to foreign parts and something tells me that India needs the help of my poor services'.[45] For many men, the missionary call emerged seamlessly out of their training for ministry. So it was for the Revd Thomas Riddle (Presbyterian), whose subsequent lifetime of work in the New Hebrides and India presented itself as a logical next step from his being a student for ordination.[46] Other situations were more traumatic and difficult. Irene Kelling (Anglican) poignantly stated that 'a broken engagement has made that [missionary] desire doubly strong especially as it was broken by a returned soldier because I have German blood in me'. Miss L. Johnson (Anglican) sought relief both from her job as a dressmaker and costumier, and from an alcoholic father.[47] Dr Lapraik (Presbyterian) applied for medical missionary work in the New Hebrides at the age of 50, following the death of his wife.[48] Many applicants, faced with the prospects of or the need for change, employed both emotional or spiritual experience and theological concepts to re-imagine their futures. If some of these individuals simply sought to escape present circumstances, then even escape itself was still clearly thought of in theological terms and linked with consecrated, useful service.

Motivation and women

Notions of escape, and the prominence of 'life-stage transition' and 'a sense of usefulness' in New Zealand narratives indicate that women's experiences of motivation need to be considered more closely. Women made up a large proportion of the missionary workforce, as noted in Chapter One. In New Zealand as elsewhere, while married women had always been present, single women became an increasingly important factor in missionary recruitment and numbers. Although contemporaries noted this trend, there was little critical evaluation of the phenomenon until the post-World War 1 era. Most interpretative progress has been made since Beaver's seminal work of 1968.[49] More recent international and New Zealand literature on motivation has largely been framed within wider feminist or gendered discourses. As a result, we now have a more nuanced understanding of women's motivation in general, and particularly for New Zealand Presbyterian, Methodist and Baptist women.[50]

Much of this literature has stressed the relationship between first-wave feminism and the growth of women's missionary participation. Shirley Garrett argues, for example, that from the late nineteenth century the goals of American women missionaries were 'defined in the language of feminism … Most missionary tracts about women abroad were not theological, they were litanies of social problems … Women missionaries were supposed to attack these problems in one way or another. They were sent as agents of social change, church feminism on the march.'[51] Social and moral reform was a key motivational factor for women across a range of Protestant societies.[52] In this context, therefore, Sarah Coleman links motivation for New Zealand women in India with wider prevailing notions of women as 'protectors of the home' (and thus 'reformers and protectors of society in general') and with 'evangelical ideas of the feminisation of Christ' (which served to legitimise single women as missionaries in their own right).[53] There was a clearly identifiable connection between domesticity, feminist social reform and the missionary movement. This relationship, however, was not necessarily straightforward. As Jane Haggis notes, women were 'caught in a complex and contradictory web of agency and discourse which "remade" not only convert women but missionary women as well' – converts as 'wife, mother and worker', missionary wives as 'amateur appendage' and single women as 'professional woman'.[54]

A problem arises when this connection is cast as the primary factor. Was this socio-religious nexus a reality, or is it a function of more recent academic assumptions? The New Zealand evidence is ambiguous. Reforming sentiments were acutely absent from women's narratives, with only a few overt references to women's work or to issues of overseas reform. Theological imagery largely predominated. Yet such ideas were not entirely absent. Ambiguous phrases like 'a desire to uplift those in darkness' are found, and it is possible that such language was understood in both its theological and social dimensions.[55] Later NZCMS applicants had to furnish a sample Sunday school missionary lesson, for which a number of women chose a social reforming theme. Violet Bargrove, for example, linked the advances of Western civilisation with Christianity, both to highlight perceived global disparities and to accentuate the need for evangelistic and medical intervention. Similarly Ruby Lindsay drew attention, in her lesson, to the 'six out of every ten babies' in Eastern Africa 'lost through ignorance and neglect'.[56] For Baptists, the social reforming aspects of missionary work had always been highly regarded. In 1886 the Revd Alfred North graphically depicted the '100,000,000 [girls and women] sitting in darkness and the shadow of death ... Our hearts are touched by the misery of these women; we long to see them uplifted, in the social scale.'[57] Obituaries for Hopestill Pillow in 1895 drew attention to the social justice dimensions of her work.[58] Later evaluations of NZBMS work, by Baptist women commentators, were also dominated by references to social 'uplift' work among women and children.[59] Social issues were also prominent among the concerns campaigned for more broadly by New Zealand evangelical Protestant women in the 1890s, with temperance and suffrage high on the agenda. Given the country's small population, it was not surprising that the women who were stridently active in such causes, both across denominations and in groups like the Women's Christian Temperance Union, were also the same women who were prominently involved on behalf of overseas missions.[60] Missions and reform, both at home and abroad, went hand in hand.

Both single and married women missionaries expected to work almost exclusively with women or children, and missionary literature led them to expect that they would be involved in aspects of reforming work. The absence of explicit references to social amelioration, as a motivational factor, may simply reflect that it was taken for granted by many women. More importantly, this apparent omission may have reflected the gap between the idealisation and the realities of missionary work. This is certainly a question raised by Mona Dean's narrative. Missionary training in this period placed greatest emphasis on biblical and doctrinal knowledge and on practical skills. Other religions, cultures and societies were sometimes covered by curricula, but such knowledge was more often gleaned from popular missionary literature, mission study or visiting speakers. Most applicants departed New Zealand equipped with a general education or the skills of their particular profession, and full of confidence as to their part in the grand and idealised task of saving the heathen. The everyday realities of women's work – zenana visiting, medical care, school teaching and administration, teacher and nurse training, and child welfare – served over time to emphasise the social amelioration aspects of missionary work.

Perhaps social 'uplift' became a more enduring motivational theme simply as a result of its already high profile. If so, then it may be more accurate to more clearly distinguish between idealised and actual motivation. This further supports the argument that theological and spiritual motivational categories need to be treated seriously in context, because it was through these that most women (and indeed men) initially and ideally understood their identity and calling. Historical discourses that locate women's motivation within the intersecting contexts of domesticity, emancipation, reform and European colonialism are legitimate so long as they also acknowledge the theological and spiritual categories of thought that underlay and informed these other categories. In these terms, motivation in the New Zealand context was, as Yvonne Robertson helpfully points out, partly a function of a 'religious discourse' (emphasising the feminisation and empowerment of Christ's incarnation) linked with ideas of romanticist revivalism, international sisterhood and, ultimately, more traditional domestic notions of women's social and moral reforming roles.[61]

Women's narratives indicate that motivation for missionary service sometimes emerged from experiences or assumptions unique to women, and this
deserves further comment. A first observation is that, for women, some form
of family dislocation was more often a motivational factor, leaving them to
face significant life transition choices once free of family obligations. Domestic
responsibilities sometimes delayed an earlier desire to be a missionary. For
others, circumstantial change created either a dilemma or, more often, an
opportunity. Miss McKinney (Presbyterian) wrote that she had 'heard God's
voice calling me to work for Him many years ago, but have had many disap-
pointments being the eldest of a large family, home duties, sickness in the
family, etc, have detained me'. Following the death of her father in 1897,
Isabella McCallum (NZCMA) felt 'free from home ties' and 'the great need
of the heathen world was specially laid upon me'.[62] Jane Hunter notes that
the 'push of home circumstance' and the 'dramatic freedom and disorienta-
tion caused by family death' was a prominent catalyst for American women
going to China.[63] Some of Hunter's observations – for example, making a
missionary pledge as a form of penance and applying after the death of a
spouse – could also be applied to New Zealand missionaries irrespective of
their gender. Yet both the American and New Zealand narratives emphasise
the distinctive domestic and 'occupational' niches that many single women
filled in these decades. Moreover, single daughters were still expected to bear
the burden of family responsibilities, even when working in a career or occupation. When this familial role came to an end, especially for older women or
for those who had not found a career of their own, then the future was thrown
wide open in a way not so common for men.

A second observation is that the notion of 'usefulness' was increasingly
more significant in women's narratives over the period, even though it was
also important for men. Following Abraham Maslow's notion of a hierarchy of needs, it might be argued that 'being useful' met a fundamental
need for self-esteem and for self-actualisation regardless of gender.[64] Yet
the narratives indicate that there was a degree of gender differentiation.
While men and women both stressed the service aspect of being useful,
women also emphasised that they had been divinely entrusted with talents
and aptitudes that they dare not waste, and that their age and singleness
meant that they were free to render useful service. Women also accentuated
notions of 'helping' and 'doing good'. Beatrice Brunt (NZCMS) reflected
this emphasis when she wrote that 'I believe that God has given me health

and ability for the purpose of going forth to spread the great tidings of a loving Saviour.'[65]

Sarah Coleman argues that, for New Zealand women going to India, becoming a missionary was both an emancipatory act and a restatement of traditional role definitions. Single women took up a 'career of usefulness' in order to seek legitimacy outside marriage and motherhood, in a way that 'continued to utilise the traditional feminine qualities of self-sacrifice, domestic protection and moral guardianship'.[66] Lydia Hoyle helpfully casts the interpretative net a little wider here. She agrees that, in the American context, women's desire for usefulness partially reflected this perspective. At the same time, it also reflected both the potentially liberating rhetoric of mid- to late nineteenth-century evangelicalism (following the Second Awakening and the emerging holiness movement) and the growing protest over the strictures placed on women within prevailing patriarchal models of church administration and ministry.[67] In other words, women wanted to be both personally and professionally useful in the light of greater educational and work opportunities, and also in response to popular spirituality that emphasised gender equality through the agency of the Holy Spirit. These conclusions make sense for the New Zealand context, as they allow for the complex interplay of personal narrative with comparable theological and sociological factors.

At the same time, there were discernible differences within this construction of motivation. For example, New Zealand CIM women did not so readily reciprocate the self-confident tone expressed by their Presbyterian and Anglican sisters. 'Usefulness' was understood to be a result of personal surrender to God's will, bolstered by biblical texts emphasising God's all-sufficiency. This rhetorical focus accentuated the notion of God enabling an otherwise weak, sinful, wilful and undeserving human agent to obey the missionary call.[68] Indeed, the example of the emerging faith mission movement is a reminder of the limitations of categorical gendered explanations. The notion of useful service emanating from a surrendered life and dependence upon God, expressed so often by CIM and BIM missionaries, was equally attractive to women and to men. This may have meant that feminised religious sentiments had greater appeal for some male applicants, or had an abiding impact in wider church life. Alternatively, missiological frameworks less bound by church or denominational structures may have appealed to certain groups and, therefore, transcended gender boundaries.

Either way, as Peter Williams observes for the nineteenth-century English context, 'to suggest that it had a greater appeal for women is to impose a psychological theory on evidence which will yield no more than the reality of its influence on both men and women'.[69]

Finally here, it seems likely that age and marital status played an important role in catalysing or motivating women missionaries. Nearly 40 per cent of Presbyterian and NZCMA/S women were single and aged 30 or over at the time of their application, compared with just over 20 per cent of men. These were often women of considerable educational background or professional expertise, reflecting their increasing participation in these occupational categories over the period.[70] Having reached a certain age, many older single women may have perceived a missionary vocation to be either a valid lifelong option or an alternative avenue for finding a like-minded marriage partner. Overseas narrative evidence points in this direction, particularly regarding the notion of a valid alternative to marriage.[71] Myrtle Hill notes that the high ratio of single to married Irish women may have moved the former towards 'an alternative fulfilling lifestyle' in the face of receding marriage opportunities in Ireland. Different contexts may have bred different dynamics. For New Zealand society this was a period of demographic maturation. While single women immigrants in the late nineteenth century initially entered a 'male atmosphere', in which men outnumbered women, urban and rural sex ratios were moving towards equilibrium by the 1920s and 1930s. The age and sex structure was maturing, with the middle age groupings becoming a larger proportion of the total population. While the percentage of married men increased, the pool of unmarried women remained small.[72] So it would appear that the reduced opportunity for marriage was not necessarily a significant factor.

Nevertheless, some intriguing patterns were hidden within these general statistics for marital status during this period, prompting closer scrutiny of the New Zealand context. While there were always proportionally more single adult males than females, the percentage of women who were single grew markedly, from 13 to 29 per cent of women between 1874 and 1906. By the 1930s there was a surplus of single urban women aged over 45.[73] The *rate* at which the number of single women grew was also significantly more than for single men between the 1870s and the 1920s, particularly for women aged between 25 and 35 (1880s–1890s) and for women over 35 (1896–1906).[74] Geographically, Otago and Canterbury were the only two regions to return a notable excess of single women over single men.[75] It would appear, then, that the marked growth in missionary departures and interest from the 1890s coincided with a period of growth in the numbers and proportions of single women, particularly those aged 25 and over. Coincidentally, too, the two regions that initially contributed a large number of missionaries were also those with an excess of single females. It thus seems fair to speculate that there was some connection between this demographic transition, increased missionary rhetoric, an initial dearth of service opportunities in the home churches, and the perception by some older single women that marriage or vocation might therefore be more gainfully found in missionary employment.

Most single women missionaries remained single for the duration of their service – a little over 70 per cent, as opposed to just over 30 per cent of single male missionaries. Of those women who married, many wed another missionary and remained living and working in a missionary context, or married non-New Zealand men in other occupations. If marriage was a motivational factor, it was not necessarily a primary consideration. There was perhaps a more profound dynamic at work. In a short posthumous biography of the Australian Baptist missionary Ellen Arnold, Donovan Mitchell suggested that she was the closest thing there was to a 'Baptist Nun'. He referred to her self-discipline, asceticism and devotion to both Christ and others. In his opinion, writing in 1932, the time was ripe 'for the Protestant Churches to remind themselves that without taking vows of celibacy, and without cutting themselves off from the world, hosts of Protestant women are living lives of extreme devotion to Christ and the Church'.[76] This is a relatively unexplored but intriguing avenue for investigation, bolstered by more recent research on women missionaries and deaconesses both in New Zealand and abroad.[77] If valid, it combined a variety of elements – demographic trends, marital status, age, vocation, 'usefulness', spiritual devotion and the notion of divinely entrusted ability – into a powerfully sustaining motivational mix for single women.

Conclusion

When applying to work in southern China, Annie Hancock (Presbyterian) wrote feelingly, 'I shall leave so many advantages and privileges behind me, that possibly no other inducement would be sufficient to make me wish to spend my life in a foreign country, than the foreign mission purpose.'[78]

Theological and gendered perspectives are a salutary reminder that missionary motivation should be contextually evaluated and understood, as far as possible, from the standpoint of those involved. In the New Zealand context, missionary motivation prior to World War II emanated from a complex mix of idealism and pragmatism; gender differences, opportunities and constraints; personal circumstances and historical context; and both religious and mundane factors. In this chapter I have highlighted the 'religious' dimensions simply to argue that these were fundamentally important in participants' minds. The adoption of a contextual narrative approach also indicates that these underlying religious categories interacted with and were influenced by a range of factors specific to the late nineteenth and early twentieth centuries. This approach also synthesises what were, in effect, some 1000 individual stories. While not intending to diminish the uniquely different circumstances of these individual lives, the approach taken here assumes that individual motivation must be treated on its own terms and also be set within its equally distinctive geographical, ideological, theological, socio-economic and historical contexts.

As Mona Dean's case has indicated, however, there was a difference between how the missionary task was perceived or idealised and how it may have played out on the ground. In other words, idealism (whether religiously, pragmatically, heroically or romantically conceived) was a significant underlying force of missionary propulsion. From Bolivia, Annie Cresswell (BIM) wrote tellingly to her supporters in 1914 that '[t]o the worker at home, especially to one whose lot is cast among what might be termed "common tasks", the labour of her sister in a foreign land seems all important ... We ... know that the difference is not so great as some imagine ... Circumstances and conditions certainly are different, but ... there is little romance about the life of a missionary.'[79] In the next chapter, I examine the notion of the missionary movement as a mentalité (mentality or world view) – that is, as an enduring mode of thought that became deeply embedded in colonial religious culture and which influenced such idealistic approaches to the missionary endeavour. Here we note that application narratives and complementary data indicate the extent to which this mentalité had taken root in New Zealand by the 1930s.

One indicator of this was the relatively long time period between the initial interest shown by applicants and the actual date of application, and the early age at which interest was often registered. Interest in mission work was clearly not an overnight phenomenon. Many applicants displayed a prolonged interest over many years, on average between five and nine years prior to application. In some cases this interest had been maintained over decades. A large proportion of applicants further signalled that their interest dated back to childhood and, more commonly, to their teenage years. Two thirds of women, compared with just under a half of men, dated their attraction to missionary work back to their formative decades. A long-nurtured missionary mentalité thus enveloped the decision to enquire about or apply for missionary service.

The second indicator suggests that, for many New Zealand church-goers, there was by the early twentieth century a well-entrenched sense that missionary service represented the pinnacle of Christian life and service – a belief also evidenced among Australian Protestants and in the Keswick movement in Britain.[80] This line of reasoning can be discerned in Mona Dean's enquiries. It was further hinted at in a number of applicant narratives, such as Alice Hercus's (Presbyterian) assertion: 'I feel that I cannot settle to work at home, until Foreign Work has been found inadvisable.' More explicitly, the Revd Oliver Kimberley reassured one unsuccessful NZCMS applicant by saying, 'there is just this satisfaction, that you have faced the question which so many have failed to do, and thus cannot blame yourself for remaining in the homeland'.[81] This expectation was often highly internalised, as evidenced by the various degrees of mental and emotional anguish experienced by some applicants. This was exemplified by Kate Cooper's (Anglican) struggle for several months over the decision to apply for missionary service, spurred on by the 1910 Church of England Mission to New Zealand's Anglican churches.[82] Having initially assumed that she should offer herself for service, it was with a good deal of remorse (and perhaps a hint of relief) that she finally retracted her initial offer to the NZCMA:

> I went home and fought it out all that night before I retired. God was very, very near to me … He showed me so plainly that I had only offered or rather wanted to offer myself for foreign work because I was dissatisfied with my work and surroundings here … just because I found my life here rather hard and trying at times, I just made myself feel that it was God's wish that I should go. How thankful I am that I came to myself before too late. May Christ help me to do my duty here … Surely our lives here can be just as dedicated as those who go

forth on the mission field and God can consecrate for His great use just where we happen to be ... Oh, how sincerely I regret the great mistake I made. It is not my surroundings that needed changing it is only myself.[83]

Despite the individual struggle presented here, Kate's self-pressure or expectation also reflected a fair degree of perceived public pressure to conform to a commonly accepted norm. Missionary service, as a concrete expression of this underlying mentalité, was an increasingly accepted ideal both in corporate church life and in the spiritual understanding of individual New Zealand Protestants of this period. In this way, it leant powerful and sustaining force to those whose self-apprehension led them to consider a missionary lifestyle or vocation, and fed into the religiously framed world view that was so sincerely communicated through their motivational narratives.

Clockwise starting above:
Rosalie Macgeorge was the first NZBMS missionary to East Bengal, sent by Hanover Street Church, Dunedin, in 1886. She died prematurely, in 1891, while returning through Colombo, Sri Lanka (Ceylon), to New Zealand. *NZBMS Archive, Ayson Clifford Library*

Annie Newcombe was the second NZBMS missionary to East Bengal in 1897. She resigned in 1889 from ill health and later, as Mrs Annie Driver, began a missionary training home in Dunedin. She was a founding member of the Baptist Women's Missionary Union. *NZBMS Archive, Ayson Clifford Library*

Hopestill Pillow was the third NZBMS missionary to East Bengal, sent by Oxford Terrace Baptist Church, Christchurch, in 1889. She also died tragically before being able to return home for furlough in 1895, and was buried in Kolkata (Calcutta). *NZBMS Archive, Ayson Clifford Library*

Annie Bacon, a trained nurse, was the fourth NZBMS missionary to East Bengal, sent by Hanover Street Baptist Church, Dunedin, in 1890. She married another Baptist missionary and they returned to New Zealand in 1899. *NZBMS Archive, Ayson Clifford Library*

Above: The NZBMS Roll of Honour depicting all NZBMS missionaries who left New Zealand up to 1914. This used to hang in the Oxford Terrace Baptist Church, Christchurch. *NZBMS Archive, Ayson Clifford Library*

Right: The original founders of the New Zealand Church Missionary Association in 1892. Bishop E.C. Stuart (Waiapu Diocese) returned to missionary work in 1894 with the English Church Missionary Society in Persia along with his daughter Anne, who was a nurse. *New Zealand Church Missionary Society Archive, John Kinder Theological Library*

THE FOUNDERS OF THE N.Z. CHURCH MISSIONARY SOCIETY 1892

Alice L. Wilson, from Auckland's St Sepulchre Anglican Church on Khyber Pass, was the third missionary of the NZCMA. She worked in Nigeria 1894–1908 before ill health forced her return home where she continued in YWCA and welfare home work. *New Zealand Church Missionary Society Archive, John Kinder Theological Library*

Elizabeth Colenso (left) and Julia Farr with Melanesian women, Melanesian Mission, Norfolk Island, 1890s. Born in New Zealand, Elizabeth was the daughter of English CMS missionaries at Kerikeri. She married CMS missionary William Colenso, but they later separated. Julia Farr was a South Australian missionary who lived and worked on Norfolk Island 1894–1900. *Church of Melanesia Collection, John Kinder Theological Library*

Melanesian Mission staff, Norfolk Island, c. 1905. Identified individuals include: Miss Herbert (woman standing on the left), Revd Commins (middle, front row) and probably Mrs Commins (to his left), Mrs Godden (front row in dark dress), Sister Kate Ivens (front row right). Others probably include Miss Coombe, Miss Kitchen and Daisy Palmer. *Church of Melanesia Collection, John Kinder Theological Library*

Missionaries and staff in front of one of two mission hospitals in Ranaghat, India (north of Kolkata). Vivienne Opie is one of the unidentified people in the front row (this photo comes from her album). Vivienne lived and worked at Ranaghat as a nurse, nursing superintendent and educator from 1919 until her retirement in 1955. *New Zealand Church Missionary Society Archive, John Kinder Theological Library*

'Miss [Elizabeth] Prentice with her nurses and village women [with their babies] at Kong T'suen hospital', Guangzhou, China. Elizabeth was a trained nurse from Mosgiel who worked with the Presbyterian Church's Canton Villages Mission 1910–23, when she retired back to New Zealand due to ill health. These babies had been born in the hospital, and were brought back daily to be washed and dressed in order to prevent tetanus. *Presbyterian Research Centre (Archives), A-L-1.47151*

Canton Villages Mission staff, 1914 (Presbyterian Church of New Zealand). Back: Revd Herbert Davies, Dr Edward Kirk, Revd Peter Milne. Middle: Dr R. Paterson (Muriel, held), Catherine Paterson, Elizabeth Prentice, Winifred Stubbs, Annie Hancock, Annie James, Annie McEwan, Hazel Milne, Revd William Mawson (George, held). Front: Jean McNeur, Margaret Davies (Jock Davies, held), Margaret McNeur, Revd George McNeur, Sara Mawson. Very Front: Ellen Wright, Margaret Mawson, Gordon Mawson. *Presbyterian Research Centre (Archives), A-L-1.11-13*

'Mrs Andrew Miller and Nancy itinerating', 1920s. Ellen Wright, from Dunedin, worked with the Canton Villages Mission staff 1911–19 when she married the Revd Andrew Miller. They continued there until the ill health of their daughter Jean forced them home in 1929. Tragically their daughter Nancy died from tropical fever in 1926. *Presbyterian Research Centre (Archives), A-L-1.23-69*

Busy Bee Hive, St Andrew's Presbyterian Church, Dunedin (c. 1910s). Children organised into Busy Bee groups quickly became ubiquitous in New Zealand Presbyterian churches as enduring sites of children's and young people's missionary support and further socialisation. *Presbyterian Research Centre (Archives), P-A62.7-21*

Missionary tableau at a missionary exhibition, Dunedin (c. 1910s). Such exhibitions were a common feature of local church life, giving the wider public ready access to both missionary information and the artefacts of other geographical locations and cultures. *Presbyterian Research Centre (Archives), P-A62.10-30*

Outdoor group photo of the Milne family members and relations on Nguna Island,
New Hebrides (Vanuatu), c. 1913. Back (from left): Revd W. Anderson, Nurse
Kennedy, Revd M. Frater, Revd William V. Milne. Middle: Kate Anderson, Keith

Anderson (held), Janie Frater, Revd Peter Milne (Snr), Isobel Milne (later Riddle), Jemima Milne. Front: Violet Veitch Anderson, Isobel Anderson, Allan Frater, Alec Frater, Laurie Milne, Ian Milne. *Presbyterian Research Centre (Archives), A-S30-162.41-50*

The Revd Oscar Michelsen and others on a four-wheel buggy on the island of Tongoa, New Hebrides (Vanuatu), c. 1910. L-R: Buggy driver (unidentified), Revd Oscar Michelsen, Miss Plaisted, Alba Michelsen, Mrs Newman and (possibly) Roy Mill. *Presbyterian Research Centre (Archives), A-L-2.51-130*

Group photograph of the Nguna Busy Bees, New Hebrides (Vanuatu) 1926, taken outside the church at Taloa. Many of the children are displaying handcrafted items. Mrs Jemima Milne is standing third from the right in the centre row. *Presbyterian Research Centre (Archives), A-S30-163.19-29*

'First party of missionaries to sail from New Zealand to Argentina in 1898 [South American Evangelical Mission]: Mr. and Mrs. George Allan [front], Mr. Ernest Heycock [left] and Mr. Charles Wilson [right].' The Allans moved to Bolivia in 1903 and subsequently established the Bolivian Indian Mission. Charles Wilson returned to Dunedin in 1905 after the mission fell apart, and Ernest Heycock continued working in the Argentine until his death in 1923. He married Jessica Jackson, a Baptist missionary from Ashburton. *Reproduced from Margarita Hudspith,* Ripening Fruit: A history of the Bolivian Indian Mission *(New Jersey: Harrington Press, 1958)*

'Mr. and Mrs. George Allan, Margarita and Joseph, Bolivian Indian Mission, ready to return to Bolivia in 1909.' For at least seven years George led the mission's work in San Pedro while Mary lived a good part of each year with the children in La Paz, where they attended an American primary school. *Reproduced from Margarita Hudspith, Ripening Fruit: A history of the Bolivian Indian Mission (New Jersey: Harrington Press, 1958)*

Margarita Allan and pupils of San Pedro Boys' School, c. 1920s. Margarita returned to Dunedin where she attended Columba College before returning to work for the Bolivian Indian Mission. She married English BIM missionary Thomas Hudspith. *Reproduced from Margarita Hudspith,* Ripening Fruit: A history of the Bolivian Indian Mission *(New Jersey: Harrington Press, 1958)*

'Mr and Mrs George Mackenzie, of Queenstown, N.Z., at Pandita Ramabai's home at Mukti, Poona, India. Widows and children.' Otago Witness, *20 January 1909, 45, reproduced with the permission of the Hocken Collections, Uare Taoka o Hakena, University of Otago*

'Sister Clare (Miss Cole), formerly of Dunedin, and Mrs George Mackenzie, with small band of Indian widows.' Otago Witness, *20 January 1909, 45, reproduced with the permission of the Hocken Collections, Uare Taoka o Hakena, University of Otago*

'The China Inland Missions, Tu Shuen Station. Mr and Mrs John Webster, formerly of Dunedin (seated.)' Otago Witness, *27 January 1909, reproduced with the permission of the Hocken Collections, Uare Taoka o Hakena, University of Otago*

'Oriental bazaar and sale of work in aid of Pandita Ramabai's Mission to the Child-widows of India, Choral Hall, Dunedin, October 26–28: Some of the committee and workers.' Otago Witness, *9 November 1904, 41, reproduced with the permission of the Hocken Collections, Uare Taoka o Hakena, University of Otago*

'A snapshot of one of the Indian stalls at the recent oriental bazaar in the choral hall.' Otago Witness, *9 November 1904, 41, reproduced with the permission of the Hocken Collections, Uare Taoka o Hakena, University of Otago*

PART TWO

GLOBAL CONNECTIONS

CHAPTER 5

Overseas Missions and the Writing of New Zealand History

UP TO THIS POINT we have considered the broad details of how and why a missionary consciousness emerged among settler Protestant churches from the late nineteenth century, and what that movement looked like from both corporate and individual perspectives. It is clear, from this discussion, that to properly understand this aspect of New Zealand's religious history we have to 'read' it theologically, sociologically and culturally. To do so is to take seriously both the self-understanding of the historical participants and the various factors (domestic and international, religious, social and cultural) that were influential over many decades. In the following four chapters, I now turn to the wider question of 'so what?' In other words, what is significant about considering the history of overseas missionary involvement and links in these terms? In particular, I consider the relationship between New Zealand overseas missions and their wider historical context by way of selected themes – most notably, nation, empire, childhood and reflex impact. Here I enter into dialogue with a diversity of scholarship in order to arrive at a more nuanced and contextualised understanding of the missionary movement, and to indicate the value of integrating this movement into the broader history of settler societies like New Zealand. In this chapter, my focus is on how thinking about overseas missions might contribute to the writing of national history – in this case, the history of New Zealand as a settler society and emerging nation. I argue that by attending to the missionary element, as one significant linkage between nation-state and global society, national histories might be greatly enriched.

Of maps and things

A brief historical vignette provides a useful entry point into this discussion, and raises some intriguing questions. On a week night in late 1929 a crowd of people jammed into Auckland's Baptist Tabernacle, at the top end of Queen Street, for the annual graduation ceremony of the New Zealand Bible Training Institute (NZBTI). The 'BTI', as it affectionately became known, was founded in 1922 by the intrepid evangelical Baptist the Revd Joseph Kemp.[1] As we have seen, it emerged in the 1920s as a key institution for ministry and missionary training outside of the denominational colleges.[2] It was one of many such evangelical lay educational 'institutes' that proliferated during the early 1900s across Australasia, North America and Britain, and which were foundationally important as recruiting grounds for mission organisations.[3] Between 1922 and 1939 at least 182 men and women – over 50 per cent of the NZBTI's total graduates – left New Zealand as overseas missionaries, and a good number of others became home-based missionaries in different contexts.[4] As a tribute to this achievement, and to provide a climax to the 1929 proceedings, a large map of the world was raised at the front of the auditorium. From 'the elevated pulpit of the Tabernacle students threw among the audience coloured streamers which were pinned on to a large map of the world, the position of the various mission fields being thus clearly indicated. Streamers thus connected relatives and friends with loved ones who had left all and followed the Lord Jesus to the great beckoning fields of India, China, Islands of the Pacific, Africa, Palestine, and South America.' The exhortation, by the writer observing these events, was for those 'who remain at home' to 'hold the ropes' and to 'be faithful labourers in prayer on their behalf'.[5]

Maps of the world were prevalent in the promotional literature of the NZBTI (most notably the *Reaper*),[6] as they were in many similar institutional and missionary publications both in New Zealand and other Western nations. Educational by intent, they were also complex tools of colonisation and a means of asserting particular ideological emphases such as nationalism.[7] Maps, and the technologies that made them possible, helped to reshape attitudes to landscapes and geographies, as well as re-inscribing the landscapes themselves. At the same time, they provided a means for colonisers to build geographical knowledge in order to control and co-opt territories and peoples and, conversely, for colonised peoples to perform acts of resistance and geographical re-appropriation.[8] In the specific missionary context of the era under consideration this process was epitomised in the production of the *World Atlas of Christian Missions* in 1911,[9] the climax of a burgeoning nineteenth-century statistical movement that corralled the world, and its component parts, within a massive array of discursive statistical and visual representations.[10]

The NZBTI map also raises other questions about colonial or settler identity. How, for example, did these early twentieth-century participants view their geographical location, and therefore their socio-political situation, in an era that much recent historiography has viewed as pivotal to emerging national identity? In the map printed in the October 1925 issue of the *Reaper*, New Zealand was physically central and proximate to locations of mission overseas, with both Great Britain and North America situated on the map's margins. However else the folk attending the Auckland graduation ceremony felt linked to their historical and cultural origins, their most immediate and important linkages seemed to be with the so-called non-evangelised or non-Christian spaces (and inhabitants) of the world. In this respect there was a great similarity, for example, with the BWMU membership card discussed in Chapter Two, which indicated that Baptist identity in New Zealand was very much linked to East Bengal. Irrespective of the other ways in which New Zealand identity was being constructed in their minds, it certainly raises questions about the extent to which this identity was spatially and culturally discrete, contiguous (with British or 'Western' identity), or multi-layered; and about the ways in which identity was conceived, by this time, as local, national, regional or global. Any answers to these questions must surely lend subtlety and complexity, at least, to the ongoing debate over colonial, settler and national identity in the wider historiography of Aotearoa New Zealand.

Missionaries and national history: An uneasy relationship?

While much has been written about the missionaries who came to New Zealand to work among Māori,[11] missionaries such as those departing the halls of the NZBTI have not been nearly so prominent in our written histories. We have already noted Allan Davidson's critique of this in the Introduction, indicating ways in which this gap potentially impoverishes our view of the historical record.[12] Yet it is worth pondering this point further with respect to the writing of New Zealand history, venturing beyond the terms of Davidson's initial essay. It is possible that the gap he identified also results from historians not knowing what to do with a phenomenon that now appears so anachronistic. Many aspects of past missionary thinking and activity do not sit easily alongside the sensibilities and sensitivities of the early twenty-first century. It is perhaps an easy option to therefore dismiss them as esoteric and marginal. Yet, as Pocock astutely observes, in a completely different context, one of the historian's tasks is not 'to show that belief systems are ridiculous, but to discover why they were not ridiculous once'.[13] In other words, the apparent strangeness of the past should act to stimulate a further excavation and interpretation of its perceived strangeness.

More profoundly, New Zealand's overseas missionary history has perhaps been implicitly marginalised by other concerns deemed to be far more central, as John Stenhouse has so ably outlined in a series of thoughtful and provocatively framed essays (see Introduction). Prime among these concerns, in recent decades, is what Erik Olssen calls the 'principle of nationality' that has 'operated as a controlling device' for how New Zealand history is to be interpreted and represented.[14] This has been understandably integral to the larger quest for Antipodean self-understanding. Yet that very quest, increasingly attentive to the discourses of globalisation and pluralism, is inherently problematic if it is activated within such a singular and insular paradigm as 'national identity' or 'nationhood'. In turn this paradigm, if taken as normative, may further marginalise those groups and cultures that do not so easily come within its purview. Such an approach amounts to an act of implicit cultural colonisation that, to quote one commentator, does not simply constitute historical representations but also 'practices with real and continuing consequences'.[15]

Missionaries and missions, as an element of religious history, constitute one such category that potentially misses out through a focus on the nation. Missionary involvement and support reflect a mindset that was distinctly transnational, as indicated by the NZBTI map. Missionaries and their supporters were people whose identities and self-definition did not necessarily fit neatly into such categories as nationhood, or at least rendered them ambiguous. These were people who possibly, or increasingly, thought and lived their lives in quasi-global terms, as much as they also worked, lived, studied and played in their own particular colonial or national setting. If the national identity paradigm is the only one available to make sense of this complexity then the prognosis is bleak, because it renders missionaries and their supporters as just another historical, or indeed historiographical, minority or curiosity. They are left at the margins of this paradigm either because they are irrelevant to it or because they do not easily fit it – or, indeed, because their presence in the historical record uncomfortably subverts the prevailing paradigm.

As I signposted in the Introduction, this is not a radically new interpretation of religious or mission history on at least two counts. In the first instance, it was implicitly raised in 1979 by religious historian Ian Breward, in a seminal essay that mapped out what he saw as the significant gaps in the historiography and the pressing issues or themes still to be considered. Breward questioned the appropriateness of using a 'framework of national history (a method which assumes that this was the most formative factor)' for the writing of New Zealand religious history. He argued among other things that nineteenth-century colonial religion, in particular, might be more usefully seen as 'an extension of the histories of British churches'. Protestant literature and 'intellectual vitality' were largely derivative, and homegrown theological and liturgical controversies were 'essentially provincial echoes of disputes that had their origins in Europe or Britain'. International linkages, he argued, were even more critical for a proper understanding of the colony's Roman Catholic history.[16] If this position now seems a little overstated, or at least needs to also acknowledge other international influences beyond Europe or Britain, it was certainly at odds with the prevailing historiographical sentiments of the 1970s and was helpfully prescient. As we have already noted, this focus on wider British and European connections also lies at the heart of Stenhouse's important analysis of the evolution of settler Christianity and its relationship to wider New Zealand society.[17] This view of our religious history is now by no means an isolated one and has helped to rebalance our religious and social self-understanding.[18]

In the second place, wider historiographical debate over the last decade or so provides further legitimacy for deliberately including missionary history into broader historical thinking and practice. This debate, again signposted in the Introduction and like Breward's argument, has led to the questioning of an exclusively 'nation-focused' history, leading further to the formulation of various historical approaches that range from the local to the global as either an alternative or as complementary to it. The work of New Zealand historian Peter Gibbons has been central to this 'seismic shift' in both 'history writing' and the 'ways in which we think about what comprises 'history' and what constitutes 'New Zealand'.[19] It has been the springboard for subsequent research and thinking marked by those themes, noted in the Introduction, currently being explored by other historians – the relationship between indigenous and Western historiographies; the efficacy of placing the 'nation' at the centre of historical narratives and explanation; and the extent to which 'colonialism' was historically definitive or remains an ongoing experience. With respect to the 'nation', Gibbons argues that:

> The construction by Pakeha [sic] of a New Zealand national identity was not a sign that the colonization phase of history was over, but was instead an important part of the ongoing (and still incomplete) processes of colonization. He suggests that we interrogate the seemingly innocent terms 'New Zealand' and 'New Zealand national identity', and that the term 'New Zealand' is itself a discursive construction, a shorthand device for referring to a multiplicity of places, peoples, products, practices and histories.[20]

Gibbons' provocations, either directly or indirectly, have prompted a growing body of scholarship that seeks to complicate the nation as an historical category, to the extent that this is no longer a marginalised cry in the historiographical wilderness. The recently published *New Oxford History of New Zealand*, for example, is a deliberately transnational treatment that offers a 'new interpretation of New Zealand history that seeks to complicate, rather than simplify, the past experience of New Zealand and its people'.[21] New Zealand is now variously interpreted in terms of 'transnational' or 'transcolonial' histories, and in reference to 'the webs of empire', all of which 'brings New Zealand and India [for example] into one analytical space'.[22] Our historical self-understanding is being reconfigured along a continuum of influences from the local to the global, with our historical stories tied, for example, as much to South Asia and China as to Britain or Europe.[23] Here surely is a fruitful intersection of ideas within which a discussion of New Zealand's overseas missionary involvement might make a useful contribution.

What follows, therefore, is an attempt at a 'conversation' with one element of Gibbons' work, in which he makes a plea for a decentred and globally dynamic approach to New Zealand's history and which seriously questions the potentially unhelpful discursive notion of 'national identity'.[24] In his search for alternative 'explicatory frameworks', Gibbons suggests that there might be much to gain from a combination of macro- and micro-historical perspectives that, in turn, focus on New Zealand's place in the world, the 'world's place in New Zealand', and the historical particularities that have arisen with respect to gender, class, ethnicity, geographical location and community type. Among other things, he argues that we might more effectively 'explore the convergences of experiences in these parts of the world with experiences of peoples in other parts of the world, emphasizing the exchange and accumulations and redistributions of material culture'.[25] This is an inherently dynamic and comparative approach that recognises the importance of understanding the material, cultural and social exchanges taking place on a global scale. Gibbons argues that '[i]t is through trade that peoples meet, whether actually or vicariously and within and between and through these contacts ideas, values and attitudes are exchanged and adjusted along with the goods. Though a very materialist perspective on the world, it does not ignore non-material aspects of life.'[26] This line of thinking, I would suggest, becomes especially fertile when we consider how the missionary phenomenon might further inform, or be more effectively integrated into, settler (New Zealand) history.

Case study: The Bolivian Indian Mission

How might we, then, begin to tease out the ways in which missionary history might contribute to national history along the lines suggested above? Included on the large map presented at the NZBTI graduation in 1929 were the names of four men and four women graduates working among Bolivia's Quechua Indians, under the aegis of the Bolivian Indian Mission (BIM). These graduates were the most recent of 26 New Zealanders who worked with this organisation or its antecedents up until 1939, and were among at least 111 others who went as missionaries to South America over this period. The BIM is both an indicative and representative example of how mission history might add real value to the national histories of settler societies like New Zealand. On the one hand, the BIM was thoroughly representative of contemporary denominational and non-denominational organisations and of the religious sentiment expressed in this period. On the other hand, its origins and early support were almost exclusively New Zealand-based. Furthermore, the organisation enables us to consider aspects of Gibbons' 'explicatory framework' that may provide another way by which to understand and assess the significance of the missionary phenomenon in the context of New Zealand history.

A brief account of the BIM's origins and early development introduces some of the themes relevant to this discussion.[27] Although the mission was formally constituted in 1908, it had effectively evolved, over the previous nine years, out of two pre-existing missions to South America: the Toronto-based South American Evangelical Mission and then the Melbourne-based Australasian South American Mission. Central to the mission's story were two southern New Zealanders, George and Mary Allan. George was the son and grandson of Ulster Irish settlers who had emigrated in 1842 and established a network of farms and identities in southern New Zealand. Little is known about Mary Allan's (née Stirling) background, except that she also lived in the south and met George while he worked locally on his brother's farm. New Zealand interest in South America in the 1890s intersected with growing international interest, especially among North American Protestants. George and Mary's personal interest was first aroused around 1895 when they were involved in a Presbyterian Christian Endeavour group, and was further fed by reading Lucy Guinness's book *The Neglected Continent*. Their sense of vocation came later, in 1898, while training together at Angas College in Adelaide. They subsequently applied to and were accepted by the South American Evangelical Mission, and were instrumental in establishing support committees in Australia and New Zealand. In 1899 six New Zealanders, including George and Mary, left to work with the mission, initially settling in the Argentine. A further three of their compatriots joined them between 1903 and 1905. In 1903 George and Mary relocated to Bolivia to focus on work among the Quechua Indians.

George and Mary Allan eventually formed the BIM in 1908 after the previous mission ventures disintegrated. In terms of its operation and ethos, it was consciously modelled on the CIM, as an evangelical faith mission with a self-perceived mandate to work specifically among Bolivia's Indians.[28] While control was vested in the Bolivian Field Council, Australasian support and interest was fostered through a Home Council based in Dunedin, whose members were known and respected by George Allan. This southern council initially formed the hub of a small network of local committees dotted all around New Zealand by 1916. While missionaries and finances came particularly from the southern regions of Otago and Southland, the geographical parameters of New Zealand interest and support widened significantly in later years. By the 1920s George Allan and other BIM speakers had secured a platform in a variety of larger national contexts – especially at the annual Christian conventions held at Pounawea (South Otago) and Ngaruawahia (Waikato), and the NZBTI in Auckland.

Recruits and financial support for the BIM came predominantly from New Zealand up to World War I. In 1917 George Allan carried out a concerted recruitment campaign in New York, Chicago and Los Angeles, from which time American missionaries became progressively more predominant in the organisation. By 1930 they comprised over two-thirds of the mission's workforce, and American finances had also become critically important. Australian and British missionaries further contributed to the increasingly international makeup of the BIM. George and Mary continued to dominate the mission's leadership and direction right up until their deaths in 1939 (Mary) and 1941 (George). In their obituaries, they were reverently and warmly referred to as the 'mother' and 'father' of the BIM.[29]

The BIM, missionaries and material linkages

The BIM, and groups like it, materially linked New Zealand with the wider world. Three examples may suffice. First, the BIM acted as a conduit through which New Zealand currency flowed overseas. Although the financial sources are fragmentary, what survives is suggestive nonetheless. In the early phase, up to 1906, the Dunedin committee remitted a total of just over £2000 to Bolivia. Between 1910 and 1917 at least another £2000 was sent.[30] Significant initial financial support came from a few unidentified benefactors, probably of Otago and Southland origin. By the 1910s it appears that financial support was more widely spread. This was by no means an isolated phenomenon. Stevan Eldred-Grigg, for instance, notes in general terms the 'significant transfer of wealth and skills from the dominion to China' through missionary work.[31] When other missions are also taken into account, by the 1920s upwards of £20,000 was being remitted annually by New Zealand churches and individuals to support missionaries, capital projects and various relief programmes overseas.[32] For a small population, these offshore financial transfers were not insignificant.

Second, material linkages can also be discerned in the range of cultural artefacts brought back into New Zealand by returning missionaries. When

Dunedin enthusiasts farewelled Isabel Elder back to Peru in 1926, they were treated to a popular hymn sung in Spanish by the ex-pioneer BIM missionary, Charles Wilson.[33] More generally, public meetings, youth rallies, women's events and missionary exhibitions were common venues at which missionaries displayed the exotic colour and vivacity of the otherwise inaccessible 'other'. It was not uncommon for a visiting missionary speaker to appear before an audience 'robed in the dress of a Chinese teacher', or for songs and hymns to be sung at such gatherings in the Chinese language.[34] In particular, missionary exhibitions replicated or paralleled a wider proliferation of cultural exhibitions that acted as 'an extremely effective means for people … to learn more about Asians' – occasions that were 'underpinned by imperial networks of exchange and discourses on the connections between civilisation, science and empire-building'.[35]

In the pre-World War I period, this phenomenon was epitomised by the 1910 Missionary Exhibition held at Dunedin's Knox Presbyterian Church. Over the space of three days, the Dunedin public listened to missionary speakers, saw and heard presentations in other languages and viewed a wide range of displays depicting life in various parts of the world.[36] Reports noted that the halls were continually packed with visitors. The displays were constituted from at least 968 items donated by individuals and groups. Some belonged to missionaries, but many were privately owned by individuals who had previously bought them from missionary retail outlets or at publicity events. New Hebridean shell beads, sacred stones, bows, arrows, clubs and clothing sat alongside Chinese opium-smoking apparatus, carved ivory ornaments and a geomantic compass, an Indian idol car and Congolese animal skins, witch doctors' charms and execution knives.

Such one-off events were not the only means by which the missionary movement introduced exotic material culture into New Zealand. Local churches and Bible classes sometimes curated such items, often brought back by their own visiting missionaries, into permanent 'missionary museums'.[37] Presbyterian women from at least the 1880s regularly bought arrowroot from the New Hebrides and distributed it through congregational channels. This was a revenue-raising venture by New Hebridean Christian communities which had a direct and long-lived market among New Zealand Presbyterian missionary supporters.[38] 'Oriental depots' run by the PWMU imported and sold on a great range of material goods from overseas localities. Profits were directed back into Presbyterian missionary projects. By the mid-1920s up to 62 women were acting as retail agents for these depots, and the evidence suggests that those people buying goods were not just Presbyterian churchgoers.[39] In some respects, these outlets and institutions prefigured the many Save the Children Fund and Trade Aid shops that are now such a familiar part of the New Zealand retailing landscape, and which seek to connect consumers with the material contexts and issues of the contemporary world.

Third, and perhaps most significant of all, was the volume and wide range of international literature introduced into New Zealand through missionary agency. Most missions had their own magazine by which they kept their constituency informed and through which financial needs could be publicised. The BIM was no exception, printing and distributing its own bi-monthly magazine from 1911. Early subscriptions totalled around 225, comprised mainly of Otago and Southland residents.[40] By the 1920s the *Bolivian Indian* was a firm fixture. It was read internationally, driven editorially by George Allan, and carried articles written by its missionaries. These ranged widely from initial impressions to well-thought-out essays on Bolivian life, from personal testimony to theological treatise, and from the pragmatic to what could be more recognisably identified as propaganda for the cause. In the wider New Zealand context, however, this was simply the tip of the iceberg. All denominations had their own missionary magazines, or regular missionary inserts, that drew on both New Zealand and overseas sources. For children and young people in particular, titles like *The Young Folks Missionary Messenger* (Baptist), *The Break of Day* (Presbyterian) and *The Lotu* (Methodist) became decades-long household names.

Furthermore, there were substantial public and private missionary libraries that offered a wide range of international titles. Advertisements for retail bookshops, in denominational newspapers, indicated that there was domestic demand for imported missionary titles. By 1910 significant numbers of churchgoers, especially women, were involved in formal missionary study circles, using sophisticated educational literature produced both locally and sourced from abroad. Children were also an important market for periodical literature, and the *Bolivian Indian*'s contributors often wrote for a specifically juvenile audience. While women's and children's literature will be treated separately in Chapters Seven and Eight, it is worth simply noting here, in very general terms, that through such cultural texts non-Western women and children were often cast in a negative light as heathen, benighted, wretched, helpless, down-trodden people who needed the religious, educative and curative technologies of the West. At the same time the clamant needs of the missions were made known. At the very least, the domestic spaces of many New Zealand homes were adorned with texts and pictures from around the world on a weekly and monthly basis – in a way not unlike the ubiquitous *National Geographic* in more recent decades.

A missionary view of the world

The BIM indicates the ways in which New Zealand was simply one site on an international pathway, along which flowed material goods and information. To restrict discussion to material elements, however, would be to neglect other factors, as earlier chapters have argued. In this respect, the BIM pointed to the profound ways in which many New Zealanders' perceptions of and attitudes to the world were shaped by distinctly international influences. Its experience highlighted an underlying and pervasive transnational Protestant missionary mentalité or 'world view'.[41] Derived from the French *Annales* school of historical thought, this concept places an emphasis on 'collective attitudes', on 'unspoken or unconscious assumptions, on perception [and] on conscious thoughts or elaborated theories', and a 'concern with the structure of beliefs … with categories, with metaphors and symbols, with how people think as well as what they think'.[42] It is a useful concept in the context of the present discussion, because it focuses attention on *how* people thought, as opposed to the content of their thought, and it helps to explain further their response to the world through involvement as missionaries and missionary supporters.

In effect, the BIM was both the inheritor and exemplar of a largely imported missionary mentalité, which had dual historical roots in the conversionist emphases of nineteenth-century British evangelicalism and in Enlightenment optimism about human progress and the socially transformative power of Christianity. These were both further reshaped by Australian and American influences. As I indicated in Chapter Two, this approach to the world was profoundly theological, and although cast within a broadly evangelical framework it was noticeably variegated in how it was defined and expressed until at least the end of World War I. For individuals, this theologically shaped missionary mentalité was perceived through increasingly privatised spiritual lenses. The spirituality that resulted emphasised an individualised or personal Higher Calling, personal consecration and surrender, useful and empowered service, and sacrificial commitment. The so-called 'Great Commission' (of Matthew 28:19–20 or Mark 16:15) was interpreted as a call to individual believers, from which no one was exempt. As outlined in Chapter Four, missionary motivation issued out of this complex mix of internalised theological and spiritual imperatives. Furthermore, it intersected with contemporary imperialist sentiments and was sometimes differentiated along lines of gender and doctrine.

This, then, was the wider matrix within which the Christian faith and missionary calling of BIM missionaries was shaped. George and Mary Allan, for example, were raised in rural Presbyterian churches in Otago and Southland, in an atmosphere pervaded by evangelical revivalism.[43] Their early faith had been further enlivened by involvement with the Christian Endeavour movement, with its emphasis on conversion, a consecrated life and outward-looking sacrificial service and which, as a global movement, was missionary in outlook. It was in this theological context that George and Mary first perceived both the needs of South America and a calling to train for Christian ministry. George confided to his sister in 1895 that it was a Christian responsibility to 'show forth [Jesus'] wondrous love' to those who did not know it and that, despite the task's enormity, 'our Saviour knows our weakness and has promised to strengthen us'.[44] In 1909 at a supporters' meeting in Wellington, Mary Allan developed this theme:

> I am glad that we are going back ... Out there you look into the face of thousands, and in none does one see the light which alone can bring liberty to the soul, and joy and peace of mind. We carry the joyous news that has made us free. I feel pleased and honoured that God had called us to the work again. Those people do not know the Lord Jesus, although they have images of Him. Cruelty and illtreatment [sic] rules there. We know what a change it makes in one's life when Jesus comes in bringing peace and gladness. How much more then does it mean to these people whose circumstances are so entirely different to ours![45]

In the ongoing development of the BIM's work, these sentiments endured. The emphasis remained on conversion, as it was perceived that the Bolivian Indians were devoid of personal religion, and because it was thought that their social regeneration would come primarily from personal regeneration. By the early 1920s all of the mission's New Zealand recruits were graduates of the NZBTI. As a result, unlike many other missionary ventures around the globe, the BIM never undertook large-scale medical work. Rather, it laid an early emphasis on setting up schools for children and, in the longer term, on itinerant village evangelism and church planting, indigenous lay theological training, literature distribution and especially on the translation of the Bible into the Quechua language.

If Gibbons' macro-historical approach encourages a materialist interpretation of New Zealand's place in the world, then the the example of the BIM emphasises that there were other profoundly non-materialist elements that need to be considered. By focusing on theology and mentalité, it is possible to show that settler New Zealanders were also the importers, consumers and reshapers of international modes of thought and consequent practice.

Other conceptual possibilities

The case of the BIM further suggests two qualifications to Gibbons' original thesis. First, if the focus is on the place in the 'world economic system' of an emerging society like New Zealand, then the historical microscope needs to be refocused to discern nuances within that system. The BIM, as a representative mission, lends support to his contention that New Zealand was not globally isolated, but rather that it was securely located on the main oceanic 'highways' and firmly linked to an 'archipelago of urban centres'.[46] More specifically, however, it indicates that there were significant linkages within two particular regions: Australasia and the Pacific Rim. We have already explored this set of linkages. In the context of this chapter, however, it is worth noting that the BIM's origins and early development provide further evidence of a two-way trans-Tasman relationship. Its missionaries were certainly trained in Australia up until the founding of the NZBTI in 1922, and Melbourne was its administrative locus until 1906. Yet George Allan was instrumental in fostering enthusiasm for the mission and its antecedents in both Australia and New Zealand, and he encouraged the administrative shift from Melbourne to Dunedin in 1908. Furthermore, with respect to North America, the BIM narrative indicates a long and significant relationship – from its origins in the Canadian-based South American Evangelical Mission, to the influences exerted by Christian Endeavour from the 1890s and further, after World War I, to an array of conservative evangelical American churches and training institutions primarily in New York, Chicago and Los Angeles. By this stage George Allan was firmly entrenched in his opposition to perceived liberalising trends in wider Protestantism.[47] Thus he found ready and strong allies among American conservative evangelicals. In more practical terms, these BIM missionaries proceeded to steam and horse-trek their way along the axes of a new regional triangle, linking New Zealand directly with both the South and North American continents.

The second qualification concerns Gibbons' contention that macro- and micro-historical perspectives on New Zealand history might converge, among other things, with 'material culture, especially the consumption of goods'.[48] While the BIM narrative adds credence to this notion of converging macro- and micro-perspectives, it once again suggests that material culture can only constitute one such convergence point. Geography, popular religion and missionary enthusiasm mark another possible set of convergences. One example may suffice. The southern New Zealand region of Otago and Southland provided much of the BIM's early support. The region provided half of its New Zealand workers up to 1939, along with a number of unsuccessful applicants. This was only part of a larger picture. Of all New Zealand's missionaries up to 1939, at least 46 (nearly 5 per cent) came from Southland alone. At least another 30 people unsuccessfully applied for missionary service from this region. Over half of these people came from the farming valleys radiating out at a distance of up to 20 kilometres from the rural service town of Gore, in Central Southland. This small area also rated highly in terms of financial giving to Presbyterian overseas missions over this period. It was obvious, however, that enthusiasm in Southland was spread across the denominations, and that enduring interest was vested in a range of missionary organisations. This was a region which had been influenced by revivalism and evangelistic activities since the 1880s.[49] Popular religion was further nurtured by Christian Endeavour, the Presbyterian young people's Bible class movement, annual conventions at nearby Pounawea and, from the early 1920s, strong links with the NZBTI in Auckland.

If New Zealand was integrally linked to a set of 'world systems', which influentially shaped how New Zealanders understood, thought about and related to the wider world, then it seems that the dynamics of that system need to be analysed at the localised level of specific geographical regions and communities. In other words, macro- and micro-historical perspectives converge in the churches, country halls, kitchens and lounges of individuals and families – the evidence for which must be painstakingly excavated from parish and congregational records, family journals, correspondence and private diaries. Local, national and transnational factors are all equally important.[50] There is much yet to be understood, then, concerning the intricate relationships between enduring but localised popular and enthusiastic religion, missionary support, cultural practices, gender and individual or communal values. Among other things, it will be necessary to ask how these elements were shaped by a pervasive missionary mentalité and, ultimately, how they were nationally and globally linked.

Identity(ies)

In conclusion we return to the notion of identity, because this issue provides a useful gauge by which to provisionally assess the significance of the missionary phenomenon for wider historiographical concerns. It is here that the Southland example is also apposite. Margaret Allen, in her exploratory study of late nineteenth-century Australian Baptist women missionaries in India, draws attention to an apparent paradox. She argues that the identities of these women were highly contestable, as they variously identified themselves as 'British, English, South Australian, colonial, Australian, white, Christian and Baptist'.[51] In making this point, Allen is drawing on a considerable body of literature on the contested identities of men and women in colonial and imperial contexts. If Southland Protestant missionaries and their supporters were asked how they primarily identified themselves in that same period, their responses may have been just as varied, as would those of other contemporary New Zealand missionaries and their supporters.

Allegiance and identity were multi-dimensional elements that were ambiguously interwoven. Early BIM missionaries, for instance, were New Zealand born but genealogically close to the migration process. Both George and Mary Allan were within one generation of their settler ancestors.[52] It is unclear in what terms they would have primarily described themselves. It is quite possible, however, to detect a pioneering theme interwoven through the early narrative of their mission to Bolivia. Consequently, up to 1918 the BIM had the feel of a small, close-knit, pioneering family embarking

on yet another adventure into the rugged unknown. Prospective missionaries of this period were instructed, for example, to take to Bolivia things
like 'a few instruments for extracting teeth', a 'garden hoe and rake' and
'several yards of steel fencing wire' for stretching wire bed mattresses. They
were also instructed to master the art of horse riding.[53] In the mission's
first decade, George looked simultaneously to Australia, New Zealand and
England for support and recruitment. By the 1920s the New Zealanders
on whom the BIM drew had a more urbane, sophisticated air about them.
Moreover, their inspiration was just as likely to be American in origin as
British or Australasian. Yet throughout the 1920s this sense of ambiguous
identity remained, and is hinted at in the pages of the mission's magazine,
the *Bolivian Indian*. Bi-monthly missionary lists continued to categorise the
New Zealanders as 'British' up until 1928, when the category changed to
'New Zealand'.[54]

When the BIM data is placed within the context of the wider New
Zealand missionary movement of this period, the following general picture
emerges. Allegiance and identity were multi-dimensional concepts, perhaps
paralleling the notion of co-existing but 'competing discourses of identity'
identified by Esther Breitenbach for the Scottish missionary context, among
which 'nation' was but one defining element.[55] 'Identity' simultaneously
embraced such descriptors as 'New Zealand', 'British', 'Empire citizen',
'settler', 'female' and 'male', as well as more particular denominational and
regional labels. In a sense, all of these were held in tension, but for many
Protestants they were also framed within a wider set of allegiances that
were theological and spiritual by definition.[56] Consequently, many New
Zealanders saw themselves as world citizens whose primary allegiance was to
the all-embracing Kingdom of Christ. As such, they had a deeply ingrained
sense of theological connectedness with and obligation to the rest of the
world, suggesting that there was an important spatial dimension to the
late colonial missionary mentalité. As a result, many missionary supporters
and participants, as world citizens, had a comparatively well-informed and
nuanced understanding of the wider world. At the same time, this knowledge
contributed to the world becoming spatially differentiated, in the popular
mind, along lines of race, culture and religion. The world was conceptually
broken up into 'the great beckoning fields', and these fields were invariably
a synonym for the non-European and non-Christian regions of the world.
The frequently used phrase 'regions beyond' accentuated this sense of spatial,

cultural, religious and physical dissonance. It also reinforced the prevailing binary construction of Christendom and heathen non-Christendom. While the basic distinction was between those 'saved' and 'unsaved', the popular construction of potentially racist and demonstrably Euro-centric anthropological hierarchies was not an unexpected outcome.

There is an apparent paradox here, in that missionary supporters can be thought of as being both globally well-informed while at the same time perpetuating stereotypical representations of that world. Missionary supporters potentially knew a good deal about the world (geography, peoples and cultures) and about the increasingly complex global issues that marked this period. Yet it seems that this knowledge was often framed in such a way that implicit anthropological hierarchies were still accepted as the norm. Furthermore, this knowledge did not exist on its own merits, but was subordinated to or employed for a greater purpose, the Christianisation of non-Christian peoples. Again, however, the truth of the matter is much better teased out with respect to particular contexts, and to this end there is much still to be done for the colonial or settler society context – modelled, for example, on the imaginative work of Nicholas Thomas.[57] In Chapter Eight, I expand this discussion in the context of Presbyterian women. As with the large NZBTI world map discussed earlier in the chapter, geographically marginal societies like New Zealand and Australia were perceived to be at the global centre, while the other regions were on the periphery. In this sense, identity was also intertwined with prevailing imperialist and nationalist views of the world.[58] This was particularly noticeable during conflicts such as the South African War and World War I. New Zealand settler Christians may not all have seen themselves as colonisers or imperialists. Yet at heart they identified with the Christianised West, particularly but not exclusively with the British Empire, and were therefore firmly and comfortably enmeshed within prevailing power structures.

Conclusion

The New Zealand missionaries of the Bolivian Indian Mission and of other organisations in the same period, along with the many people and communities that supported them, may never rock the historiographical boat nor loom large in the historical record. But neither were they insignificant, as I have attempted to demonstrate in this chapter in the context of discussing writing and thinking about national history. This has been amply recognised in the literature of other 'British' world societies. In the Scottish context, for example, an admittedly larger body of people and organisations (but still, in Breitenbach's estimation, one that was numerically small in terms of total population) had a disproportionate influence on shaping national and imperial sentiments within wider Scottish society. In particular, missionaries and their organisations, missionary supporters and the churches through which they expressed themselves proved to be an important associational (as opposed to political) influence on the eventual 'articulation of Scottish national identity in the nineteenth and twentieth centuries'.[59] As other historians have begun to show over the last decade or so in the New Zealand context, the 'missionary factor' was also important for emerging national and transnational colonial identities – especially if we think of the hitherto nationally bounded stories of New Zealand being intertwined with the stories of such other regions as China and South Asia.

The intriguing possibilities of a more careful integration of the 'missionary factor' within New Zealand's historical narratives are neatly caught and showcased in Eldred-Grigg's recent history of the China–New Zealand relationship. In dedicating it to the 'memory of Joe Kum Yung and Edith Searell',[60] Eldred-Grigg has chosen two 'martyrs', one on either side of this particular relationship, as a subtle centrepiece for the book. One, Joe Kum Yung, was the man brutally murdered on a Wellington street in 1905 by Lionel Terry. The other, Edith Searell, was the only New Zealand Protestant missionary (CIM) to be murdered in Shanxi Province in 1900 during the Boxer War.[61] Edith's story does not dominate the text and she is certainly not treated uncritically. Furthermore, it might be possible to interpret the placing of these names in more than one way. What is significant for this discussion, however, is that Edith Searell's life is deemed to be important to a history that links two sets of cultures across the nineteenth and twentieth centuries. By extension, the two-way national relationship fed into New Zealand's story and 'identity', and in this New Zealand missionaries were an integral, if not completely uncontested, part of that story. When we approach New Zealand's history from this more transnational, comparative or relational angle (as opposed to the perspective of the bounded nation), then people like the BIM missionaries and Edith Searell are seen to matter.

As the practice and pursuit of historical enquiry becomes increasingly decentred, and as historians explore more fluid and dynamic explanatory paradigms, it appears that there is much to be gleaned from what were once thought of as the 'margins' (if indeed those 'margins' ever existed). In recent decades missionaries and their ilk have occupied the conceptual or historiographical margins, and it has been difficult for many historians to know what to do with them. In this chapter, in concert with a growing body of literature and scholarship, I have argued that analysis of the missionary movement provides one way of moving towards a more dynamic and less nationally bounded historiography. The missionary movement, therefore, might also usefully contribute to an understanding of the evolution of colonial or settler social and cultural identities, of which religion was intrinsically and inseparably a part, and of the ways in which New Zealand's fortunes have been intricately bound up with those of the wider world.

Overseas Missions and
the British Empire

A SECOND SUBJECT to consider in more detail is the nature of the relationship that existed between New Zealand overseas missions and imperial sentiments or actions. In many respects, for the period up to the 1920s at least, it is difficult to think of 'the nation' without reference to 'the British Empire'. As Katie Pickles notes for the Canadian context, there was a 'complex relationship between Britishness and national identity',[1] an observation that is equally pertinent to the New Zealand setting of the late nineteenth and early twentieth centuries. As I show in this chapter, the relationship between missions and empire is a fertile area of debate within wider Anglo-American historiography. It is also relevant here, in that increased settler missionary support coincided exactly with a sustained period of imperial enthusiasm. This boiled over during the South African War of 1899–1902, the first properly international conflict in which New Zealand soldiers were involved in significant and sustained numbers. In 1900 New Zealanders, along with others around the British Empire, followed with great interest the siege and relief of Ladysmith. The secular and religious press reflected this interest in equal measure, carrying stirring stories and images. The Salvation Army's paper *The War Cry* included a striking cover illustration which reverberated with both imperial and religious sentiments (Figure 6.1).

This cover image was accompanied by an article that reflected on the incident and questioned its wider meaning. The writer asked pointedly what disgrace there would be in surrendering the British flag to the Boer. The response was unequivocally affirmative. The 'glorious flag represented the history of centuries; that indelibly woven with its three colours were

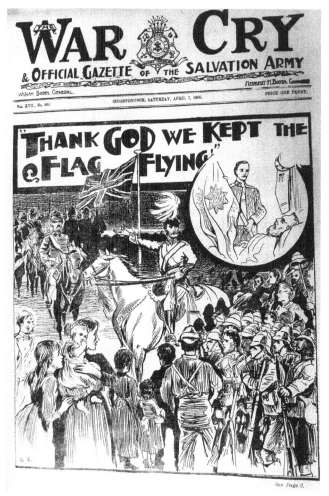

FIGURE 6.1. 'Thank God we Kept the Flag Flying', 1900[2]

the most marvellous deeds of the three countries, England, Scotland, and Ireland. To them that flag represented Britain's honour, and they must not, dare not, suffer it to be lowered by the hands of a foreign foe.' However lofty these ideals might be, New Zealand Salvationists were further prompted to think about deeper lessons of faith and allegiance. To uphold a second tri-coloured flag, the Army's 'yellow, red and blue', was to give allegiance to a 'wider empire', one that proclaimed 'salvation to the uttermost for all the nations'. Employing popular military rhetoric, the writer incited readers to cry, 'No surrender! We fought to the last; we have been true to the Blood and Fire. Thank God, we've kept the flag flying!'[3]

Colonial Salvationists undoubtedly reflected prevailing sentiments that were entrenched among the settler populations of all the British societies in this era of high imperialism. In this, they were certainly not dissimilar to other Protestant denominations, missionary organisations and individual leaders. They were also representative of the ways in which imperial and religious sentiments kept close company. In this chapter I seek to shed further light on this relationship. I argue that New Zealand missionaries and supporters, reflecting their wider social, cultural and religious milieu, maintained a range of both positive and negative positions towards the empire. Of course, this is not an original argument or conclusion, and it is hardly surprising that British attitudes were replicated. At the same time, settler societies like New Zealand were not a carbon copy of the metropole. Sites of religion and empire become important, then, both for their commonalities and their differences.

New Zealand missions and empire in context

The connections between European imperialistic expansion, the creation of colonial space, religious sentiment and the missionary movement have been extensively documented and interrogated since Stephen Neill's seminal overview in 1966.[4] This relationship has become 'one of the unquestioned orthodoxies of general historical knowledge', although the ways in which it has been considered have become increasingly nuanced according to location and context.[5] In the wider field of imperial history, historians have been slower to recognise the relationships between religion, the missionary movement, imperialism and colonialism. In a relatively recent book examining this relationship in colonial India, Jeffrey Cox records that an early nineteenth-century columnist once 'described the Baptist missionaries in Bengal as "little detachments of maniacs".' Cox goes on to observe that 'this presumption of marginality, if not of insanity, has been carried over from the imperial establishment into the imperial history that they fostered, a history that is undergoing an interesting resurgence'.[6]

This 'resurgence' has been most visible over at least the last decade, and is represented by a broad sweep of literature embracing such categories as postcolonialism, cultural history, revisionist mission and religious history, imperial history and a whole raft of studies dissecting the manifold relationships between colonialism, gender, race, class, nationalism, culture and religion. Tony Ballantyne suggests that such 'critical reflections on the connections between religion, of which the missionary movement was a part, and empire building, have been central to the rekindling of interest in the history of the British Empire over the past two decades'.[7] Such research, to quote the anthropologist Johannes Fabian, must:

> 'go beneath the surface of colonial ideology and practice ... [and] get to the roots of this enterprise, the famed *oeuvre civilisatrice* that once fired the imagination and enthusiasm of honest and intelligent people ... [In these terms, the] role which religion – via the missions – played in formulating and sustaining colonialism cannot be reduced to mere ideological justification or pragmatic collaboration.'[8]

This challenge has been helpfully taken up, with respect to British mission history, in the recent works of Andrew Porter and Jeffrey Cox. It is also being answered in the dispersed writings of other scholars in the 'British' world context.[9]

In the New Zealand context, the literature on the missions–empire relationship is still in its infancy and is largely based on the late Edward Said's influential works on 'Orientalism' and the culture–imperialism nexus, and the interdisciplinary body of postcolonial literature that has emerged in Said's wake. This local literature remains largely unpublished and untested, as indicated in the Introduction. At first glance, the debate over overseas missions and empire might be perceived as being less relevant for Australia and New Zealand, both of which were British colonies and therefore colonised rather than colonising powers. This view of course is wide open to debate, with respect to New Zealand as a missionary receiving society that essentially colonised its own indigenous population. This misperception, however, is partly a product of what Damon Salesa refers to as the 'purposeful and studied ignorance [in New Zealand historiography] of the "other Pacific Islands"' – that is, a neglect of the South West Pacific, of which New Zealand is geographically a part – and of 'a century and a half of New Zealand's imperial manoeuvring and colonial rule in the Pacific'.[10] It is also a product of the kinds of bounded historical narratives of 'nation' and 'national identity', identified and challenged in Chapter Five, which tend to focus more exclusively on domestic colonisation. New Zealand's beginnings were fundamentally imperial, in the sense of being technically and legally a part of the British Empire, both in terms of accepting the mindset of territorial expansion and acquisition, and in the manner in which particular cultural attitudes were both held and deployed.[11] These elements of our national history are forgotten at our peril, and are brought into sharper relief, again, when we bring into the discussion colonial missionaries and their organisations that operated within and across other imperial spaces, or whose presence and impact were made possible partly as a consequence of the values and attitudes that accompanied empire.

With respect to overseas missions, current interest in the wider 'British' world is indicative of a complex and mutually sustaining relationship between Britain and colonies like New Zealand and Australia.[12] In turn, the evidence for the New Zealand context clearly indicates that the colonists were also colonisers; this is, as I noted in the previous chapter, one of the fundamental themes and issues of historical and contemporary New Zealand. But such forces were not exclusively domestic. Again, the relationship with the South West Pacific is apposite. It is easy to point, for example, to those late nineteenth-century settler politicians who held aspirations towards creating imperial space in the South Pacific, and how those aspirations were intricately bound up with allegiance to the British Empire. New Zealand's disastrous involvement in post-World War I Samoa provides a further caveat.[13] Furthermore, there were occasions when church, missionary and political aspirations in the South Pacific intersected. This was apparent, for instance, when both the Anglican and Presbyterian Churches, under pressure from missionary leaders, lobbied the New Zealand parliament in the 1880s over their concerns about both the Queensland Melanesian labour trade and French aspirations in Melanesia.[14] Yet, if we think again of colonial New Zealand's relationship to the Pacific then it is possible, as Salesa argues, to read these as merely episodic examples of a wider imperial intention. In effect, by World War I, New Zealand 'possessed a fully fledged overseas empire of its own', encompassing such territories as the Cook Islands, Niue and Samoa, and epitomised by the Pioneer Battalion composed of these nationalities as well as Māori – New Zealand's very own 'imperial army'. New Zealand could thus be thought of as an 'empire-state', rather than as a 'nation' or a 'colony'.[15] In these terms, missionary projects in the South West Pacific could be seen as logical extensions of an imperial mentality reflecting both domestic and wider British imperial aspirations – even if they were not ultimately or exclusively defined by those aspirations.

The relevance of imperialism to this discussion, and the ambiguities it engendered, is further highlighted in Margaret Allen's exploratory study, referred to in the previous chapter, of early Australian Baptist women missionaries in India, which alerts us to the paradoxes of allegiance and identity in the colonial context.[16] In another essay, she argues further that Australians 'enjoyed the freedom to travel to and work and spread the Christian gospel in India' precisely because they were 'white British subjects'. Indians, on the other hand, were 'effectively debarred from the enjoyment of reciprocal rights in Australia' by the White Australia Policy. Thus the 'mobility of modernity was reserved for those deemed white'.[17] In making these observations, Allen could also be writing about New Zealanders in the same era, including both those who were missionaries and those who were connected to them as kin or supporters.

In this chapter I pick up on some of these themes by outlining the general New Zealand Protestant thinking about the British Empire that was prevalent in missionary circles, literature and organisations. While the rhetoric was British in tone, it was complicated by patterns of geographical and organisational affiliation. Such thinking was also complicated by the intersection of localised and globalised influences, so that specific missionary 'sites' and denominational issues need to be considered alongside more broadly identifiable factors. New Zealand's involvement and interest in India, while not unique, highlights how factors local to the New Zealand context reshaped or confounded broader influences of imperial citizenship and loyalty. My treatment of Indian involvement, as a case study, is neither adulatory nor condemnatory in its intent or conclusions. It is exploratory, non-exhaustive and broad in its approach. Rather than making judgements, I signpost the kinds of historiographical and methodological issues and possibilities that might be raised by approaching the relationship between the missionary endeavour and imperialism from a 'non-metropole' or decentred perspective.

The rhetoric of New Zealand missionaries and their supporters

Theological and philosophical thinking about missions in late nineteenth and early twentieth-century New Zealand was not easily disentangled from language extolling the virtues of Western civilisation, and more particularly those that marked the British Empire. As a result, acceptance and criticism sat together. Two historically discrete sets of comments exemplify the problematic mixed messages that prevailed over several decades. The first comes from a small treatise on Christian missions written in 1881 by the Revd John Inglis, in the light of long missionary service in the New Hebrides:

> It is not Christianity which causes the decrease in the population [referring to population decline primarily from disease and the labour trade] … It is not civilisation … But it is the vices and diseases of civilised life so largely imported; the selfishness of traders and colonists … and also the ignorance of the poor natives themselves … In many … cases, the transition from barbarism to civilisation is too rapid; an injudicious use is often made of the conveniences and advantages of civilised life, which is injurious, instead of being beneficial to health and life.

At the same time, Inglis understood Christianity and civilisation to be a partnership which, together, might raise the 'heathen inhabitants of the South Pacific … from their present state of ignorance and degradation, to enjoy all the blessings and all the advantages of pure and undefiled religion, of scriptural education, and of general civilisation …'[18] The second comment was made 35 years later. In 1916, against the backdrop of the horrors of war in Europe, veteran Baptist missionary John Takle again demonstrated the same apparent ambivalence towards Western civilisation and imperialism, this time with England specifically in mind. Addressing the Baptist Union Conference he stated:

> The Apostle Paul was proud of being a citizen of the Roman Empire, which in his day controlled practically the whole of the Mediterranean world. So every true Britisher thrills with the privilege of belonging to an Empire so extensive that nearly one quarter of the world's population has come under its sway, an Empire that has done more than any other for the emancipation of peoples, and for the evangelisation of the native races. She is destined to do still more for the uplift and unity of humanity.

Yet in the same speech, he was also quick to remind his audience that the Christian community should be more concerned with 'a greater Imperium, to whose Imperator we have bowed in reverence, obedience and loyal submission. Our supreme interest is the Kingdom of God … That Kingdom is now passing through the seed and leaven stages of great expansion and quiet gradual development, preparatory to the final consummation which, some day, all faithful souls will surely behold, for Christ shall reign.'[19]

In New Zealand such sentiments were born out of historical, cultural and familial British roots. They were relatively consistent across time, class and gender. Perhaps they were voiced most stridently in times of heightened imperial awareness such as a war or the death of a monarch. Against the backdrop of the South African War, and alluding to 1 Chronicles 12:18, Anglican minister the Revd George MacMurray suggested in 1900 that:

> To-day the British Empire is passing through a time of trouble and it seems as if God's Spirit had prompted her Colonies throughout the world to say ... 'Thine are we, and on thy side; peace, peace, peace unto thee, and peace be to thy helpers, for thy God helpeth thee' ... To-day the colonies in ranging themselves on Britain's side ... believing that God will help her helpers, are taking their due share of the Empire's responsibilities, and are making many sacrifices to maintain her role.[20]

Queen Victoria died in January 1901. Adult and juvenile missionary newspapers alike marked her death with a range of tributes indicative of the deep-seated support for the monarchy among New Zealand Protestants. In Otago, where missionary and evangelical enthusiasm was high at the turn of the centuries, 'Baptists, Methodists and Congregationalists were,' observes Alison Clarke, 'as much loyal monarchists as their Anglican and Presbyterian brethren.'[21] Earlier missionary thinking about the empire was also bundled up with a cluster of theological images that emphasised the expansionist nature of Christianity, especially up to World War I. Imperial imagery was often employed to point churchgoers to a set of higher responsibilities above and beyond the call for service to country or empire. Thus the Anglican bishop of Nelson told NZCMA supporters in 1915 that the 'Church existed for the building up of the Empire of Christ and the Kingdom of God'.[22]

The relationship between Church and empire was clearly evolving and was largely perceived in a positive light by New Zealanders throughout this broad period. Popular rhetoric tended to emphasise a cluster of commonly held ideas across the denominational spectrum. In the first instance, the British Empire was seen as a means of international unity, symbolised by the monarchy, and as a guarantor of freedom and security for all 'races, religions and degrees of civilization'.[23] These were common sentiments in Church and society, and were not dissimilar to those voiced in the Protestant churches of England in the same period.[24] Christianity was integral to this conception. England was seen through progressive lenses, conceived as a Christian and Protestant nation endowed with a responsibility to evangelise the world. Some perceived England's imperial role to be accidental; its leaders had been 'impelled towards an object which they had not consciously aimed at, as by some invisible force'. More popularly, many viewed the empire's expansion as providential, so that spiritual responsibilities were high on the agenda for colonisation and the forging of imperial relationships. In this respect, the British Empire meant more than the 'selling of calico and opening doors of commerce'.[25] In wider New Zealand society during this period, the moral qualities of imperial citizenship were loudly extolled among adults and juveniles alike. There is considerable evidence that an imperial pedagogy also permeated church education for children and young people in these years.

Embedded within this rhetoric was the broadly held notion of 'trusteeship'. Non-Christian peoples and geographic regions within the British Empire were perceived as being the special and often paternal responsibility of New Zealand Christians. India and its peoples were most prominent in this respect. However, 'trusteeship' might also encourage criticism. The empire was founded upon God's providence and Britain had been entrusted with a set of wider moral responsibilities. These had to be upheld. Jessie MacKay, for example, exhorted New Zealand Women's Christian Temperance Union members, as 'Britons, as citizens', to protest the policy that 'has kept Armenia a bleeding tortured sacrifice for the peace and aggrandisement of the British Empire'.[26] This protest was aimed particularly at the plight of Armenian women, and was indicative that neither distance nor geography was a barrier to the global awareness of New Zealanders in this period. Similar comments were offered over Britain's role in China's opium trade.[27] Other New Zealanders understood that Western civilisation in general could be detrimental to indigenous populations. Christian mission might ameliorate its negative effects.[28] By the 1920s a handful were bold enough to publicly argue that Western imperialism per se constituted a hindrance to the progress of indigenised Christianity.[29]

Christian mission was therefore viewed by New Zealanders as essential to the ongoing welfare of the empire, both at home and abroad. Arguably, New Zealanders were some of the empire's staunchest defenders; these 'better Britons' living in the farthest corner of that empire expected most of it, and might therefore be bold in criticising its deficiencies. The Revd George MacMurray reminded an Anglican audience in 1900 that the colonies 'must remember that the spiritual expansion of the empire must keep pace with the physical, if it is to have the abiding blessing of God upon it. It is only by doing the will of God, and by doing it with Christ-like service and self-sacrifice that the British Empire can secure God's peace and blessing.'[30]

Not all groups or individuals agreed with the status quo, and following World War I a more internationalist perspective began to emerge. By the late 1920s Methodist religious education material was appealing as much to the model League of Nations as to older models of international relations, and provocatively used quotes from Lenin and the African leader James Aggrey to foster discussion among young people.[31] This was a transitional period in terms of New Zealand's emerging sense of national identity, and in some church circles there was evident ambivalence with regard to the connections with England. As early as 1906, some Auckland Anglicans had vigorously debated the benefits and demerits of empire and the New Zealand Church's connection with its English counterpart.[32] The lack of references to national or imperial allegiance in the narratives of non-denominational missionaries possibly reflected perceived priorities that transcended imperial allegiance; while indicating archival silences that might also indicate tacit imperial support or the ways in which the imperial factor was taken for granted. New Zealand's non-denominational missionaries also appeared to distance themselves from colonial authorities in order to focus on pioneer evangelism and church planting. Their formal and informal narratives made repeated reference to the virtues of surrender, submission, service and sacrifice in obedience to God and for the sake of the 'heathen'. That they did so as New Zealanders or empire citizens appeared to be secondary to a wider set of theological and spiritual imperatives and assumptions which took priority over imperial allegiances. Debates over mission among post-1918 student movements also indicated that wider internationalist concepts were gaining currency, especially the League of Nations and the brotherhood of man. Mission was seen by some as a cooperative exercise with indigenous peoples and churches. Renate Howe suggests that post-1918 Australian women student volunteers 'saw themselves as a new type of missionary who aimed to build up indigenous resources in church and society'.[33] While imperial imagery and allegiance was important to New Zealand missionaries and their supporters, these postwar observations serve notice that the relationship with the British Empire progressively became complicated by other factors.

Geographical and organisational dimensions of missionary involvement

Another way of asking how far New Zealand's missionaries were enmeshed within or dependent on the British Empire is to look at where these people went, and with which organisations. Taking a broad view, the empire provided a physical, as well as an ideological or theological, framework for the New Zealand movement. This assertion needs to be scrutinised more closely, however, with particular reference to geographical and institutional patterns of missionary service.

In Chapter One I outlined the general pattern of missionary destinations, noting the dominance of the South Pacific, India, China and, to a lesser extent, South America. Useful as this information is, it hides a number of more nuanced details pertinent to the present discussion. With respect to the South West Pacific, early colonial Methodist and Anglican ventures were certainly an aspect of the missionary thrust that emanated from Britain in the first two decades of the nineteenth century. But by mid-century such ventures were very much in local hands, with the formation of the Anglican Melanesian Mission in 1849 and the transfer of Wesleyan Methodist Pacific missions to Australasian control in 1855.[34] New Zealand missionary interests, especially in the Solomon Islands and the New Hebrides, predated British expansion and control there by at least 30 years, and were either initiatives of local denominational and non-denominational ventures, or part of such international co-operatives as the Presbyterian New Hebrides Mission. At the same time, they could be read as one expression of what Salesa refers to as 'public interest in a Pacific empire'. By the late nineteenth century this interest was often 'specific', being 'concentrated in certain locations or among particular groups', and was typically 'clustered around concrete formations', among which were the churches. In these respects, the Melanesian Mission epitomised the 'deep entanglements' between New Zealand and its 'Pacific empire', from relatively early on in the colony's history.[35]

Some of New Zealand's extensive missionary involvement in India was predicated on the pre-existence of British missions on the subcontinent – particularly those of the Church Missionary Society, the Baptist Missionary Society, the Church of Scotland, the Free Church of Scotland, the London Missionary Society and the Society for the Propagation of the Gospel. However, other ventures that arose from the 1890s onwards were less dependent on the British connection, and are discussed further in the concluding section of this chapter.

China also loomed large as a major destination for New Zealand missionaries up to their expulsion in 1952. Two thirds of New Zealand missionaries worked either with the China Inland Mission (and therefore were often placed well beyond the geographical margins of British influence in China) or with the New Zealand Presbyterian Church's Canton Villages Mission in the vicinity of Guangzhou.[36] This latter mission, which would later enter into Union ventures in education and health with other international missions, was born out of unique circumstances. Missionary work initially began among villages in the Guangzhou region, from whence came many of the Chinese gold miners who worked in southern New Zealand in the 1860s. The impetus for missionary work that began in 1901 arose partly out of the network of relationships established between the Presbyterian Church in New Zealand, Chinese immigrants, and their families and communities in southern China over subsequent decades.

While Africa was not a major continental destination, it did attract a number of New Zealand missionaries who were to be found in a variety of British African colonies. Some, like Associated Churches of Christ missionaries in southern Rhodesia and Sudan United Mission workers in the Sudan, formally participated in colonial projects such as primary and secondary education. There were also a number who operated in non-British territories, especially the Belgian Congo, Abyssinia and Eritrea, and Portuguese East Africa. Many of these were Open (Plymouth) Brethren missionaries who were working in Africa primarily because of their links with the international Brethren community, rather than from any specific attachment to the empire.[37]

Finally, involvement in the South American continent constituted the most notable instance of missionary interest in a region more or less completely outside the British Empire's bounds. In total, at least 111 New Zealanders lived as missionaries in South America up to 1939 (just over 10 per cent of total New Zealand Protestant missionaries), some of whom worked with British organisations like the Regions Beyond Missionary Union and the Evangelical Union of South America. As with Africa, there were also a significant number of independent Open Brethren missionaries working in transnational missionary projects. As already noted, the BIM emerged as a completely home-grown venture, almost exclusively maintained by New Zealand and Australian missionaries and money up until World War I, but which was increasingly tied thereafter into links with the North American continent and conservative American evangelicalism.

With respect to institutional patterns, New Zealand missionaries worked under the direction of, or in partnership with, at least 78 different denominational or non-denominational organisations up to 1939 (see Appendix 1). Many of these people were of British origin, or had British links. Again, however, the situation was more complex. For example, 29 of these organisations were specifically Australasian in origin, even if British church leaders had sometimes been instrumental in their formation. Moreover, when we take the period as a whole, there were discernible changes in the organisational affiliation of New Zealand missionaries. British organisations were always influential, employing just over half of all New Zealand missionaries up to 1919. They were popular for a number of reasons, namely denominational and family links, the geographical location of their operations, and individuals' previous educational or work experience in Britain. Yet these organisations attracted a shrinking proportion of New Zealanders from the 1920s. North American organisations became increasingly attractive after World War I, especially among evangelical constituencies drawn to the faith mission movement. The overriding trend, however, was the involvement of New Zealanders, from the very beginning, with a wide range of denominational and non-denominational organisations emerging from within New Zealand and Australia.

Contexts, intersections and sites

In dissecting the motivation of New Zealand Methodist women working in the Solomon Islands, Lisa Early usefully suggests that a combination of 'patriotism, nationalist sentiment, and imperialistic beliefs intertwined with evangelical Christianity' provided a 'supportive context for the idea of mission' among these women.[38] If imperial sentiments or notions of Western superiority were present in New Zealanders' constructions of the missionary project then, as I emphasised in Chapters Three and Four, they co-existed with a range of other influences, both domestic and imported. New Zealand missionaries were perhaps not so much initiators of empire as they were often confident participants in empire. In a general sense, there is plenty of evidence, for example, that while specifically imperial motives were absent from discourses like motivational narratives, New Zealand missionaries worked within a wider Western mindset that offset or juxtaposed Western progress and Christianity against the 'heathen', non-progressive 'other'. Motivational narratives, for example, were replete with what might be termed the language of pity. William Searle, of the BIM, wanted to 'have the joy of leading the poor sin stricken [sic] Indians of Bolivia to our Lord and Master and incidentally to a better and purer life'.[39] In many narratives there was a common concern for those in the 'dark', 'suffering' or in 'need', who had 'never heard' about Christ, or who needed to be raised to a 'higher plane'.

Ultimately, it is only the marriage of macro and micro perspectives that will allow us to realistically understand the relationship between colonial missionaries and the wider British Empire. In this respect, the relationship also needs to be examined with respect to how missions were theologically conceived, gendered and activated within particular sites of missionary activity. The concept of 'site', here, is both spatial and discursive in meaning. It derives in particular from recent scholarship in human geography and social anthropology, and has been most particularly applied to intersections of gender and space, as well as to thinking about the historical outworking of colonialism.[40] It refers both to 'physical entities in socially and culturally mapped space' – that are demarcated by 'particularity', 'interaction' and 'frameworks' of meaning – and to a 'domain or a cluster of social practices and ideas that are expressed in a variety of physical spaces'.[41] This is by no means a new argument; for instance, it echoes recent scholarship on the British missionary movement by historians such as Andrew Walls and Andrew Porter.[42] Their contention is that the relationship between British missionaries and empire must be teased out within specific temporal, spatial, national and cultural contexts, simply because the relationships were so complex and variable. Furthermore, the concept of sites sits well with Tony Ballantyne's notion of empire as a web-like structure with multiple, mutually constitutive ties and influences holding together disparate locations (once thought of in terms of 'centre' and 'periphery') as co-equally important to the expression, construction or maintenance of empire.[43] In this sense, sites are not discrete and closed-off localities, but rather spaces that 'are interconnected, "open and porous" embracing both local and global dimensions'.[44]

Case Study: India as a 'site' of New Zealand missionary interest and involvement

This chapter concludes, then, with an exploration of some of the issues that might be considered within such a contextual approach, using New Zealand's missionary involvement in India as a particular site. Up until at least World War I, India was the main focus for New Zealand Protestants. This reflected a wider British, North American and Australian missionary focus on India by the late nineteenth century.[45] Most colonial Protestant denominations had missionary representatives in India, and New Zealanders worked there with at least another 18 domestic or international organisations. This high level of interest was linked, at least in part, to wider imperial ties and sentiments. In 1900, for example, New Zealand parliamentarians unanimously supported the payment of £5000 for Indian famine relief after a nationwide fundraising campaign received widespread support.[46] New Zealand's relative geographical proximity to South Asia was also a factor. Ceylon and the Indian mainland were the first truly foreign ports of call for those settler New Zealanders travelling home to Britain in the pre-Panama Canal era.

It is worth noting, however, that missionary involvement was but one expression of a broader and complex relationship between New Zealand and imperial India. New Zealand's presence in India was evident through people like colonial administrators, teachers, Christian clerics and missionaries. However, recent trends in historiography have thrown the emphasis on 'India in New Zealand', where 'consumption culture, intellectual and religious life and demographic composition' were all 'more real and substantial than has been generally acknowledged'.[47] Thus there was a sustained two-way flow of peoples (with the earliest Indian migrants dating from the early 1800s), commodities (especially tea and cultural artifacts), ideas (Christianity and Theosophy), and money, among other things.[48] Missionary engagement thus intersected with a growing Indian profile in settler New Zealand and an interest in a host of ideas, things and peoples from the subcontinent (albeit often structured around Western or Christian cultural priorities and expectations). When this relationship between New Zealand overseas missions and India as a complex imperial site is considered more closely, two clusters of factors emerge which, while not exhaustive, again indicate the same inherent ambiguities and complexities identified in the preceding general discussion.

(a) Cluster 1: Imperial ties or colonial autonomy?
First, because the turn of the nineteenth and twentieth centuries marked a transition in New Zealand's political and cultural status within the empire, it is important to examine the extent to which involvement in India was either an expression of imperial ties or an assertion of autonomy and independence. India held a special place in the sentiments and thinking of churchgoing New Zealanders. It was seen as a special responsibility because of a sense of imperial belonging, one accentuated by geographic proximity. These sentiments were borne out in the statement of one Presbyterian missionary applicant, written in 1906. William Blair suggested that 'India is part of the British Empire; is peopled by a virile race, and is one of the strongholds of the great religion, destined … to be the most powerful opponents [sic] of Christianity. Hence, as a British student, I feel a responsibility to the people of India.'[49] Although Blair was New Zealand-born and had previously worked as a missionary trader in the New Hebrides, he located himself within a wider set of imperial definitions and responsibilities. His sentiments were further reflected in the comments of other Presbyterian missionary applicants in the same period. When asked to explain their preference for a missionary destination, they variously noted that 'as part of our Empire, India seems to be our peculiar trust'; that it was 'a British possession' and a 'part of our own Empire'; and that 'India is British and our responsibility'.[50] Likewise, the Revd Harry Driver, author of the first history of the NZBMS, noted somewhat romantically that in choosing East Bengal as a field of Baptist operations,

> We felt that India had peculiar claims upon us, because it formed a large part of the mighty Empire to which we also belonged. It was ruled by the sceptre of our own Sovereign. Its wealth enriched our national treasury. Its splendour and beauty added to the glory of our nation. This vast Empire, with its 313,000,000 people, with its marvellous history reaching back to remote ages, with all its mystery and majesty, had in the providence of God, come under Britain's sway, and we believed that this had not been brought to pass merely to add to the power and prestige of Britain, but chiefly in order that we might give to India the Gospel to which our nation owed its greatness … Patriotism as well as piety called us to this glorious crusade.[51]

While these sentiments seemed to clearly indicate the importance of imperial ties, the picture was complicated. The first New Zealand missionaries in India were certainly there as employees of British missions, such as the Zenana Bible and Medical Mission (from 1875), the Church Missionary Society (from the early 1880s), the Free Church of Scotland (from 1892), the London Missionary Society (from 1893), and the Church of Scotland (from 1897). British missions would continue to attract New Zealanders over succeeding decades. Some early New Zealand ventures in India, especially those of the NZBMS, the NZCMA and Brethren missionaries, rode on the coat-tails of British missions in a subsidiary, younger sibling role, or else complemented the work of British missions. Yet the bulk of missionaries to India from the mid-1880s onwards were sent through the agency of newly emergent New Zealand and Australian missionary societies or groups. One of these, the independent Australasian-based PIVM, has already been discussed in Chapter Three. A second Indian venture was the Punjab Mission, established by the Presbyterian Church of New Zealand in the vicinity of Jagadhri and Ludhiana in northern India.[52] New Zealand Presbyterian women had been missionaries in the Madras region, under the various Presbyterian churches of Scotland, since 1892. In 1910, however, the New Zealand Church initiated its own venture, with an initial focus on medical work and village evangelism but a later emphasis on primary and secondary education. This was a project undertaken in partnership with the American Presbyterian Mission already established in northern India. Until the 1960s at least, this mission was a firm marker of Presbyterian identity in New Zealand itself.

These examples suggest that turn-of-the-centuries missionary involvement in India was simultaneously an expression of imperial ties, a reflection of wider international influences, and also an assertion of colonial autonomy. Furthermore, this mix of factors needs to be understood within the context of particular Protestant denominations. In the case of the Baptists, for instance, some of the strongest pro-empire statements in relation to India, at least in the period up to 1914, came from the pen of the Revd Harry Driver in Dunedin, who was an influential force in colonial Baptist missionary circles. English-born and theologically trained at Spurgeon's College, Croydon, he was strong on administrative skills, secretary of the NZBMS from its formation in 1885 until 1902 and, most influentially, the editor of the *New Zealand Baptist* from 1906 to 1915.[53] It is questionable, however, to what extent his comments were representative of all Baptists; and it is obvious, in such a small denomination, that people in key positions could wield disproportionate influence.

It may also be the case that the Baptist venture in India, at least in its early stages up to 1900, was driven by sentiments of 'better Britonism' as much as by imperial or theological obligation and responsibility. Better Britonism refers to a set of sentiments, albeit waxing and waning over time, that colonial New Zealand was British par excellence, a society that embraced and exemplified all that was best in being British. Between 1886 and 1900, 19 NZBMS missionaries were sent to East Bengal from a denomination barely making up 2 per cent of New Zealand's population. Seven of them went in the space of just two years, between 1895 and 1896. This was rapid growth for a small denomination with a limited budget. While it reflected an activism that was fundamental to the colonial Baptist ethos, it also begs a further question. Was it a definable way by which colonial Baptists could assert their independence from Britain, and indeed from Australia, and show that they were more than capable of the task of carrying the missionary burden themselves?[54] If so, it was a risky way of making a statement. By 1895 two of the three original missionaries had died in India and the third was convalesced home. In 1899 the whole venture almost unravelled with the dismissal or resignation of six further missionaries. Injudicious expansion, poor support structures, and the dominating influence of one particular Baptist leader, the Revd Alfred North, indicated that hubris and bravado were poor substitutes for organisation and planned growth.[55]

Particular missionary sites may have also acted as the crucibles in which a sense of New Zealand self-identity was forged or reinforced. While nationhood is a clearly contested category of historical interpretation, it is evident that the interwar years were pivotal in the emergence of at least a sense of a more defined national identity. If so, then the Indian context suggests that this was a fraught process. Diane Rixon's study of New Zealand Presbyterian missionaries caught up in the nationalist debates that wracked India in the interwar period indicates that some of them occupied a middle ground. She argues that most of these missionaries understood that Indian self-rule was inevitable and that they showed varying degrees of sympathy. While some were more reluctant to concede the possibility of political or ecclesiastical autonomy, others were 'filled with optimism at the thought of working with them'. She observes further that New Zealand missionaries in this period 'lived [somewhat uncomfortably] on the periphery of both Indian and Anglo-Indian society'.[56] Again, India was certainly important to the emerging self-identity of particular denominations, perhaps none more so than the New Zealand Baptists for whom East Bengal remained the sole missionary focus until the 1950s. This connection has remained to the present day, with the NZBMS still in an active partnership role with the Bangladesh Baptist Fellowship.[57]

(b) Cluster 2: The influence of domestic factors

While New Zealand missionary involvement in India reflected wider global connections and the cultural influences of British citizenship, there was also a second cluster of local or domestic factors at play. The period from the 1890s onwards was one of growing economic recovery and prosperity for the entire colony (following a period of warfare and economic depression), of greater social modernisation (marked in particular by increasing urbanisation), and of political sophistication. These developments had a consequent impact on or were reflected in the life and fortunes of local churches. Financial growth in missionary budgets and giving was moderate up to 1900. This reflected the relatively late economic development of New Zealand's North Island, the impact of the New Zealand Wars, the long depression of the 1880s and the struggle for colonial denominations to cope with the constant debt resulting from building programmes.[58] While church finances were primarily focused on capital works such as church building, projects of a more general nature were also budgeted for and these included overseas missionary work. Missionary recruiters were able to tap into a growing reservoir of educated women and men, and to target particular communities for the requisite finances. Each denomination had specific local churches and regions that historically showed more enthusiasm and wielded more financial power when it came to sending missionaries. However, by the 1930s missionary enthusiasm, as witnessed in budgets and in giving, was fairly widespread with respect both to denomination and to geography. Missionary involvement was an important indicator of the maturing character of both society and institutional religion in the interwar period. Against this background, India was an important focus until at least World War II.

There are three other sets of local factors linked to the Indian site, which were just as important as imperial and other entanglements for understanding missionary motivation. First, India was an important focus and vocational outlet for women in an era of growing public opportunities and political freedoms. In the New Zealand context, first-wave feminism was in part linked to Protestant evangelical communities, was focused around the issue of alcohol prohibition and temperance, and was an influential factor in the attainment of universal suffrage for women in 1893.[59] The missionary thrust towards India from the late 1880s coincided with this great rush of energy and changing societal attitudes towards the public roles of women. While the attraction of India for women is unquestioned, what does beg further reflection is the extent to which women either supported or subverted imperial allegiances. European women missionaries in India of all denominations, including those from New Zealand, were placed in a variety of evangelistic, domestic, educational, health, welfare and administrative positions. A summary glance at the available data suggests that there was little to distinguish New Zealand women from their international 'white sisters', in terms of how they understood (or were understood by) their missionary subjects. While they used the rhetoric of sisterhood, as Sarah Coleman notes, this construction consisted of inherent racial hierarchies which created the perception that 'superior' Western women were there to rescue their 'inferior' Indian sisters.[60] Yet, as noted in the Introduction and expanded on further in Chapter Four, such analysis has been predominantly framed within non-theological academic discourses that have too quickly adopted international conclusions for the New Zealand context, and which have not paid due attention to potential nuances within this construction.

Second, India as a missionary site was also an important factor in shaping the lives and sensibilities of many Protestant children in New Zealand. This is the focus of the next chapter. Some initial observations, however, are worth making for the present discussion. The period up to World War I recorded the highest levels of children's participation in institutional religion,[61] and marshalling juvenile energies and finances for the missionary cause was a significant feature of missionary committee activity. At a general level, children's involvement was significant for the financial support of missions. Yet more important, from an adult perspective, was the concern to develop a lifelong sense of missionary citizenship among children. The Baptist experience again serves as a useful introductory example. New Zealand Baptist children were made aware of India from the inception of NZBMS activities there in the mid-1880s, helping to foster a sense of colonial Baptist identity as much as a concern for India per se. To that end, children's enthusiasm was very quickly engaged through a great range of juvenile projects: the Missionary Pence Association and the Missionary

Houseboat Share Certificate scheme (1897–98); Birthday Bands and the Missionary Brick scheme (1903); publication of the *Young Folk's Missionary Messenger* (from 1904); a missionary section of the annual Scriptural Examinations (1920); and the Ropeholders' League (1926). Strong mental links in the national psyche, between India and the British Empire, rubbed off on Baptist children through their prolonged and focused involvement with India. The Baptist case is not an isolated one. By tracing the missionary support of Methodists for the South Pacific, or Presbyterian children for southern China, the same kinds of influences and results can be found.

In the final instance, the focus on India also reflected the impact of evangelical revivalism on New Zealand Protestants more generally. There is growing evidence that revivalism was a dynamic, but not always uniform, feature of Christianity in New Zealand from the late nineteenth century onwards.[62] Revivalism served to heighten religious enthusiasm as much as it increased the numbers of churchgoers, and was further nourished by Australian, British and North American influences. There is a strong case for arguing that missionary support and involvement was increasingly viewed, from the 1890s onwards, as an outcome of this heightened religious enthusiasm. Places such as India provided a significant outlet for these new energies. As noted in Chapter Three, however, the case of the Poona and Indian Village Mission also illustrates that such enthusiasm might stimulate further ventures. This seems particularly likely for both the Anglican and the Presbyterian Churches, which perceived the newly emergent faith missions as a threat to their own missionary finances and recruitment.[63]

Conclusion

Empire is a complex construct, understood differently in various times and places. It is, argues Linda Colley, 'one of the most enduring, versatile and ubiquitous forms of political organization',[64] a form that endures even in the present day. Its meaning varies across a range of spectra, falling between such binary opposites as coloniser and colonised, contemporary and historical, male and female, or indigenous and settler. When we consider the concept in relationship to the missionary movement emanating from a colonial setting like New Zealand, the Indian site indicates clearly the complex interplay of factors in the colonial context. My remarks here signal only a beginning in this task, as does the work by Margaret Allen on Australia.

Our efforts form part of a wider concern to understand the operation of the 'British' world not just from the perspective of colonised peoples or the metropole, but also from the perspective of other settler or colonial constituents caught up in the 'webs of empire', who themselves wittingly or unwittingly transmitted or imposed cultural values and expectations. In this chapter, I offer a tentative and generalised conclusion: that the participation of New Zealand Protestants in the missionary movement and their relationship with the British Empire was not uniform in its shape or content. They imbibed the cultural mores of their day and reflected them in their words and actions. At the same time, they were shaped, motivated and sustained by a complex interplay of local and even global factors. Their participation in particular missionary sites influenced how they worked, thought and reacted to the multiple worlds of missionaries and 'missionary subjects', and in turn shaped how they conveyed news of those worlds back to their domestic and denominational constituencies. New Zealand Protestant missionaries and their supporters faced the same problems and challenges of cultural translation that all of us face in any age.

CHAPTER 7

Protestant Children, Overseas Missions and Empire

A THIRD AREA to consider is the important relationship that had clearly emerged, by the late nineteenth century, between Protestant children and overseas missions, and to ponder further their relationship to imperial rhetoric and messages. Religious settler childhoods were shaped by a number of factors, not least of which was the missionary work under consideration here. By the early decades of the 1900s this had become a firmly established religious feature for children and young people in the Protestant denominations. This influence was expressed, for example, in August 1922 when the Revd Charles Laws (newly established as president of the New Zealand Methodist Conference) wrote specifically and candidly to the children of his denomination. Recounting a trip he had previously made in Asia, he contrasted the faces of children he had seen there – 'full of sunshine and laughter' – with those of Asian adults, whom he perceived to be 'full of sorrow, and disappointment, and even of *Fear*'. With Methodist work in the Solomon Islands firmly in mind, he went on to assert that

> heathenism takes all the beauty and joy out of life, and turns happy boys and girls into sad and clouded men and women. It is so in the Solomon Islands to-day … You must remember the thousands of young folk, as dear to Jesus as yourselves, for whom Fear is waiting, and you must pray for them, and give and collect so that in every village the story of Jesus may be heard, and when in later life God calls some of you to go forth across the sea to work in His great harvest fields, you must say, 'Here am I, send me.'[1]

Laws wrote these words as a presidential address in the inaugural issue of the children's missionary magazine, *The Lotu*. It was clearly framed to reinforce the New Zealand Methodist Church's recently devolved responsibility for Solomon Islands mission work. 'Lotu' was a Tongan term that referred variously to Christianity or religion, to the Church generically or as a place, and to the specific elements of prayer and worship.[2] This magazine became a firm fixture in the memories of several generations of young Methodist New Zealanders. What Laws wrote here was typical of the magazine's content over the next two decades, and also typical of the messages heard by all colonial Protestant children throughout the period.

Children's relationship to the Anglo-American missionary movement has been treated haphazardly in historical scholarship.[3] Most commonly the focus has been on colonised children, particularly with respect to missionary education. The children of missionaries form a relatively neglected category, although this is now beginning to be addressed by scholarship. With respect to children as missionary supporters, earlier studies typically dealt with such themes as financial support, socialisation, missionary literature and pedagogy, and racial attitudes.[4] More recently, the focus has been on children's material culture and their relationship to missionary literature, with a focus on wider cultural, political and religious discursive frameworks.[5]

The nexus of children, missions and empire is also a relatively underdeveloped area of study. Therefore, in this chapter I extend the theme of missions and empire by focusing on settler New Zealand children as missionary supporters. My focus here is primarily on the cultivation of juvenile support for overseas missions, and on the ways in which imperial sentiments were presented in Sunday school and Bible class pedagogy and missionary rhetoric. As I indicated in the previous chapter, it was in this period that white New Zealanders, at least, took seriously their constituent membership of the British Empire. According to Pocock, their imported imperial culture was not 'imposed', but rather viewed as 'their inheritance'.[6] They perceived themselves, simultaneously, as inhabitants of a southern hemisphere colony only just coming to terms with its own identity, and as citizens of the wider British world. At the same time, settler children's religion and missionary awareness was also increasingly being shaped by American materials and influences.

Children as missionary supporters

The organisation of British children's energies and sentiments in the cause of overseas missions, particularly on behalf of the evangelical societies, followed fast on the heels of the explosion of missionary endeavour from the 1790s. While the concerted marshalling of children's support dates from the early 1840s, earlier and more sporadic efforts were evident from the first decade of Protestant missionary activity.[7] By the end of the nineteenth century British children were firmly established as a formidable force of missionary supporters. In the London context alone, Francis Prochaska estimates that juvenile missionary societies 'numbered in the thousands, some of them with thousands of members. The pennies added up to millions of pounds.' In some cases, such as the Methodist Missionary Society, children's donations may have amounted to 20 per cent of annual income by the early 1900s.[8] Susan Thorne likewise estimates that Congregational Sunday schools in England contributed at least a quarter of LMS funds throughout the nineteenth century.[9] At the same time, these children were also willing participants in the regional and national rallies and missionary exhibitions that became annual rituals, and they were voracious consumers of an array of missionary magazines and other literature.

The same pattern can be discerned in the New Zealand context. Protestant children and young people were quickly caught up into the movement from the 1880s onwards – primarily through denominational Sunday schools and, later, Bible classes. Around 80 per cent of the juvenile population between the 1880s and 1930s were Protestant; Roman Catholic children made up a further 13 to 14 per cent.[10] Those attending Sunday schools – often but not exclusively taught by women – ranged between five and 14 in age. Those in the Bible classes typically were young to mid-aged adolescents, with young adults regularly engaged as leaders. Both boys and girls participated in equal numbers in the Sunday schools. By adolescence, the formation of Young Men's and Young Women's Bible Class Unions ensured that males and females participated and contributed in equal proportions. Children and adolescents were also keen missionary supporters through the various Christian Endeavour societies, and educated young adults through the Student Volunteer Movement and the Australasian Student Christian Union (later the Student Christian Movement).

That these patterns of support and involvement in late nineteenth-century New Zealand replicated those found in Britain in the earlier decades was not insignificant. Denominational leaders and those over-seeing children's work were barely a generation removed from their British roots. Indeed many, like Jane Bannerman (née Burns) from Scotland, had been supporters of missions as children in Britain prior to emigration.[11] Furthermore, many of the early involvements of New Zealand mission-aries had occurred either in such British-administered territories as India or been twinned with British organisations and personnel. British literature and other propaganda materials remained influential for children across the period until at least World War I.

By the early 1900s there were a number of well-established children's and young people's institutions for missionary support. Baptist examples of such schemes were canvassed in Chapter Six. They were age-appropriate (such as the birthday clubs) and project-specific (for example, supporting a missionary house-boat), with the emphasis on systematic and habitual support (see Figures 7.1 and 7.2).

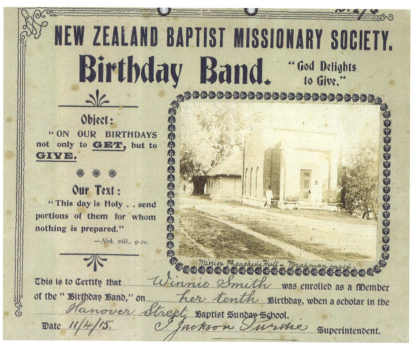

FIGURE 7.1. NZBMS Children's Birthday Band Membership Card, 1915[12]

FIGURE 7.2. NZBMS Children's Missionary House-boat Share Certificate, 1898[13]

Across the Protestant denominations, juveniles were drawn into these kinds of schemes in ways that were both emotional and intellectual,[14] although it is not always possible to properly discern the gendered nature of such involvement. Proximity to Melanesian and Polynesian spheres of activity meant that mission personnel and vessels were often highly accessible. On a visit to Wellington in 1877, the Melanesian Mission's Bishop John Selwyn took Anglican children for a day cruise on the mission's ship the *Southern Cross*, replete with 'an unlimited supply of buns, ginger beer etc'.[15] By this date Anglican children were already supporting Melanesian school children on Norfolk Island. Similar visits by the New Hebrides mission ship the *Dayspring* from the late 1860s gave Presbyterian children a first-hand glimpse of missionary realities and reinforced their ongoing financial support.[16]

Children were quickly catered for by denominational literature and through such trans-denominational publications as *China's Millions* and *White Already to Harvest*. Initially, children read imported British literature that was progressively supplemented and then replaced by local materials. The Southland and Otago Presbyterian Synod, for example, subscribed to a number of English and Scottish publications on behalf of its Sunday schools.[17] Specific children's publications like the Presbyterian *Break of Day*, the Methodist magazine *The Lotu*, and the Baptist *Young Folk's Missionary Messenger* did not appear until after 1900. Together, these formed a local extension of a well-established literary institution among British children, exemplified by publications like the *Juvenile Missionary Record* (Church of Scotland) and *Children's Missionary Record* (Free Church of Scotland), *Church Missionary Juvenile Instructor* and the *Wesleyan Juvenile Offering*. Over the longer term, children's and young people's support was sought with ever increasing sophistication and innovation, with an obvious focus on fostering financial support.[18]

As with children's support in Britain, it was not always clear whether juvenile missionary money derived from parents' giving or from child-sponsored activities and collections.[19] Herein lies a fundamental issue that is both theoretical and methodological in nature: children's historical agency with respect to missionary support. It is a widely recognised issue that remains at the forefront of children's historical research, and which revolves around problems of sources and accessibility.[20] In the New Zealand context an initial survey of data suggests that there are some grounds for thinking that children were both agents and subjects in this respect. Presbyterian statistics, for example, indicate that children and young people were significant conduits and sources of financial support. Sunday school financial records suggest that southern scholars gave proportionately more than their northern counterparts until the early 1900s. By the 1920s donations to various missionary causes consistently made up around one third of all Presbyterian Sunday school giving in this decade, and up to two-thirds of Bible class giving.[21] Juvenile money, then, formed a significant bloc of missionary income for Presbyterians.

Just as significant was the array of ways in which money was raised, along with increased missionary awareness. Across the denominations fundraising activities became regular rituals that kept missionary support and interest alive. These also had a ring of great fun about them, which may have resulted in the missionary cause being regarded later with some warmth in the collective memory of adult churchgoers. Baptist young people staged dramatic presentations, ran photography and cooking competitions, held missionary evenings and participated in missionary rallies.[22] They also enrolled in a diverse range of well-subscribed schemes aimed at supporting specific projects. Anglican youngsters were catechised, held sales and concerts, combined for mission festivals, and dedicated gifts on the annual church Christmas tree for overseas children.[23] Presbyterian 'Busy Bees' were organised into 'hives' to make 'pots of honey' (money) through making crafts, sales, collections (of bottles, rags, pinecones and wood), and selling vegetables. They also visited the sick and lonely and received instruction by way of catechism and literature.[24] 'Busy Bees' was a Presbyterian missionary support movement for both boys and girls that emerged in 1909, initiated by two daughters of the Presbyterian minister at Bluff – Muriel and Dorothy Laishley – but which was eventually re-organised and institutionalised through the Presbyterian Women's Missionary Union.[25] In the Busy Bees, as for the Christian Endeavour groups, older children and adolescents were instrumental in providing and maintaining the energy, inspiration, junior leadership and longevity of such ventures. Special children's services and young people's days were a further Presbyterian feature. An annual Presbyterian children's Christmas collection sponsored by the *Break of Day* – whereby children competed with each other to save their small change, either donated or earned for a specified missionary project (in New Zealand or abroad) – saw at least £8000 raised for Māori Mission and overseas mission projects between 1909 and 1940.[26]

Socialising children through education

In the longer term, however, finances were perceived to be secondary to the primary goal: to cultivate a lifetime of missionary awareness and responsibility. This was summed up in 1919 by one Baptist minister when he urged the New Zealand Baptist Union to 'make this movement educational if it is to affect effectually our children … If we indoctrinate our children with the claims of missions, home and foreign, and instruct them in relation to the need for them, the high service they render, and the Lord Christ's commands concerning them, we may hope to develop a generation who will intelligently and conscientiously cultivate missionary enthusiasm and generosity towards this, the greatest enterprise of all.'[27]

The Christian home, Sunday schools, Christian Endeavour and Bible classes, sustained by missionary literature, were the main sites and influences in this process. Long-term 'intelligent' and 'conscientious' enthusiasm was the primary goal: educated givers were better in the long run. But the goal was also couched in more directly evangelistic terms. Another Baptist commentator suggested that if the saying was true that 'you can evangelise the world in a single generation if you educate the generation to do it', then the responsibility of the Church was to give children a 'broad, full conception of Christian religion – one which will carry with it a clear, intelligent understanding of the universal Fatherhood of God and the real brotherhood of man'.[28] As always, adult motivations for garnering children's support were mixed.

These sentiments were programmatically mapped out by leading Presbyterian minister the Revd Rutherford Waddell as early as 1883, in an address on 'The Sabbath-school and Missions' to a national gathering of Presbyterian Sunday school teachers in Dunedin.[29] Waddell took it for granted that missions were an important element of children's education, but he did not assume that his adult audience would all agree. In particular, he focused on the need for character development rather than on the money that could be leveraged out of children. Juveniles were foundationally important because they were 'the future church', and childhood was the key developmental phase in which to inculcate missionary enthusiasm. Overseas missions deserved a 'prominent place in Sabbath-school teaching'. In turn, this required teachers who were 'possessed' with the 'missionary spirit'; that is, people who would concentrate their efforts 'not upon filling the missionary-box, but upon filling the child's soul with the Spirit of Christ'. Consequently, pedagogy should be focused on two priorities. The first was to teach children to have 'wide sympathies'. In other words, children should become more aware of the wider world 'outside their family, their friends, or even their country and race'. The second priority was the need to teach them the 'joy and heroism of doing good'. Children should understand 'the nobility of doing good, the nobility of helping and serving others, and especially the nobility of a missionary life'. People were 'all too slow,' he suggested, 'to imitate the heroism of God's example'.

This basic philosophy endured throughout the period, although it was evident that it was one that needed constant emphasis and reworking. The narratives of many New Zealand missionary applicants indicate that home and parents were enduring influences that helped to perpetuate an awareness of missions throughout childhood. Home and community were important sites of settler child formation, both secular and religious.[30] Violet Latham (NZCMS) talked of her mother's encouragement towards missionary service, and John Muir (CIM) wrote of how his mother 'consecrated her two young children to the Lord' for missionary service; John went to China and Molly to the Solomon Islands.[31] As indicated in Chapter Four, many of the men and women applying for missionary service in this period located their first missionary interest either in childhood or late adolescence. This suggests that childhood was an enduring crucible within which longer-held missionary aspirations were nurtured.[32] Missions were also a focus for family prayers in the home. The cycle of devotional prayers and Bible readings introduced by the Presbyterian Church in 1917 typically included petitions for '"our missionaries" to the "Maoris" [sic]', the 'Chinese and other foreigners within our borders', and those 'beyond the seas – in the New Hebrides, the Canton Villages, the Panjâb [sic], India, and elsewhere'.[33]

Yet it was also thought, by the early 1900s, that the Sunday school and Bible class was a more effective vehicle for promoting the 'wide sympathies' that Waddell had earlier highlighted. Properly trained teachers, a well-designed syllabus and 'systematic instruction' were preferable to a haphazard reliance on the home. This was conceived of in at least two broad ways. One approach was to designate regular missionary days on a monthly or annual basis.[34] A second approach built on this by arguing for a syllabus that included regular missionary lessons spanning all age levels of Sunday school work. This latter approach required deliberate teacher training, thoughtful resources and a mixture of both regular lessons and special one-off events. As late as 1914, the Revd George Jupp echoed Waddell's earlier call by suggesting that Sunday schools should 'Begin young and you will imbue the men and women of the next generation with the missionary idea … The story for the child; the heroic for the growing boy and girl; the appeal with the heroic as its foundation for the youth – this will win missionary recruits among boys and girls.'[35]

From the 1910s the systematic inclusion of missionary subjects within cycles of graded syllabi became commonplace in Protestant Sunday schools and Bible classes. By the late 1920s denominations were joining forces to produce teaching materials that systematically integrated missionary themes into their annual schedules. The Methodist Bible Classes' *Manual of Missions* (1933) perhaps offered the most advanced example of such progress.[36]

Teachers were increasingly better supported, both in terms of instructional notes and hands-on resources. A set of Presbyterian mission lessons for 1918, focusing on Japan, had its own textbook, information sheets, large outline maps, pictures, sheet music and even a set of cut-out cardboard Japanese model houses.[37] Both internationally and nationally, this was a period in which religious education became more systematic, creative and 'modern'.[38] New Zealand Sunday schools adopted both British and American pedagogical materials, such as the *Arnold's Practical Sabbath-School Commentary* series, as well as developing their own. The focus was on both emotional and intellectual learning. Weekly activities were complemented by the continued use of missionary catechisms, annual children's services with a missionary theme, and end-of-year examinations that included questions on the missionary work of the churches.

Imperial sentiments and missionary pedagogy

In the British context, Francis Prochaska suggests that the children's missionary movement helps to shed significant light on at least three broader features of nineteenth-century English society and culture: children's recreation, changing conceptions of childhood, and the 'formation of prejudice'. It is the last feature that is most apposite for the present discussion. In a somewhat speculative paragraph, he argues that the 'power of the missionary societies to form racial and cultural attitudes in the young' was their 'most enduring legacy'.[39] 'Racialism', argues Colin Kidd, was certainly an 'omnipresent factor in nineteenth-century intellectual life',[40] one that in part both emanated from and affected religious sentiments. Taken together, private homes, Sunday schools and missionary associations, bolstered by a huge body of literature, were all important sites for the formation of a distinctively racialised British children's world view. This was especially so in the period prior to formal state education, in the early to mid-nineteenth century.

Can we extend this same argument to the context of children in late nineteenth- and early twentieth-century New Zealand where, from 1877, there was a functioning state education system, compulsory schooling and significantly improving rates of school attendance?[41] To what extent were children presented with and influenced by imperial sentiments through their contact with missionary pedagogy and rhetoric, especially through Sunday school attendance? David Keen argues that this was indeed the case; that colonial Sunday schools 'through their publicising of and support for overseas missionary work … helped to develop a broader context for New Zealand's nascent sense of national identity, indirectly reinforcing the cultural and political imperialism of the period'. Keen writes further that

> For all the generosity of intent, it was a paternalistic example of mission which the Otago Sunday schools held up for the emulation of their young. Children of the Covenant were left in no doubt that they were heirs to a superior culture, the mission gospel was proclaimed *de haut en bas* … The curriculum offered to Sunday school children … in the later nineteenth century encapsulated the world view of the settlement's religious leaders. Otago's young people were socialized by the Sunday school into a microcosm of Empire, into the life of a colony planted in faith and affirmed by the material evidence of its own development. The Sunday schools fostered both individual confidence and patriotic pride, while tempering these with a keen sense of dependence on the sustaining power of God.

Against this background, 'Sunday school children were made aware of their godly heritage, and of their several duties to defend, share and sustain it.'[42]

Keen's focus was on the southern part of New Zealand up to 1901, rather than on the whole colony or period, and was framed within an historiographical discourse of national identity formation. Therefore, it could be argued that his observations are limited in both their scope and application. As the previous chapter made abundantly clear, however, there are many indications that these regionally specific sentiments were representative of wider New Zealand society in the same period. Bishop Cowie, Anglican bishop of Auckland, welcomed the Duke and Duchess of Cornwall in 1901 by expressing the clear opinion that 'we are whole-hearted in our loyalty to His Majesty King Edward. Under him we believe that the Empire, of which New Zealand is an integral part, will continue to advance in the cherishing of liberty, justice, and brotherhood throughout its extent; and that the morality and the religion of our King's subjects everywhere will always be to him matters of supreme interest.'[43] Such sentiments were strongly expressed in times of heightened imperial fervour. In the wake of Queen Victoria's death in 1901, it was suggested to Australasian Christian Endeavour members that her death 'appeals to us each personally. We experience a sense of individual loss.'[44]

At the same time, by the early 1900s the Sunday school was established as the 'centrepiece of Protestant religious education', becoming a 'normal part of childhood experience'. Enrolment rates peaked at between 65 and 69 per cent of all children aged 5–14 by 1911, and continued to be high for some decades.[45] Pedagogy became more child-centred and technologically sophisticated. Methodist children, for example, were taught by means of 'blackboards, easels, sandtables, [and] large figures'. Many denominations adopted the children's 'cradle roll' as a way of encouraging regular attendance.[46] These pedagogical institutions continued to be important sites for education, socialisation and attitudinal formation, well beyond the period and geographical boundaries that delimit the study by Keen.

Wider evidence from both secular and religious records suggests that children were continually exposed to pro-imperial information and sentiments until the late 1920s if not longer. Bible class syllabi continued to focus young people's attention, at least in part, on British missionary stories. Although individuals such as David Livingstone and Mary Slessor were still popular, earlier British missionaries like St Wilfrid or St Chad also had their stories told.[47] Likewise, missionary geography often centred on those territories most commonly linked with the empire – Africa, India and the South Pacific – or on imperial colonies like New Zealand. Imperial content and jingoism was much evident in the books given as end-of-year prizes. Like their English counterparts, these books were often distinctly gendered in the way that they presented their stories and themes, and their focus was exclusively on European missionaries and Christians.[48]

The evidence for the cultivation of imperial sentiment is found most explicitly in a range of polemical overtures as well as in these many textual references to places and people. A sample Sunday school lesson submitted to the NZCMA as part of an application in 1915 by Vivienne Opie was representative of this material. Her lesson was entitled 'The British Flag: What does it stand for?'[49] In her opinion, the flag differentiated those who lived in 'Freedom [and] Peace' from those who lived in 'fear of one another, fear of spirits, fear of death', who were imbued with a 'spirit of hate and cannibalism' or despoiled by 'the deaths of the little children'. The flag represented such qualities as 'love and trust' between people and was marked by 'wealth and possessions'. If the British Empire had anything to offer, it was because Christianity lay at its heart and formed its foundation. As empire citizens, therefore, New Zealand's Anglican children and adults alike were entrusted with a great and terrible responsibility. 'God has opened up the way for us and given us all means,' wrote Opie, '[and] we must obey or expect to have our privileges taken from us.' Her words amplified the kinds of late nineteenth-century sentiments already identified by Keen, and reflected the wider educational discourse that was common in all New Zealand schools by the 1910s. School corridors and Sunday school halls alike reverberated with many of the same imperial themes.

Although the British Empire was not always so explicitly present in what missionaries and their supporters wrote for children, its shadow can be discerned in the language used. Again, racial and other dualities were often not far below the surface of both the theological and polemical imagery that was employed. Throughout the period, New Zealand Sunday school children were regularly offered such images as sad Chinese praying to 'dumb wooden or stone idols', 'poor kaffirs' from southern Africa, and the 'ignorant men and women ... and little children' of India.[50] In 1918 the jubilee history of the Presbyterian mission in the New Hebrides, designed as a study text for young people, was tellingly given the title *Light in Dark Isles*. It was a before and after story of a 'people in darkness' contrasted with the 'children of light'. The darkness was physiological and racial, but also psychic, marked by perceived character traits that included a love of war, fickleness, impulsiveness, treachery, indolence and filthiness. Study questions counterpoised the unhappiness of the Melanesians with the happiness of the colonial juvenile. The light of Christianity brought freedom from fear, prayerfulness, a simple faith, generosity, hope and responsibility.[51] While not readily accessible, there is some evidence that systematic exposure to this rhetoric resulted in potentially conflicted attitudes and perceptions on behalf of settler children readers. Methodist children's letters written in 1928 to their counterparts in the Solomon Islands, for example, are at least indicative: counterposing expressions of familial belonging ('I feel that we belong to the one big family over which our Heavenly Father reigns') with stereotypical perceptions (references to 'our dear brown brothers and sisters', expectations of material deprivation, and assumptions that all Solomon Island children 'must love singing ... for it seems so natural that you can sing so well').[52]

It is worth noting that these sentiments were not the entire sum of 50 or more years of Christianisation in the New Hebrides or the Solomons. Furthermore, it is dangerously convenient to cast everything under the rubric of 'cultural imperialism'.[53] As Geoffrey Oddie observes, for nine-teenth-century evangelical Protestants at least, 'the most important polarity was not to be found in race or culture, but in the individual's morality and relationship with God ... [Therefore] "the other" was not only represented by Orientals, but also by less fortunate country-men.'[54] This is also a key theme in Alison Twells' work on 'civilising mission' both in and from early to mid-nineteenth-century England.[55] Nevertheless, the imagery of racial privilege was pervasive in children's religious literature and, as in other white societies, it served to accentuate a hierarchy of more and less deserving non-European peoples in the minds of its young readers.[56]

Such sentiments were also represented pictorially. One example, intro-duced in Chapter Two, comes from an Anglican missionary magazine. Distributed monthly by the New Zealand Anglican Board of Missions, the *Reaper* sought to publicise and support the diverse missionary involvements of Anglicans, irrespective of diocese, mission or ecclesiology. While prima-rily targeted at adults, it also fostered children's interest through dedicated columns and a regular cartoon series drawn by the Revd Noel Luker, a local clergyman of British origins.[57] Throughout 1932 children read about the 'adventures of Inky and Nugget', supposedly 'two little African boys'. The sequence of seven locally produced cartoon strips related how Inky and Nugget, in league with a resident European missionary, challenged the power and influence of the local witch doctors. The inference was that Inky and Nugget were already Christian or Christianised. There was a clear juxtaposition between perceived native simplicity and childlikeness, on the one hand, and the urbane, sophisticated Western missionary, on the other. Yet the missionary was not necessarily centre-stage. Throughout the series Inky and Nugget were instrumental in the conversion of their own village and witch doctor, and they actively effected the same changes in neigh-bouring villages. Theirs was an intensely practical Christianity, tinged with humour and compassion. At the same time this portrayal of Africans and of the missionary may well have served to reinforce a dualistic sense of 'them' and 'us' in the minds of New Zealand Anglican child readers. Africa was still, in the mentality of the early 1930s, a geographical site that needed to be changed for the better, both spiritually and materially.

Conclusion

In this chapter I have begun to tease out the ways in which colonial children and young people participated as empire citizens through the missionary movement, and the ways in which they were confronted with empire as it was mediated through religious pedagogy and rhetoric. At least three sets of issues emerge from the present discussion.

There is, firstly, a cluster of issues revolving around the notion of empire itself. The New Zealand case suggests that 'empire' was primarily mediated or represented to children, through both secular and religious pedagogy, as a set of virtues and values. Empire citizenship was to be aspired to, emulated and lived out in both childhood and adulthood, and it carried clear responsibilities and obligations. That the British Empire existed as a political, spatial, commercial, military and cultural entity appears to have been a secondary or consequential consideration. For children in Sunday schools and missionary groups, however, there was a clear underlying message that Christianity legitimated and empowered the empire; an empire not sustained by Christian convictions, morality and ethics was an illegitimate and doomed enterprise. There also appears to be a direct line of continuity between the rhetoric of religious global citizenship used by Rutherford Waddell in the 1880s and the language of secular imperial citizenship expressed in New Zealand schools during the 1920s. At the very least, Christian character and imperial citizenship became conflated over this period. There is also a strongly discursive element to be considered. A narrative emerged that was readily adopted, irrespective of secular or religious pedagogical context, and which seems to have reinforced a dualistic view of the world among colonial children.

Secondly, however, there were a number of potentially complicating factors that need to be considered. Race was one such factor. In a society like New Zealand, where two quite different pictures of childhood were emerging by 1900,[58] the notion of dualistic world views needs to be interrogated further. To what extent was this world view adopted by both colonised indigenous and colonial settler children? Further, to what extent did it entrench a dualism by which colonial settler children saw their indigenous counterparts as other and alien? Changing international influences constituted another factor that potentially muddied the waters of imperial influence. Children's pedagogy, in New Zealand, was increasingly influenced by Australian and American ideas and materials. Children heard missionary speakers and stories that were more often than not American in origin. From 1918 they were also taught about the League of Nations, encountered internationalist notions of peace and development, and considered the implications of Western paternalism for missionary churches in the non-West. From an international perspective this was in keeping with the rhetoric heard in other contemporary youth organisations like the Girl Guides.[59] Denominational loyalty was yet another potential complicating factor. Significant minority denominations existed around the fringes of Protestant Christianity, in particular the Salvation Army and Plymouth Brethren. These groups, because of their small size, tended to embrace an identity that was both national and international. This is not to say that they were not enmeshed or implicated in an imperial discourse. The Salvation Army, for instance, was a force for imperial 'regeneration' among Britain's juvenile population, and actively reinforced the 'White Australia' policy through assisted juvenile migration.[60] The Army's case does, however, provide a useful warning about too conveniently anticipating that all denominations, because they were white and 'British', exclusively socialised their children to be empire citizens.

Thirdly, analysis now needs to turn from the representations of Christianity and empire, in both pedagogy and literature, to the ways in which children actually responded to or interacted with such representations. This returns us to the vexed issue of children's historical agency as missionary supporters. On the one hand, this is a methodological problem in that sources are often 'scattered', 'sketchy', 'inconsistent' and, more often than not, produced by adults with adult agendas.[61] Previous discussion makes it very clear that the sources for the New Zealand context, as for other Western settler societies, are problematic. Children's voices were co-opted, redacted, manipulated and only occasionally heard in a semi-unfiltered fashion. At the same time, the written and pedagogical rhetoric around empire was almost exclusively an adult production.

As a counterpoint to this, Mary Jo Maynes' penetrating discussion of adults' personal narratives, as one entry point for considering childhood, indicates that adult dominance is by no means an impasse for excavating evidence of agency. In the New Zealand context, for example, the handwritten narratives of Anglican and Presbyterian missionary applicants contain substantial material about childhood, and the influences on their adult thinking of those earlier years. These narratives are as potentially informative for their rhetorical structures as they are for their content.[62]

On the other hand, the issue of agency is not just methodological. As Maynes indicates further, it is also a theoretical one – particularly if the focus is on individual actions, or if interest is centred on notions of marginalisation or powerlessness.[63] At this juncture, two of six questions posed for childhood history by Joseph Hawes and Ray Hiner may serve as a useful focus for further research apposite to the missionary context. They suggest that it is fundamentally important to address 'how children influenced adults and each other' and 'what institutions have been most important in defining children's lives and experiences'.[64] In particular Hawes and Hiner question the assumption that children's perceived powerlessness equated to a lack of influence, and they highlight the importance of understanding religious sites of influence and interaction. As this chapter has indicated, both questions are important for the New Zealand context as a hypothetically typical 'British' world society. A comparative or transnational approach, then, should elucidate further the extent to which such patterns were ubiquitous and similar within or across colonial societies.[65]

Over the period under study, secular pedagogy increasingly co-opted religious imagery and language to bolster notions of national and imperial citizenship. In turn, religious and missionary pedagogy co-opted imperial rhetoric to draw children into what might be called a form of Christian imperialism. The subtext, however, was never far below the surface. If settler children were being called in this period to an imperial allegiance then, even more so, they were also being called to give their allegiance to a 'greater imperium'. In the case of colonial New Zealand, it appears that they were constantly caught between the two.

CHAPTER 8

The Impact of Overseas Missions at Home

A FINAL AREA to consider is the extent to which the missionary activity promoted from and supported within colonial New Zealand had a significant impact on its point of origin. That this is a potent idea for further reflection is amply indicated in the discussion of children and missions in Chapter Seven. The 'reflex impact' of missions was an enduring theme across the Anglo-European movement, particularly at points when the efficacy or financial viability of overseas missionary endeavour came under scrutiny, both within churches and wider settler society. Contemporaries had a clear sense of the pervasiveness of missionary propaganda and its potential to influence knowledge and opinions. Quoting from the *London Quarterly Review* of 1856, for example, Susan Thorne notes that, in mid-nineteenth-century Britain, 'many a small tradesman or rustic knows more of African or Polynesian life than London journalists'.[1] In a similar vein, Jeffrey Cox notes that, for a majority of nineteenth-century British children, it was likely that 'the single largest source of information about what foreign people were like came from the foreign missionary societies of their respective denominations'.[2]

So it was in New Zealand. The colony's newspapers and denominational literature were constantly reporting missionary events, news and items over the full length of the period under review. By the 1930s missionary support and involvement was a firmly established part of the mental furniture and an accepted physical expression of Antipodean Protestant Christianity. As we have seen, New Zealanders were to be found in many parts of the world as missionaries. Their supporters across the denominational spectrum viewed this as a natural outcome and expression of Christian belief and practice. Missionaries and supporters together were simultaneously citizens of a newly emergent settler nation, of the British Empire and of the Kingdom of God. They had gone out to the world and the world had come to them.

At the same time, there was a vocal minority of detractors who criticised overseas missionary involvement. This was more than hinted at in Auckland's *Observer* newspaper in October 1897 in a column that questioned:

> *Is there no mission work at Home?*
>
> Every religion commands our respect and veneration, and yet, in view of the fact that additional young women in this city are preparing themselves for inland mission work in China and India, we feel ourselves justified in giving utterance to some kind of remonstrance. China and India are a long way off; the fruits of self-denying missionary labours in these distant lands are problematical. Is there not a wide and fruitful field for missionary labours in the slums of our own large towns?[3]

The newspaper criticised such missionary activity for financial and resource reasons, in that the New Zealand church was perceived to be losing valuable revenue and personnel. The supposed heroism of overseas involvement was contrasted with the perceived less heroic but eminently noble humanitarian work still to be done at home. It questioned the possibility or worth of conversion of the so-called 'heathen' on both cultural and theological grounds. There was also a note of male criticism. Men apparently understood the true nature of urban poverty in the colony and were more likely to give money, because the alleviation of urban poverty was a 'noble and useful work, far exceeding in profit and fruitfulness any proselytizing labours, wherever carried on'. The *Observer* article encapsulated the main objections that were sporadically thrown at overseas missionary involvement in the period up to 1939. Critics variously asserted that overseas missions neglected domestic priorities, wasted limited money and resources, and were doomed to failure. Over subsequent decades, missionary apologists rebutted these arguments as well as answering the popular assertion by the 1920s that all religions had equal merit, or that all religions would eventually evolve into Christianity.[4]

Missionary enthusiasts called such thinking short-sighted, arguing more particularly that overseas missions should have what they called a positive reflex impact on local congregational life. Others considered such objections to be 'minor criticisms' that more significantly obscured 'the fact that the poverty of our own spiritual life is the real cause of our belittling of [missionary] work'.[5] In their opinion, the objectors' general anonymity meant either that they were small in number or that they were unwilling to openly challenge prevailing modes of thought. Appealing to the notion of 'reflex impact' was a recurring refrain in the defence of mission, and it is to this idea that my final chapter now turns. In it I evaluate representative ways in which mission impacted on Protestant Christianity in New Zealand, taking the 1910 Edinburgh World Missionary Conference and its aftermath as a specific case study.

Defining and measuring the reflex impact of overseas missions

The notion that overseas missionary activity and support could benefit churches and churchgoers at home was communicated at all levels, from the parish upwards. In 1928 Bishop Walter Averill told the Auckland Anglican Diocesan Synod that a parish's missionary interest was a 'sure indication' of its spiritual life, and that the 'attitude of the Vicar to Missions and his zeal for the cause which Christ committed to His Church' was an important determinant.[6] At an even higher level, a gathering of Australasian Anglican bishops and clergy were reminded in 1906 that 'active participation in missionary effort always proves the most effective method for securing the spiritual uplifting of a diocese or a parish and the betterment of its material concerns'. Bishop Selwyn and the Revd Samuel Marsden before him were offered as church leaders who exemplified how domestic and overseas missions could go hand in hand, and benefit the church both in the short and longer term.[7]

The notion of overseas missions having reflexive value was one to be found across places, creeds and time, and finds a resonance in various other sub-fields of historical enquiry. Antoinette Burton, for example, considers the impact on Britain of what she calls the 'reverse flow' of liberal political ideas from the settler colonies in the late nineteenth century. Likewise, Catherine Hall and Sonya Rose note the long mutual relationship between 'British state formation and empire building' that stretched back to the 'premodern period'.[8] For the missionary context, this was certainly not the only motivational message, but it was commonly heard in the early twentieth century and was simply assumed by many people. As a result, many statements made in its defence were frustratingly thin on detail. Typically, such statements declared baldly that 'foreign missionary work has brought to the Church in return a boundless blessing'. Conversely, 'to stop all this [missionary] work for the world would bring upon the Church paralysis and death'.[9] Where the notion was elaborated on, it was often personalised in terms of a blessing or reward.[10] As one New Zealand Baptist writer suggested, 'God has graciously arranged it that we never try to do good to others without getting good to our own hearts; and although the good should be done without any regard to the recompense that will reward it, we may fairly find encouragement in the fact that in seeking the welfare of others we are benefited ourselves.'[11] Alternatively, public rhetoric often predicated the quality of life of the home churches on the degree to which they extended their generosity and aid overseas. Such were the sentiments paraded, at the first American Catholic Congress held in 1909, for example, where one speaker linked evangelistic success at home to the extent of engagement abroad. 'Every parish,' he declared, should have a 'mother's love' for clergy and missionaries 'striving for Christ in the wilderness beyond the frontiers'.[12]

Such rhetoric sat comfortably in an era in which the world was conceived of in terms of discrete geographical and religious spheres. It was also perhaps a convenient marketing ploy to counter those who argued for 'home missions' first, and by which to bolster finances. Some of this reasoning was certainly implicit in the findings of Commission VI on 'The Home Base' at the 1910 World Missionary Conference in Edinburgh. Yet even this commission took as read the wider benefits accruing to the home base: '[T]he reflex influence of foreign missions on the home Church is so marked and far-reaching, that an examination of the nature and extent of that influence must be full of encouragement to those who believe in that work, and must go far to remove the difficulties of those who think that the development of the work abroad must be prejudicial to that which so urgently needs to be done at home.'[13] While these sentiments were marked by their historical context, this notion still finds a resonance in contemporary thinking. Scottish missiologist Kenneth Ross, for instance, argues that vigorous non-Western Christianity, previously viewed by the West as peripheral and dependent, may yet have a key role in reflexively rejuvenating Western Christianity.[14]

It is difficult to definitively assess the reflex impact of mission on domestic church life, although examples from the international literature certainly indicate some possibilities. For North America, the focus has been on the 'social and cultural role' of missionaries – with respect to such things as international policy and diplomacy, popular culture and domestic forms of religion – and on the formation of both public perceptions and academic disciplines.[15] In the British context, we have already noted the observation that children's missionary contact and involvement, as supporters and consumers, most probably helped to shape or entrench cultural or racial attitudes.[16] There are further relevant examples. Alison Twells argues that 'civilising mission', both at home and abroad, was an important influence on the formation of middle-class identity and culture in mid-nineteenth-century England.[17] Likewise, Esther Breitenbach focuses on how missionary support contributed to later nineteenth-century Scottish perceptions of empire and colonised peoples, and notions of Scottish civic identity. It was one of many interwoven 'threads', she argues, that helped to form the 'meaning of empire for Scots at home, how they understood it, and how it was shaped in their imaginings'.[18] Susan Thorne's work on the impact of mission on Victorian-era Protestant religion further indicates the dynamic nature of this reflex impact – where, for example, the ability of English missionaries and organisations to influence national politics waned markedly through the nineteenth century, and missionary support fed the tensions that existed at local and regional levels between working and middle-class English Congregationalists.[19] Closer to home, Stuart Piggin hypothesises at least 12 'marks' of mission reflex impact in the Australian setting. These range from the missionary contributions to Australian spirituality after experiencing revival in mission contexts to the impact on scholarship and the emergence of women's roles in Australian public life.[20] In sum, an uneven and often impressionistic mix of both quantitative and qualitative measures again highlights the difficulties involved in assessing the domestic impact of the missionary endeavour. Contexts of time and place are certainly important to note.

By the early twentieth century there was a broad consensus among Anglo-American and European contemporaries over the ways in which churches might be benefited through missionary enthusiasm and involvement. Edinburgh's Commission VI report on the home base of missions is a representative document, bringing together many of the disparate arguments to be found elsewhere. It was compiled from the written responses of a broad cross-section of Anglo-American and European church and missionary leaders, among whom there was a high degree of independently stated agreement. This enabled the commission to note that the 'similarity of the replies in stating that only good and not evil has come to the Church from its labours of love and sacrifice is most striking'.[21] Common responses fell broadly into six categories: educational value; the creation of greater public 'sympathy' or concern; ecclesial unity; increased generosity; greater evangelistic energy and enthusiasm; and a more general 'strengthening and deepening of the faith of the Church'.[22]

Again, these categories were by their nature impressionistic and are extremely difficult to measure. They were the perceptions of mostly male leaders immersed in daily parish life as much as they were the observations of missionary leaders and participants. In many cases, they were more idealistic than realistic. That missionary involvement should result in such things as increased general giving and evangelistic zeal did make logical sense, but whether or not it produced these benefits in reality remains a moot and indeterminate point.

Measuring reflex impact in the New Zealand context

In New Zealand most of these ideas were echoed two decades later by the Revd William Mawson, Presbyterian Foreign Missions Committee secretary and an ex-South China missionary. Speaking at the General Assembly of 1930, Mawson noted the broad impact of missionary involvement on a more general 'spirit of giving', broadened vision and interests, an enriched sense of denominational history, the quality of church leadership, and the harnessed energies of youth. He suggested that 'through it all there has been the quickening of faith, the stirring of compassion, the call to earnest prayer, the incentive to high endeavour, which has helped to bring forth the best from our people in the life and work of the Church. I believe that we have been a greater Church, and have done a greater work in New Zealand, because of our efforts to send the Gospel abroad.'[23]

Three categories of reflex impact are easier to assess in an empirical or observable sense. Two derive from Commission VI findings – 'educational value' and greater 'church unity' – while the third, women's public participation in religious life, went beyond the concerns of Edinburgh. In the first instance, missionary involvement appears to have gone hand in hand with a broadening of church-based 'education' across boundaries of both age and gender. The Commission VI report noted the international proliferation of missionary literature and the 'rapid development of organised missionary study'.[24] The same observations were true for New Zealand in the early 1900s, especially with respect to periodicals, books and mission study. All denominations, parishes and congregations had their periodicals, newspapers, supplements and newsletters. Missionary content was a regular feature of such publications. Existing subscription and circulation figures suggest that readership was widespread. For example, among Baptists nearly half of the children or young people and up to a third of all adults were subscribing to periodical literature with substantial missionary content by 1915.[25] If any single magazine was read by at least a household full of people, then such publications must have reached a reasonably wide audience and been partially influential in providing information and in shaping attitudes. These periodicals, as we have seen, were especially important for children's and young people's engagement with missions over a long period from the early twentieth century.[26]

People were also well informed through books. While missionary books were widely advertised, sold and given as prizes, the growing trend was towards the creation of missionary libraries and the establishment of denominational publishing houses. The Presbyterian FMC, for example, administered a lending library that included equal numbers of biographies, regional studies, books on missionary history and theology, and children's titles. Individual churches and Sunday schools also had their own libraries. As the Church's missionary work matured, the FMC also began publishing its own titles for denominational consumption. In 1925 a Presbyterian Bookroom was established, both as a publishing venture and a retail outlet, and quickly reported wide interest and sales.[27] By the 1940s it was publishing missionary titles and through these a number of missionaries became household names. It is difficult to determine the readership and sales of such books. The evidence from many missionary applicants indicated that they read a wide range of devotional, theological and missionary books, both bought and borrowed. There were also many smaller private collections of missionary literature. Taken altogether, these literary sources must have had an abiding influence on successive generations of readers, for whom private reading itself was an important recreational and educational activity in the pre-radio age. Formal missionary study also grew in popularity by the second decade of the 1900s, spurred on in part by the Edinburgh conference. This is examined in more detail below.

In the second instance, missionary interest and involvement also helped to foster a greater sense of 'church unity'. An early British precedent was set for this in the formation of the LMS as an initially ecumenical missionary organisation.[28] A range of examples illustrate how this was worked out in New Zealand, at both the denominational and trans-denominational levels. At the denominational level it may be more helpful to use the term identity rather than unity, in that missionary activity helped to form a sense of who people were as Anglicans, Methodists, Presbyterians, and so on. As I have shown in previous chapters, denominational identity gave people at least one further point around which to rally. Furthermore, this tended to work itself out at both the national and regional levels. For Anglicans, regional identity was partially mediated through particularised missionary links. Auckland Anglicans identified with the Melanesian Mission in the Solomon Islands, largely as a result of the historical connections with Bishop Selwyn in the early to mid-nineteenth century. For at least a century, the Melanesian Mission was the missionary focus in official diocesan literature and the focus of the annual Diocesan Synod missionary meetings. Earlier discussion has indicated that specific geographic fields of operation also contributed to the national identity of other Protestant denominations.

Missionary involvement also served to bring various degrees of cohesion to small, disparate denominations otherwise separated by a mixture of ecclesiology and attenuated geography. This was perhaps most significant for New Zealand Baptist and Open Brethren churches. While Baptist union, in 1882, was probably the necessary precursor to the formation of the NZBMS in 1886, ongoing missionary projects provided some of the glue that held this fragile union together over successive decades.[29] Likewise, increased missionary participation from the late 1890s gradually propelled individual Brethren assemblies to seek ways of co-operating over finances and information. As a result, two Brethren institutions emerged in 1899 that are still active today and that aided significantly in the creation of a sense of national Brethren identity: the *Treasury* magazine and the Missionary Funds Service (later to be renamed Missionary Funds (NZ) Incorporated, and then Missionary Services New Zealand).[30]

At the trans-denominational level, missionary involvement contributed to an evolving ecumenism. As in Australia, this ecumenism tended to be more organic than structural, and ultimately is best understood in reference to such movements as evangelicalism or revivalism.[31] Churches were energised by the mutually sustaining combination of missionary interest and personal activism explicit in Christian Endeavour, the various young people's Bible Class Unions, the Student Volunteer Movement, and both the Student Christian Movement and later the Crusader movement and Evangelical Unions. Student missionary conferences in 1896 and 1903 provided a model for trans-denominational engagement, and many of the participants became significant missionary and church leaders. In turn, these two conferences prefigured the 1926 National Missionary Conference and the subsequent formation of the National Missionary Council. This was the first nationally cooperative mission-oriented venture with wide denominational and non-denominational support and representation. The council also provided churches with a collective lobbying voice in both the parliament and the media, especially in the new age of radio, and was foundational for the later ecumenical movement. In 1945 the council merged with the National Council of Churches, formed in 1941, and was instrumental in both the development of post-World War II interchurch aid and New Zealand's links with the international ecumenical movement.[32]

In the third instance, mission also appears to have had a profound reflex impact on the involvement of Protestant women. This is not to ignore masculine religiosity. Rather, it is a response to a body of scholarship that now highlights the place of women in the public religious life of New Zealand.[33] As we have seen, increased missionary support from the late nineteenth century in New Zealand coincided with the expansion of vocational opportunities for single women in the international missionary movement and, on the domestic front, for women's ministry through the various deaconess movements.[34] It also coincided with the heightened participation of women in domestic political campaigns revolving around prohibition and women's suffrage. Rather than ask to what extent one affected the other, it is perhaps more apposite to note the interwoven nature of women's involvement in both public politics and religion, and to appreciate the great energy that resulted. These developments certainly did not lead automatically to greater religious power-sharing between the genders; such changes did not take place until at least the 1920s.[35] It is increasingly clear, however, that although women were largely excluded from podium, pulpit and political power, they were involved in broad areas of church life. Missionary support was both a feature of such involvement and a significant vehicle for wider women's influence, and indeed for the slow progression towards greater equality.

At an extremely conservative estimate, there were at least 10,000 New Zealand Protestant women active in missionary support by the 1920s and 1930s.[36] Each denomination had its own structures through which they were actively involved. Regional women's missionary unions or auxiliaries were gradually reshaped into well-run national organisations for Baptists (BWMU 1903), Presbyterians (PWMU 1905) and Methodists (MWMU 1915). Anglican women were prominently involved in the running of diocesan and parochial Gleaners' Unions, and missionary support was also a part of the more broadly based Mother's Union, formed in 1886.

The PWMU provides a good example of how women's missionary involvement was worked out. Growth in membership and regional branches paralleled wider growth in the Presbyterian Church by the mid-1920s.[37] It is difficult to establish the proportion of women who were active as supporters and members. Financial statistics indicate that the PWMU was generating over 20 per cent of Presbyterian missionary income by the 1920s, and possibly more women than men left legacies and bequests for mission projects.[38] The PWMU steadily increased its range of activities and created administrative structures to guarantee both growth and quality. By 1915 this range of activities and responsibilities was quite staggering: a bi-monthly magazine, missionary correspondence, international networking, mission study circles, fundraising, the Māori Missions' Birthday League and the Scattered Members' League, the Presbyterian Women's Training Institute, the Girls' Auxiliary, Busy Bees, and 'Oriental Depots' selling overseas goods.[39] In 1911 the first paid travelling secretary was employed to increase, encourage and strengthen branches, with noticeable membership growth occurring over the following two decades.[40] Longer term, the PWMU proved to be a foundational plank of one of the Presbyterian Church's most important and enduring institutions, the Association of Presbyterian Women.[41]

This wide influence of women is an important topic which is yet to be more fully written about and explained. Women's influence through public religious involvement was foundationally important in the New

Zealand context with respect to children's religiosity, international links, literary outputs, enduring denominational narratives and mythologies, and denominational financial schemes, among other things. It was also inevitable that women's increased participation, as missionaries or deaconesses, would lead eventually to ordination and eldership. As this book's final act, then, I focus further on Presbyterian women's engagement with the 1910 Edinburgh conference and its legacy, in an attempt to understand in more detail the ways in which mission impacted on church life and participation in New Zealand.

Case Study: Edinburgh 1910, Presbyterian women and global awareness

Brian Stanley rightly argues in broad fashion that the role of women in mission was 'one of the least obvious yet conceivably most far-reaching consequences' of the Edinburgh conference, which made a valuable contribution to the provision of new opportunities for women's missionary study and training.[42] It stands to reason that this event would have had a discernible reflexive imprint on the churches and mission societies of the young dominion. This assumption is predicated on the extent to which the Edinburgh conference marked the high point of Euro-American missions, and the degree to which such non-metropole British societies as New Zealand were enmeshed in this movement.

(a) New Zealand involvement

The conference was well advertised among churches and was perhaps anticipated by some more than others. Among evangelical Anglicans it was promoted as the possible catalyst for 'an increase of devoted thoroughness at Home and a more perfect service in the mission field'. Presbyterians, by contrast, referred to it as an 'ecumenical missionary conference'.[43] In the official account of its proceedings, W.H. Gairdner waxed lyrical about the conference's worldwide constituency represented by the 'English-speaking delegations'. Here were 'delegates from the United States of America, from Great Britain and Ireland, and from "All the Britains" across the sea – Canada, Australia, New Zealand, South Africa'.[44] Gairdner was much too generous. Brian Stanley estimates more soberly that there were 27 representatives from South Africa, the Australian states and New Zealand.[45] New

Zealand's share of this was very small: a handful of Australian or British-based personnel deputised on behalf of Anglicans and Methodists, one Anglican missionary, two Presbyterian ministers and a lay Baptist. This was due as much to the limits set on the criteria for representation as to factors of distance. All were male.

At least three other people not named in the list of formal delegates sat through the conference's parallel programme in the Synod Hall: Mrs Kaye and Mrs MacKenzie from Christchurch, and a Miss Morris from Gisborne.[46] Mrs MacKenzie accompanied her ordained husband, who was an official Presbyterian delegate; they represented the PWMU unofficially, as the PWMU did not meet the criteria set for annual income or missionary representation. This certainly did not dilute the enthusiasm of these three women; they lapped up what was presented through plenary addresses and discussions. Mrs Kaye also attended the discussion session for the Commission VI report on 'The Home Base of Missions'. This was perhaps the aspect of the conference that left its most indelible mark on these delegates and those with whom they worked. In turn, they reported back through the PWMU's monthly magazine *Harvest Field* and in a published booklet, copies of which are no longer extant.[47]

In the conference's wake, denominational newspapers and mission societies reported at varying lengths. These reports tended to paraphrase conference findings or capture some kind of essence, rather than dwell exhaustively on the details. The one exception was Mrs Kaye, who tried to cover both the depth and breadth of conference proceedings in her reports back to the PWMU. The issues of 'unity' and 'liberality' appears to have resonated most strongly with many New Zealand commentators. However, it is very difficult to identify concrete outcomes or strategies derived from the conference in the ongoing missionary thinking of the various denominations. The impression given is that, in a very broad fashion, the Edinburgh conference served to feed into and underpin already existing Protestant assumptions, structures, strategies and energies.

(b) The PWMU and Edinburgh 1910

The responses of the Presbyterian women sitting through the sessions in the Synod Hall indicate that this was not the whole story, however. As with its sister organisations worldwide, the PWMU's brief was all-encompassing. Members were reminded prior to the conference that they worked 'not only for our own people, not only for the Church, not only for the heathen, but for Christ'.[48] The PWMU was a deeply spiritual or devotional movement whose purview encompassed the notion of 'mission' in a broad sense. Mrs Kaye drew quite deliberate attention to a comment from a report on Commission I to the Synod Hall attendees, that 'the crucial factor in the missionary enterprise was the spiritual condition of the Home Church'. This fundamental belief that mission began at home helps to explain why the reports on Commission VI in particular struck such a chord with both the PWMU delegates and their constituency. In a later reflection on the conference's outcomes, Mrs MacKenzie argued that 'a real live church, filled with missionary zeal, and with devotion to Jesus Christ assuredly means success in the work abroad'. In her view, as 'co-workers with God', women's missionary organisations were consequently well-placed to advance the home base through spiritual devotion, prayer, systematic giving, missionary recruitment and education.[49]

Other members proceeded to pick up this focus on education. One writer outlined a quasi-programmatic and pedagogical framework that encompassed both the PWMU and the wider life of the Presbyterian Church.[50] Education was critical both for prospective women missionaries, because of who they would influence, and for children and adults at home. The goal was to produce 'intelligently interested' church members. For this to happen more effectively, at least three things were required: the development of curricula with systematic missionary lessons for children and young people; the publication and distribution of good literature; and the appointment of a full-time organising secretary for the PWMU. All three aims were realised within a few years.

(c) The PWMU, mission study and education

Mission study emerged as one of the more explicit outcomes of this debate in the wake of Edinburgh. One PWMU member, reflecting further, argued that if its members were to be better educated about missions, then this would 'not come of itself, but must be created by systematic, organized, and persistent effort; whatever else we do this must not be left undone'.[51] Mission study was not new to the PWMU or to the wider church. Various denominational and non-denominational Protestant groups had sporadically adopted formal, group-based mission study techniques since at least 1902. The Edinburgh conference gave a sense of urgency to the further extension of the concept. PWMU members were encouraged to facilitate and promote 'the regular systematic study of missions amongst all classes of Students and among the *rank and file* [original emphasis] of church members', and urged their own denomination to develop trans-denominational links to foster this as a broader study movement.[52] This theme was picked up many times over the next couple of years. A Mrs Baird suggested that such systematic study helped to 'fill the mind with ideas'. There was a cycle, she thought, wherein 'knowledge awakens thought, thought passes into feeling, and feeling leads to active endeavour'. Mrs MacKenzie understood such study to have communal dimensions. She argued that knowledge would 'stimulate their interest, and it would not be long before this increased interest would spread to others'.[53]

A strategy was unveiled through successive issues of the *Harvest Field*. Mission study circles were promoted as providing a mix of intellectual challenge, personal engagement and uplift, and a springboard for action. This was, as Nancy Hardesty suggests for the North American context, the 'scientific study of missions',[54] but packaged in a way that might appeal to a broad spectrum of participants and replicated across the English-speaking world. According to one set of guidelines, up to 12 women meeting fortnightly could engage with a set text, consider a range of questions, present short talks, study maps and pictures, and encompass the whole experience with prayer.[55] Further guidelines personalised this process by inviting readers into an imagined study circle meeting, an exercise clearly designed to allay potential members' fears. As things became more organised, leaders received or acquired prepared resources. Columns with topical information irregularly appeared in the *Harvest Field*, as did a set of guidelines for a study booklet titled *The Church Afield*, produced by the Presbyterian FMC in 1913.[56] Throughout 1914, an extensive set of study outlines were published in the *Harvest Field* to accompany a reading of John Mott's *The Decisive Hour of Christian Missions*. The precedent for this type of approach had already been set. For example, a study schedule for Canadian Presbyterian young women was based on Surendra Kumar Datta's *The Desire of India*, published by the CMS in 1908.[57] Increasingly, however, the studies were centred on locally published literature that was often, but not exclusively, focused on Presbyterian mission 'fields'.

(d) Edinburgh, Presbyterian women and the issues

This was the situation, then, in the half decade or so following the Edinburgh conference. The rhetoric was strident and progressive, anticipating a missionary 'forward movement' among the dominion's Presbyterians if not the wider Protestant community. As Nancy Hardesty notes more generally, this was a period in which 'progress reigned; the millennium was at hand', when through the agency of Christian women '[t]he whole world could be made homelike'.[58] How did this sense of optimism work itself out when the New Zealand case is looked at more closely? Three non-exclusive questions may help to map the way ahead.

First, to what extent was the push for mission study an enduring, widespread or influential outcome of Edinburgh? For the specific 'mission study circle' concept, the evidence is not conclusive. By 1916 there were barely 20 such circles operating among 226 PWMU branches. A decade on there were only 'two or three [Presbyterian] study circles' nationwide; 30 years on the author of the PWMU jubilee history still felt compelled to write that 'more and more women are realizing the necessity for definite study of missionary work'.[59] Mission study required constant attention and publicity.

Formal groups were only one of several ways in which mission study took place. It also occurred in the regular meetings of the PWMU, as well as those of the Presbyterian Laymen's Missionary Movement, in Sunday Schools and Bible classes, and in many regular gatherings of clergy. The concept was applied across the denomination under the influence of the PWMU. The FMC, partly on the PWMU's behalf, regularly ordered and distributed large numbers of set texts, copies of its annual reports and other study material. There were also sporadic attempts to cross denominational boundaries. An interdenominational 'Mission Study Council', formed in Christchurch in 1912, appears to have engaged the energies of Presbyterian women and men for some years.[60] The *Harvest Field* continued to carry substantial articles and essays and to publicise denominational missionary news. By 1930 this material was more strictly organised as an annual set 'syllabus' of topics.[61] PWMU branches built up regional missionary libraries and tapped into the FMC's larger library. Women also contributed to a growing body of locally written and published Presbyterian missionary literature. In sum, the PWMU promoted intelligent missionary engagement through the wider organs of the Church, as well as through its own channels. All the activities outlined here continued to be enduring features of Presbyterian life in New Zealand until at least the 1960s.

The focus on literature prompts a second question: to what extent was this Presbyterian literary output an indicator of enlightened global awareness, or simply prejudice wrapped up in respectable scientific dust jackets? This question is apposite when set against two wider contextual observations. The first is Prochaska's observation cited in the previous chapter, that the 'power of the missionary societies to form racial and cultural attitudes in the young' was their 'most enduring legacy'.[62] Was this also the case for women's groups like the PWMU? The second observation is that, in the same period, New Zealand state school curricula were underscored by a prevailing British imperialist discourse.[63] From the 1930s until at least the 1960s, an American-influenced social studies syllabus attempted to engage students with broader concepts of democratic citizenship, but with implicit notions of European cultural superiority.[64] Thus it is questionable as to what extent PWMU materials and ideas, promoted through mission study, were substantively different from the wider cultural and educational milieu.

One way to assess this is to look at the broad spread of topics, themes and resources offered through PWMU study and reading material, and to ask whether study and reading may have helped to form a significant core of people with a relatively nuanced global understanding. The educative element of such material cannot be fully grasped in hindsight. There is no direct way of knowing how this material made an impact – a point observed for other contexts such as late nineteenth-century working-class England, where 'the fact that they consumed missionary material does not in itself reveal the consequences of their so doing'.[65] Nevertheless, a wide array of textual and illustrative material, presented on a regular basis, did introduce the wider world to a broad spectrum of Presbyterian women. In an age that predated in-home entertainment and large-scale international tourism, this must have been a significant means by which the world outside was apprehended and viewed.

However broad this education might have been, it was tempered by other tendencies evident in the extant literature. A *Harvest Field* article from 1913 captured prevailing sentiments in its conception of non-Christian religions as 'inadequate', because they could 'provide no cure, no remedy for the sin-stained soul'. Conversely, Christianity was 'perfect', entirely adequate to remedy sin, and thus completely 'universal' in its application.[66] Women's literature and study material tended to reinforce rather than subvert prevailing Western stereotypes of non-Western peoples and religions. One of the enduring theological motifs was that non-Christian religions were degraded, inhabiting spiritually barren geographical spaces. Another motif focused on the great need of the non-Western world, and a third reflected Joan Brumberg's observation, for the American context, that non-Western women were constantly portrayed as intellectually deprived, domestically oppressed and sexually degraded.[67] Up to the 1950s such themes could be understood as the product of a predominantly monocultural environment, wherein indigenous Māori were often still missionary subjects and in which Christianity was still the main religious influence. For New Zealand, this situation began to change from the 1960s onwards with the growth of Pacific and later Asian immigration and the increasing disengagement of its population from organised Christianity.

As we have seen, applying categorical racial discourses to religious and missionary rhetoric is a fraught process. By the 1920s, in particular, race was becoming much more 'plastic' in its definition and application. Again, this was reflected in the New Zealand context. There were noticeable attitudinal shifts taking place in PWMU literature, with persistent stereotypes often juxtaposed with newer sentiments. As early as 1930 this was indicated by the inclusion of an Australian essay in the *Harvest Field* on the celebrated Ghanaian Christian leader and educationalist James Kwegyir Aggrey, titled 'Black without blemish'. Aggrey was directly quoted in this essay, without editorial comment:

> I am glad I am black. God knew his business when He made me so, and He wants to do something through me. The real African idea of purity, which you find in their sacrifices, for instance, is that the colour should be there in its purity: black 'without blemish' and white 'without blemish!' ... You white folks ... may bring your gold, your great banks, your sanitation, and other marvellous achievements to the Manger, but that will not be enough. Let the Chinese and the Japanese and the Indians bring their incense of ceremony, but that will not be enough. We black people must step in with our myrrh of childlike faith ... If you take our childlikeness, our love for God, our belief in humanity, our belief in God, and our love for you, whether you hate us or not, then the gifts will be complete – the gold, the frankincense and the myrrh.[68]

Obvious stereotypes abounded in both this quote and the essay in which these words were embedded. Yet it is the editorial intent that should be noted. A wind shift in thinking, perhaps reflecting the 1928 Jerusalem conference more than Edinburgh, was beginning to be felt among the Presbyterian women of New Zealand. By the late 1940s, they were reading about the lives of both Western and non-Western Christians – people like Aggrey and the Indian medical doctor Hilda Lazarus at the 'ecumenical' Vellore Christian Medical College. Mission was as much about the 'healing of the nations' as it was about 'the spread of the Gospel'.[69] Gradually, the textual messages and the illustrations changed. By the early 1960s artwork and photographs in the *Harvest Field* carried the message that Christianity was not always expressed or conveyed in purely Western terms. It was becoming more truly global with respect to how New Zealand women read about and understood their faith.

The final question to be asked, then, is: to what extent was this missionary focus really a desire for global awareness and engagement, or more an expression of entrenched denominationalism? As I have argued throughout this book, settler Protestant Christianity was, in many ways, a denominational religion. It had been so since the mid- to late nineteenth century. Denominations became markers of distinctive identity and served as channels for institutionalised piety. Certainly, a large amount of the material that appeared in PWMU literature and study material up to the 1950s related to the Presbyterian Church's four main historical mission fields: New Zealand Māori, the New Hebrides, southern China and northern India. Denominational identity was very much invested in these 'fields' and their personnel. While other groups and denominations were not unimportant, being proudly 'Presbyterian' deliberately included these distinctive connections as significant identity markers.

There seems to be a certain amount of truth to the notion that PWMU energy and activity reflected entrenched denominationalism rather than a genuine desire to be globally engaged. At the same time, two final observations add some balance. The first picks up a point already noted in Chapter Two: that from their inception, women's groups like the PWMU sought to be broadly linked with sister groups in other denominations and overseas. Early PWMU links were forged and maintained with Protestant and Reformed women's groups in Australia, Britain, Canada and the United States of America. Typically, this was done through an international or corresponding secretary, who sought to keep the PWMU linked to 'this "girdle round the earth" of missionary service'.[70] The ideal was international sisterhood which, in theory, extended to those sisters in the mission fields. Hierarchies of race and gender certainly existed within such a construction of sisterhood. Furthermore, it is questionable how far women's missionary rhetoric was aimed at the task of mission, or to what extent it was about creating emotional communities of women in the home churches.[71] The reality was probably somewhere in between. What resulted was a sense of connection between New Zealand women at home, their missionaries overseas and the people with whom they worked. These connections naturally led to interest in other ways of life, other issues, problems and solutions.

The second observation is that being Presbyterian, and therefore engaging with specifically Presbyterian overseas interests, did not negate the genuine ways in which Presbyterian women became globally connected within these denominational parameters. The rhetoric and discourses may have changed from 1910 onwards, and women may have been guilty of supporting relational hierarchies erected between themselves and their 'missionary subjects'. Yet the tone of these writings, both public and private, indicates a genuine sense of concern and compassion for others immediately beyond their own world. Over the *longue durée* of the twentieth century, the PWMU itself changed. In 1963 it was formally reconstituted as the Association of Presbyterian Women (APW), just one year before the first women were ordained into the church as ministers.[72] Mission now became just one of a number of priorities for the APW and was gradually redefined much more broadly. Yet, as the pages of the *Harvest Field* attest, global linkages and partnerships remained vital elements of the APW's ongoing life. In 1994, some 30 years on, the APW annual conference received the following message from Idau Nafuki of the Presbyterian Church in Vanuatu:

> I bring warm Christian greetings from the PWMU Annual Conference, National Executive and members in Vanuatu. May I take this chance to thank you for your love, concerns and prayers. Thank you for your help which you give in so many ways. We have nothing to give you in return, but we assure you, our Presbyterian sisters, that we pray for you because we all have a common aim to serve the Lord and make his love known throughout the world … It is good to have one common aim and we are asking you to pray together for us earnestly to God our Father, to raise up among us women of strong character and faith to help extend God's mission in our country.[73]

Conclusion

When discussing the reflex impact of missions on the home Church there are some useful parallels in thinking about the impact of the British Empire on the so-called British metropole. In previewing the notion of the 'empire at home', Hall and Rose talk about its 'taken-for-granted' character for British people, its 'unconscious acceptance', and its 'undoubtedly uneven' impact. It was variously hidden and 'highly visible', and it certainly had an impact, 'fatal or not'. But this was not the point. Whatever its profile or however people thought at particular times, argue Hall and Rose, 'their everyday lives were infused with an imperial presence'. Thus the important question to ponder is: how was empire lived across everyday practices? And therefore to what extent was it simply assumed, existing as a 'part of the given world that had made [British people] who they were'[74]?

These references to empire, and the notion of an underlying and all-suffusing influence, could be translated directly across to the missionary phenomenon among New Zealand Protestants considered here. In many Protestant churches and denominations, up to the 1980s at least, overseas missionary involvement was seen as normative and essential. The period prior to 1939 was the crucible within which this mindset had developed. It became axiomatic that an outward focus on the world beyond the shores of Aotearoa would contribute to the domestic life and quality of New Zealand's churches and people. In this chapter I have argued that, while difficult to measure, there are a number of indications that this claim for the reflex impact of missions was justified. It is most notably evident with respect to education, evolving denominational identity, a developing, 'organic' ecumenism and women's participation and influence in public religion. This is a pertinent reminder that it is perilous to dissect an entity like 'the Church' or 'Christianity' into component parts, rather than to seek a cohesive view of those parts. Missionary endeavours, for example, have often been left out of accounts of 'Church' or 'Christian' history, or have been seen as peripheral to narratives focused on parish, clergy and church structures. It is indeed true that missionaries were often seen as 'little detachments of maniacs', and that not everyone agreed that churches should be so taken up with missionary projects and finances. Yet this chapter indicates that such activity needs to be narrated and understood for its own sake, and for the ways in which it was interwoven with domestic church polity and life. In Hall and Rose's terms, mission was lived out across the 'everyday practices' of significant numbers of New Zealanders, and was 'a part of the given world', physical and mental, that they inhabited.

Reflex impact is also a concept that deserves renewed consideration in the light of the huge global shifts that are taking place within Christianity. Idau Nafuki's appeal to the Presbyterian women of Aotearoa New Zealand in 1994 is an interesting note on which to conclude this chapter. Here, 84 years after the Edinburgh conference, the rhetoric was redirected to the so-called 'home base' by those who were originally 'missionary subjects' in earlier years. Here were the fruits of a century or more of Presbyterian women's global engagement, for all the wrong and right reasons. How much was the Edinburgh conference the cause of this? Directly, of course, it is difficult to say. Indirectly, however, Edinburgh fed into, nurtured and gave further significant impetus to women's deliberate and thoughtful global engagement through missions. It is the nature of Christianity, of cultures and of history that this impetus did not atrophy, but mutated along the way. And so it will continue.

CHAPTER 9

The Question of Significance

THE PATTERNS OF MISSIONARY involvement, support and commitment established among the Protestant churches of colonial New Zealand up to 1939 represented both the foundation for further engagement and the climax of a particular way of thinking about the wider world beyond the shores of Aotearoa. It remains, then, to conclude by considering both the longer-term trajectory and the wider significance of this early period of engagement. I have argued throughout this book that the missionary phenomenon, as it was expressed by and among New Zealand's Protestants in the formative decades up to 1939, was significant for both historical and historiographical reasons. Here, by way of conclusion, the issue of significance is laid out more broadly with respect to the historical patterns of mission context and New Zealand religion, and to the historiographical issues intrinsic to settler religion and missions.

In 1929 the Presbyterian Foreign Missions Committee once again recruited the services of the now-retired Revd Rutherford Waddell to write an article for the dominion's Presbyterians on the centrality of overseas missions in church life.[1] Waddell had earned a reputation as a missionary enthusiast, among other things, while serving as minister at St Andrew's Dunedin between 1879 and 1919, and had pioneered the 'own missionary' scheme whereby Presbyterian congregations adopted and fully supported individual missionaries. By 1929 the economic depression that would plague denominational missionary finances throughout the 1930s was just beginning to bite. Against this background, his commission was to signal once again the importance of supporting missions by emphasising the principles that defined the Church's missionary character. Waddell took up the challenge, albeit with his characteristic reticence to be thought of as an expert. The resulting article was a state-of-the-nation address on how missions ought to be viewed, and provides a useful reflection of how many settler Protestants had come to think by the 1920s and 1930s.

In Waddell's mind the primary motive for missions was theological, irrespective of other contextual or pragmatic considerations. The missionary imperative was centrally located in the words of the risen Christ, who 'regarded [missions] as the primary and pressing business of His future Church', and was intimately linked with the coming of the Holy Spirit. In other words, the so-called Great Commission texts so commonly found in earlier New Zealand Protestant sources had become theologically pivotal to the conception of missions by 1930. He argued that if the Spirit was genuinely allowed to indwell both the Church and individual believers, then 'missionary activity [should be] as natural and necessary as breathing', and the outward actions of missionary support and participation should follow effortlessly and without conscious thought. Thus, in Waddell's estimation, such involvement was a 'subtle and searching test of the reality of one's own religion', as it was 'impossible to be under the control and possession of the spirit of Christ and not to be concerned as He was, with having others to share our peace and power'.[2]

At the same time, this central theological motive was linked to other imperatives that were more culturally and politically framed. If 'a man's only practical business is to win the world for Christ', wrote Waddell, then the time had come when 'if this is not undertaken in earnest, the world is headed for perdition'. Here Waddell had a number of concerns in mind as he observed the world of the interwar years, concerns already made clear by such visitors as John R. Mott in the mid-1920s. These included the shrinkage of time and distance, with the consequent proximity of other races and cultures; the sense that all of humanity must equally be cared for in both moral and physical terms; and the obligations and opportunities offered by advances in science and technology. He considered that the Church in New Zealand was inevitably a part of a much more 'internationalised' community than had hitherto existed, demanding that its gaze be on a 'world horizon' rather than on its own little geographical or cultural corner. Overshadowing all of this, however, was the fear of racial conflict as a result of the 'sudden intermingling of all the races of the world'.[3] Missions, in his estimation, might serve as a bulwark against such forces or as a leavening influence in places like Africa or India, where societies and peoples were slowly but inexorably moving towards independence. In countering the arguments of those who pushed for home missions before overseas missions, Waddell gave a positive estimation of New Zealand Presbyterians' role to date: 'Our Church has been seeking to play its part in this great issue. It has obeyed the command of Christ to begin at Jerusalem – that is, to evangelise its own kith and kin, and the Maoris [sic] whose country we have occupied. It has gone on, in obedience to this same command, to occupy the islands of the Pacific, and, further still, to India and China.' Then, in answer to what differentiated modern British people from their once heathen Anglo-Saxon ancestors, he went on to suggest,

> we have an object lesson of it before our very eyes in this Dominion. What was it made the difference between us here to-day and the unciv-ilised Maoris [sic] of two generations ago, and the savages of the South Sea Islands? It was because one wave of the great Western migration of the Aryan races from India come [sic] in contact with the Cross and St. Paul and the early Christian missionaries, and the other wave which came southward did not. We meet them face to face to-day, and are trying to pay our debt to them as 'stewards of the manifold grace of God'.[4]

This mix of theological obligation and cultural imperative formed the core of a missionary mentalité that framed New Zealand Protestant overseas engagements in the early twentieth century, and continued to do so well into the post-World War II era – as it has continued to do for some Prot-estant missionaries of other nations.[5] While the depression and war years of the 1930s and 1940s dented missionary numbers and budgets (particularly for the denominations), the years that followed were ones of significant growth. The numbers of departing missionaries working for projects run by their own denominations rose demonstrably after World War II: for example, Presbyterian missionaries increased from 14 in the 1940s to 68 in the 1960s (over 300 per cent growth) and Methodists from 21 in the 1940s to 67 in the 1960s (over 200 per cent growth).[6] In response to changing global politics some geographical locations were restricted while new areas of possibility opened up. Missionaries working for the Presbyterian Church in the 1960s, for example, no longer went to China (closed off to missionaries from 1952), but were now to be found in Hong Kong, Singapore, Malaysia, Indonesia and Papua New Guinea, as well as in India and Vanuatu. Angli-cans remained committed to a broad range of projects and locations around the world. Missionary commitment also remained strong among Brethren and Baptists. From 1950 to 1980 an estimated 432 Open Brethren and 560 Baptist New Zealanders participated overseas in various missionary roles.[7] In many cases they worked for other organisations quite separate from their own denominations, but this in turn indicated the extent to which Baptist and Brethren churches continued to see overseas engagement as a priority well into the late twentieth century.

Comparisons with global statistics confirm the sustained nature of this growth and commitment, indicating that the trends of the period up to 1939 were not anomalous.[8] At the time of the Edinburgh World Missionary Conference in 1910, an estimated 38 Australian and New Zealand missionaries were being sent overseas for every million Australasian Christians. By 2010 this figure had increased to 327 per million Christians, putting the Australasian region in sixth place on a world ranking of missionaries sent. At the same time, these statistics also indicate changing realities. While white New Zealanders and Australians made up the bulk of missionaries from Oceania in 1910, this had changed significantly a century later. In 2010 Polynesia as a grouping was ranked first in the world as a missionary-sending region, with Western Samoans, American Samoans and Tongans making up the bulk, albeit mostly working within the wider ambit of Oceania.

The emergence of world Christianity in the late twentieth century, marked by the creation of indigenous church structures achieving greater autonomy from their missionary antecedents, meant that the way missions were thought of had to change. This had been signalled as early as 1932 when an American 'laymen's enquiry' into 're-thinking missions' noted that 'in the last few years there have been signs of such change. The old fervor [sic] appears to have been succeeded in some quarters by questionings if not by indifference ... There is a growing conviction that the mission enterprise is at a fork in the road, and that momentous decisions are called for.'[9] A succession of international missionary conferences from 1928 onwards tackled the changing realities of global Christianity and politics. Substantive change was effected on both sides of the missionary relationship. Among the original sending nations, the creation of the World Council of Churches in 1948 served to refocus many churches on ecumenical and political engagement, and accentuated the differences between conciliar and evangelical elements. Political upheavals and independence movements also forced change. From 1949 the rise of Communist China seemed to spell the end of missions as traditionally conceived – or so it appeared at the time.[10] In the early 1970s the All-African Council of Churches acted out this perception by calling for a moratorium on missionaries. A succession of evangelical congresses from the early 1970s indicated that evangelicals were themselves developing a broader and deeper conception of missions for the realities of the late twentieth century.[11]

In response to this changing climate, New Zealand denominational missions effected a broad transition away from paternalism and towards partnership over this period. In the Presbyterian Church, for example, this was characterised by moves towards autonomy and partnership with respect to mission work in New Zealand among Māori, in India and in the New Hebrides; the formation of a joint Presbyterian–Methodist Council for Mission and Ecumenical Co-operation; and a more specific focus on aid and development.[12] Partnerships became more common for Baptist and Anglican missionary ventures, and non-denominational missions were also forced to change their patterns of geographical and structural involvement, even if this was not always accompanied by a change in basic philosophy of approach and intent. Even so, churches and related organisations remained committed to overseas engagement.

The significance of the missionary activity itself remains an open question and is one that is not easily answered. It is obvious that those who engaged in missionary activity at the time thought it to be pivotally important, as did those churches and organisations that gave them support. In hindsight, they did not always see their endeavours through rose-tinted spectacles, or at least their self-evaluations were mixed. Looking back over four decades of work in the New Hebrides and India, the Revd Thomas Riddle (Presbyterian missionary) noted that while the missionary task was 'no simple one ... none of us can say that he has shown the God-life to those of other faiths in any adequate way, but as we look back through the years we see that the Gospel seed has grown, we know not how, till it has become a great tree'.[13] Motifs of service and sacrifice common in motivational narratives were still important in the words used by missionaries at retirement. So too was the sense of something new being created as a result of these projects. Commonly this was couched in religious terms. When asked if 32 years spent in India had been worth it, Catharine Eade (NZBMS) replied, 'yes, it was worth it to see men and women, boys and girls come to a knowledge of God and His son, Jesus Christ. What is there to show? There is a Christian Union in Tripura of just over 5,000 baptised believers who are carrying on witnessing to their own people, trained and equipped to present Christ as the Living Saviour.'[14]

From a missionary perspective, these were important and perhaps self-evident outcomes. Of course, the difficulty with such evaluations is that they are also self-legitimating. They raise obvious questions about the extent to which the people they impacted saw things in the same way, and they create the impression that the missionaries were often the only significant factor in the creation of new communities of faith and belief. Scholarship now clearly indicates the complexities involved, indicating that these outcomes were never purely religious and that their non-religious consequences were often unintentional. Recent work on American Protestant missionaries in a range of nineteenth- and twentieth-century settings outlines the ways in which the missionary impact was as much political and cultural as it was religious, and that this was significant for the societies involved.[15] With respect to New Zealand women's missionary work and support, as noted at various points throughout the book, while this focused on idealised notions of 'sisterhood' it may have also contributed to the creation of both imagined and real racial or hierarchical distinctions between settler, missionary and indigenous women.

In academic assessments, it is commonplace to highlight the ways in which missionary activity was discursively imperialistic in its cultural impact, or inextricably enmeshed in colonial projects. Monolithic conclusions hold several grains of truth but they are not necessarily helpful, as Andrew Porter has outlined in his critique of the wholesale application of the concept of 'cultural imperialism' as a way of interpreting missionary impact in the context of colonialism.[16] More specifically, anthropologist Bronwen Douglas sagely warns that 'if we merely deplore [missionary and colonial] tropes as politically and morally obnoxious signs in a mission tropology, we run the risk of reinscribing them through negation: of accepting as monolithic and uncontested a hegemony which on the ground was always uncertain, disputed and locally reconfigured'.[17] Lisa Early's study of New Zealand Methodist women missionaries in early to mid-twentieth-century Solomon Islands indicates the importance of evaluating significance on a case-by-case basis. She concludes that while these women certainly 'shared in the racialist ideas of the day', they also 'offered a model to [Solomon Islands women], based on equality before God, sisterhood, Christian service and caring, quite unlike other expatriates'.[18] Likewise, in the context of China, Rachel Gillett challenges the notion that British missionary women had little impact on the social emancipation of Chinese women. It was very likely that the act of becoming a 'Bible woman' or deaconess, a teacher, a headmistress, a nurse or a doctor was a profound act of liberation for many women impacted by the New Zealand Presbyterian mission in southern China from 1901.[19]

On a broader front, it is now clear that one of the legacies of historical mission work, albeit often indirect, is the tremendous modern growth of Christianity in nations of the global 'South', particularly in sub-Saharan Africa, parts of Asia, and the length of Latin America.[20] In particular, while modern church structures are now substantively different, and indeed the expressions of indigenous Christianity are much changed from their missionary origins, there is still a strong continuity between the two. For example, Philip Jenkins notes, in the African context, that while the African Independent Churches are now numerically and culturally significant, there are still many millions more African Protestants and Catholics within the mainstream churches and denominations with clear and conscious links to their missionary foundations.[21]

The communication from the PWMU of Vanuatu to Presbyterian women in 1994, cited in Chapter Eight, indicates that these continuities were also important for the New Zealand context. New Zealand missionaries and organisations never loomed large in terms of overall numbers and impact. Yet their presence in myriad global locations served to link Christian communities in New Zealand and overseas in ways indicated by the Vanuatu example, and which are congruent with the global pattern of links between the missionary-dependent past and the indigenous independent present. In some cases that link can be identified quite specifically. One legacy of the BIM, for example, was the ultimate creation of the Bolivian Union of Evangelical Churches which, by the 1990s, had 600 congregations with around 45,000 members.[22] More commonly, the activities of many other missionaries quietly and progressively contributed to local Christian communities that, in turn, formed the foundations of a multiplicity of modern indigenous and wholly independent churches. This was so in locations as widely spread as South Sudan and Nigeria, northern and eastern India (now Bangladesh), southern China, the Solomon Islands and Andean South America. In these places, New Zealand remains in the collective memory of local and indigenous Christian communities. Likewise, many individual New Zealanders contributed to these churches and societies in ways that were measurable at the time and that have also lodged in the local memory – as clergy, evangelists, educators, nurses and doctors, welfare and social workers, administrators and more. These were people like Charles Fox in the Solomon Islands, Peter Milne in Vanuatu, Rosalie Macgeorge and Morton Ryburn in India, and academics Jocelyn Murray and Harold Turner in Africa.[23] In the odd case, that impact went well beyond the original intentions of missionary work, perhaps best exemplified in Garfield Todd's period as a politician and as prime minister in Southern Rhodesia in the 1950s, following his initial years as an Associated Churches of Christ missionary from New Zealand.[24]

While the legacies of mission were often complex, contentious or controversial, as well as more positive or benign, these observations are at best indicative of the ways in which New Zealand missionary involvement up to World War II left its mark overseas. Ultimately, a proper assessment of these legacies requires more missionary site-based research that measures the impact of New Zealand Protestant missions from the perspectives of both local communities and of the sending churches, and which attends to multiple voices from both sides of the relationship. The potential for this is evident, for example, in a recently completed doctoral thesis by Sylvia Yuan on New Zealand missionary engagement in China, which utilises oral and archival sources from both New Zealand and Chinese participants.[25] However, because the focus of the present book is on the New Zealand side of the relationship, the question of significance is perhaps more accurately assessed by attending to domestic 'contours' and issues.

Throughout this book, a case has been made that the major impact of missionary activity was on the sending churches and communities of New Zealand. This is now a well-attested observation for the Anglo-American missionary-sending nations of the nineteenth and early twentieth centuries.[26] For the New Zealand context this reflex impact was no less important and has been identified in myriad ways throughout the book, especially with respect to imperial and national identity, women, children, education, denominational and regional identity, and ecumenical engagement. In the period at least up until World War I, missionary and evangelical energies were intertwined, imbricating colonial Protestant men, women and children in an activist Christianity that was outward-looking, both within and beyond New Zealand's geographical borders. It is certainly true that this was a crucial factor in the ongoing formation of Baptist and Brethren identity as avowedly evangelical communities, and of a growing number of missionary agencies that self-identified as evangelical. At the same time, this undercurrent of activism that lay at the heart of missionary endeavour also remained important for the likes of Anglican, Methodist and Presbyterian churches, irrespective of their position on the emerging 'evangelical–liberal' theological spectrum. Furthermore, this activism was not exclusively restricted to Pākehā Christian communities. As the pages of the Māori Anglican newspaper *Te Pipiwharauroa: He Kupu Whakamarama* attest, exhortations urging missionary support were regularly to be found by the late nineteenth century.[27] Certainly, too, women's and children's support groups existed by the 1920s among Presbyterian Māori communities and in the schools run by the Presbyterian Māori Mission in the central and eastern North Island. While Māori engagement as overseas missionaries was a minor feature of Māori Christianity in these decades, home-based engagement was more obvious – albeit often controlled by settler-dominated church structures and priorities, or channelled through such institutional magazines as the *Break of Day* or the *Harvest Field*.

We could compile a long list of the many specific examples of how this reflex influence of overseas missionary involvement impacted on churches and church life in colonial New Zealand up to 1939. In a sense, this has already been done through the previous chapters. However, by way of final conclusion, a wider lens is applied to this phenomenon as a means of identifying elements of greater significance at play here. This broader significance is suggested by the experience of New Zealand women supporters of missionary work. As we have seen, missions were pivotally important for the religious lives of New Zealand Protestant women. From the late nineteenth century onwards women were pioneers, both in mission contexts from India to Bolivia, and also at home as organisers and strategists for missionary support. Groups like the Anglican Mothers' Union or the Baptist, Methodist and Presbyterian women's missionary unions were long-lasting core institutions in settler church life. In this – like their Scottish Presbyterian counterparts, for example – such groups were among the 'first and in many respects the most important large-scale' women's organisations. Women's groups, while not without their tensions with wider church structures and authorities, constituted a 'network of information and support, which received regular injections of fresh ideas and challenges', and in which women 'gradually developed new skills and confidence'.[28] That similar kinds of groups with similar experiences co-existed in various parts of the world in this period was no accident or coincidence. They operated through a multiplicity of internationally configured connections, shared knowledge, experiences and deliberate engagement. In these terms, they were not simply parallel organisations. While operating autonomously within the context of their own religious, political and socio-cultural milieux, they activated a globalised web or network of relationships between women in a range of missionary-sending settings worldwide. In so doing, they gave form to 'feminized discourses of spirituality' that 'collapsed the gap' between 'the centre and the periphery'.[29]

Women's missionary engagement, however, was but one reflexive element that indicated the broader extent to which overseas missionary involvement shaped or contributed to settler religious communities. Missionary engagement reinforced the initial early to mid-nineteenth-century religious links between colony and British homelands. Over the longer term, it also ensured that settler religion remained both local and global in its configurations, its influence and its place within wider colonial society. Here we return to the language of 'centre' and 'periphery' canvassed in the Introduction, to the historiographical concerns raised both in the Introduction and Chapter Five over the writing of New Zealand history, and to the photograph on the cover of this book. Whatever the precise imagery employed – be it Peter Gibbons' notion of colonial New Zealand sitting on a global oceanic highway linked to an 'archipelago of urban centres'; or Tony Ballantyne's reconceptualisation of New Zealand's constituent position or role within the 'web-like structure' of the British Empire;[30] or perhaps even the image of history moving backwards and forwards along a continuum from the local to the global – it is clear that a single or a static interpretive paradigm is inadequate. Over the last two to three decades, historians have sought 'new analytical stances, novel ways of framing [histories], seeking out new – or little-used sources, finding fresh ways of reading old analytical concerns, and critically reflecting upon some of the basic assumptions that govern understandings of New Zealand history'.[31] Intrinsic to that search has been the concerted attempt to write New Zealand's history from more avowedly transnational and comparative perspectives.[32] As I argued in Chapter Five, this is a point at which a nuanced historical understanding of New Zealand's missionary engagement might usefully contribute to a wider reading of New Zealand history.

To a degree, these developments are also becoming apparent in the writing of New Zealand's religious history more specifically,[33] but perhaps less quickly due to reasons intrinsic to this particular historical sub-field. Traditionally, our religious history has been conceived of in national and denominational terms, a feature that was challenged by religious historian Ian Breward as early as 1979 (see Chapter Five).[34] While many of Breward's original concerns are now being addressed,[35] it is worth noting that this is not a problem limited solely to societies such as New Zealand. The advent of global or world Christianity in the late twentieth century has necessarily forced us to rethink the pedagogies and the writing of Christian history, resulting in a move away from Euro-centric perspectives, narratives and content. Furthermore, the religious histories of settler societies are themselves being reconceived or reconfigured, with fresh writings emerging on how American religion has been historically shaped by influences from Asia and Africa, for example.[36] Likewise, recent research into the Destiny Church phenomenon adds a corrective by considering indigenous expressions of contemporary religion while indicating how neo-Pentecostalism in New Zealand has been partially shaped by black Pentecostal churches in America that, in turn, owe some of their origins to African churches and African-American missionaries.[37]

In light of this historiographical turn, the deliberate writing of New Zealand's missionary engagement into the narratives of national religious history would serve to more effectively connect that history with the wider narratives of regional and global Christianity and, in turn, to produce a local religious history that is more dynamic in its contours. For example, Hilary Carey's recent study of the relationship between nineteenth-century British colonialism and denominational initiatives in the white settler colonies has more definitively linked the origins of New Zealand's, and other settler societies', religious structures to those of the wider British world.[38] Even this approach or set of narratives remains limited, however, as it largely ignores the contemporaneous reverse thrust of religious people and ideas outwards from the colonies and the subsequent ways in which this reflexively shaped or influenced religion back in the colonies. Weaving the history of overseas missionary engagement from these colonies more deliberately and thoughtfully into the religious history of colonial society could potentially broaden this picture even further. It might create a better sense of how New Zealand's religious history has not only been defined by its British roots (or indeed, by its relationship to other British or Anglo-world contexts), but also by a multiplicity of other global locations, cultures and world views. In this way, New Zealand's religious history becomes both a history of the local and a history of the global; both are required for a fully orbed understanding of our religious past.[39] From this perspective, the distinctions between centre and periphery are blurred, turned upside down or indeed collapsed – in a way that is fitting for a post-Christendom world that is now marked by a less hierarchical set of global Christian networks and pathways. The challenge still facing us, I suggest, is the need for a new religious history of New Zealand written from the perspectives of both the local and the global.

By way of a postscript, the integration of the local and the global are neatly represented by the photograph on the cover of this book and by three small, engraved, ivory-lined and carved wooden boxes that sit on my study shelves (Figure 9.1). In January 1903, Miss Manoramabai, daughter of the celebrated high-caste Brahmin Christian convert and social reformer Pandita Ramabai, spoke at conventions arranged on her behalf in Queenstown and Dunedin. At some point, she signed books on her mother's work.[40] Nearly two years later, in October 1904, an 'oriental bazaar' was held in Dunedin to further support the work of Pandita and Manoramabai among 'child widows' (Mukti Mission) in Pune, western India.[41] Either one of my maternal grandparents, or possibly a great-grandparent, attended that bazaar, where they bought one of the signed books and the three wooden boxes: a glove box, a jewellery box and a small trinket box. These have remained in our family ever since.

That these events happened, it seems, was due to the energies of two Queenstown Presbyterians, George and Jane Mackenzie.[43] Through them, a support committee was formed around 1898, organising annual gifts of money and materials, and over the next several years at least four New Zealand women went to India to work in the Mukti Mission.[44] In 1908 when George was 70 years old and just five years shy of his death in 1913, the Mackenzies followed up their commitment with a visit to the mission in India, where 'they were photographed with the bands of young women and children supported by their efforts'.[45] This is the subject of the photograph on the cover of this book. Their visit was duly reported back in Dunedin through the pages of the *Otago Witness*.[46] In particular, this image appeared as one of a montage of photographs of the Mackenzies with Pandita, the Indian women and children, and New Zealand worker Sister

FIGURE 9.1. Bazaar items bought at event for the Ramabai Mukti Mission, c. 1904[42]

Clare Cole. On the same page were other 'exotic' photographs connecting Dunedin to the wider world; of 'Sioni', a 'motherless New Guinea baby' to be adopted by Dunedin's Trinity Methodist Sunday School, and of a giraffe belonging to the Wirth Brothers' travelling circus. In reporting back to the public, the Mackenzies noted the ways in which the material help of New Zealand Protestants had made a difference for the young Indian women they encountered. In particular they mused that the 'Bible was now their meat and drink' and that 'Christianity had worked entire reformation in their lives'. At the same time, George turned these observations on their head by also commenting on the 'earnestness with which the natives at the mission prayed, not only for their own people, but for other nations, and for New Zealand – not emotionally, but really and truly striving for a divine blessing'. Thus, the influence and significance of missions was directed equally both outwards and inwards.

The Mackenzies, along with fellow supporters and the missionaries of the late nineteenth and early twentieth centuries, were clearly people of their times. Their lives occupied and traversed a mental landscape that now seems strange and foreign to many people. They did so with a largesse of spirit and an apparent naivety that seem astonishing in hindsight. At the same time, they were global citizens before their time. Their lives and actions prefigured the large-scale interchanges of cultures and commodities that now characterise the present era of globalisation. They sought to influence the world for good, through the Christian message. In the process, they helped to bring the world to New Zealand and the West to the world. The past they represent may be a 'foreign country' for many readers today.[47] Yet in a shrunken world, in which New Zealanders of all walks of life have always been willing or adventurous globetrotters, the strangeness of that past is surely an invitation for further exploration. And who is to say that there are still not valuable treasures to be unearthed beneath the surface of that 'foreign country' that is our colonial past?

Summary of New Zealand
Missionary Data, 1827–1939

MISSIONARY ORGANISATION[1]	First Known NZ Missionary	Total Known	Main Denomination	Main Destination
Australasian Wesleyan / NZ Methodist Church	1827?	125	Wesleyan Methodist	Solomons Fiji
Melanesian Mission	1852	64	Anglican	Solomons
Presbyterian Church of New Zealand	1869	128	Presbyterian	South China North India New Hebrides
Zenana Bible and Medical Mission	1875	3	Baptist	India
British and Foreign Bible Society	1877	1	Presbyterian?	China
Kanaka Queensland Mission	1882	1	Brethren	Australia
Church Missionary Society	1884	8	Anglican	Persia Nigeria India
New Zealand Baptist Missionary Society	1886	55	Baptist	India
China Inland Mission (Australasia)	1891	84	Baptist	China
United Free Church of Scotland	1892	3	Presbyterian	India

1. Mission names are as they were in the period up to 1939.

MISSIONARY ORGANISATION	First Known NZ Missionary	Total Known	Main Denomination	Main Destination
New Zealand Church Missionary Association[2]	1893	39	Anglican	China India
London Missionary Society	1893	14	Congregational	India Samoa China
Unknown	1894	17	Baptist	Various
Independent	1894	6	Various	New Hebrides
Congo Balolo Mission	1896	1	Presbyterian	Upper Congo
Telegu Mission	1896	1	Presbyterian	India
Poona and Indian Village Mission	1896	54	Various	India
Open Brethren (Plymouth)	1896	153	Brethren	India China South America
New South Wales Baptist Missionary Society	1896	2	Baptist	India
Church of Scotland	1897	9	Presbyterian	India China
Associated Churches of Christ (ACC)	1898	18	ACC	Southern Rhodesia
South American Evangelical Mission[3]	1899	2	Baptist	Argentine
Regions Beyond Missionary Union	1900	8	Baptist	Argentine
Christian and Missionary Alliance	1903	1	C & MA	?
Ramabai Mukti Mission	1904	3	?	India
Missionary Settlement for University Women	1906	1	?	India

2. Renamed New Zealand Church Missionary Society in 1916.
3. Reformed as the Australasian South American Mission in 1901.

MISSIONARY ORGANISATION	First Known NZ Missionary	Total Known	Main Denomination	Main Destination
Salvation Army (New Zealand)	1906	14	Salvation Army	India China
Bolivian Indian Mission	1908	25	Presbyterian Baptist	Bolivia
Anglican Papuan Mission	1909	1	Anglican	Papua
Evangelical Union of South America	1909	7	Baptist	Brazil Peru
Presbyterian Church of Tasmania	1909	1	Presbyterian	New Hebrides
Church of England Zenana Missionary Society	1909	3	Anglican	India
Society for the Propagation of the Gospel	1909	9	Anglican	China
Egypt General Mission	1909	8	Baptist	Egypt
Baptist Missionary Society	1910	3	Baptist	Congo India
South Sea Evangelical Mission	1911	27	Baptist	Solomons
United Aborigines Mission	1912	1	?	Australia
Algiers Mission Band	1912	2	Baptist	Algeria
Sudan United Mission	1912	22	Baptist	Sudan
Presbyterian Church of Victoria	1912	2	Presbyterian	Korea
Presbyterian Church of New South Wales	1914	1	Presbyterian	India
South Australia Baptist Missionary Society	1915	2	Baptist	India
Mission to Lepers	1918	2	Baptist	India
St Andrew's Colonial Homes	1918	1	Baptist	India
Universities Mission to Central Africa	1919	1	Anglican	Uganda

MISSIONARY ORGANISATION	First Known NZ Missionary	Total Known	Main Denomination	Main Destination
New Zealand Anglican Board of Missions	1920s	3	Anglican	India
South African Wesleyan Church	1920s	2	Methodist	South Africa
China Inland Mission	1920	3	Baptist	China
New Zealand Student Christian Movement	1920	1	?	India
Sudan Interior Mission (SIM International)	1921	21	Baptist	Sudan, Ethiopia and Nigeria
African Inland Mission	1921	4	Baptist	Central Africa Kenya
Kwato Extension Association	1923	4	Baptist	Papua and New Guinea
Anglican Diocese of Polynesia	1924	12	Anglican	Fiji
Pentecostal Church of New Zealand	1926	4	Pentecostal	Fiji
American Pentecostal Mission	1926	4	AOG and Pentecostal	Fiji Tonga
YWCA	1926	1	?	Pacific Malaya
YMCA	1927	2	?	Singapore
Welsh Presbyterian Church	1927	2	Baptist Presbyterian	India China
Assemblies of God	1927	2	AOG	India
Cairo Nile Mission Press	1928	1	Baptist	Egypt
Latin American Prayer Fellowship	1928	2	Baptist	Mexico
Australian Board of Mission (Anglican)	1929	1	Anglican	China

MISSIONARY ORGANISATION	First Known NZ Missionary	Total Known	Main Denomination	Main Destination
Emmanuel Mission to Seamen	1930	1	Congregational	Ceylon Australia
Congo Evangelistic Mission	1930	3	AOG	Belgian Congo
Ceylon and India General Mission	1930	6	Baptist	India
Dutch Reformed Church	1930	1	Baptist	Sumatra
Unevangelized Fields Mission (UFM)	1932	5	Baptist	Brazil
Oriental Missionary Society (OMS)	1933	1	Baptist	Japan
British Syrian Mission	1934	2	Presbyterian Baptist	Lebanon
World Evangelization Crusade (WEC International)	1935	5	Baptist Presbyterian	Colombia
Roodeport Compounds Mission	1935	2	Baptist	Transvaal
Central Japan Pioneer Mission	1937	2	Baptist	Japan
Japan Apostolic Mission	1937	3	Apostolic	Japan
Australian Baptist Missionary Society	1937	1	Baptist	India
Papua UK Mission	1937	1	Baptist	Papua
Shanghai Hebrew Mission	1937	1	Baptist	China
Central Asia Mission	1938	4	Baptist	India
Jerusalem and the East Mission	1939	1	Anglican	Palestine
Oswald Smith's Mission	1939	1	Presbyterian	Cuba West Indies

Notes on the Sources of
New Zealand Missionary
and Applicant Data

Bolivian Indian Mission (BIM)

Missionary and applicant names for both the South American Evangelical Mission and the Australasian South American Mission (1899–1908) were extracted from a combination of the Minutes of the Dunedin Committee of the South American Evangelical Mission, 1899–1908; the Correspondence of the Dunedin Committee of the South American Evangelical Mission, 1900–02; and the Correspondence of the Australasian South American Mission, 1902–08. Further missionary and applicant names for the Bolivian Indian Mission (1908–39) were extracted from a handwritten 'Listing of Bolivian Indian Missionaries, 1909–1945', and crosschecked against the Minutes of the New Zealand Council of the Bolivian Indian Mission, 1908–16, and the Minutes of the Field Conferences of the Bolivian Indian Mission, 1913–45. All of these sources, plus the three magazines listed below, are physically located in the SIM International Resource Centre, Fort Mill, South Carolina, USA. Biographical details were found in a wide range of BIM material including miscellaneous personnel files; the *South American Messenger*, 1897–99; the *South American News*, 1904–06; *The Bolivian Indian*, 1911–30 (initially entitled *Tahuantin Suyu*); the Student Record Cards of the New Zealand Bible Training Institute (Laidlaw College); the literature of other New Zealand denominations; and newspapers. In addition, both the magazines *Tahuantin Suyu* and *The Bolivian Indian* are now archived in pdf form at: http://archives.sim.org/.

Brethren missionaries

The list of names of missionaries from Brethren assemblies (1896–1939) was exclusively extracted from Les Marsh, *In His Name: A record of assembly missionary outreach from New Zealand* (Palmerston North: G.P.H. Society, 1974), and from the updated version: Les Marsh and Harry Erlam, *In His Name: A record of Brethren assembly missionary outreach from New Zealand* (Palmerston North: G.P.H. Society, 1987). No attempt has been made to work directly with Brethren primary source material due to difficulty of access and time constraints. A complete run of the Brethren magazine *Treasury* is archived at the GPH offices in Palmerston North, but these have only been surveyed with respect to children's material. Miscellaneous biographical details have also been sourced from J.G. Harvey, *Brief Records of Service for Christ in Many Lands, 1896–1947* (Palmerston North: Gospel Publishing House, 1947); materials relating to the Poona and Indian Village Mission; biographies; other New Zealand denominational literature; the Student Record Cards of the New Zealand Bible Training Institute (Laidlaw College); and the private collection of Dr John Hitchen, Auckland.

China Inland Mission (CIM)

The list of missionary names for the China Inland Mission in New Zealand, 1894–1939, was initially constructed from a combination of the lists in Marcus Loane, *The Story of the China Inland Mission in Australia and New Zealand, 1890–1964* (Sydney: Overseas Missionary Fellowship, 1965), 151–64, and Matthew Dalzell, *New Zealanders in Republican China 1912–1949* (Auckland: The University of Auckland New Zealand Asia Institute, 1995), 184–85. Applicant names, for the North Island only, were listed in the 'CIM Register of Candidates, 1893–1937'. Biographical details were also found in the 'CIM Register', as well as in miscellaneous personnel files and in the Mission's magazine, *China's Millions*, 1893–1939 (Australasian edition). These are held either in the Overseas Missionary Fellowship Archives, Auckland, or in the Evangelical Archive at Laidlaw College, Auckland. Further details were found in the literature of New Zealand denominations and in the Student Record Cards of the New Zealand Bible Training Institute (Laidlaw College). There is also some New Zealand CIM personnel information in the Australia CIM archives held at the Melbourne School of Theology, Victoria, including applicant names and an incomplete set of individual missionary files. There are gaps in the personnel data for some South Island CIM missionaries because the official records of the South Island council (up until its amalgamation with the North Island council in 1939) seem to have been lost or destroyed. Substantial efforts to locate these were unsuccessful. Again, the Australian CIM records provide material to fill some of these gaps, particularly the identification of South Island applicants who did not go on to missionary service. Finally, a very important updated attempt to catalogue all New Zealand Protestant missionaries in China up to 1952, including those of the CIM, is to be found in Sylvia Yang Yuan, '"Kiwis" in the Middle Kingdom: A sociological interpretation of the history of New Zealand missionaries in China from 1877 to 1952 and beyond' (PhD thesis, Massey University (Albany), 2013).

London Missionary Society (LMS)

Names for New Zealand LMS missionaries (1893–1939) were initially found in a wide range of sources, including local newspapers and the Minute Book of the London Missionary Society, New Zealand Auxiliary, Otago Branch, 1900–32. These were then crosschecked and supplemented by more complete material in James Sibree (ed.), *London Missionary Society: A register of missionaries, deputations, etc, 1796–1923* (London: London Missionary Society, 1923) and Norman Goodall, *A History of the London Missionary Society, 1895–1945* (London: Oxford University Press, 1954), Appendix III, 595–623.

Melanesian Mission

Missionary names only were initially extracted from a range of sources including W.P. Morrell, *The Anglican Church in New Zealand* (Dunedin: Anglican Church of the Province of New Zealand, 1973); E.S. Armstrong, *The History of the Melanesian Mission* (London: Isbister, 1900); D. Hilliard, *God's Gentlemen: A history of the Melanesian Mission, 1849–1942* (St Lucia, Queensland: Queensland University Press, 1978); Janet Crawford, '"Christian Wives for Christian Lads": Aspects of women's work in the Melanesian Mission, 1849–1877', in *With All Humility and Gentleness*, Allan K. Davidson and Godfrey Nicholson (eds) (Auckland: St John's College, 1991), 51–66; the *Proceedings of the General Synod*, 1896–1900; the Minutes of the

Christchurch Gleaners' Union, 1893–1923; and the *Annual Reports of the New Zealand Anglican Board of Missions*, 1920–21, 1924–39. These names were further crosschecked against the 'List of Melanesian Missionaries Compiled at the London Office of the Mission', a copy of which is located in the Alexander Turnbull Library, Wellington. Biographical material was also extracted from these sources, as well as from the *Southern Cross Log*, 1895–1926; the [NZABM] *Reaper*, 1923–39; Gerald Anderson (ed.), *Biographical Dictionary of Christian Missions* (New York: MacMillan Reference USA, 1998); and Robert Glen (ed.), *Mission and Moko: Aspects of the work of the Church Missionary Society in New Zealand, 1824–1882* (Christchurch: Latimer Fellowship of New Zealand, 1992). Further biographical details can also be found in the *Blain Biographical Directory of Anglican Clergy in the South Pacific* at: http://anglicanhistory.org/nz/blain_directory/directory.pdf

Methodist Overseas Mission (MOM)

A list of Methodist missionaries (1886–1939) was constructed initially from George C. Carter, *A Family Affair: A brief survey of New Zealand Methodism's involvement in mission overseas* (Proceedings Wesley Historical Society of New Zealand, vol. 28, nos. 3–4, Auckland: Wesley Historical Society (NZ), 1973), Appendix II. There was no further attempt to work directly with primary source material, although children's material was surveyed in the Methodist Church's Christchurch-based archive. Biographical details were extracted from *A Family Affair*, other Wesley Historical Publications (noted in the bibliography), and from two theses on New Zealand Methodist women missionaries: Daphne Beniston, 'New Zealand women of the Methodist Solomons Mission 1922–1992' (MA thesis, University of Auckland, 1992), 184–99; and Lisa Early, '"If we win the women": The lives and work of Methodist missionary women in the Solomon Islands, 1902–1942' (PhD thesis, University of Otago, 1998), 350–61.

New Zealand Baptist Missionary Society (NZBMS)

The list of missionary names for the NZBMS (1886–1939) was initially drawn from S.L. Edgar and M.J. Eade, *Towards the Sunrise: The centenary history of the New Zealand Baptist Missionary Society* (Auckland: New Zealand Baptist Historical Society for the New Zealand Baptist Missionary Society,

1985), 272–73. These names were crosschecked against E.P.Y. Simpson, 'A history of the N.Z. Baptist Missionary Society, 1885–1947' (MA thesis, Canterbury University College, 1948), 171–73. Applicant names were extracted from the Minutes of NZBMS Committee Meetings, 1885–1939 (held in the Carey Baptist College Library, Auckland). Biographical details were found in a combination of miscellaneous personnel files; the *NZBU Handbook*, 1903–39 (annual lists of Baptist missionaries working for both the NZBMS and other agencies or denominations); the *New Zealand Baptist*, 1886–1939; the *Missionary Messenger*, 1886–1939; and the Student Record Cards of the New Zealand Bible Training Institute (Laidlaw College).

New Zealand Church Missionary Association/Society (NZCMA/S)

An initial list of missionary names for the NZCMA (1893–1916) and the NZCMS (1916–39) was extracted from Kenneth Gregory, *Stretching Out Continually: Whaatoro tonu atu: A history of the New Zealand Church Missionary Society, 1892–1972* (Christchurch: The author, 1972), and supplemented by Dalzell, *New Zealanders in Republican China 1912–1949*, 189. This list was then crosschecked against a full listing of missionaries given in the catalogue of the NZCMS Archives, Series Three. Names of applicants were also extracted from Series Three. Biographical details were found primarily in the application records and personnel files of both missionaries and applicants, located in the Correspondence of the New Zealand Church Missionary Association/Society, 1893–1939 (Series Three). Further biographical details can also be found in the *Blain Biographical Directory of Anglican Clergy in the South Pacific* at: http://anglicanhistory.org/nz/blain_directory/directory.pdf

Poona and Indian Village Mission (PIVM)

The list of names for New Zealand missionaries with the Poona and Indian Village Mission (1896–1939) was extracted from a combination of the mission's magazine, *White Already to Harvest*, 1899–1939 (located in the SIM International Resource Centre, Fort Mill, South Carolina, USA); references to missionaries in New Zealand denominational publications (especially the *NZBU Handbook*, 1903–39); the Student Record Cards of the

New Zealand Bible Training Institute (Laidlaw College); and the Minutes of the Christchurch Gleaners' Union, 1893–1923. Applicant records do not exist. Biographical details were found in the same sources as those listed above. In addition, the magazine *White Already to Harvest* is now archived in pdf form at: http://archives.sim.org/

Presbyterian Church of New Zealand Foreign Missions Committee (PCNZ FMC)

An initial list of names of missionaries sent out by both the Presbyterian Synod of Southland and Otago (1869–1901) and by the Presbyterian Church of New Zealand (1869–1939) was constructed from a combination of the following: J.R. Elder, *The History of the Presbyterian Church of New Zealand, 1840–1940* (Christchurch: Presbyterian Bookroom, 1940); J.S. Murray, *A Century of Growth: Presbyterian overseas mission work, 1869–1969*, (Christchurch: Presbyterian Bookroom, 1969), 110–12; and Dalzell, *New Zealanders in Republican China 1912–1949*, 187–88. This list was then crosschecked using Ian Fraser, 'Register of Ministers and Missionaries, 1840–1989', Presbyterian Research Centre, 1990. This register is now accessible as an online 'Register of New Zealand Presbyterian Ministers, Deaconesses and Missionaries', 1840–2014, at: www.archives.presbyterian.org.nz/page143.htm. Applicant and missionary names and biographical details were supplemented from: the Staff Files, Series Six, Canton Villages Mission Archives (1901–39); the Staff Files, Series Six, Punjab Mission Archives (1908–39); the Staff Files, Series Six, New Hebrides Mission Archives (1869–1939); and from Missionary Candidates, Series Three, PCNZ Foreign Missions Committee Archives (1905–39). The most comprehensive collection of formal application records, for both missionaries and unsuccessful applicants, has only been kept from 1905 onwards. Biographical details were also found in various Presbyterian publications plus miscellaneous personnel files.

Student volunteers (SVM/ASCU/NZSCM)

The names and details of New Zealand Student Volunteers (1896–1918) were constructed from two extant lists: an undated 'Listing of NZ Student Volunteers', located in the NZSCM Collection in the Alexander Turnbull

Library, Wellington, and a 1916 'List of [Australasian] Student Volunteers' (G549.111), located in the World Student's Christian Federation Archives, Special Collections, Yale Divinity School Library, Yale University, USA. An effort was made to track down the original application papers filled out by New Zealand Student Volunteers (which exist for their North American counterparts). These were probably sent either to the central office of the Australasian Students Christian Union (first in Sydney and then in Melbourne) or directly to the missionary organisations being applied to, but they do not seem to have survived. Further biographical information was also found in NZCMA/S and PCNZ application records.

Other missions and missionaries

Missionary names for the other diverse range of missionary organisations were found in a wide array of sources. Primarily, these were the publications of the various New Zealand denominations (already cited), as well as the [NZBTI] *Reaper*, 1923–39, regional newspapers, various biographies, and historical accounts of some of the missions (see Bibliography). Some biographical information for missionaries departing between 1922 and 1939 was also found in the Student Record Cards of the New Zealand Bible Training Institute (Laidlaw College). Further biographical information was found in Anderson (ed.), *Biographical Dictionary of Christian Missions*; Brian Dickie (ed.), *The Australian Dictionary of Evangelical Biography* (Sydney: Evangelical History Association, 1994); the online Presbyterian 'Register of Presbyterian Ministers, Deaconesses and Missionaries'; and the multi-volume *Dictionary of New Zealand Biography* now hosted online by *Te Ara – The Encyclopedia of New Zealand* at: www.teara.govt.nz/en/biographies. Again, because this listing of 'other missionaries' is incomplete, the working assumption should be that overall missionary numbers are underestimated for the period up to 1939.

Introduction

1 Transcript of John Takle's Diary, 1896, John Takle Papers, Folder 1, Box 0201, New Zealand Baptist Missionary Society Archives (NZBMS Archives), Carey Baptist College, Auckland, New Zealand.

2 Graeme A. Murray, 'John Takle', in *Biographical Dictionary of Christian Missions*, Gerald Anderson (ed.), (New York: Macmillan Reference USA, 1998), 656; see also Tony Ballantyne, *Webs of Empire: Locating New Zealand's colonial past* (Wellington: Bridget Williams Books, 2012), 94–95.

3 Throughout the book the terms 'foreign' and 'overseas' are used interchangeably. 'Overseas' is the more modern and usual rendering of the word 'foreign', and is used in preference except where context dictates otherwise.

4 The details and sources for most of these people are more fully documented in Hugh Morrison, '"It is our bounden duty": The emergence of the New Zealand Protestant missionary movement, 1868–1926' (PhD thesis, Massey University, 2004), 280–86, 296–351.

5 Missionary statistics were voluminous and useful, but are open to debate and variable interpretation; see Steven S. Maughan, *Mighty England Do Good: Culture, faith, empire, and world in the foreign missions of the Church of England, 1850–1915* (Grand Rapids, Michigan, and Cambridge, UK: William Eerdmans, 2014), 470–72. For the British context, one estimate is that British Protestant missionary numbers grew from 4232 in 1889 to a peak of 8699 by 1925. Another estimate is that overall Protestant missionary numbers grew from 21,000 in 1911 to over 29,000 by 1925, of whom half came from North America. See Jeffrey Cox, *The British Missionary Enterprise since 1700* (New York and London: Routledge, 2008), 267; and Gerald H. Anderson, 'American Protestants in pursuit of mission: 1886–1986', *International Bulletin of Missionary Research* 12, no. 3 (1988): 105.

6 Todd M. Johnson and Kenneth R. Ross (eds), *Atlas of Global Christianity* (Edinburgh: Edinburgh University Press, 2009), 286–89.

7 See further Pamela Welch, 'Constructing colonial Christianities: With particular reference to Anglicanism in Australia, ca 1850–1940', *Journal of Religious History* 32, no. 2 (2008): 234–55; Hilary Carey, *God's Empire: Religion and colonialism in the British world, c.1801–1908* (Cambridge: Cambridge University Press, 2011).

8 See, for example, Geoffrey Troughton and Hugh Morrison (eds), *The Spirit of the Past: Essays on Christianity in New Zealand history* (Wellington: Victoria University Press, 2011); Hugh Morrison, 'Globally and locally positioned: New Zealand perspectives on the current practice of religious history', *Journal of Religious History* 35, no. 2 (2011): 181–98; and John Stenhouse, 'God's own silence: Secular nationalism, Christianity and the writing of New

Zealand history', *New Zealand Journal of History* (*NZJH*) 38, no. 1 (2004): 52–71. The bibliographies published annually in the *New Zealand Religious History Newsletter* also reflect this trend (archived at: http://researchspace. auckland.ac.nz/handle/2292/1961).

9   Two exceptions to this are Ian Breward, *A History of the Churches in Australasia* (Oxford: Oxford University Press, 2001); and Allan K. Davidson, *Christianity in Aotearoa: A history of church and society* (Wellington: The New Zealand Education for Ministry Board, 2004).

10   Allan K. Davidson, 'The New Zealand overseas missionary contribution: The need for further research', in *With All Humility and Gentleness*, Allan K. Davidson and Godfrey Nicholson (eds), (Auckland: St John's College, 1991), 41–50.

11   For the sake of space, where a large group of New Zealand titles are referred to here, the footnotes in this chapter will give author and date only. The fuller references can be found in the bibliography.

12   In addition to the two titles by Driver and Don, see also Stock, 1913; Gregory, 1972; Fox, 1958; Edgar and Eade, 1985; Murray, 1969; Carter, 1973; Trew, 1996.

13   For example: Breward, 2001; McEldowney, 1990.

14   Representative examples are Loane, 1965; Hudspith, 1958.

15   Eugene Stock, *The History of the Church Missionary Society*, 4 vols (London: Church Missionary Society, 1899 and 1916).

16   Savage, 1980; Trew, 1996; Murray, 1969.

17   Representative examples are Dineen, 1933; Henderson, 1947; Clapham, 1966; Carter, 1985.

18   For example, MacDiarmid, 1968; Roke, 2003.

19   For example, Newnham, 2000; McGregor, 2006; Ogilvie, 1994.

20   R. Pierce Beaver, *All Loves Excelling: American Protestant women in world mission* (Grand Rapids, Michigan: Eerdmans, 1968), 143–55; Dana Robert, *American Women in Mission: A social history of their thought and practice* (Macon, Georgia: Mercer University Press, 1997), 257–72.

21   Joan Brumberg, 'Zenanas and girlless villages: The ethnology of American evangelical women, 1870–1910', *The Journal of American History* 69, no. 2 (1982): 347–71; Judith Rowbotham, '"Hear an Indian sister's plea": Reporting the work of 19th-century British female missionaries', *Women's Studies International Forum* 21, no. 3 (1998): 247–61.

22   Simpson, 1948; Parsonson, 1941.

23   Roberts, 1977; Marshall, 1967.

24   Brash, 1948; Henderson, 1939.

25   Davidson, 'The New Zealand overseas missionary contribution'; Peter J. Lineham, 'Missions in the consciousness of the New Zealand churches', *Stimulus* 7, no. 2 (1999): 33–39; and Peter J. Lineham, 'Missionary motivation in New Zealand', in New Zealand Association of Mission Studies Conference (collected papers), Auckland, November 2000.

26 This is well represented by the annual conferences of the Yale-Edinbugh
    Group on the History of the Missionary Movement and World Christianity
    (details archived at http://divinity-adhoc.library.yale.edu/Yale-Edinburgh/).
    For further selected examples, see the 'Empires of Religion' Conference,
    Dublin 2006, with papers published in Hilary M. Carey (ed.), *Empires
    of Religion*, Cambridge Imperial and Post-Colonial Studies (Houndmills,
    Basingstoke: Palgrave Macmillan, 2008); the 'Evangelists of Empire'
    Conference, Melbourne 2008, with papers published in Patricia Grimshaw
    and Peter Sherlock (eds), *Evangelists of Empire?: Missionaries in colonial
    history*, History Conference and Seminar Series 18 (Melbourne: eScholarship
    Research Centre, 2008); and the 'Changing Face of Missionary Education'
    Conference, Münster 2014, with papers to be published in a special issue of
    the journal *Itinerario* in 2016.

27 Dana Robert, 'From missions to mission to beyond missions: The
    historiography of American Protestant missions since World War II',
    International Bulletin of Missionary Research 18, no. 4 (1994): 146–62.

28 John Stuart, 'Introduction: Mission and empire', *Social Sciences and Missions*
    21, no. 1 (2008): 4; Tony Ballantyne, 'Review essay: Religion, difference
    and the limits of British imperial history', *Victorian Studies* 47, no. 3 (2005):
    427–55.

29 Cox, *The British Missionary Enterprise since 1700*, 5, 7.

30 Two examples: A. Austin and J.S. Scott (eds), *Canadian Missionaries,
    Indigenous Peoples: Representing religion at home and abroad* (Toronto,
    Buffalo, London: University of Toronto Press, 2005), 7; Patricia Grimshaw
    and Andrew May (eds), *Missionaries, Indigenous Peoples and Cultural Exchange*
    (Brighton, England & Portland, Or.: Sussex Academic Press, 2010).

31 Giselle Byrnes and Catharine Coleborne, 'Editorial introduction: The utility
    and futility of "the nation" in histories of Aotearoa New Zealand', *NZJH* 45,
    no. 1 (2011): 1–14; and Giselle Byrnes (ed.), *The New Oxford History of New
    Zealand* (Oxford and Melbourne: Oxford University Press, 2009).

32 Byrnes and Coleborne, 'Editorial introduction', 6–8.

33 John Stenhouse, 'Religion and society', in *The New Oxford History of New
    Zealand*, 344.

34 See, in particular, John Stenhouse, 'The controversy over the recognition
    of religious factors in New Zealand history: Some reflections', in *The Spirit
    of the Past: Essays on Christianity in New Zealand history*, 43–54; Stenhouse,
    'God's own silence'; and Stenhouse, 'God, the Devil, and gender', in *Sites
    of Gender: Women, men and modernity in southern Dunedin, 1890–1939*,
    Barbara Brookes, Annabel Cooper and Robyn Law (eds), (Auckland:
    Auckland University Press, 2003), 313–47.

35 Tony Ballantyne, *Orientalism and Race: Aryanism in the British Empire*
    (Houndmills, Basingstoke and New York: Palgrave, 2002), 1. See further
    Brian Moloughney, 'Translating culture: Rethinking New Zealand's
    Chineseness', in *East by South: China in the Australasian imagination*,

Charles Ferrall, Paul Millar and Keren Smith (eds), (Wellington: Victoria University Press, 2005), 389–404; Tony Ballantyne & Brian Moloughney, 'Asia in Murihiku: Towards a transnational history of colonial culture', in *Disputed Histories: Imagining New Zealand's past*, Tony Ballantyne and Brian Moloughney (eds), (Dunedin: Otago University Press, 2006), 65–92; and Sekhar Bandyopadhyay, 'Introduction', in *India in New Zealand: Local identities, global relations*, Sekhar Bandyopadhyay (ed.), (Dunedin: Otago University Press, 2010), 7–18.

36 Stefan Berger and Chris Lorenz (eds), *The Contested Nation: Ethnicity, class, religion and gender in national histories* (Houndmills, Basingstoke: Palgrave Macmillan, 2008).

37 Cox, *The British Missionary Enterprise since 1700*, 263–71.

38 Ruth Compton Brouwer, *New Women for God: Canadian Presbyterian women and India missions, 1876–1914* (Toronto: University of Toronto Press, 1990); Maughan, *Mighty England Do Good*, 2014.

39 Daniel Bays and Grant Wacker (eds), *The Foreign Missionary Enterprise at Home: Explorations in North American cultural history* (Tuscaloosa and London: University of Alabama Press, 2003); Mark Hutchinson and Greg Treloar (eds), *This Gospel Shall Be Preached: Essays on the Australian contribution to world mission* (Sydney: Centre for the Study of Australian Christianity, 1998).

40 Esther Breitenbach, *Empire and Scottish Society: The impact of foreign missions at home, c. 1790 to c. 1914* (Edinburgh: Edinburgh University Press, 2009); Alison Twells, *The Civilising Mission and the English Middle Class, 1792–1850: The 'heathen' at home and overseas* (New York: Palgrave Macmillan, 2008); Susan Thorne, *Congregational Missions and the Making of an Imperial Culture in 19th-century England* (Stanford, California: Stanford University Press, 1999).

41 See the essays by Wayne Te Kaawa ('A gifted people: Māori and Pākehā covenants within the Presbyterian Church') and Lachy Paterson ('The rise and fall of women field workers within the Presbyterian Māori Mission') in *Mana Māori and Christianity*, Hugh Morrison, Lachy Paterson, Brett Knowles and Murray Rae (eds), (Wellington: Huia Publishers, 2012), 3–21, 179–204.

42 Peter J. Lineham, 'How institutionalised was Protestant piety in nineteenth century New Zealand?', *Journal of Religious History* 13, no. 4 (1985): 370–82.

43 *New Zealand Census*, 1871–1936.

44 William Svelmoe, 'Faith Missions' in *Encyclopedia of Mission and Missionaries*, Jonathan J. Bonk (ed.), (New York and London: Routledge, 2007), 155.

45 Allan K. Davidson, 'The interaction of missionary and colonial Christianity in nineteenth century New Zealand', *Studies in World Christianity* 2, no. 2 (1996): 145–66.

46 Geoffrey Troughton, 'Between the wars, 1919–1940', in *Living Legacy: A history of the Anglican Diocese of Auckland*, Allan K. Davidson (ed.),

(Auckland: Anglican Diocese of Auckland, 2011), 190; 'Miss Eunice Preece, Missionary', *Early New Zealand Families*: http://tortoise.orconhosting.net. nz/eunicepreece.html.

47 See further, Hirini Kaa, '"Te wiwi nati": The cultural economy of Ngati Porou, 1926–1939' (MA thesis, University of Auckland, 2000); and Monty Soutar, 'Ngāti Porou leadership: Rāpata Wahawaha and the politics of conflict: "Kei te ora nei hoki tātou, me tō tātou whenua"' (PhD thesis, Massey University, 2000).

CHAPTER ONE

1 Andrew Walls and Cathy Ross (eds), *Mission in the 21st Century: Exploring the fives marks of global mission* (Maryknoll, New York: Orbis Books, 2008), 202; Mark Noll, *The New Shape of World Christianity: How American experience reflects global faith* (Downers Grove, Illinois: IVP Academic, 2009), 10.

2 Rollo Arnold, *The Farthest Promised Land: English villagers, New Zealand immigrants of the 1870s* (Wellington: Victoria University Press, 1981), 354.

3 Jock Phillips and Terry Hearn, *Settlers: New Zealand immigrants from England, Ireland & Scotland 1800–1945* (Auckland: Auckland University Press, 2008), 27, 34–45.

4 Allan K. Davidson and Peter J. Lineham, *Transplanted Christianity: Documents illustrating aspects of New Zealand church history* (Palmerston North: Dunmore Press, 1989), 36.

5 James Irwin, *An Introduction to Maori Religion* (South Australia: Australian Association for the Study of Religions, 1984), 5–12; Timothy Yates, *The Conversion of the Māori: Years of religious and social change, 1814–1842* (Grand Rapids, MI, and Cambridge, UK: William B. Eerdmans, 2013), 1–9. For wider context see: Robert Glen (ed.), *Mission and Moko: The Church Missionary Society in New Zealand 1814–1882* (Christchurch: The Latimer Fellowship of New Zealand, 1992); and Allan K. Davidson, Stuart M. Lange, Peter J. Lineham and Adrienne Puckey (eds), *Te Rongopai 1814 'Takoto Te Pai!': Bicentenary reflections on Christian beginnings and developments in Aotearoa New Zealand* (Auckland: The General Synod Office, 'Tuia', of the Anglican Church in Aotearoa New Zealand and Polynesia, 2014); and Tony Ballantyne, *Entanglements of Empire: Missionaries, Māori, and the question of the body* (Auckland: Auckland University Press, 2015).

6 James Belich, *Making Peoples: From Polynesian settlement to the end of the nineteenth century* (Auckland: Allen Lane The Penguin Press, 1996), 156–78.

7 Robert Glen (ed.), *Mission and Moko: The Church Missionary Society in New Zealand 1814–1882* (Christchurch: Latimer Fellowship of New Zealand, 1992); Peter J. Lineham, *Bible and Society: A sesquicentennial history of the Bible Society in New Zealand* (Wellington: Daphne Brasell Associates Press and the Bible Society in New Zealand (Inc.), 1996); Larry Prochner, Helen

May and Baljit Kaur, '"The blessings of civilisation"': Nineteenth-century missionary infant schools for young native children in three colonial settings – India, Canada and New Zealand 1820s–1840s', *Paedagogica Historica* 45, no. 1/2 (2009): 83–102.

8   Allan K. Davidson, *Christianity in Aotearoa: A history of church and society in New Zealand* (Wellington: The New Zealand Education for Ministry Board, 2004), 17–18; Raeburn Lange, *Island Ministers: Indigenous leadership in nineteenth century Pacific islands Christianity* (Canberra: Pandanus Books, 2005); Allan K. Davidson (ed.), *Semisi Nau, the Story of my Life: The autobiography of a Tongan Methodist missionary who worked at Ontong Java in the Solomon Islands* (Suva: Institute of Pacific Studies, University of the South Pacific, 1996).

9   Raeburn Lange, 'Indigenous agents of religious change in New Zealand, 1830–1860', *Journal of Religious History* 24, no. 3 (2000): 279–80.

10 Nathan Matthews, 'Kaikatikīhama: "Our most precious resource"', in *Mana Māori and Christianity*, 141–58; and Paterson, 'The rise and fall of women field workers within the Presbyterian Maori Mission, 1907–1970', 179–204.

11 George C. Carter, *A Family Affair: A brief survey of New Zealand Methodism's involvement in mission overseas* (Auckland: Wesley Historical Society NZ, 1973), 3–4, 10–17.

12 C.E. Fox, *Lord of the Southern Isles: Being the story of the Anglican mission in Melanesia 1849–1949* (London: A.R. Mowbray, 1958), 209; J.P. Te Paa, 'Māori and the Melanesian Mission: Two "sees" or oceans apart?', in *The Church of Melanesia 1849–1999*, Allan K. Davidson (ed.), (Auckland: The College of St John the Evangelist, 2000), 146–49, 154.

13 Michael Blain, 'Hawkins' and 'Papahia', *Blain Biographical Directory of Anglican Clergy in the South Pacific*: http://anglicanhistory.org/nz/blain_directory/directory.pdf

14 Fox, *Lord of the Southern Isles*, 208–09.

15 Hilary Carey, *God's Empire: Religion and colonialism in the British world, c. 1801–1908* (Cambridge: Cambridge University Press, 2011), 341–42, 344–46.

16 *New Zealand Census*, 1871, x.

17 Davidson, *Christianity in Aotearoa*, 55–56, 134–35. Robert Joseph, 'Intercultural exchange, matakite Māori and the Mormon Church', in *Mana Māori and Christianity*, 43–72.

18 Helen Bethea Gardner, *Gathering for God: George Brown in Oceania* (Dunedin: Otago University Press, 2006), 28–29; Carter, *A Family Affair*, Appendix II.

19 J.R. Elder, *The History of the Presbyterian Church in New Zealand 1840–1940* (Christchurch: Presbyterian Bookroom, 1940), 34, 57–58; Darrell Whiteman, 'Inglis, John', in *Biographical Dictionary of Christian Missions*, 318.

20 David Hilliard, *God's Gentlemen: A history of the Melanesian Mission, 1849–*

1942 (St Lucia, Queensland: Queensland University Press, 1978), 1.

21 For a recent, wide-ranging treatment of Bishop Selwyn see Allan K. Davidson (ed.), *A Controversial Churchman: Essays on George Selwyn, bishop of New Zealand and Lichfield, and Sarah Selwyn* (Wellington: Bridget Williams Books, 2011).

22 A.K. Davidson, '"An interesting experiment": The founding of the Melanesian Mission', in Davidson, *The Church of Melanesia*, 19; and Hilliard, *God's Gentlemen*, 2.

23 Esther Breitenbach, 'Religious literature and discourses of empire: The Scottish Presbyterian foreign mission movement', in *Empires of Religion*, 84–86; D. Chambers, 'The Church of Scotland's nineteenth century foreign missions scheme: Evangelical or moderate revival?', *Journal of Religious History* 9, no. 2 (1976): 115, 125; John Roxborogh, *Thomas Chalmers: Enthusiast for mission. The Christian good of Scotland and the rise of the missionary movement* (Carlisle, Cumbria: Paternoster Publishing, 1999), 160–74.

24 Bishop Julius quoted in the *Annual Report of the New Zealand Anglican Board of Missions*, 1924–1925, 5.

25 Kenneth Scott Latourette, *A History of the Expansion of Christianity*, vol. 4 (London: Eyre and Spottiswoode, 1938), 2–3, 7.

26 15 October 1856, Minute Book of the Presbytery of Auckland 1856–1869, MS 1501.P928, Box 1, Auckland War Memorial Museum Library, Auckland, New Zealand.

27 For a fuller treatment of the early New Hebrides Mission, see Gordon Parsonson, 'Early Protestant missions in the New Hebrides, 1839–1861' (MA thesis, University of Otago, 1941).

28 J.S. Murray, *A Century of Growth: Presbyterian overseas mission work, 1869–1969* (Christchurch: Presbyterian Bookroom, 1969), 11–14.

29 *The Evangelist* 1:3 (1869): 7–10.

30 *The Evangelist*, April 1872, 123; 'Missions Report, 1883', *Proceedings of the General Assembly of the Presbyterian Church of New Zealand* [*PCNZ PGA*], 41.

31 'Missions Report, 1926', *PCNZ PGA*, 110.

32 'Missions Report, 1913', *PCNZ PGA*, 82–83; 'Missions Report, 1929', *PCNZ PGA*, 151.

33 'Missions Report, 1909', *PCNZ PGA*, 90–91; 'Missions Report, 1913, *PCNZ PGA*, 81–82; 'Missions Report, 1923, *PCNZ PGA*, 134.

34 Murray, *A Century of Growth*, 50, 51.

35 'Missions Report, 1940', *PCNZ PGA*, 72.

36 Data are derived from Appendix One in Morrison, 'It is our bounden duty', 280–82.

37 Malcolm Prentis, 'Binding or loosing in Australasia: Some trans-Tasman Protestant connections', *Journal of Religious History* 34, no. 3 (2010): 316–18; Carter, *A Family Affair*, 94–103.

38 Cox, *The British Missionary Enterprise since 1700*, 213–15.

39 All statistics and statistical representations that follow are derived from a

database of New Zealand missionary departures collated by the author. The original version is in the appendices of Morrison, 'It is our bounden duty', 280–351. Notes on the sources for these data appear in Appendix 2 of this book. Here, 1852 is the first reliable date for identifying individually named missionaries departing from New Zealand.

40 J.D. Salmond, *By Love Serve: The story of the Order of the Deaconesses of the Presbyterian Church of N.Z.* (Christchurch: Presbyterian Bookroom, 1962), 67–69.

41 W.P. Morrell, *The Anglican Church in New Zealand* (Dunedin: Anglican Church of the Province of New Zealand, 1973), 192–95.

42 Latourette, *A History of the Expansion of Christianity*, vol. 7, 16.

43 Stuart Lange, *A Rising Tide: Evangelical Christianity in New Zealand 1930– 1965* (Dunedin: Otago University Press, 2013), 16–21.

44 J. Oswald Sanders, *Expanding Horizons: The story of the New Zealand Bible Training Institute* (Auckland: Institute Press, 1971), 94, 96.

45 David Thorns and Charles Sedgewick, *Understanding Aotearoa/New Zealand: Historical statistics* (Palmerston North: Dunmore Press, 1997), 32–33.

46 Again, a more in-depth coverage of these statistics and trends is offered in Morrison, 'It is our bounden duty', particularly 35–37, 65–73, 107–13 and 134–41.

47 All data in this table relate to missionaries at the time of their departure only. Median figures are given as a more reliable descriptive statistic than mean figures. Highest educational attainment and occupational background prior to departure is not known for all people in this database, so that these figures are an estimate based on known data. 'Other tertiary' refers primarily to missionaries trained in post-secondary educational institutions outside of the universities, of which nursing and teacher training, and lay ministry/Bible institute training were the dominant categories. Again, 1852 is the most reliable date from which to begin analysing missionary statistics.

48 Occupational categories are derived from an occupational taxonomy developed for the New Zealand historical context, 1890–1940. See Erik Olssen and Maureen Hickey, *Class and Occupation: The New Zealand reality* (Dunedin: University of Otago Press, 2005), 57–90, 155–252.

49 Dorothy Page, 'The first lady graduates: Women with degrees from Otago University', in *Women in History 2: Essays on women in New Zealand*, Barbara Brookes, Charlotte Macdonald and Margaret Tennant (eds), (Wellington: Bridget Williams Books, 1992), 112–13.

50 Revd John Inglis, *Thesis – The doctrine of Christian missions, with special reference to the South Sea islands* (Edinburgh: Morrison & Gibb, 1881), 39–40; 'London Missionary Society', *The Press*, 23 August 1877, 3.

CHAPTER TWO

1   *New Zealand Baptist*, November 1890, 162.
2   *Bolivian Indian*, April 1916, 3–4.
3   Thomas Askew, 'The 1888 London Centenary Missions Conference: Ecumenical disappointment or American missions coming of age?', *International Bulletin of Missionary Research* 18, no. 3 (1994): 114.
4   Revd Peter Milne, 'The certainty and means of the world's conversion', *The Evangelist*, 1 October 1874: 12.
5   Askew, 'The 1888 London Centenary Missions Conference', 114, 116.
6   15 October 1856, Minute Book of the Presbytery of Auckland, 1856–1869, Auckland War Memorial Museum Library.
7   Based on comments and key phrases drawn from 623 individual documentary sources for the period 1890–1930: 122 Anglican, 127 Baptist, 217 Presbyterian, 58 China Inland Mission, 45 Bolivian Indian Mission, and 54 from other sources. Documentary sources for the period prior to 1890 are much more fragmentary, and it is not clear to what extent these descriptors would have been wholly representative of the earlier period. These data were initially presented in Morrison, 'It is our bounden duty', 38–42, 73–80, 113–19 and 142–49.
8   Extracted from the same data as for Table 2.1.
9   David Bosch, *Transforming Mission: Paradigm shifts in theology of mission* (Maryknoll, New York: Orbis Books, 1991), 339–41.
10 *The Press* (Christchurch), 24 October 1892; *China's Millions*, Supplement, January 1902, 156.
11 *Nelson Evening Mail* (Nelson), 19 January 1899 and 20 January 1899.
12 Dana L. Robert, 'The origin of the Student Volunteer watchword: "The evangelization of the world in this generation"', *International Bulletin of Missionary Research* 10, No. 4 (1986): 146–48; Dana L. Robert, '"The crisis of missions": Premillennial mission theory and the origins of independent evangelical missions', in *Earthen Vessels: American evangelicals and foreign missions, 1880–1980*, J.A. Carpenter and W.R. Shenk (eds), (Grand Rapids, Michigan: Eerdmans, 1990), 33–37.
13 J.R. Mott, *The Evangelization of the World in this Generation* (London: Student Volunteer Missionary Union, 1900), 7–8.
14 'Ivens', ANG 143/3.70, Box 10, Archives of the New Zealand Church Missionary Society [NZCMS Archives], John Kinder Theological Library, St John's College, Auckland, New Zealand.
15 *The South American Messenger* 3, no. 3 (1899): 170–71.
16 *New Zealand Baptist Union Baptist Handbook*, 1903–04, 14–23.
17 Herbert Davies, *Four Studies in World-wide Evangelisation* (Dunedin: ASCU, 1909), 5–7.
18 B. Broomhall, *The Evangelisation of the World. A Missionary Band: A record of consecration, and an appeal*, 3rd edn (London: Morgan & Scott, 1889), Frontispiece.

19 See again Brumberg, 'Zenanas and girlless villages' and Rowbotham, 'Hear an Indian sister's plea'.

20 'Missions Report, 1910', *PCNZ PGA*, 1116.

21 'Doris Wilks', ANG 143/3.124, Box 17, NZCMS Archives.

22 *The Outlook*, 23 August 1910, 8.

23 'Australasian Baptist Missions in Bengal, Prayer List Calendar', 1905, Folder 1, Box 0026, NZBMS Archives.

24 James Belich, *Paradise Reforged: A history of the New Zealanders from the 1880s to the year 2000* (Auckland: Allen Lane The Penguin Press, 2001), 95–96, 116–17.

25 'NZBMS Report, 1915', *NZBU Baptist Handbook*, 1915–16, 78.

26 *New Zealand Baptist*, January 1922, 3.

27 'Dorothy Mathew', 6.17, Folder 1, Punjab Mission (GA0149), Series 6, Staff Files, Presbyterian Church of Aotearoa New Zealand [PCANZ Archives], Presbyterian Research Centre, Dunedin, New Zealand.

28 From the hymn 'O'er the Gloomy Hills of Darkness', one that was also popular in nineteenth-century British missionary meetings. In 'Hymns', Folder 1, Box 0026, NZBMS Archives.

29 Timothy Yates, *Christian Mission in the Twentieth Century* (Cambridge: Cambridge University Press, 1994), 7–21.

30 *China's Millions*, June 1922, 63.

31 *New Zealand Baptist*, November 1927, 341–42.

32 'Missions Report, 1923', *PCNZ PGA*, 129.

33 J.H. Oldham, *Christianity and the Race Problem* (London: Student Christian Movement, 1924), vii.

34 J.R. Mott, 'The Race Problem', in *Report of the New Zealand Missionary Conference Held at Dunedin April 27 to April 29, 1926*, Anonymous (ed.), (Dunedin: New Zealand Missionary Conference Committee, 1926), 25.

35 Revd George McNeur, 1926, *Otago Daily Times* clipping in George Hunter McNeur Papers, 95–012, ARC-038, Hocken Library [Hocken], Dunedin, New Zealand.

36 *New Zealand Baptist*, January 1923, 10.

37 Tom Brooking and Roberto Rabel, 'Neither British nor Polynesian: A brief history of New Zealand's other immigrants', in *Immigration and National Identity in New Zealand: One people, two peoples, many peoples?*, Stuart Greif (ed.), (Palmerston North: Dunmore Press, 1995), 23.

38 'BWMU Member's Card', undated, Folder 1, Box 0036, New Zealand Baptist Historical Society Archives [NZBHS Archives], Carey Baptist College, Auckland, New Zealand.

39 'PWMU Report, 1899', *Presbyterian Church of Southland–Otago Proceedings of Synod*, [PCSO PS] 74; 'PWMU Report, 1900', ibid. 111; 'BWMU Report, 1913', *NZBU Baptist Handbook*, 1913–14, 101. For further discussion of this theme, see Yvonne Robertson, *Girdle Round the Earth: New Zealand Presbyterian women's ideal of universal sisterhood, 1878–1918*, Annual

Lecture, Auckland 1993 (Dunedin: Presbyterian Historical Society of New Zealand, 1994); and Jane Haggis and Margaret Allen, 'Imperial emotions: Affective communities of mission in British Protestant women's missionary publications c1880–1920', *Journal of Social History* (Spring 2008): 691–716.

40   Bosch, *Transforming Mission*, 285–91, 339–41.

41   Hudspith, *Ripening Fruit*, 16–19; *Bolivian Indian*, January–February 1929, 8.

42   For example, 'NZBMS Report, 1903', *NZBU Baptist Handbook*, 1903–04, 68.

43   H.D. Morrison, 'The Keeper of Paradise: Quarantine as a measure of communicable disease control in late nineteenth-century New Zealand' (BA(Hons) dissertation, University of Otago, 1981), 3–10.

44   Yates, *Christian Mission in the Twentieth Century*, 57.

45   *Our Bond*, January 1912, 11–12.

46   'Report of the commission appointed to consider the missionary policy of the NZSCM', c. 1925–26, Miscellaneous Publications, MS-Papers-1617-503, New Zealand Student Christian Movement Collection, Alexander Turnbull Library [Turnbull], Wellington, New Zealand.

47   Typewritten report found in 'Pacific Basin Tour 1926 – NZ', Series VII, Biographical Documentation, 2590/156, Mott Papers, 45, Yale Divinity School Library [Yale], New Haven, Connecticut, USA.

48   'Missions Report, 1928', *PCNZ PGA*, 177.

49   *Reaper* [New Zealand Anglican Board of Missions], February 1932, 6.

50   Viv Grigg, *Companion to the Poor* (Australia: Albatross Books, 1984); Jenni Craig, *Servants Among the Poor* (Manila: OMF Literature Inc., 1998).

CHAPTER THREE

1   *New Zealand Baptist*, August 1895, 113.

2   Anne J.P. Driver, *Missionary Memories* (Dunedin: H.H. Driver, 1930), 5–10.

3   Alf Roke, *They Went Forth: Trials and triumphs of a pioneer SIM missionary in Ethiopia* (Auckland: Alf Roke, 2001).

4   Belich, *Paradise Reforged: A history of the New Zealanders from the 1880s to the year 2000* (Auckland: Allen Lane The Penguin Press, 2001), 29–30, 53–86; James Belich, *Replenishing the Earth: The settler revolution and the rise of the Angloworld* (Oxford: Oxford University Press, 2009).

5   Miles Fairburn, 'Is there a good case for New Zealand exceptionalism?' in *Disputed Histories: Imagining New Zealand's past*, 143–67, 259–65.

6   James Bennett, *'Rats and Revolutionaries': The Labour movement in Australia and New Zealand 1890–1940* (Dunedin: University of Otago Press, 2004), 10.

7   Donald Denoon, 'Re-Membering Australasia: A repressed memory', *Australian Historical Studies* 34, no. 122 (October 2003): 290–304; Phillippa Mein Smith, 'The ties that bind (and divide) Australia and New Zealand', *History Now* 9, no. 4 (Autumn 2004): 4–12.

8   Donald Denoon, Philippa Mein Smith and Marivic Wyndham, *A History of Australia, New Zealand and the Pacific* (Oxford: Blackwell Publishers, 2000); *Anzac Neighbours*: www.nzac.ac.nz/index.html; and Philippa Mein Smith, Peter Hempenstall and Shaun Goldfinch, *Remaking the Tasman World* (Christchurch: Canterbury University Press, 2008).

9   Hugh Jackson, *Churches and People in Australia and New Zealand, 1860–1930* (Wellington: Unwin and Allen, 1987).

10   Ian Breward, *A History of the Churches in Australasia* (Oxford: Oxford University Press, 2001).

11   Malcolm Prentis, 'Binding or loosing in Australasia: Some trans-Tasman Protestant connections', *Journal of Religious History* 34, no. 3 (2010): 312–34; and Mein Smith et al, *Remaking the Tasman World*, 147–55.

12   Ibid., 331–32.

13   Paul Tonson, *A Handful of Grain: The centenary history of the Baptist Union of New Zealand, Volume 1: 1851–1882* (Wellington: The New Zealand Baptist Historical Society, 1982), 2–5, 50; *Census of New Zealand*, 1881, 217, 221; Martin Sutherland, 'Seeking a turangawaewae: Constructing a Baptist identity in New Zealand', *Baptist History and Heritage* 36 (Winter/Spring 2001): 232–50.

14   *New Zealand Baptist*, November 1883, 355.

15   Margaret Allen, '"White already to harvest": South Australian women missionaries in India', *Feminist Review* 65 (Summer 2000): 96, 101; Ros Gooden, '"We trust them to establish the work": Significant roles for early Australian Baptist women in overseas mission, 1864–1913', in *This Gospel Shall be Preached: Essays on the Australian contribution to world mission*, M. Hutchinson and G. Treloar (eds), (Sydney: Centre for the Study of Australian Christianity, 1998), 132–33.

16   *New Zealand Baptist*, January 1885, 10–12.

17   *New Zealand Baptist*, May 1885, 65–66.

18   Ibid., 10.

19   *New Zealand Baptist*, March 1885, 41; April 1885, 56–57; May 1885, 65–66.

20   Gooden, 'We trust them to establish the work', 134; Donovan F. Mitchell, *Ellen Arnold: Pioneer and pathfinder* (Adelaide: South Australian Baptist Union Foreign Missionary and Book and Publication Departments, 1932).

21   *New Zealand Baptist*, March 1885, 41.

22   *New Zealand Baptist*, May 1885, 71.

23   'Minutes of the New Zealand Baptist Union Conference, 1885', in *New Zealand Baptist*, November 1885, 166.

24   Stuart Piggin, *Spirit of a Nation: The story of Australia's Christian heritage* (Sydney: Strand Publishing, 2004), 49–50. See also Jackson, *Churches and People*, 48–65.

25   Jackson, *Churches and People*, 63.

26   Piggin, *Spirit of a Nation*, 66.

NOTES 241

27 Brian Dickey (ed.), *The Australian Dictionary of Evangelical Biography* (Sydney: Evangelical History Association, 1994); Charles F. Reeve, 'How to obtain Pentecostal Christianity', *White Already to Harvest*, November 1899, 154.

28 Whittall, G., 'Charles Frederick Reeve, his life and work', (Unpublished mss, no date), quoted in Ian Welch, 'Poona (Pune) and Indian Village Mission (PIVM)', Working Paper, August 2014, 2: https://digitalcollections.anu.edu.au/bitstream/1885/13041/1/Welch%20Poona%202014.pdf

29 For a brief outline of origins, see 'SIM History': www.sim.org/index.php/content/sim-history

30 Welch, 'Poona (Pune) and Indian Village Mission (PIVM)', 3.

31 Reports in the *New Zealand Baptist*, January 1899, 11; February 1899, 28; April 1897, 59; May 1897, 75; *The Press* (Christchurch), 8 March 1897; 12 April 1897; and the *Otago Witness*, 14 January 1897. See also 'List of New Zealand Council Members', *White Already to Harvest*, January 1898, 13.

32 Morrison, 'It is our bounden duty', 86–87, 296–351.

33 *Christian Outlook*, 4 September 1897, 376.

34 *Christian Outlook*, 9 October 1897, 443–44; 16 October 1897, 456.

35 Eugene Stock, *The History of the Church Missionary Society*, 4 vols (London: Church Missionary Society, 1899 and 1916), 674–75.

36 'Report on Canton Village Mission', in 'McNeur', Series 6, Staff Files, Canton Villages Mission, GA0148, PCANZ Archives.

37 'Missions Report, 1899', *PCSO PS*, 68–69; 'George and Margaret McNeur', Register of Missionaries, Deaconesses and Missionaries; Henry H. Barton, *George Hunter McNeur: A Pioneer missionary in South China* (Christchurch and Dunedin: Presbyterian Bookroom, 1955), 3; 'Australasian China Inland Mission Record of Applications', 69, Melbourne School of Theology Archives, Melbourne, Australia.

38 'Missions Report, 1903', *PCNZ PGA*, 101, 160.

39 E.C. Millard, *The Same Lord: An account of the mission tour of the Rev. George. C. Grubb* (London: E. Marlborough, 1893), 356.

40 W. Lockhart Morton, *Drifting Wreckage: A story of rescue in two parts* (London, New York and Toronto: Hodder and Stoughton, 1912), 259–309; David Parker, 'Lockhart Morton', in *Australasian Dictionary of Evangelical Biography*, Brian Dickey (ed.), (Sydney: Evangelical History Association, 1994), 269–70.

41 *Church Missionary Intelligencer*, June 1893, 458–60.

42 Martin to Chatterton, 25 January 1894, ANG143/3.22, Box 6, NZCMS Archives.

43 Barnes to Holloway, 10 September 1903, ANG143/3.9, NZCMS Archives.

44 'Prospectuses, Exam Papers', in Ephemera (6), ANG143/5.3, NZCMS Archives.

45 'Preparation of Missionaries', in Historical and General Papers, ANG143/1.6, NZCMS Archives.

46 Quoted in Martin to Chatterton, 25 January 1894, ANG143/3.22, NZCMS Archives.

47 See Martha Vicinus, *Independent Women: Work and community for single women, 1850–1920* (London: Virago Press, 1980), 163–87; Correspondence: Barnes to Carr, 28 March 1908, ANG143/3.9, NZCMS Archives; Woods to Kimberley, 1 August 1919, ANG143/3.130, NZCMS Archives.

48 Typed extract from NZCMA Ladies' Committee Minute Book, 10 December 1907, ANG143/3.112, NZCMS Archives.

49 Notes, n.d., ANG143/3.112, NZCMS Archives.

50 Barnes to Carr, 28 March 1908, ANG143/3.9, NZCMS Archives.

51 Ibid.

52 Dr J.J. Kitchen to NZCMA, 15 February 1908, ANG143/3.112, NZCMS Archives.

53 See, for example, M.P. Lissington, *New Zealand and the United States 1840–1944* (Wellington: Historical Publications Branch, Department of Internal Affairs, 1972), 1–23; Deborah Montgomerie, *The Women's War: New Zealand women 1939–45* (Auckland: Auckland University Press, 2001), 162–69.

54 Chris Hilliard, 'Colonial culture and the province of cultural history', *NZJH* 36, no. 1 (2002): 92.

55 Colin Brown, 'The American connection: The United States of America and churches in New Zealand', in *Religious Studies in Dialogue*, Maurice Andrew et al. (eds), (Dunedin: Faculty of Theology, University of Otago, 1991), 153–62; Bryan Gilling, 'Rescuing the perishing', *Stimulus* 1, no. 2 (1993): 28–36.

56 Geoffrey Troughton, 'Richard Booth and Gospel temperance revivalism', in Geoffrey Troughton and Hugh Morrison (eds), *The Spirit of the Past: Essays on Christianity in New Zealand history* (Wellington: Victoria University Press, 2011), 112–25.

57 Hugh Morrison, 'Rew(r)i(gh)ting an "unfortunate neglect"?: John R. Mott and individual agency in New Zealand mission history', *Colloquium* 44, no. 1 (2012): 59–77.

58 Gerald Anderson, 'American Protestants in pursuit of mission, 1886–1986', *International Bulletin of Missionary Research* 12, no. 3 (1988): 98–118; Timothy Yates, *Christian Mission in the Twentieth Century* (Cambridge: Cambridge University Press, 1994), 8.

59 Dana Robert, *Christian Mission: How Christianity became a world religion* (Chichester: Wiley-Blackwell, 2009), 57–58.

60 For example: Amos R. Wells, *The Missionary Manual: A handbook of methods for missionary work in young people's societies* (Boston and Chicago: United Society of Christian Endeavour, 1899); John Burnham (ed.), *Christian Endeavour Melodies* (London: W. Nicholson & Sons, nd).

61 *New Zealand Baptist*, October 1892, 158; December 1907, 292. See further, Henry Bush and J.E. Kerrison (eds), *First Fifty Years: The story of Christian*

Endeavour under the Southern Cross (Sydney: National Christian Endeavour Union of Australia and New Zealand, 1938), 12.

62 *New Zealand Baptist*, February 1893, 25; 'Committee on the State of Religion Report', *PCSO PS*, 1893, 47; *New Zealand Baptist*, October 1894, 159; January 1898, 15.

63 *New Zealand Baptist*, May 1894, 77; *Church Gazette*, November 1895, 201.

64 *The Society of Christian Endeavour* (undated pamphlet, probably c. 1912), 10, Terrace Congregational Church, Wellington, Miscellaneous Records, 1896–1941, 96-059-3/12, Turnbull.

65 20 December 1896, Knapdale Christian Endeavour Minutes, 1896–99, AN2/1, PCANZ Archives.

66 *The Society of Christian Endeavour* (undated pamphlet), 31–32.

67 27 September 1896, Knapdale Christian Endeavour Minutes, 1896–99, PCANZ Archives.

68 Knapdale Christian Endeavour Minutes, 1896–99, PCANZ Archives; Taranaki Street Wesleyan Young People's Society for Christian Endeavour Minute Books, 1892–96 and 1898–1905, MSY-0482, Turnbull; and the Christchurch Central Mission Endeavour Society, reported in the *Press*, 25 April 1896.

69 *The Society of Christian Endeavour* (undated pamphlet), 11.

70 From an anonymous poem entitled 'Tired', *New Zealand Baptist*, May 1897, 76–77.

71 *The Society of Christian Endeavour* (undated pamphlet), 31–32; *Otago Witness*, 25 June 1896.

72 Revd Francis Clark speaking in Auckland, *New Zealand Baptist*, October 1892, 157–58.

73 See Judith Rowbotham, '"Soldiers of Christ"? Images of female missionaries in late nineteenth-century Britain: Issues of heroism and martyrdom', *Gender and History* 12, no. 1 (2000): 82–106.

74 'Stubbs', 6.45, Staff Files, 1901–30, CVM (GA0148), Series 6, PCANZ Archives.

75 Robert, *Christian Mission*, 58.

76 Dana L. Robert, 'The origin of the Student Volunteer watchword: "The evangelization of the world in this generation"', *International Bulletin of Missionary Research* 10, no. 4 (1986): 146.

77 Clifton J. Phillips, 'Changing attitudes in the Student Volunteer Movement of Great Britain and North America, 1886–1928', in *Missionary Ideologies in the Imperialist Era, 1880–1920*, T. Christensen and W.R. Hutchison (eds), (Aarhus: Aros, 1982), 132–35; Anderson, 'American Protestants in pursuit of mission', 106.

78 See further, Renate Howe, *A Century of Influence: The Australasian Student Christian Movement 1896–1996* (Sydney: UNSW Press, 2009), 23–38, 54–61.

79 'Constitution of the ASCU, 1896', 4, Series G310: Australasia, 2015/244,

Archives of the World Student Christian Federation (WSCF), 46/8, Yale; 'The Missionary Department of the ASCU, c. 1896', World Trip – Australia and New Zealand, Series VII, Biographical Documentation, 2506/150, Mott Papers, 45, Yale.

80   P.E. Sutton, 'The New Zealand Student Christian Movement, 1896–1936' (MA thesis, Victoria University College, 1946); Christine Berry, *The New Zealand Student Christian Movement, 1896–1996: A centennial history* (Christchurch: The Student Christian Movement of Aotearoa, 1998).

81   Based on 'Listing of NZ Student Volunteers', New Zealand Student Christian Movement Collection (NZSCM), MS Papers 1617, Folder 4, Turnbull; and 'List of Student Volunteers, 1916', G549.111, 2033/246, WSCF, 46/8, Yale; Jessie Reeve, *The Missionary Uprising among Australasian Students* (Melbourne: ASCU, 1910), 24.

82   'Work in Australasia, Part 1', 1, John Mott Report Letters, 1895–99, A912E, 344/42B, WSCF, 46/1, Yale.

83   Renate Howe, 'The Australian Student Christian Movement and women's activism in the Asia–Pacific region, 1890s–1920s', *Australian Feminist Studies* 16, no. 36 (2001): 312.

84   'Constitution of the ASCU, 1896', 4.

85   'Otago University Christian Union Membership Application Form', undated, Series G610.3, Australasia, 2036/246, WSCF, 46/8, Yale.

86   'Otago Christian Union Syllabus, 1896', Mott's Notes, Series G100, Australasia, 2009/244, WSCF, 46/8, Yale; Sample Syllabi for New Zealand Christian Union Meetings, 1900 and 1903, Series G615.004, Australasia, 2037/246, WSCF, 46/8, Yale.

87   'The Endeavour Movement on its trial', *New Zealand Baptist*, April 1898, 1.

88   'Suggestions to Volunteers', undated, Series G540.3, Australasia, 2027/246, WSCF, 46/8, Yale.

89   'University Christian Movements', *Otago Daily Times*, 23 April 1896.

90   'A Seven Year Contrast in Australasia', 1903, 1–2, Series III, Report Letters, Journals and Diaries, 1937/117, Mott Papers, 45, Yale.

91   Robert, 'The origin of the Student Volunteer watchword', 148; Phillips, 'Changing attitudes in the Student Volunteer Movement', 134.

92   *Nelson Evening Mail*, 19 January 1899; 20 January 1899.

93   Peter J. Lineham, 'Finding a space for evangelicalism: Evangelical youth movements in New Zealand', in *Voluntary Religion*, W.J. Sheils and D. Woods (eds), (Oxford: Basil Blackwell, 1986), 477–94; Stuart Lange, *A Rising Tide: Evangelical Christianity in New Zealand 1930–1965* (Dunedin: Otago University Press, 2013), 42–46, 50–54, 72–83.

94   *Outlook*, 16 May 1903, 3–38.

95   22 May and 16 June 1903, Minutes of the Presbyterian Church of New Zealand Foreign Missionary Committee, 1901–13, Series 1, GA0001, PCANZ Archives; 6 October 1903, Minutes of the Executive Committee of the New Zealand Church Missionary Association, 1900–12, ANG 143/1.2,

Box 1, NZCMS Archives.

96 Mark Noll, *The New Shape of World Christianity: How American experience reflects global faith* (Downers Grove, Illinois: IVP Academic, 2009), 191.

97 See, for example, Malcolm Prentis, 'Guthrie Wilson and the trans-Tasman educational career', *History of Education Review* 42, no. 1 (2013): 69–84.

98 Denoon et al, *A History of Australia, New Zealand and the Pacific*, 195-97; Philippa Mein Smith, *A Concise History of New Zealand* (Cambridge: Cambridge University Press, 2005), 112-16; Philippa Mein Smith, 'The Tasman World', in *The New Oxford History of New Zealand*, 306–08; and Mein Smith et al, *Remaking the Tasman World*, 40–45.

99 Quoted in Andrew Walls, *The Missionary Movement in Christian History: Studies in the transmission of faith* (Maryknoll, New York: Orbis Books, 1996), 221, 222.

100 Noll, *The New Shape of World Christianity*, 13.

101 Ian Tyrrell, 'American exceptionalism in an age of international history', *American Historical Review* 96, no. 4 (1991): 1031–55; Ian Tyrrell, 'Making nations/making states: American historians in the context of empire', *Journal of American History* 86, no. 3 (1999): 1015–44.

102 Andrew Porter, 'Church history, history of Christianity, religious history: Some reflections on British missionary enterprise since the late eighteenth century', *Church History* 71, no. 13 (2002): 556–58; Walls, *The Missionary Movement in Christian History*, 223, 223–27; Alvyn Austin, 'Only connect: The China Inland Mission and transatlantic evangelicalism', in *North American Foreign Missions, 1810–1914: Theology, theory, and policy*, Wilbert Shenk (ed.), (Grand Rapids, Michigan and Cambridge, UK: William B. Eerdmans, 2004), 281–313.

CHAPTER FOUR

1   Myrtle Hill, 'Women in the Irish Protestant foreign missions c. 1873–1914: Representations and motivations', in *Missions and Missionaries*, Pieter N Holtrop and Hugh McLeod (eds), (Woodbridge, UK: Boydell Press, 2000), 181.

2   'Mona Dean', ANG 143/3.35, Box 8, NZCMS Archives.

3   Kimberley to Dean, 23 April 1913 and 22 October 1913, ANG 143/3.35, Box 8, NZCMS Archives.

4   Dean to Kimberley, 9 November 1913, ANG 143/3.35, Box 8, NZCMS Archives.

5   Dean to Kimberley, 12 February 1916, ANG 143/3.35, Box 8, NZCMS Archives.

6   Robert Glen, 'Those odious evangelicals: The origins and background of CMS missionaries in New Zealand', in Robert Glen (ed.), *Mission and Moko: The Church Missionary Society in New Zealand 1814–1882* (Christchurch: Latimer Fellowship of New Zealand, 1992), 35.

7   See, for example, S. Piggin, 'Assessing nineteenth century missionary

motivation: Some considerations of theory and methods', in *Religious Motivation: Biographical and sociological problems for the church historian*, D. Baker (ed.), (Oxford: Basil Blackwell, 1978), 333.

8   R. Pierce Beaver, 'Missionary motivation through three centuries', in *Reinterpretation in American church history*, Jerald C. Brauer (ed.), (Chicago and London: University of Chicago Press, 1968), 113–51; Johannes van den Berg, *Constrained by Jesus' Love: An inquiry into the motives of the missionary awakening in Great Britain in the period between 1698 and 1815* (Kampen: J.H. Kok, n.v., 1956).

9   Representative among these are: N.A. Etherington, 'American errand into the South African wilderness', *Church History* 39, no. 1 (1970): 62–71; Wayne J. Flynt and Gerald W. Berkley, *Taking Christianity to China: Alabama missionaries in the Middle Kingdom, 1850–1950* (Tuscaloosa: University of Alabama Press, 1997); Diane Langmore, *Missionary Lives: Papua, 1874–1914*; G.A. Oddie, 'India and missionary motives c. 1850–1900', *Journal of Ecclesiastical History* 25, no. 1 (1974): 61–74; Andrew Porter, 'Evangelical enthusiasm, missionary motivation and West Africa in the late nineteenth century: The career of G.W. Brooke', *Journal of Imperial and Commonwealth History* 6, no. 1 (1977): 23–46; Stuart Piggin, *Making Evangelical Missionaries, 1789–1858: The social background, motives and training of British Protestant missionaries to India* (Abingdon: Sutton Courtenay Press, 1984).

10   Representative among these are: Derek Dow, 'Domestic response and reaction to the foreign missionary enterprises of the principal Scottish Presbyterian churches, 1873–1929' (PhD thesis, University of Edinburgh, 1977) and C.P. Williams, '"Not quite gentlemen": An examination of "middling class" Protestant missionaries from Britain, c. 1850–1900', *Journal of Ecclesiastical History* 31, no. 3 (1980): 301–15 (social history); Jane Hunter, *The Gospel of Gentility: American women missionaries in turn-of-the-century China* (New Haven: Yale University Press, 1984) and L.N. Predelli, 'Sexual control and the remaking of gender: The attempt of nineteenth-century Protestant Norwegian women to export western domesticity to Madagascar', *Journal of Women's History* 12, no. 2 (2000): 81–103 (feminist or gendered history); John and Jean Comaroff, 'Through the looking-glass: Colonial encounters of the first kind', *Journal of Historical Sociology* 1, no. 1 (1988): 6–32; and Nicholas Thomas, 'Colonial conversions: Difference, hierarchy, and history in early twentieth-century evangelical propaganda', *Comparative Studies in Society and History* 34, no. 2 (1992): 366–89 (postcolonial history).

11   Representative among these are: Sarah C. Coleman, '"Come over and help us": White women, reform and the missionary endeavour in India, 1876–1920' (MA thesis in history, University of Canterbury, 2002); Lisa Early, '"If we win the women": The lives and work of Methodist missionary women in the Solomon Islands, 1902–1942' (PhD thesis in history, University of

Otago, 1998); E. Johnston, '"Cannibals won for Christ": Oscar Michelsen Presbyterian missionary in the New Hebrides, 1878–1932' (MA thesis in history, University of Auckland, 1995); and Brooke Whitelaw, 'A message for the missahibs: New Zealand Presbyterian missionaries in the Punjab, 1910–1940' (MA thesis in history, University of Otago, 2001).

12 Myrtle Hill, 'Gender, culture and "the spiritual empire": The Irish Protestant female missionary experience', *Women's History Review* 16, no. 2 (2007): 203–26.

13 Beaver, 'Missionary motivation through three centuries', 148.

14 15 October 1856, Minute Book of the Presbytery of Auckland, 1856–1869, MS 1501.P928, Box 1, Auckland War Memorial Museum Library.

15 'Motives for missionaries', *White Already to Harvest*, June 1901, 84.

16 Revd John Inglis, *Thesis – The doctrine of Christian missions, with special reference to the South Sea islands* (Edinburgh: Morrison & Gibb, 1881), 5; NZCMA Report, 1899–1900, 4.

17 Gustav Warneck, *Outline of a History of Protestant Missions from the Reformation to the Present Time* (Edinburgh & London: Oliphant, Anderson & Ferrier, 1906), 3–4.

18 Missionary sermon preached to the NZBU Conference, *Missionary Messenger*, January 1917, 2.

19 Ruth Rouse, 'A study of missionary vocation', *International Review of Missions* 6, no. 22 (1917): 255–57.

20 Revd A.H. Collins, 'The new motive in religion', [unpublished] 15 July 1894, 6, Box 0194, NZBHS Archives.

21 Herbert Davies, *Four Studies in World-wide Evangelisation* (Dunedin: ASCU, 1909), 7.

22 Mrs McLean, 'Our attitude towards the non-Christian world', *Harvest Field*, November 1913, iii.

23 'The permanent missionary motive', *Outlook*, 15 December 1900, 17–18; 'Student volunteer recruitment', undated, Series IV, Notes and Notebooks, 2105/130, Mott Papers, 45, Yale.

24 *Christian Outlook*, 7 March 1896, 72. There was a general 'decline in the importance of the "perishing heathen" as a motive': Langmore, *Missionary Lives*, 41–42. It is possible, however, that organisations like the CIM continued to emphasise this as a motive, as evidenced in Rita Dobson's narrative written prior to her departure in 1928; see *China's Millions*, November 1928, 165.

25 Rhonda Semple, *Missionary Women: Gender, professionalism, and the Victorian idea of Christian mission* (Woodbridge, Suffolk, and Rochester, NY: Boydell Press, 2003), 17.

26 Langmore, *Missionary Lives*, 39–40; Piggin, 'Assessing nineteenth century missionary motivation', 328–30; Whitelaw, 'A message for the missahibs', 41–48.

27 One exception to this was an early survey of missionary motives conducted

by Ruth Rouse and published as 'A study of missionary vocation'. A brief consideration of motivation is also found in Rosemary Seton, '"Open doors for female labourers": Women candidates of the London Missionary Society, 1875–1914', in *Missionary Encounters: Sources and issues*, Robert Bickers and Rosemary Seton (eds), (Richmond, Surrey: Curzon Press, 1996), 57.

28 These calculations are based on known factors for 44 per cent of total applicants – NZBMS 10 per cent, BIM and CIM both 27 per cent, NZCMA/S 67 per cent, and PCNZ FMC 64 per cent.

29 It may be that 'life-stage transition' and 'life-stage dissatisfaction' should have been grouped together. The choice was made, however, to separate these factors because the dynamics involved appeared to be fundamentally different.

30 Van den Berg's categories are listed in Max Warren, *The Missionary Movement from Britain in Modern History* (London: SCM Press, 1965), 45–48; Piggin, *Making Evangelical Missionaries*, 124–49.

31 These calculations are based on known motivational factors for 39 per cent of total applicants – NZBMS 10 per cent, BIM 25 per cent, CIM 28 per cent, NZCMS/A 73 per cent, and PCNZ FMC 49 per cent.

32 The discussion that follows is based on the documented 'spiritual experience' of 31 per cent of Presbyterian applicants and missionaries; 19 per cent of NZCMA/S applicants and missionaries; 38 per cent of BIM missionaries; and 45 per cent of CIM missionaries. Equivalent material does not appear to exist for BIM and CIM applicants, or for NZBMS applicants and missionaries.

33 'Elsie Goodson', 6.11, CVM (GA0148), Series 6, Staff Files, PCANZ Archives; 'Obituary for Nellie MacDuff', *China's Millions*, September 1927, 131.

34 'Christina Anderson', 'Eveline Arthur', 'William Byrt', 'Reginald Judson', 'Joseph Venables', PCNZ FMC (GA0001), Series 3, Missionary Candidates, PCANZ Archives; 'Arthur Carr', ANG 143/3.19, Box 6, and 'Florence Smith', ANG 143/3.105, Box 14, NZCMS Archives.

35 'Katherine Ensor', ANG 143/3.40, Box 9, NZCMS Archives.

36 'New Year Retrospect and Prospect, 1896', Diaries of George McNeur, 1890–1900, George Hunter McNeur Papers, MS-1007, ARC-038, Hocken Library, Dunedin, New Zealand.

37 Alice Henderson, *My Yesterdays in Sunshine and Shadow* (Christchurch: Presbyterian Church of New Zealand, 1947), 8.

38 See James Fowler, *Stages of Faith: The psychology of development and the quest for meaning* (Blackburn, Victoria: Dove Communications, 1981).

39 For an extended discussion of the prevalent discourses emerging within nineteenth-century British evangelicalism, and particularly the notion of gendered evangelical narrative structures, see Callum G. Brown, *The Death of Christian Britain: Understanding secularisation, 1800–2000* (London: Routledge, 2001), 35–57, 58–114, 115–44. For a response to Brown's thesis and an updated survey of the historiography of modern British secularisation

also see Jeremy Morris, 'The Strange Death of Christian Britain: Another Look at the Secularization Debate', *The Historical Journal* 46, no. 4 (2003): 963–76; and Jeremy Morris, 'Secularization and Religious Experience: Arguments in the historiography of modern British religion', *The Historical Journal* 55, no. 1 (2012): 195–219.

40 'Name withheld', ANG 143/3.68, Box 10; 'Form No. 3, NZCMA, Questions for Candidates', ANG 143/3.8, Box 4, NZCMS Archives.

41 'Annie Hancock', 6.13, CVM (GA0148), Series 6, Staff Files, PCANZ Archives.

42 John Olley to James Clapham, November 1917, quoted in J.W. Clapham, *John Olley, Pioneer Missionary to the Chad*, rev. edn (London: Pickering & Inglis, 1966), 32.

43 This table combines the two categories of 'life-stage transition' (Tables 4.1 and 4.2) and 'life-stage dissatisfaction' (Table 4.1). It is based primarily on Presbyterian and NZCMA/S data.

44 'Annie Astbury', 6.02, CVM (GA0148), Series 6, Staff Files, PCANZ Archives.

45 'Patrick Lane', ANG 143/3.80, Box 11, NZCMS Archives.

46 T.E. Riddle, *The Light of Other Days* (Christchurch and Dunedin: Presbyterian Bookroom, 1949), 46.

47 Kelling to C.H. Grant, 18 January 1919, in 'Irene Kelling', ANG 143/3.75, Box 11; 'Miss L. Johnson', ANG 143/3.73, Box 10, NZCMS Archives.

48 'Dr Lapraik', PCNZ FMC (GA0001), Series 3, Missionary Candidates 1905–35, PCANZ Archives.

49 William Ernest Hocking (ed.), *Re-Thinking Missions: A laymen's inquiry after one hundred years* (New York and London: Harper & Brothers, 1932), 255–86; R. Pierce Beaver, *All Loves Excelling: American Protestant women in world mission* (Grand Rapids, Michigan: Eerdmans, 1968), 143–55.

50 See earlier references in this chapter as well as: Daphne Beniston, 'New Zealand women of the Methodist Solomons Mission 1922–1992' (MA thesis, University of Auckland, 1992); Rachel Gillett, 'Helpmeets and handmaidens: The role of women in mission discourse' (BA (Hons) dissertation, University of Otago, 1998); and Diane Rixon, 'New Zealand mission and nationalism in the Punjab: The missionaries of the Presbyterian Church of New Zealand in the Punjab and their encounter with Indian nationalism between 1910 and 1932' (BA (Hons) dissertation, University of Otago, 1997).

51 Shirley S. Garrett, 'Sisters all: Feminism and the American women's missionary movement', in *Missionary Ideologies in the Imperialist Era, 1880–1920*, T. Christensen and W.R. Hutchison (eds), (Aarhus: Aros, 1982), 221, 224.

52 See, for example: Jean Allman, 'Making mothers: Missionaries, medical officers and women's work in colonial Asante, 1924–1945', *History Workshop* 38 (1994): 23–47; Delia Davin, 'British women missionaries in nineteenth century China', *Women's History Review* 1, no. 2 (1992): 257–71; Leslie A.

Flemming, 'A new humanity: American missionaries' ideals for women in North India, 1870–1930', in *Western Women and Imperialism: Complicity and resistance*, N. Chaudhuri and M. Strobel (eds), (Bloomington: Indiana University Press, 1992), 191–206; Margaret Jolly, '"To save the girls for brighter and better lives": Presbyterian missions and women in the south of Vanuatu, 1848–1870', *Journal of Pacific History* 26, no. 1 (1991): 27–48; and Ann White, 'Counting the cost of faith: America's early female missionaries', *Church History* 57, no. 1 (1988): 19–30.

53 Coleman, 'White women, reform and the missionary endeavour in India, 1876–1920', 197–98.

54 Jane Haggis, 'Ironies of emancipation: Changing configurations of "women's work" in the "mission of sisterhood" to Indian women', *Feminist Review* 65 (Summer 2000): 108–26.

55 'Christina Anderson', PCNZ FMC (GA0001), Series 3, Missionary Candidates 1905–35, PCANZ Archives.

56 'Violet Bargrove', ANG 143/3.7, Box 4; 'Ruby Lindsay', ANG 143/3.85, Box 11, NZCMS Archives.

57 Valedictory Address for Rosalie Macgeorge, *New Zealand Baptist*, November 1886, 174.

58 *New Zealand Baptist*, August 1895, 113–16; September 1895, 135.

59 *Our Bond*, 24:1 (1918), 4–5; 12 October 1925; Minutes of the Annual Meetings of the BWMU, 1905–28; and 'Presidential Address by Emma Beckingsale, 1935' [unpublished], in BWMU Records, Folder 1, Box 0036, NZBHS Archives.

60 See further John Stenhouse, 'God, the Devil, and gender', in *Sites of Gender: Women, men and modernity in southern Dunedin, 1890–1939*, Barbara Brookes, Annabel Cooper and Robyn Law (eds), (Auckland: Auckland University Press, 2003), 327–28.

61 Yvonne Robertson, *Girdle Round the Earth: New Zealand Presbyterian women's ideal of universal sisterhood, 1878–1918*, Annual Lecture, Auckland 1993 (Dunedin: Presbyterian Historical Society of New Zealand, 1994), 12–21. Elements of this argument are echoed in Jane Haggis, '"A heart that has felt the love of God and longs for others to know it": Conventions of gender, tensions of self and constructions of difference in offering to be a lady missionary', *Women's History Review* 7, no. 2 (1998): 171–92.

62 'Miss McKinney', PCNZ FMC (GA0001), Series 3, Missionary Candidates 1905–35, PCANZ Archives; 'Isabella McCallum', ANG 143/3.86, Box 12, NZCMS Archives.

63 Hunter, *The Gospel of Gentility*, 40–42.

64 Abraham Maslow, *Motivation and Personality*, 2nd edn (New York: Harper & Row, Publishers, 1970), 45–47.

65 'Beatrice Brunt', ANG 143/3.17, Box 6, NZCMS Archives.

66 Coleman, 'White women, reform and the missionary endeavour in India, 1876–1920', 56–57. Janet Lee advances a similar argument in 'Between

subordination and she-tiger: Social constructions of white femininity in the lives of single, Protestant missionaries in China, 1905–1930', *Women's Studies International Forum* 19, no. 6 (1996): 621–32.

67 Lydia Hoyle, 'Nineteenth century single women and motivation for mission', *International Bulletin of Missionary Research* 20, no. 2 (1996): 58–59.

68 Based on candidates' testimonies published in *China's Millions* between 1912 and 1930.

69 Peter Williams, '"The missing link": The recruitment of women missionaries in some English evangelical missionary societies in the nineteenth century', in *Women and Missions: Past and present, anthropological and historical perspectives*, F. Bowie, D. Kirkwood and S. Ardener (eds), (Providence & Oxford: Berg Publishers, 1993), 62–63.

70 See, for example: Michael Belgrave, 'A subtle containment: Women in New Zealand medicine, 1893–1941', *NZJH* 22, no. 1 (1988): 44–55; Antoinette Burton, 'Contesting the zenana: The mission to make "lady doctors for India", 1874–1885', *Journal of British Studies* 35 (1996): 368–97; Dorothy Page, 'The first lady graduates: Women with degrees from Otago University, 1885–1900', in *Women in History 2: Essays on women in New Zealand*, Barbara Brookes, Charlotte Macdonald and Margaret Tennant (eds), (Wellington: Bridget Williams Books, 1992), 98–128.

71 Hunter, *The Gospel of Gentility*, 38; Myrtle Hill, 'Women in the Irish Protestant foreign missions c. 1873–1914', 177.

72 Andrée Lévesque, 'Prescribers and rebels: Attitudes to European women's sexuality in New Zealand, 1860–1916', in *Women in History: Essays on European women in New Zealand*, Barbara Brookes, Charlotte Macdonald and Margaret Tennant (eds), (Wellington: Allen & Unwin New Zealand, 1986), 1; Erik Olssen, 'Towards a new society', in *The Oxford History of New Zealand*, W.H. Oliver and Bridget Williams (eds), (Wellington: Oxford University Press, 1981), 250–53; R.J. Warwick Neville and C. James O'Neill (eds), *The Population of New Zealand: Interdisciplinary perspectives* (Auckland: Longman Paul, 1979), 150–84.

73 Olssen, 'Towards a new society', 252.

74 *Census of New Zealand*, 1916, Part VII, 'Conjugal Condition': 2; ibid., 1926, Volume IV, 'Conjugal Condition', Tables 4 and 5:7.

75 In 1896 Canterbury had 78 bachelors to every 100 spinsters and Otago had 91. By 1906 Canterbury had 91 and Otago 96. *Census of New Zealand*, 1896, part V. 'Conjugal Condition', Table IV, 195; ibid., 1906, 'Part V, 'Conjugal Condition', Table IV, 243.

76 Donovan F. Mitchell, *Ellen Arnold: Pioneer and pathfinder* (Adelaide: South Australian Baptist Union Foreign Missionary and Book and Publication Departments, 1932), 17–21.

77 An initial exploration of this phenomenon is found in Diane Langmore's comparison of Protestant and Catholic women working in Papua, and Margaret Tennant's preliminary analysis of the early deaconess movement

in New Zealand. See Diane Langmore, 'A neglected force: White women missionaries in Papua, 1874–1914', *Journal of Pacific History* 17, no. 3 (1982): 138–50, and 'Exchanging earth for heaven: Death in the Papuan missionfields', *Journal of Religious History* 13, no. 3 (1985): 383–92; Margaret Tennant, 'Sisterly ministrations. The social work of Protestant deaconesses in New Zealand 1890–1940', *NZJH* 32, no. 1 (1998): 3–22. The notion of Protestant orders for women (established in the 1890s) is also helpfully outlined in two local Anglican histories: Ruth Fry, *The Community of the Sacred Name: A centennial history* (Christchurch: Community of the Sacred Name, 1993); and Margaret McClure, *Saving the City: The history of the Order of the Good Shepherd and the Community of the Holy Name in Auckland, 1894–2000* (Auckland: David Ling, 2002). See also: J.D. Salmond, *By Love Serve: The story of the Order of Deaconesses of the Presbyterian Church of New Zealand* (Christchurch: Presbyterian Bookroom, 1962); and Martha Vicinus, *Independent Women: Work and community for single women, 1850–1920* (London: Virago Press, 1985), 46–84.

78 'Annie Hancock', 6.13, CVM (GA0148), Series 6, Staff Files, PCANZ Archives.

79 *Tahuantin Suyu*, March 1914, 28–30.

80 Stuart Piggin, *Spirit of a Nation: The story of Australia's Christian heritage* (Sydney: Strand, 2004), 66–74; Andrew Porter, 'Cambridge, Keswick and late nineteenth century attitudes to Africa', *Journal of Imperial and Commonwealth History* 5, no. 1 (1976): 5–34.

81 'Alice Hercus', PCNZ FMC (GA0001), Series 3, Missionary Candidates, PCANZ Archives; Kimberley to Revd Henry Wright, 25 June 1919, 'Wright', ANG 143/3.131, Box 17, NZCMS Archives.

82 For further details of this mission, see Hugh Morrison, 'Maintaining the church in unsettled times, 1899–1918', in *Living Legacy: A history of the Anglican diocese of Auckland*, Allan K. Davidson (ed.), (Auckland: Anglican Diocese of Auckland, 2011), 129–30.

83 'Cooper', ANG 143/3.28, Box 8, NZCMS Archives.

CHAPTER FIVE

1 Jane Simpson, 'Joseph W. Kemp: Prime interpreter of American fundamentalism in New Zealand in the 1920s', in *'Rescue the Perishing': Comparative perspectives on evangelism and revivalism*, Douglas Pratt (ed,), (Auckland: College Communications, 1989), 23–41.

2 For further references to its growing influence on the development of twentieth-century evangelicalism in New Zealand, see Stuart Lange, *A Rising Tide: Evangelical Christianity in New Zealand 1930–1965* (Dunedin: Otago University Press, 2013), 35–36; and Peter Lineham, 'The foundation of the Bible Training Institute', in *Gospel, Truth and Interpretation: Evangelical identity in Aotearoa New Zealand*, Tim Meadowcroft and Myk Habets (eds),

(Auckland: Archer Press, 2012), 49–67.

3   For the North American context, for example, see Joel A. Carpenter, 'Propagating the faith once delivered: The fundamentalist missionary enterprise, 1920–1945', in *Earthen Vessels: American evangelicals and foreign missions, 1880–1980*, Joel A. Carpenter and Wilbert R. Shenk (eds), (Grand Rapids, Michigan: Eerdmans, 1990), 102–06.

4   J. Oswald Sanders, *Expanding Horizons: The story of the New Zealand Bible Training Institute* (Auckland: Institute Press, 1971), 94, 96.

5   Stanley Muir, 'A memorable gathering', [NZBTI] *Reaper*, October 1929, 269.

6   Annotated map entitled 'After Three Years! N.Z.B.T.I. Graduates on Every Continent', [NZBTI] *Reaper*, October 1925, 224. Note that from 1923 there was also an unrelated *Reaper* magazine produced by the New Zealand Anglican Board of Missions.

7   See, for example, Jeremy Black, *Maps and History: Constructing images of the past* (New Haven and London: Yale University Press, 2000), 51–80.

8   Representative examples of a wide body of literature on this subject are: Giselle Byrnes, *Boundary Markers: Land surveying and the colonisation of New Zealand* (Wellington: Bridget Williams Books, 2001); Simon Dench, 'Invading the Waikato: A postcolonial review', *NZJH* 45, no. 1 (2011): 33–49; and Sujit Suvasandaram, *Islanded: Britain, Sri Lanka & the bounds of an Indian Ocean colony* (Chicago and London: University of Chicago Press, 2013), 209–45.

9   James S. Dennis, Harlan P. Beach and Charles H. Fahs (eds), *World Atlas of Christian Missions* (New York: Student Volunteer Movement for Foreign Missions, 1911).

10   For a brief introduction to the statistical movement in Victorian Britain, see Pat Hudson, *History by Numbers: An introduction to quantitative approaches* (London: Arnold, 2000), 32–40.

11   This is now an extensive body of literature in its own right. A useful survey of the subject's trajectory can be found in Timothy Yates, *The Conversion of the Māori: Years of religious and social change, 1814–1842* (Grand Rapids, MI, and Cambridge, UK: William B. Eerdmans, 2013). The broad contours of the longer debate over Māori conversion can also be traced through the following representative works: J.M.R Owens, 'New Zealand before annexation', in *The Oxford History of New Zealand*, W.H. Oliver and B.R. Williams (eds), (Wellington: Oxford University Press, 1981), 36–39; James Belich, *Making Peoples: From Polynesian settlement to the end of the nineteenth century* (Auckland: Allen Lane The Penguin Press, 1996), 156–211; Michael King, *The Penguin History of New Zealand* (Auckland, New Zealand: Penguin, 2003), 139–50; Judith Binney, 'History and memory: The wood of the whau tree, 1766–2005', in Giselle Byrnes (ed.), *The New Oxford History of New Zealand* (Oxford and Melbourne: Oxford University Press, 2009), 76–82; and Tony Ballantyne, *Entanglements of Empire: Missionaries, Māori*

and the question of the body (Auckland: Auckland University Press, 2015). This is also the subject of ongoing postgraduate thesis research.

12 Allan K. Davidson, 'The New Zealand overseas missionary contribution: The need for further research', in *With All Humility and Gentleness*, Allan K. Davison and Godfrey Nicholson (eds), (Auckland: St John's College, 1991), 41–50.

13 J.G.A. Pocock, 'Tangata whenua and Enlightenment anthropology', *NZJH* 26, no. 1 (1992): 29.

14 Erik Olssen, 'Where to from here? Reflections on the twentieth-century historiography of nineteenth-century New Zealand', *NZJH* 26, no. 1 (1992): 70.

15 Peter Gibbons, 'Cultural colonization and national identity', *NZJH* 36, no. 1 (2002): 14.

16 Ian Breward, 'Religion and New Zealand society', *NZJH* 13, no. 2 (1979): 141.

17 Stenhouse, 'Religion and society', in *The New Oxford History of New Zealand*, 344.

18 See, for example, the following essays in Geoffrey Troughton and Hugh Morrison (eds), *The Spirit of the Past: Essays on Christianity in New Zealand history* (Wellington: Victoria University Press, 2011): Adrienne Puckey, 'Who you know: Māori, missionaries and the economy', 83–97; Geoffrey Troughton, 'Richard Booth and gospel temperance revivalism', 112–25; Christopher J. van der Krogt, '"The evils of mixed marriages": Catholic teaching and practice', 142–55; and Nicholas Reid, 'A new world through a new youth: The life and death of the Catholic Youth Movement in New Zealand', 156–68.

19 Giselle Byrnes and Catharine Coleborne, 'Editorial introduction: The utility and futility of "the nation" in histories of Aotearoa New Zealand', *NZJH* 45, no. 1 (2011), 2.

20 Ibid., 4.

21 Giselle Byrnes, 'Introduction: Reframing New Zealand history', in *The New Oxford History of New Zealand*, 1.

22 Byrnes and Coleborne, 'Editorial introduction', 3.

23 See, for example: Tony Ballantyne, *Orientalism and Race: Aryanism in the British Empire* (Houndmills, Basingstoke, and New York: Palgrave, 2002); Ballantyne, *Webs of Empire: Locating New Zealand's colonial past* (Wellington: Bridget Williams Books, 2012); Brian Moloughney, 'Translating culture: Rethinking New Zealand's Chineseness', in *East by South: China in the Australasian imagination*, Charles Ferrall, Paul Millar and Keren Smith (eds), (Wellington: Victoria University Press, 2005), 389–404; Tony Ballantyne and Brian Moloughney, 'Asia in Murihiku: Towards a transnational history of colonial culture', in *Disputed Histories: Imagining New Zealand's past*, Tony Ballantyne and Brian Moloughney (eds), (Dunedin: Otago University Press, 2006), 65–92; and Sekhar Bandyopadhyay, 'Introduction', in *India in*

New Zealand: Local identities, global relations, Sekhar Bandyopadhyay (ed.), (Dunedin: Otago University Press, 2010), 7–18.

24 Peter Gibbons, 'The far side of the search for identity: Reconsidering New Zealand history', *NZJH* 37, no. 1 (2003): 39–46, 39.

25 Ibid., 47.

26 Ibid., 41.

27 The fuller narrative plus sources can be found in Hugh Morrison, '"It is our bounden duty": The emergence of the New Zealand Protestant missionary movement, 1868–1926' (PhD thesis, Massey University, 2004), 96–106. Two histories of the BIM have been published: Margarita Allan Hudspith, *Ripening Fruit: A history of the Bolivian Indian Mission* (New Jersey: Harrington Press, 1958); and James L. Hansen (ed.), *A Heart to Serve: Ordinary people with an extraordinary God* (Cochabamba: Mision Andina Evangelica, 2007). An in-depth study of the BIM's educational mission can be found in Hugh Morrison, 'Theorising missionary education: The Bolivian Indian Mission 1908–1920', *History of Education Review* 42, no. 1 (2013): 4–23.

28 'Bolivian Indian Mission Principles and Practice, 1908', Minutes of the New Zealand Council of the BIM, 1908–16, Box 5; and 'Principles and Practice of the Bolivian Indian Mission, 1927', in Minutes of the Field Conferences of the BIM, 1913–45 [Bound Volume], BIM Archives.

29 'Obituary', *Bolivian Indian*, May–June 1939, 138–40; 'Obituary', *Bolivian Indian*, January–March 1942, 3–6.

30 Correspondence of the Dunedin and New Zealand Committee of the SAEM, the ASAM and the BIM, 1900–13; *Tahuantin Suyu*, 1911–14 and the *Bolivian Indian*, 1914–30.

31 Stevan Eldred-Grigg and Zeng Dazheng, *White Ghosts, Yellow Peril: China and New Zealand 1790–1950* (Dunedin: Otago University Press, 2014), 139.

32 This estimate is based on a broad survey of the annual reports of representative missions (namely, Baptist Church, BIM, CIM, Methodist Church, NZBMS, NZCMA/S and Presbyterian Church).

33 *Otago Witness*, 12 October 1926.

34 Eldred-Grigg and Zeng Dazheng, *White Ghosts, Yellow Peril*, 138 (in turn quoting from *The Colonist*, 1 February 1899).

35 Ballantyne and Moloughney, 'Asia in Murihiku', 87.

36 'Official Handbook, Grand Missionary Exhibition', Subject Files, Series 4, GA0001, PCANZ Archives; *Outlook*, 23 August 1910, 8.

37 Anon., *St Andrew's Presbyterian Church: A brief survey of the first sixty years and an illustrated history of the years 1923–1963* (Dunedin: Editorial Committee, 1963), 43–44.

38 Alexander Don, *Light in Dark Isles: A jubilee record and study of the New Hebrides Mission of the Presbyterian Church of New Zealand* (Dunedin: Foreign Missions Committee, Presbyterian Church of New Zealand, 1918), 44, 45, 46.

39 'Annual Report of the South Island Oriental Depot, 1924–1925' [unpublished], PWMU South Island Oriental Depot Minutes, 1924–30, Box AF3/1, PCANZ Archives.

40 Aitchison to Allan, 16 December 1911, Correspondence of the ASAM/BIM, 1905–13, Box 5, BIM Archives.

41 See further Peter Burke, 'Strengths and weaknesses of the history of mentalities', *History of European Ideas* 7, no. 5 (1986): 439–51, for some background on this influential French school of historical thought.

42 Ibid., 439.

43 Robert Evans and Roy McKenzie, *Evangelical Revivals in New Zealand* (Paihia: ColCom, 1999), 58–62; Peter J. Lineham, *There We Found Brethren: A history of assemblies of Brethren in New Zealand* (Palmerston North: GPH Society, 1977), 96–102.

44 George Allan to Jean, 20 January 1895, in 'Allan Correspondence, 1895–1925', George and Mary Allan Personal Collection, Box 11, BIM Archives.

45 'Farewell address in St John's Presbyterian Church, Wellington, 21 April 1909', in 'Allan Correspondence, 1895–1925', George and Mary Allan Personal Collection, Box 11, BIM Archives.

46 Gibbons, 'The far side of the search for identity', 41, 44.

47 *Bolivian Indian*, April 1916, 3–4.

48 Gibbons, 'The far side of the search for identity', 45.

49 David Jull, 'The Knapdale revival (1881): Social context and religious conviction in 19th century New Zealand', *Australasian Pentecostal Studies* 7 (2003): http://webjournals.alphacrucis.edu.au/journals/aps/issue-7

50 Tony Ballantyne, 'Thinking local: Knowledge, sociability and community in Gore's intellectual life, 1875–1914', *NZJH* 44, no. 2 (2010): 138–56.

51 Margaret Allen, '"White already to harvest": South Australian women missionaries in India', *Feminist Review* 65 (Summer 2000): 98.

52 See M. Thayer, *The Taieri Allans and their Descendants* (Dunedin: University of Otago Printery, 1990); and J.A. Thomson, *The Taieri Allans and Related Families: A page out of the early history of Otago* (Dunedin: NZ Bible and Book Society, 1929).

53 'Bolivian Indian Mission Outfit Instructions' and 'How to Get to Bolivia from New Zealand', Miscellaneous Documents, Box 9, BIM Archives.

54 *Bolivian Indian*, 1922–28; *Bolivian Indian*, January–February 1928, back cover.

55 Esther Breitenbach, *Empire and Scottish Society: The impact of foreign missions at home, c. 1790 to c. 1914* (Edinburgh: Edinburgh University Press, 2009), 180.

56 That this was so more generally is hinted at in Rosalind McClean, '"How we prepare them in India": British diasporic imaginings and migration to New Zealand', *NZJH* 37, no. 2 (2003): 147.

57 See Nicholas Thomas, 'Colonial conversions: Difference, hierarchy, and history in early twentieth-century evangelical propaganda', *Comparative*

Studies in Society and History 34, no. 2 (1992): 366–89; and Nicholas Thomas, *Colonialism's Culture: Anthropology, travel and government* (Cambridge, UK: Polity Press in association with Blackwell Publishers, 1994), 105–42.

58 These complexities are helpfully introduced in Adrian Hastings, 'The clash of nationalism and universalism within twentieth-century missionary Christianity', in *Missions, Nationalism, and the End of Empire*, Brian Stanley (ed.), (Grand Rapids, Michigan: William B. Eerdmans, 2003), 15–33.

59 Breitenbach, *Empire and Scottish Society*, 181.

60 Eldred-Grigg and Zeng, *White Ghosts, Yellow Peril*, facing Contents page.

61 Ibid., 126–27, 182–83.

CHAPTER SIX

1 Katie Pickles, *Female Imperialism and National Identity: Imperial Order Daughters of the Empire* (Manchester: Manchester University Press, 2002), 5

2 Cover, *The War Cry*, 7 April 1900.

3 'Keep the flag flying: A stirring appeal to Salvationists of all ranks', *The War Cry*, 7 April 1900, 2.

4 Stephen Neill, *Colonialism and Christian Missions* (London: Lutterworth Press, 1966).

5 Brian Stanley, *The Bible and the Flag: Protestant missions and British imperialism in the nineteenth and twentieth centuries* (Leicester: Apollos, 1990), 12. See further as examples: John and Jean Comaroff, 'Through the looking-glass: Colonial encounters of the first kind', *Journal of Historical Sociology* 1, no. 1 (1988): 6–32; J.H. Proctor, 'Scottish missionaries in India: An inquiry into motivation', *South Asia: Journal of South Asian Studies* 13, no. 1 (1990): 43–61.

6 Jeffrey Cox, *Imperial Fault Lines: Christianity and colonial power in India, 1818–1940* (Stanford, California: Stanford University Press, 2002), 8.

7 Tony Ballantyne, 'Review essay: Religion, difference, and the limits of British imperial history', *Victorian Studies* 47, 3 (2005): 427.

8 Johannes Fabian, 'Religious and secular colonization: Common ground', *History and Anthropology* 4 (1990): 339, 352.

9 Andrew Porter, 'Review essay: Evangelical visions and colonial realities', *Journal of Imperial and Commonwealth History* 38, no. 1 (2010): 145–55.

10 Damon Salesa, 'New Zealand's Pacific', in *The New Oxford History of New Zealand*, Giselle Byrnes (ed.), (Oxford and Melbourne: Oxford University Press, 2009), 149.

11 See further, for example: Mark Hickford, *Lords of the Land: Indigenous property rights and the jurisprudence of empire* (Oxford: Oxford University Press, 2011); and Damon Salesa, *Racial Crossings: Race, intermarriage, and the Victorian British Empire* (Oxford: Oxford University Press, 2011).

12 For example: David Cannadine, *Ornamentalism: How the British saw their empire* (Oxford: Oxford University Press, 2001); Carl Bridge and

Kent Fedorowich, 'Mapping the British world', *Journal of Imperial and Commonwealth History* 31, no. 2 (2003): 1–15. Over the last decade a succession of international conferences and an explosion of publications have placed the 'British world' squarely in the centre of historical enquiry and ongoing debate.

13 Angus Ross, *New Zealand Aspirations in the Pacific in the Nineteenth Century* (Oxford: Oxford University Press, 1964), 288–304; Mary Boyd, 'Racial attitudes of New Zealand officials in Western Samoa', *NZJH* 21, no. 1 (1987): 139–55.

14 Ross, *New Zealand Aspirations*, 70–88, 131–48, 206–29; J.A. Salmond, 'New Zealand and the New Hebrides', in *The Feel of Truth: Essays in New Zealand and Pacific history*, Peter Munz (ed.), (Wellington: A.H. & A.W. Reed, 1969), 113–35.

15 Salesa, 'New Zealand's Pacific', 150, 153.

16 Margaret Allen, '"White already to harvest": South Australian women missionaries in India', *Feminist Review* 65 (Summer 2000): 104.

17 Margaret Allen, '"Innocents abroad" and "prohibited immigrants": Australians in India and Indians in Australia 1890–1910', in *Connected Worlds: History in transnational perspective*, Ann Curthoys and Marilyn Lake (eds), (Canberra: ANU E Press, 2005), 124.

18 Revd John Inglis, *Thesis – The doctrine of Christian missions, with special reference to the South Sea islands* (Edinburgh: Morrison & Gibb, 1881), 31, 39–40.

19 J. Takle, 'The inspiration of the imperium in India', *New Zealand Baptist*, November 1916, 210.

20 *Annual Report of the New Zealand Church Missionary Association*, 1900, 1, 2.

21 Alison Clarke, '"With one accord rejoice on this glad day": Celebrating the monarchy in nineteenth-century Otago', *NZJH* 36, no. 2 (2002): 155–56.

22 *Annual Report of the New Zealand Church Missionary Association*, 1915, 38–39.

23 Bishop Octavius Hadfield, *Proceedings of the General Synod*, 1898, 3–4; 'A Hymn of Praise for Queen Victoria's Diamond Jubilee', *New Zealand Baptist*, July 1897, 99; H.H. Driver to John Takle, 11 March 1901, Miscellaneous Correspondence, Folder 1, Box 0211, NZBMS Archives.

24 See David Bebbington, 'Atonement, sin, and empire, 1880–1914', in *The Imperial Horizons of British Protestant Missions, 1880–1914*, Andrew Porter (ed.), (Grand Rapids, Michigan: William B. Eerdmans, 2003), 14–31; Hugh McLeod, 'Protestantism and British national identity, 1815–1945', in *Nation and Religion: Perspectives on Europe and Asia*, Peter van der Veer and Hartmut Lehmann (eds), (Princeton, New Jersey: Princeton University Press, 1999), 44–70.

25 *Annual Report of the New Zealand Church Missionary Association*, 1900, 2; 1899, 1, 13; 1900, 1–3, 11–12; 1915, 38–39.

26 'Letter to Editor', *White Ribbon*, September 1896, 5.

27   *Outlook*, 15 December 1900, 17–18; *PCNZ PGA*, 1909, 107; 1917, 90.

28   Bishop John Selwyn, quoted in the *New Zealand Church News*, April 1877, 77–8; John Takle, 'Hindrances in the mission field' *New Zealand Baptist*, October 1903, 149.

29   For example, Pastor So (New Zealand Baptist Chinese missioner) addressing St Alban's Baptist Church in Christchurch, *St Alban's Baptist Church Messenger*, May 1927, Folder 1, Box 0160, NZBHS Archives.

30   *Annual Report of the New Zealand Church Missionary Association*, 1900, 2–3.

31   Anonymous, *Widening Horizons: Four studies compiled for Dominion Camp, Easter 1929* (Christchurch: New Zealand Methodist Young Women's Bible Class Movement, 1929), 17–19; Anonymous, *One Increasing Purpose: Four studies for Easter 1930* (Christchurch: Methodist Young Women's Bible Class Movement, 1930), 8.

32   *Church Gazette*, February 1906, 36–37; March, 58; April, 73–75; May, 99–100; June, 121–22.

33   Renate Howe, 'The Australian Student Christian Movement and women's activism in the Asia–Pacific region, 1890s–1920s', *Australian Feminist Studies* 16, no. 36 (2001): 317.

34   A.K. Davidson, '"An interesting experiment": The founding of the Melanesian Mission', in *The Church of Melanesia 1849–1999*, Allan K. Davidson (ed.), (Auckland: The College of St John the Evangelist, 2000), 13–48; J.W. Burton, *The First Century of Missionary Adventure, 1855–1955* (Sydney: Methodist Overseas Missions, 1955), 26.

35   Salesa, 'New Zealand's Pacific', 154.

36   J.S. Murray, *A Century of Growth: Presbyterian overseas mission work, 1869–1969* (Christchurch: Presbyterian Bookroom, 1969), 22–24; Matthew Dalzell, *New Zealanders in Republican China, 1912–1949* (Auckland: The University of Auckland New Zealand Asia Institute, 1995), 20–108; and Sylvia Yang Yuan, '"Kiwis" in the Middle Kingdom: A sociological interpretation of the history of New Zealand missionaries in China from 1877 to 1952 and beyond' (PhD thesis, Massey University (Albany), 2013).

37   Murray J. Savage, *Forward into Freedom: Associated Churches of Christ in New Zealand missionary outreach, 1949–1979* (Nelson: Associated Churches of Christ Overseas Missionary Department, 1980); George Trew (ed.), *Looking Back, Forging Ahead: A century of participation in overseas mission by New Zealand Brethren Assemblies*, 1st edn (Palmerston North: Missionary Services New Zealand, 1996), 29–54.

38   Lisa Early, '"If we win the women": The lives and work of Methodist missionary women in the Solomon Islands, 1902–1942' (PhD thesis, University of Otago, 1998), 129.

39   'Searle, William and Margaret', Miscellaneous Personnel Files, Box 25, BIM Archives.

40   See in particular, N. Laurie, C. Dwyer, S.L. Holloway and F.M. Smith, *Geographies of New Femininities* (Harlow, UK: Longman, 1999); and Giselle

Byrnes and Catharine Coleborne, 'Editorial introduction: The utility and
futility of "the nation" in histories of Aotearoa New Zealand', *NZJH* 45, no.
1 (2011), 5. For the missionary context, the concept is applied in more detail
in Hugh Morrison, 'Theorising missionary education: The Bolivian Indian
Mission 1908–1920', *History of Education Review* 42, no. 1 (2013): 4–23.

41 Barbara Brookes, Annabel Cooper and Robin Law, 'Situating gender', in
Sites of Gender: Women, men and modernity in southern Dunedin, 1890–1939,
Barbara Brookes, Annabel Cooper and Robyn Law (eds), (Auckland:
Auckland University Press, 2003), 11–12.

42 Andrew Porter, *Religion Versus Empire? British Protestant missionaries and
overseas expansion, 1700–1914* (Manchester and New York: Manchester
University Press, 2004); 'Religion and empire: British expansion in the long
nineteenth century 1780–1914', *Journal of Imperial and Commonwealth
History* 20, no. 3 (1992): 370–90; '"Cultural imperialism" and Protestant
missionary enterprise, 1780–1914', *Journal of Imperial and Commonwealth
History* 25, no. 3 (1997): 367–91; Andrew Walls, *The Missionary Movement
in Christian History* (Maryknoll, New York: Orbis Books, 1996) and *The
Cross-Cultural Process in Christian History* (Maryknoll, New York: Orbis
Books, 2002).

43 Tony Ballantyne, *Orientalism and Race: Aryanism in the British Empire*
(Houndmills, Basingstoke and New York: Palgrave, 2002), 14–16;
Ballantyne, *Webs of Empire: Locating New Zealand's colonial past* (Wellington:
Bridget Williams Books, 2012), 14–16, 24–47.

44 Morrison, 'Theorising Missionary Education', 9, quoting in turn from Laurie
et al., *Geographies of New Femininities*, 13.

45 'Statistical Summary of Foreign Missions Throughout the World' in
Ecumenical Missionary Conference, New York 1900, vol. 1, Edwin M. Bliss
et al. (eds), (New York and London: American Tract Society and Religious
Tract Society, 1900), 424–34.

46 *Appendices to the Journals of the House of Representatives*, vol. 3, 1900, H.-30,
Miscellaneous, 1–3 and H.-30A, Miscellaneous, 1–9.

47 Sekhar Bandyopadhyay, 'Introduction', in *India in New Zealand: Local
identities, global relations*, Sekhar Bandyopadhyay (ed.), (Dunedin: Otago
University Press, 2010), 10.

48 See, for example, Ballantyne, *Webs of Empire*, 82–104; Jacqueline Leckie,
'A long diaspora', in *India in New Zealand: Local identities, global relations*,
Sekhar Bandyopadhyay (ed.), (Dunedin: Otago University Press, 2010),
48–49.

49 'William Blair', PCNZ FMC (GA0001), Series 3, Missionary Candidates
1905–35, PCANZ Archives.

50 'Andrew Smaill', Series 3.50, Missionary Candidates 1905–35; 'Peter
Milne', Series 6.34, CVM Staff Files, 1901–30; 'Josiah Ryburn', Series 6.33
and 'Violet Sutherland', Series 6.39, Punjab Mission Staff Files, 1910–30,
PCANZ Archives.

51   H.H. Driver, *Our Work for God in India: A brief history of the New Zealand Baptist Missionary Society* (Dunedin: H.H. Driver, 1914), 20–21.

52   Murray, *A Century of Growth*, 39–47; W.M. Ryburn, *Through Shadow and Sunshine: The history of the Punjab Mission of the Presbyterian Church of New Zealand, 1909–1959* (Christchurch: Presbyterian Bookroom, 1961).

53   Martin Sutherland (ed.), *Baptists in Colonial New Zealand: Documents illustrating Baptist life and development* (Auckland: New Zealand Baptist Research and Historical Society, 2002), 213–14.

54   Informal conversation with Dr Martin Sutherland, Auckland, New Zealand, 2005.

55   Hugh Morrison, '"It is our bounden duty": The emergence of the New Zealand Protestant missionary movement, 1868–1926' (PhD thesis, Massey University, 2004), 89–91; Martin Sutherland, '"Better to ignore the past": New Zealand Baptists, scandal, and historical memory', *Fides et Historia* 36, no. 1 (2004): 47–51.

56   Diane Rixon, 'New Zealand mission and nationalism in the Punjab: The missionaries of the Presbyterian Church of New Zealand in the Punjab and their encounter with Indian nationalism between 1910 and 1932' (BA(Hons) dissertation, University of Otago, 1997), 4, 105–06.

57   S.L. Edgar and M.J. Eade, *Toward the Sunrise: The centenary history of the New Zealand Baptist Missionary Society* (Wellington: New Zealand Baptist Historical Society, 1985), 90–101; 'New Zealand Baptists Reaching the World': www.baptist.org.nz

58   See, for example, Geoffrey Troughton, 'Christianity and community: Aspects of religious life and attitudes in the Wanganui–Manawatu region, 1870–1885' (MA thesis, Massey University, 1995), 34–35.

59   John Stenhouse, 'God, the Devil, and gender', in *Sites of Gender: Women, men and modernity in southern Dunedin, 1890–1939*, 313–47.

60   Sarah C. Coleman, '"Come over and help us": White women, reform and the missionary endeavour in India, 1876–1920' (MA thesis, University of Canterbury, 2002), 198–99. This point is elaborated on, in the wider context of the British world, in Haggis and Allen, 'Imperial emotions: Affective communities of mission in British Protestant women's missionary publications c. 1880–1920'.

61   Geoffrey Troughton, 'Religion, churches and childhood in New Zealand, c. 1900–1940', *NZJH* 40, no. 1 (2006): 39–40.

62   For example: Bryan Gilling, 'Retelling the old, old story: A study of six mass evangelistic missions in twentieth century New Zealand' (PhD thesis, University of Waikato, 1990), 63–85; H.R. Jackson, *Churches and People in Australia and New Zealand, 1860–1930* (Wellington: Allen and Unwin, 1987), 48–65; Peter J. Lineham, '"When the roll is called up yonder, who'll be there?": An analysis of nineteenth century trans-Atlantic revivalism in New Zealand and Canada', in *'Rescue the Perishing': Comparative perspectives on evangelism and revivalism*, Douglas Pratt (ed.), (Auckland: College

Communications, 1989), 1–19.

63 Eugene Stock, *The History of the Church Missionary Society*, vol 3 (London: Church Missionary Society, 1899 and 1916), 674–75; *Church Gazette*, 12 July 1898; Minutes of the Presbyterian Church of New Zealand Foreign Missions Committee, 1888–1901, Series 1, PCANZ Archives.

64 Linda Colley, 'The difficulties of empire: Present, past and future', *Historical Research* 79, no. 205 (2006): 368.

CHAPTER SEVEN

1 'A Message from the President', *The Lotu*, August 1922, 3.

2 *The Lotu*, August 1922, 2–3.

3 (1) Colonised children: Fiona Leach, 'African girls, nineteenth-century mission education and the patriarchal imperative', *Gender and Education* 20, no. 4 (2008): 335–47; Hayden J. Bellenoit, 'Missionary education, religion and knowledge in India, c. 1880–1915', *Modern Asian Studies* 41 (2007): 369–94; Larry Prochner, Helen May and Baljit Kaur, '"The blessings of civilisation": Nineteenth-century missionary infant schools for young native children in three colonial settings – India, Canada and New Zealand 1820s–1840s', *Paedagogica Historica* 45, nos. 1–2 (2009): 83–102. (2) Missionary children: Elizabeth Buettner, *Empire Families: Britons and late imperial India* (Oxford: Oxford University Press, 2004), 154–62; Emily J. Manktelow, *Missionary Families: Race, gender and generation on the spiritual frontier* (Manchester: University of Manchester Press, 2013); Rhonda A. Semple, '"The conversion and highest welfare of each pupil": The work of the China Inland Mission at Chefoo', *The Journal of Imperial and Commonwealth History* 31, no. 1 (2003): 29–50; and Karen A.A. Vallgårda, *Imperial Childhoods and Christian Mission: Education and emotions in South India and Denmark* (Houndmills, Basingstoke: Palgrave Macmillan, 2015).

4 For example: F.K. Prochaska, 'Little vessels: Children in the nineteenth-century English missionary movement', *Journal of Imperial and Commonwealth History* 6, no. 2 (1978): 103–18; Brian Stanley, 'Missionary regiments for Immanuel's service: Juvenile missionary organizations in English Sunday schools, 1841–1865', in *The Church and Childhood*, Diana Wood (ed.), (Oxford: Blackwell, 1994), 391–403; and David Keen, 'Feeding the lambs: The influence of Sunday schools on the socialization of children in Otago and Southland, 1848–1901' (PhD thesis, University of Otago, 1999), 191–95.

5 Sandy Brewer, 'From darkest England to the hope of the world: Protestant pedagogy and the visual culture of the London Missionary Society', *Material Religion* 1, no. 1 (2005): 98–123; Jonathan Brooke, 'Providentialist nationalism and juvenile mission literature, 1840–1870', Henry Martyn Centre Research Seminar, Westminster College, Cambridge University: http://henrymartyn.dns-systems.net/media/documents/Archive; Michelle

Elleray, 'Little builders: Coral insects, missionary culture, and the Victorian child', *Victorian Literature & Culture* 39, no. 1 (2011): 223–38; Felicity Jensz, 'Origins of missionary periodicals: Form and function of three Moravian publications', *Journal of Religious History* 36, no. 2 (2012): 234–55; and Rennie Schoepflin, 'Making doctors and nurses for Jesus: Medical missionary stories and American children', *Church History* 74, no. 3 (2005): 557–90.

6   J.G.A. Pocock, *The Discovery of Islands: Essays on British history* (Cambridge: Cambridge University Press, 2005), 6.

7   Stanley, 'Missionary regiments', 391; Prochaska, 'Little vessels', 104.

8   Prochaska, 'Little vessels', 104; F.K. Prochaska, *Women and Philanthropy in Nineteenth-Century England* (Oxford: Oxford University Press, 1980), 82–83.

9   Susan Thorne, *Congregational Missions and the Making of an Imperial Culture in 19th-century England* (Stanford, California: Stanford University Press, 1999), 133.

10 Allan K. Davidson and Peter J. Lineham, *Transplanted Christianity: Documents illustrating aspects of New Zealand church history* (Palmerston North: Dunmore Press, 1989), 181–84, 246–48.

11 'Memoirs of Jane Bannerman', Undated, Series 3/5, DA1/2, 28, 49–50, PCANZ Archives.

12 'NZBMS Birthday Band Membership Card, 1915', Folder 1, Box 0026, NZBMS Archives.

13 'NZBMS Children's House-boat Share Certificate, 1898', Folder 1, Box 0026, NZBMS Archives.

14 Hugh Morrison, '"I feel that we belong to the one big family": Protestant childhoods, missions and emotions in British world settings, 1870s–1930s', in *Emotions and Christian Missions: Historical perspectives*, Claire McLisky, Daniel Midena and Karen A.A. Vallgårda (eds), (Houndmills, UK and New York: Palgrave Macmillan, 2015), 221-25.

15 *New Zealand Church News*, May 1877, 91.

16 *The Evangelist*, March 1869, 13.

17 'Report of the Sabbath School Committee, 1883', *PCSO PS*, p. 13.

18 For further detail on children and missionary periodical literature, see Hugh Morrison, '"As the sunshine dispels the darkness of the night": Settler Protestant children's missionary magazines in New Zealand c. 1840–1940', *NZJH* 49, no. 2 (2015): 136–59.

19 Prochaska, 'Little vessels', 106.

20 See, for example: Mary Jo Maynes, 'Age as a category of historical analysis: History, agency, and narratives of childhood', *Journal of the History of Childhood and Youth* 1, no. 1 (2008): 114–24; Stephen Mintz, *Huck's Raft: A history of American childhood* (Cambridge, Mass., and London: Harvard University Press, 2004), vii–viii; Peter Stearns, 'Challenges in the history of childhood', *Journal of the History of Childhood and Youth* 1, no. 1 (2008): 35–36.

21 'Missions Report, 1886', *PCSO PS*, 69; 'Missions Report, 1890', *PCSO PS*, 1890, 62–63; *PCNZ PGA*, 1920, 120–22; ibid., 1925, 202–23; ibid., 1930, 120–21.

22 *New Zealand Baptist*, October 1901, 158; September 1903, 142; April 1909, 318–19; September 1925, 230; *NZBU Handbook*, 1925–26, 108–10.

23 *Church Gazette*, September 1895, 171; August 1904, 154; Smythe to Heron, 7 November 1921, and Lockyer to Heron, 18 December 1921, Correspondence of the Young People's Union, 1920–40, ANG 143/4.11 (1), Box 21, NZCMS Archives.

24 1920 and 1925 Reports, in *Presbyterian Women's Missionary Union Annual Reports*, 1920–21 and 1925–26, Box AF2/1, PCANZ Archives.

25 J.R. Elder, *The History of the Presbyterian Church in New Zealand 1840–1940* (Christchurch: Presbyterian Bookroom, 1940), 118–19; Laurie Barber, '1901–1930: The expanding frontier', in *Presbyterians in Aotearoa*, Dennis McEldowney (ed.), (Wellington: The Presbyterian Church of New Zealand, 1990), 75.

26 'Christmas Gift Fund', *Break of Day*, 1909–41.

27 'Financial Secretary's Report, 1918–1919', *NZBU Handbook*, 1919–20, 29.

28 G.M. Adams, 'How best to arouse and maintain the missionary enthusiasm of our Sunday schools', *New Zealand Baptist*, May 1919, 70.

29 Rutherford Waddell, 'The Sabbath-school and missions', *New Zealand Missionary Record*, February 1884, 44–49; *Otago Daily Times*, 1 December 1883.

30 Jeanine Graham, 'Young New Zealanders and the Great War: Exploring the impact and legacy of the First World War, 1914–2014', *Paedagogica Historica* 44, no. 4 (2008): 441.

31 'Violet Latham', Applicants' Correspondence, ANG 143/3.81, Box 11, NZCMS Archives; John Muir, 'Testimony', *China's Millions* [Australasian edition], November 1930, 167.

32 Hugh Morrison, '"It is our bounden duty": The emergence of the New Zealand Protestant missionary movement, 1868–1926' (PhD thesis, Massey University, 2004), 199.

33 Presbyterian Church of New Zealand, *Prayers for the Home Circle with a Selection of Bible Readings* (Dunedin: Wm. H. Adams, 1917), 70.

34 Mrs Gray, 'The education of the young in regard to missions', *Harvest Field*, December 1907, vii.

35 'An open letter to the foreign missions committee on mission lessons in the Sunday school', *Outlook*, 3 November 1914, np [photocopy].

36 Revd A.B. Chappell, *A Manual of Missions: Principles, methods, achievements, organisations, fields*, 2nd edn (Auckland: Percy Salmon, 1933).

37 Anon, 'Teachers' Notes on Mission Lessons', *Outlook*, February 1918, 1–4.

38 Geoffrey Troughton, 'Religion, churches and childhood in New Zealand, c. 1900–1940', *NZJH* 40, no. 1 (2006): 41–42.

39 Prochaska, 'Little vessels', 110, 113–14.

40 Colin Kidd, *The Forging of Races: Race and Scripture in the Protestant Atlantic world, 1600–2000* (Cambridge: Cambridge University Press, 2006), 168.

41 Colin McGeorge, 'Childhood's sole serious business: The long haul to full school attendance', *NZJH* 40, no. 1 (2006): 25–27.

42 Keen, 'Feeding the lambs', i, 192, 194, 195.

43 'Copy of Bishop Cowie's Address to Duke and Duchess of Cornwall', Auckland, 11 June 1901', S13c Bishops Administration, Folder 2, Item 8, Auckland Diocesan Archives [ADA], New Zealand.

44 'Her Late Majesty Queen Victoria', *The Golden Link*, 1 February 1901, 1.

45 Troughton, 'Religion, churches and childhood', 40.

46 Frank Hanson, *The Sunday School in New Zealand Methodism* (Auckland: Wesley Historical Society of New Zealand, 1998), 27, 28.

47 'Syllabus Studies for the New Zealand Anglican Bible Class Union', 1923–24 and 1929, ANG062/2.4 and 2.13, Boxes 2 and 6, New Zealand Anglican Bible Class Union Archives [NZABCU Archives], John Kinder Theological Library.

48 Dorothy Entwistle, 'Sunday-school book prizes for children: Rewards and socialization', in *The Church and Childhood*, Diana Wood (ed.), (Oxford: Blackwell, 1994), 405–16.

49 'Vivienne Opie', ANG143/3.97, Box 13, NZCMS Archives.

50 *New Zealand Missionary Record*, December 1882, 22; *Break of Day*, June 1909, 3; November 1909, 12.

51 Alexander Don, *Light in Dark Isles: A jubilee record and study of the New Hebrides Mission of the Presbyterian Church of New Zealand* (Dunedin: Foreign Missions Committee, Presbyterian Church of New Zealand, 1918), 98–101, 109, 146–54.

52 'Children's Letters from New Zealand to the Solomons', *The Lotu*, May and June 1928.

53 See Andrew Porter, '"Cultural imperialism" and Protestant missionary enterprise, 1780–1914', *Journal of Imperial and Commonwealth History* 25, no. 3 (1997): 367–91; Ryan Dunch, 'Beyond cultural imperialism: Cultural theory, Christian missions, and global modernity', *History and Theory* 41 (October 2002): 301–25.

54 Geoffrey Oddie, '"Orientalism" and British Protestant missionary constructions of India in the nineteenth century', *South Asia* 17, no. 2 (1994): 29–30.

55 Alison Twells, *The Civilising Mission and the English Middle Class, 1792–1850: The 'heathen' at home and overseas* (New York: Palgrave Macmillan, 2008), 2.

56 Kathryn Castle, *Britannia's Children: Reading colonialism through children's books and magazines* (Manchester: Manchester University Press, 1996), 90, 157.

57 'Noel Luker', *Blain Biographical Directory of Anglican Clergy*. http://anglicanhistory.org/nz/blain_directory/directory.pdf

58 Helen May, 'Mapping some landscapes of colonial–global childhood', *European Early Childhood Education Research Journal* 9, no. 2 (2001): 5–20.

59 See, for example, Kristine Alexander, 'The Girl Guide movement and imperial internationalism during the 1920s and 1930s', *Journal of the History of Childhood and Youth* 2, no. 1 (2009): 37–63.

60 Troy Boone, 'Remaking "lawless lads and licentious girls": The Salvation Army and the regeneration of empire', in *Christian Encounters with the Other*, John C. Hawley (ed.), (New York: New York University Press, 1998), 103–21; Esther Daniel, '"Solving an empire problem": The Salvation Army and juvenile migration to Australia', *History of Education Review* 36, no. 1 (2007): 33–48.

61 Maynes, 'Age as a category of historical analysis', 117.

62 'Correspondence of the New Zealand Church Missionary Society', ANG143, Series 3, Boxes 3–18, NZCMS Archives; 'Presbyterian Missionary Candidates', Series 3, Presbyterian Church of New Zealand Foreign Missions Committee, GA0001, PCANZ Archives.

63 Maynes, 'Age as a category of historical analysis', 116–19.

64 N.R. Hiner and J.M. Hawes, 'History of childhood: United States', in *Encyclopedia of Children and Childhood*, vol. 2, Paula Fass et al. (eds), (New York: Macmillan Reference, 2004), 428.

65 For further discussion of how this played out in colonial contexts like New Zealand and Canada, see Hugh Morrison, 'Empire, nation, and religion in Canadian and New Zealand Protestant juvenile missionary periodicals, c. 1890–1930s: "Men and women the king would wish you to be"', in *Missions and Media: The politics of missionary periodicals in the long nineteenth century*, Felicity Jensz and Hanna Acke (eds), (Stuttgart, Germany: Franz Steiner Verlag, 2013), 19–38.

CHAPTER EIGHT

1 Susan Thorne, 'Religion and empire at home', in *At Home with the Empire: Metropolitan culture and the imperial world*, Catherine Hall and Sonya Rose (eds), (Cambridge: Cambridge University Press, 2006), 144.

2 Jeffrey Cox, *The British Missionary Enterprise since 1700* (New York and London: Routledge, 2008), 101.

3 'Foreign missions', *Observer*, 23 October 1897.

4 For example, in such magazines as *New Zealand Baptist*, June 1889, 81; *Christian Outlook*, 15 February 1896, 32–33; *Church Gazette*, July 1904, 124; and *New Zealand Churchman*, January 1920, 2.

5 'Of missions', *New Zealand Churchman*, January 1920, 2.

6 'Board of Missions', *Yearbook of the Diocese of Auckland*, 1928–1929, 23.

7 C.R. Walsh, 'Missionary extension: The church's opportunity in the world', in *Report of the Church Congress held at Melbourne, 19–24 November, 1906*, Revd Henry Lowther Clarke (ed.), (Melbourne: Edgerton & Moore, Printers, 1906), 115, 116.

8   Antoinette Burton, *Empire in Question: Reading, writing, and teaching British imperialism* (Durham and London: Duke University Press, 2011), 264–72; Catherine Hall and Sonya Rose, 'Introduction: Being at home with the empire', in *At Home with the Empire*, Hall and Rose (eds), 1.

9   Revd Edward Webb, 'Reasons for taking part in efforts to save the world', *Missionary Review of the World* 8, no. 5 (1895): 367–68.

10 Revd A.J. Gordon, 'Three missionary ambitions', *Missionary Review of the World* 8, no. 2 (1895), 93–94.

11 *Missionary Messenger*, April 1894, 1–2.

12 Revd Mgr Joseph Freri, 'The foreign missions', in *The First American Catholic Missionary Congress*, Revd Francis C. Kelley (ed.), (Chicago: J.S. Hyland, 1909), 72.

13 World Missionary Conference, 1910: Report of Commission VI, *The Home Base of Missions* (Edinburgh and London: Oliphant, Anderson and Ferrier, 1910), 258.

14 Kenneth R. Ross, '"Blessed reflex": Mission as God's spiral of renewal', *International Bulletin of Missionary Research* 27, no. 4 (October 2003): 162–68.

15 Daniel Bays and Grant Wacker (eds), *The Foreign Missionary Enterprise at Home: Explorations in North American cultural history* (Tuscaloosa and London: University of Alabama Press, 2003), 2–4; A. Austin and J.S. Scott (eds), *Canadian Missionaries, Indigenous Peoples: Representing religion at home and abroad* (Toronto, Buffalo, London: University of Toronto Press, 2005), 14–17.

16 F.K. Prochaska, 'Little vessels: Children in the nineteenth-century English missionary movement', *Journal of Imperial and Commonwealth History* 6, no. 2 (1978), 113–14.

17 Alison Twells, *The Civilising Mission and the English Middle Class, 1792–1850: The 'heathen' at home and overseas* (New York: Palgrave Macmillan, 2008), 3.

18 Esther Breitenbach, *Empire and Scottish Society: The Impact of foreign missions at home, c. 1790 to c. 1914* (Edinburgh: Edinburgh University Press, 2009), 179–86, especially 179.

19 Thorne, 'Religion and empire at home', 158–65; Susan Thorne, *Congregational Missions and the Making of an Imperial Culture in 19th-century England* (Stanford, California: Stanford University Press, 1999), 124–54.

20 Stuart Piggin, 'Introduction: The reflex impact of missions on Australian Christianity', in *This Gospel Shall be Preached: Essays on the Australian contribution to world mission*, M. Hutchinson and G. Treloar (eds), (Sydney: Centre for the Study of Australian Christianity, 1998), 7–23.

21 Report of Commission VI, 259.

22 Ibid., 259–67.

23 Revd William Mawson, 'The Presbyterian Church and Foreign Missions', Subject Files, Series 4, Foreign Missions Committee GA0001, PCANZ

Archives.

24 Report of Commission VI, 260.

25 Extracted from: *NZBU Baptist Handbook* and New Zealand Baptist Missionary Society Reports, 1904–15; and *NZBU Baptist Handbook*, 1905–06, 55.

26 See again, Hugh Morrison, '"As the sunshine dispels the darkness of the night": Settler Protestant children's missionary magazines in New Zealand c. 1840–1940', *NZJH* 49, no. 2 (2015): 136–59.

27 J.R. Elder, *The History of the Presbyterian Church in New Zealand 1840–1940* (Christchurch: Presbyterian Bookroom, 1940), 214–15, 376; and 'Youth of the Church Report', Appendix XIII, *PCNZ PGA*, 1930, 118.

28 Stuart Piggin, 'Sectarianism versus ecumenism: The impact on British churches of the missionary movement to India, c. 1800–1860', *Journal of Ecclesiastical History* 27, no. 4 (1976): 387–402.

29 Martin Sutherland, 'Seeking a turangawaewae: Constructing a Baptist identity in New Zealand', *Baptist History and Heritage* 36 (Winter/Spring 2001): 232–50.

30 George Trew (ed.), *Looking Back, Forging Ahead: A century of participation in overseas mission by New Zealand Brethren Assemblies*, 1st edn (Palmerston North: Missionary Services New Zealand, 1996), 69–76.

31 Piggin, 'Introduction: The reflex impact of missions on Australian Christianity', 7–18.

32 Margaret Lovell-Smith, *No Turning Back: A history of the inter-church aid work of the National Council of Churches in New Zealand 1945–1983* (Christchurch: National Council of Churches, 1986), 9–13.

33 Caroline Daley, *Girls and Women, Men and Boys: Gender in Taradale, 1886–1930* (Auckland: Auckland University Press, 1999); John Stenhouse, 'Christianity, gender, and the working class in southern Dunedin, 1880–1940', *Journal of Religious History* 30, no. 1 (2006): 18–44.

34 Margaret Tennant, 'Sisterly ministrations. The social work of Protestant deaconesses in New Zealand 1890–1940', *NZJH* 32, no. 1 (1998): 3–22.

35 Allan Davidson, *Christianity in Aotearoa: A history of church and society in New Zealand* (Wellington: The New Zealand Education for Ministry Board, 2004), 144–49, 193–95.

36 Hugh Morrison, '"It is our bounden duty": The emergence of the New Zealand Protestant missionary movement, 1868–1926' (PhD thesis, Massey University, 2004), 1, 176.

37 *PWMU Annual Reports*, 1905–25, Box AF2/1, PCANZ Archives.

38 Extracted from *PWMU Annual Reports*, 1910–25, and cross-referenced to PCNZ FMC reports.

39 *PWMU Annual Report*, 1915–1916, 3–13, *PWMU Annual Reports*, 1905–25; Elder, *History of the Presbyterian Church*, 318.

40 'Missions Report, 1911', *PCNZ PGA*, 1911, 199.

41 Davidson, *Christianity in Aotearoa*, 149.

42 Brian Stanley, *The World Missionary Conference, Edinburgh 1910* (Grand Rapids, Michigan: Eerdmans), 312, 316.

43 'Annual Report of the NZCMA, 1909', 11; 'Foreign Missions Committee Report 1908', 97.

44 W.H. Gairdner, *Edinburgh 1910* (Edinburgh and London: Committee of the World Missionary Conference), 52.

45 Stanley, *The World Missionary Conference*, 12.

46 *Harvest Field*, April 1910, x.

47 Mrs A. Kaye, *Out of Every Nation: A brief account of the World's Missionary Conference, held in Edinburgh 1910* (Christchurch: Smith & Anthony Ltd. for Presbyterian Women's Missionary Union, 1910).

48 'Notes of the president's address', *Harvest Field*, December 1909, vi.

49 'The home base of missions', *Harvest Field*, March 1912, ii, ii–iv.

50 'Secretarial work', *Harvest Field*, February 1911, vii–x.

51 'A plea for study', *Harvest Field*, August 1911, v.

52 Ibid., v–vi.

53 *Harvest Field*, February 1912, iii; March 1912, iv.

54 Nancy Hardesty, 'The scientific study of missions: Textbooks of the Central Committee on the United Study of Foreign Missions' in *The Foreign Missionary Enterprise at Home*, D.H. Bays and G. Wacker (eds), (Tuscaloosa and London: University of Alabama Press, 2003), 106-22.

55 'How to start a study circle', *Harvest Field*, April 1911, iii–iv.

56 *Harvest Field*, March 1913, viii–ix; April 1913, iv–v; June 1913, ii–iii.

57 *The Message*, January 1915, 15.

58 Hardesty, 'The scientific study of missions', 115.

59 *PWMU Annual Report*, 1915–16, 4–59; and 1925–26, 6; Anonymous, *Women's Work for Missions* (Auckland: Presbyterian Women's Missionary Union, 1955), 29.

60 'Canterbury Mission Study Council', ANG 143/4.2, Box 19, NZCMS Archives.

61 'PWMU syllabus 1930', *Harvest Field*, February 1930, xiii–xiv.

62 Prochaska, 'Little vessels', 113–14.

63 Colin McGeorge, 'Race, empire and the Maori in the New Zealand primary school curriculum, 1880–1940' in *The Imperial Curriculum: Racial images and education in the British colonial experience*, J.A. Mangan (ed.), (London and New York: Routledge, 1993), 64–78.

64 Roger Openshaw (ed.), *New Zealand Social Studies: Past, present and future* (Palmerston North: Dunmore Press, 1992), 19–33, 34–48.

65 Thorne, *Congregational Missions and the Making of an Imperial Culture in 19th-Century England*, 125.

66 'Our attitude towards the non-Christian world', *Harvest Field*, October 1913, ii, iii.

67 Joan Brumberg, 'Zenanas and girlless villages: The ethnology of American evangelical women, 1870–1910', *The Journal of American History* 69, no. 2 (1982), 356–67.

68 'Black without blemish', *Harvest Field,* February 1930, xvi, xvii.

69 'The church in the world: An ear on the world's news', *Harvest Field,* December 1949, xxv, xxvi.

70 *PWMU Annual Report,* 1925–26, 6.

71 Sarah C. Coleman, '"Come over and help us": White women, reform and the missionary endeavour in India, 1876–1920' (MA thesis, University of Canterbury, 2002), 198–99; Haggis and Allen, 'Imperial emotions: Affective communities of mission in British Protestant women's missionary publications c. 1880–1920'.

72 J. Veitch, 'Towards the Church of a New Era', in Dennis McEldowney (ed.) *Presbyterians in Aotearoa 1840–1990* (Wellington: Presbyterian Church of New Zealand, 1990), 147–49.

73 'Greetings from Vanuatu PWMU', *Harvest Field,* July 1994, 13.

74 Hall and Rose, 'Introduction: Being at home with the empire', 2–3.

CHAPTER NINE

1 Rutherford Waddell, 'Gang o'er the fundamentals', *On Continent and Island: A missionary supplement to the Outlook,* July 1929, 2–5.

2 Ibid., 2, 3.

3 Ibid., 4.

4 Ibid., 5.

5 For example, Jane Hunter notes the enduring nature of late nineteenth-century rhetoric in some modern-day constructions of the missionary task. See Jane Hunter, 'Women's mission in historical perspective: American identity and Christian internationalism', in *Competing Kingdoms: Women, mission, nation, and the American Protestant empire, 1812–1960,* Barbara Reeves-Ellington, Kathryn Kish Sklar and Connie A. Shemo (eds), (Durham & London: Duke University Press, 2010), 19–42.

6 Numbers calculated from J.S. Murray, *A Century of Growth: Presbyterian overseas mission work 1869–1969* (Christchurch: Presbyterian Bookroom, 1969), 110–12; and G.C. Carter, *A Family Affair: A brief survey of New Zealand Methodism's involvement in mission overseas 1822–1972* (Auckland: Wesley Historical Society, 1973), Appendix II. Note, however, that these figures are under-representative as they do not all include wives with husbands.

7 Numbers calculated from George Trew (ed.), *Looking Back, Forging Ahead: A century of participation in overseas mission by New Zealand Brethren Assemblies,* 1st edn (Palmerston North: Missionary Services New Zealand, 1996), 124; and *New Zealand Baptist Union Yearbook,* 1940–80. These figures include both husbands and wives.

8 The statistics that follow are derived from 'Foreign missionaries and national workers, 2010', and 'Missionaries sent and received from continent to continent, 1910–2010', in Todd M. Johnson and Kenneth R. Ross (eds),

Atlas of Global Christianity (Edinburgh: Edinburgh University Press, 2009), 260–63.

9   William Ernest Hocking, *Re-Thinking Missions: A laymen's inquiry after one hundred years* (New York and London: Harper & Brothers, 1932), ix.

10 As noted, for example, in the Canadian context: Alvyn Austin and Jamie S. Scott, 'Introduction', in A. Austin and J.S. Scott (eds), *Canadian Missionaries, Indigenous Peoples: Representing religion at home and abroad* (Toronto, Buffalo, London: University of Toronto Press, 2005), 4.

11 Timothy Yates, *Christian Mission in the Twentieth Century* (Cambridge: Cambridge University Press, 1994), 194–209.

12 Lachy Paterson, 'The rise and fall of women field workers within the Presbyterian Māori mission, 1907–1970', in *Mana Māori and Christianity*, Hugh Morrison, Lachy Paterson, Brett Knowles and Murray Rae (eds), (Wellington: Huia Publishers, 2012), 195–97; Allan Davidson, '1931–1960: Depression, war, new life', in Dennis McEldowney (ed.), *Presbyterians in Aotearoa, 1840–1990* (Wellington: Presbyterian Church of New Zealand, 1990), 134–39; and James Veitch, '1961–1990: Towards the church for a new era', in *Presbyterians in Aotearoa, 1840–1990*, 166.

13 T.E. Riddle, *The Light of Other Days* (Christchurch and Dunedin: Presbyterian Bookroom, 1949), 222.

14 Catharine Eade, *In Heavenly Love Abiding: Memoirs of a missionary wife* (Wellington: Sarah Bennett Books, 2005), 200.

15 For example: Barbara Reeves-Ellington et al. (eds), *Competing Kingdoms*; and Heather J. Sharkey, *Cultural Conversions: Unexpected consequences of Christian missionary encounters in the Middle East, Africa, and South Asia* (Syracuse, NY: Syracuse University Press, 2013).

16 Andrew Porter, '"Cultural imperialism" and Protestant missionary enterprise, 1780–1914', *Journal of Imperial and Commonwealth History* 25, no. 3 (1997): 367–91.

17 Bronwen Douglas, 'Encounters with the enemy? Academic readings of missionary narratives on Melanesians', *Comparative Studies on Society and History* 43, no. 1 (2001): 55.

18 Lisa Early, '"If we win the women": The lives and work of female missionaries at the Solomon Islands, 1902–1942' (PhD thesis, University of Otago, 1998), ii.

19 Rachel Gillett, 'Helpmeets and handmaidens: The role of women in mission discourse' (BA(Hons) research essay, University of Otago, 1998), 40, 54. Here Gillett is responding to Delia Davin, 'British women missionaries in nineteenth century China', *Women's History Review* 1, no. 2 (1992): 257–71.

20 Noted for instance by Jeffrey Cox, *The British Missionary Enterprise since 1700* (New York and London: Routledge, 2008), 3.

21 Philip Jenkins, *The Next Christendom: The coming of global Christianity*, rev. edn (Oxford: Oxford University Press, 2007), 65–67.

22 Gary R. Corwin, 'Allan, George and Mary (Sterling)', in *Biographical*

Dictionary of Christian Missions, Gerald Anderson (ed.), (New York: MacMillan Reference, 1998), 11.

23 Allan K. Davidson, 'The New Zealand overseas missionary contribution: The need for further research', in *With All Humility and Gentleness*, Allan K. Davison and Godfrey Nicholson (eds), (Auckland: St John's College, 1991), 45–46.

24 Norman E. Thomas, 'Todd, Reginald Stephen Garfield', in *Biographical Dictionary of Christian Missions*, 674.

25 Sylvia Yang Yuan, '"Kiwis" in the Middle Kingdom: A sociological interpretation of the history of New Zealand missionaries in China from 1877 to 1952 and beyond' (PhD thesis, Massey University (Albany), 2013).

26 Stuart Piggin, 'Introduction: The reflex impact of missions on Australian Christianity', in *This Gospel Shall be Preached: Essays on the Australian contribution to world mission*, M. Hutchinson and G. Treloar (eds), (Sydney: Centre for the Study of Australian Christianity, 1998), 7.

27 *Te Pipiwharauroa: He Kupu Whakamarama*, 1898–1901; see further Lachy Paterson, *Colonial Discourses: Niupepa Māori 1855–1863* (Dunedin: Otago University Press, 2006); and Tony Ballantyne, *Webs of Empire: Locating New Zealand's colonial past* (Wellington: Bridget Williams Books, 2012), 75, 78–79.

28 Lesley A. Orr MacDonald, *A Unique and Glorious Mission: Women and Presbyterianism in Scotland, 1830–1930* (Edinburgh: John Donald Publishers, 2000), 110.

29 Elizabeth Prevost, *The Communion of Women: Missions and gender in colonial Africa and the British metropole* (Oxford: Oxford University Press, 2010), 289; and for the New Zealand context, Yvonne Robertson, *Girdle Round the Earth: New Zealand Presbyterian women's ideal of universal sisterhood, 1878–1918*, Annual Lecture, Auckland 1993 (Dunedin: Presbyterian Historical Society of New Zealand, 1994), 12–21.

30 Peter Gibbons, 'The far side of the search for identity: Reconsidering New Zealand history', *NZJH* 37, no. 1 (2003): 41, 44; Ballantyne, *Webs of Empire*, 14.

31 Tony Ballantyne and Brian Moloughney, 'Angles of vision', in *Disputed Histories: Imagining New Zealand's pasts*, Tony Ballantyne and Brian Moloughney (eds), (Dunedin: Otago University Press, 2006), 9.

32 For example, woman's suffrage in New Zealand, often seen as a marker of national progress and identity, has been re-interpreted more broadly and comparatively in Caroline Daley and Melanie Nolan (eds), *Suffrage and Beyond: International feminist perspectives* (Auckland: Auckland University Press, 1994).

33 For example, see John Stenhouse, 'Religion and society', in *The New Oxford History of New Zealand*, Giselle Byrnes (ed.), (Oxford and Melbourne: Oxford University Press, 2009), 323–56. Another edited compilation indicates the extent to which religious historiography is keeping pace with the

wider discipline in terms of influences and approaches: Geoffrey Troughton
and Hugh Morrison (eds), *The Spirit of the Past: Essays on Christianity in New
Zealand history* (Wellington: Victoria University Press, 2011).

34   Ian Breward, 'Religion and New Zealand society', *NZJH* 13, no. 2 (1979):
138–48.

35   For a further assessment of Breward's seminal essay and its impact on the
writing of New Zealand religious history, see Hugh Morrison and Geoffrey
Troughton, 'Introduction: Perspectives on Christianity and New Zealand
history', in *The Spirit of the Past*, Troughton and Morrison (eds), 14–16.

36   For example: Jay Riley Case, *An Unpredictable Gospel: American evangelicals
and world Christianity, 1812–1920* (Oxford: Oxford University Press,
2012); and Mark Noll, *The New Shape of World Christianity: How American
experience reflects global faith* (Downers Grove, Illinois: IVP Academic, 2009).

37   For more extensive analysis, see Peter Lineham, 'The rise and significance
of the Destiny Church', in *Mana Māori and Christianity*, Hugh Morrison,
Lachy Paterson, Brett Knowles and Murray Rae (eds), (Wellington: Huia
Publishers, 2012), 111–37; and Peter Lineham, *Destiny: The life and times of
a self-made apostle* (Auckland: Penguin, 2013).

38   Hilary Carey, *God's Empire: Religion and colonialism in the British world, c.
1801–1908* (Cambridge: Cambridge University Press, 2011).

39   For more detail see: Hugh Morrison, 'Globally and locally positioned: New
Zealand perspectives on the current practice of religious history', *Journal of
Religious History* 35, no. 2 (2011): 181–98.

40   'United Christian convention', *Otago Witness*, 7 January 1903, 68.

41   *Otago Witness*, 9 November 1904.

42   Glove box, jewel box and trinket box, private collection of the author.
Photograph © Hugh Morrison 2014.

43   George Mackenzie (1839–1913) and Jane Mackenzie (1853–1935) were
Presbyterian residents of Queenstown and active in their support for
church-related activities. See: www.qldc.govt.nz/cemeteries_database_search/
record/2099/forename/GEORGE and www.qldc.govt.nz/cemeteries_
database_search/record/2102/surname/mackenzie

44   'Farewell to Sister Clare', *Otago Witness*, 2 November 1904.

45   Helen S. Dyer, *Pandita Ramabai: A great life in Indian missions* (London and
Glasgow: Pickering & Inglis, 1923), 148.

46   The following observations are based on material published in the *Otago
Witness*, 20 January 1909; and 'Mission lecture', *Otago Witness*, 10 March
1909.

47   This phrase borrows from the imaginatively titled book by David Lowenthal,
The Past is a Foreign Country (Cambridge: Cambridge University Press,
1985).

BIBLIOGRAPHY

Primary Sources

Unpublished Material

Auckland Anglican Diocesan Archives, Auckland, New Zealand
Bolivian Indian Mission Archives, SIM International Resource Centre, Fort Mill, South Carolina, USA
George Hunter McNeur Papers, Hocken Library, University of Otago, Dunedin, New Zealand
Minutes of the Presbytery of Auckland, 1856–1869, Auckland War Memorial Museum Library, Auckland, New Zealand
Mott Papers, Record Group 45, Special Collections, Yale Divinity School Library, New Haven, Connecticut, USA
New Zealand Anglican Bible Class Union Archives, John Kinder Theological Library, St John's College, Auckland, New Zealand
New Zealand Baptist Historical Society Archives, Carey Baptist College, Auckland, New Zealand
New Zealand Baptist Missionary Society Archives, Carey Baptist College, Auckland, New Zealand
New Zealand Bible Training Institute Archives, Deane Memorial Library, Laidlaw College, Auckland, New Zealand
New Zealand Church Missionary Society Archives, John Kinder Theological Library, St John's College, Auckland, New Zealand
New Zealand Evangelical Archive of Christianity, Deane Memorial Library, Laidlaw College, Auckland, New Zealand
New Zealand Methodist Church Archives, Christchurch, New Zealand
New Zealand Salvation Army Archives, New Zealand Salvation Army Heritage Centre and Archives, Upper Hutt, New Zealand
New Zealand Student Christian Movement Collection, Alexander Turnbull Library, Wellington, New Zealand
Overseas Missionary Fellowship (Australia) Archives, J.W. Searle Library, Melbourne School of Theology, Australia
Overseas Missionary Fellowship (New Zealand) Archives, OMF National Office, Auckland, New Zealand
Presbyterian Church of Aotearoa New Zealand Archives, Presbyterian Research Centre, Dunedin, New Zealand
Taranaki Street Wesleyan Young People's Society for Christian Endeavour Archives, Alexander Turnbull Library, Wellington, New Zealand

Terrace Congregational Church Archives, Alexander Turnbull Library,
Wellington, New Zealand
World Student Christian Federation Archives, Record Groups 46/1 and 46/8,
Special Collections, Yale Divinity School Library, New Haven, Connecticut,
USA

Official Published Material

Appendices to the Journals of the House of Representatives, 1900
New Zealand Baptist Union Baptist Handbook, 1903–40
New Zealand Census, 1871–1936
Presbyterian Church of New Zealand Proceedings of the General Assembly,
1866–1939
Presbyterian Church of Southland–Otago Proceedings of Synod, 1866–1900
Presbyterian Women's Missionary Union Reports, 1906–39
Yearbook of the [Anglican] *Diocese of Auckland*, 1928–29

Contemporary Published Material

Adams, G.M. 'How best to arouse and maintain the missionary enthusiasm of our
Sunday schools'. *New Zealand Baptist*, May 1919, 70
Anonymous. *Official Handbook: World Missionary Conference Edinburgh 1910.*
Edinburgh: World Missionary Conference, 1910
Anonymous. 'Teachers' notes on mission lessons'. *Outlook*, February 1918, 1–4
Anonymous. *Report of the New Zealand Missionary Conference Held at Dunedin
April 27 to April 29, 1926.* Dunedin: New Zealand Missionary Conference
Committee, 1926
Anonymous. *Widening Horizons: Four studies compiled for Dominion Camp, Easter
1929.* Christchurch: New Zealand Methodist Young Women's Bible Class
Movement, 1929
Anonymous. *One Increasing Purpose: Four studies for Easter 1930.* Christchurch:
Methodist Young Women's Bible Class Movement, 1930
Broomhall, B. *The Evangelisation of the World. A Missionary Band: A record of
consecration, and an appeal,* 3rd edn. London: Morgan & Scott, 1889
Burnham, J. (ed.) *Christian Endeavour Melodies.* London: W. Nicholson & Sons,
nd
Burton, J.W. *Missionary Survey of the Pacific Islands.* London: World Dominion
Press, 1930
Cable, Mildred and Francesca French. *Something Happened.* London: Hodder &
Stoughton, 1934
Chappell, A.B. *A Manual of Missions: Principles, methods, achievements,
organisations, fields.* 2nd edn. Auckland: Percy Salmon & Co., 1933
Davies, Herbert. *The Canton Villages Mission of the Presbyterian Church of New
Zealand.* Dunedin: Foreign Missions Committee, PCNZ, 1916
_____. *Four Studies in World-wide Evangelisation.* Dunedin: ASCU, 1909

Dawson, E.C. *Missionary Heroines in Many Lands: True stories of the intrepid bravery and patient endurance of missionaries in their encounters with uncivilised man, wild beasts and the forces of nature in many parts of the world.* London: Seeley, Service & Co., 1912

Dennis, James S., Harlan P. Beach and Charles H. Fahs (eds). *World Atlas of Christian Missions.* New York: Student Volunteer Movement for Foreign Missions, 1911

Dineen, A.M.D. *Not of Gennesareth: Romance and adventure in China.* English edn. London: Zenith Press, 1933

Don, Alexander. *Light in Dark Isles: A jubilee record and study of the New Hebrides Mission of the Presbyterian Church of New Zealand.* Dunedin: Foreign Missions Committee, Presbyterian Church of New Zealand, 1918

Driver, Anne J.P. *Missionary Memories.* Dunedin: H.H. Driver, 1930

Driver, H.H. *Our Work for God in India: A brief history of the New Zealand Baptist Missionary Society.* Dunedin: H.H. Driver, 1914

Duggan, Eileen (ed.) *Blazing the Trail in the Solomons: Letters from the North Solomons of Rev. Emmet McHardy, S.M.* Sydney: Dominion Publishing, 1935

Dyer, Helen S. *Pandita Ramabai: A great life in Indian missions.* London: Pickering & Inglis, 1923

Ecumenical Missionary Conference New York. *Report of the Ecumenical Conference on Foreign Missions, Held in Carnegie Hall and Neighbouring Churches, April 21 to May 1,* 2 vols. New York: American Tract Society, 1900

Ferguson, Sir Charles. 'Empire Day 1929'. *The New Zealand School Journal: Part III,* June 1929, 133–34

Freri, Revd Mgr Joseph. 'The foreign missions'. In *The First American Catholic Missionary Congress,* Rev Francis C. Kelley (ed.), 66-72. Chicago: J.S. Hyland & Company, 1909

Gairdner, W.H.T. *Edinburgh 1910: An account and interpretation of the World Missionary Conference.* Edinburgh and London: Committee of the World Missionary Conference, 1910

Gordon, Revd A.J. 'Three missionary ambitions'. *Missionary Review of the World* 8, no. 2 (1895): 89–94

Gray, Mrs. 'The education of the young in regard to missions'. *The PWMU Harvest Field,* December 1907: vii

Henderson, Alice. *Women's Work for Missions: The story of the beginnings and growth of the Presbyterian Women's Missionary Union of New Zealand, 1905–1939.* Christchurch: Presbyterian Bookroom, 1939

Hocking, William Ernest. *Re-Thinking Missions: A laymen's inquiry after one hundred years.* New York and London: Harper & Brothers, 1932

Inglis, Revd John. *Thesis – The doctrine of Christian missions, with special reference to the South Sea Islands.* Edinburgh: Morrison & Gibb, 1881

Jansen, E.G. *Jade Engraved.* Christchurch: Presbyterian Bookroom, 1947

Johnston, Revd James (ed.) *Report of the Centenary Conference on the Protestant*

Missions of the World, London 1888. Vol. 1, 3rd edn. New York and Chicago: Fleming H. Revell, 1888

Kaye, Mrs A. *Out of Every Nation: A brief account of the World's Missionary Conference, held in Edinburgh 1910.* Christchurch: Smith & Anthony for Presbyterian Women's Missionary Union, 1910

Millard, E.C. *The Same Lord: An account of the mission tour of the Rev. George. C. Grubb.* London: E. Marlborough, 1893

Mitchell, Donovan. *Ellen Arnold: Pioneer and pathfinder.* Adelaide: South Australian Baptist Union Foreign Missionary and Book and Publication Departments, 1932

Morton, W. Lockhart. *Drifting Wreckage: A story of rescue in two parts.* London, New York and Toronto: Hodder and Stoughton, 1912

Mott, J.R. *The Evangelization of the World in this Generation.* London: Student Volunteer Missionary Union, 1900

Myers, John Brown (ed.) *The Centenary Volume of the Baptist Missionary Society, 1792–1892,* 2nd edn. London: The Baptist Missionary Society, 1892

Oldham, J.H. *Christianity and the Race Problem.* London: Student Christian Movement, 1924

Paterson, N. *The Church in York Place Hall: Some notes on its early history.* Dunedin, np, nd

Pierson, Arthur T. *The New Acts of the Apostles, or the marvels of modern missions.* London: James Nisbet, 1908

Pierson, D.L. 'South America'. *Missionary Review of the World* 8, no. 11 (1895): 851–54

Presbyterian Church of New Zealand. *Prayers for the Home Circle with a Selection of Bible Readings.* Dunedin: Wm. H. Adams, 1917

Reeve, Jessie. *The Missionary Uprising among Australasian Students.* Melbourne: ASCU, 1910

Riddle, T.E. *The Light of Other Days.* Christchurch and Dunedin: Presbyterian Bookroom, 1949

Rouse, Ruth. 'A study of missionary vocation'. *International Review of Missions* 6, no. 22 (1917): 244–57

Stock, Eugene. *The Story of the New Zealand Mission.* London: Church Missionary Society, 1913

_____. 'Review of the century'. In *Ecumenical Missionary Conference, New York 1900,* vol. 1, Edwin M. Bliss et al. (eds), 401–13. New York and London: American Tract Society and Religious Tract Society, 1900

_____. *The History of the Church Missionary Society.* Vol. 3. London: Church Missionary Society, 1899

Takle, John. 'Hindrances in the mission field'. *New Zealand Baptist,* October 1903, 149

_____. 'The inspiration of the imperium in India'. *New Zealand Baptist,* November 1916, 210

Thomson, James Allan. *The Taieri Allans and Related Families: A page out of the early history of Otago.* Dunedin: N.Z. Bible and Book Society, 1929

Waddell, Rutherford. 'The Sabbath-school and missions'. *New Zealand Missionary Record,* February 1884, 44–49

Walsh, C.R. 'Missionary extension: The church's opportunity in the world'. In *Report of the Church Congress held at Melbourne, 19-24 November, 1906,* Revd Henry Lowther Clarke (ed.), 112–18. Melbourne: Edgerton & Moore, Printers, 1906

Warneck, Gustav. *Outline of a History of Protestant Missions from the Reformation to the Present Time.* Edinburgh & London: Oliphant, Anderson & Ferrier, 1906

Webb, Revd Edward. 'Reasons for taking part in efforts to save the world'. *Missionary Review of the World* 8, no. 5 (1895): 367–68

Wells, Amos R. *The Missionary Manual: A handbook of methods for missionary work in young people's societies.* Boston and Chicago: United Society of Christian Endeavour, 1899

World Missionary Conference, 1910: Report of Commission VI. *The Home Base of Missions.* Edinburgh and London: Oliphant, Anderson and Ferrier, 1910

Young, Florence. *Pearls from the Pacific.* London and Edinburgh: Marshall Brothers, c. 1925

Contemporary Journals and Newspapers

China's Millions
Church Gazette
Church Missionary Intelligencer
Harvest Field
Missionary Messenger
Nelson Evening Mail
New Zealand Baptist
New Zealand Churchman
New Zealand Church News
New Zealand Truth
Observer
On Continent and Island
Otago Witness
Our Bond
Tahuantin Suyu
Te Pipiwharauroa: He Kupu Whakamarama
The Baptist Missionary Magazine
The Bolivian Indian
The Break of Day
The Evangelist
The Golden Link

The Lotu
The Message
The New Zealand Missionary Record
The Outlook
The Press
The Reaper [New Zealand Anglican Board of Missions]
The Reaper [New Zealand Bible Training Institute]
The South American Messenger
The War Cry
Treasury
Waiapu Church Gazette
White Already to Harvest
White Ribbon

Secondary Sources

Published

Alexander, Kristine. 'The Girl Guide movement and imperial internationalism during the 1920s and 1930s'. *Journal of the History of Childhood and Youth* 2, no. 1 (2009): 37–63

Allen, Margaret. '"Innocents abroad" and "prohibited immigrants": Australians in India and Indians in Australia 1890–1910'. In *Connected Worlds: History in transnational perspective*, Ann Curthoys and Marilyn Lake (eds), 111–24. Canberra: ANU E Press, 2005

_____. '"White already to harvest": South Australian women missionaries in India'. *Feminist Review* 65 (Summer 2000): 92–107

Allman, Jean. 'Making mothers: Missionaries, medical officers and women's work in colonial Asante, 1924–1945'. *History Workshop* 38 (1994): 23–47

Anderson, Gerald H. (ed.) *Biographical Dictionary of Christian Missions.* New York: MacMillan Reference USA, 1998

_____. 'American Protestants in pursuit of mission, 1886–1986'. *International Bulletin of Missionary Research* 12, no. 3 (1988): 98–118

Anderson, Gerald et al. (eds). *Mission Legacies: Biographical studies of leaders of the modern missionary movement.* Maryknoll, New York: Orbis Books, 1994

Anonymous. *Women's Work for Missions: The story of the beginnings and growth of the Presbyterian Women's Missionary Union of New Zealand.* Auckland: Presbyterian Women's Missionary Union, 1955

Anonymous. *St Andrew's Presbyterian Church: A brief survey of the first sixty years and an illustrated history of the years 1923–1963.* Dunedin: Editorial Committee, 1963

Arnold, Rollo. *The Farthest Promised Land: English villagers, New Zealand immigrants of the 1870s.* Wellington: Victoria University Press, 1981

Askew, Thomas. 'The 1888 London Centenary Missions Conference: Ecumenical disappointment or American missions coming of age?' *International Bulletin of Missionary Research* 18, no. 3 (1994): 113–18

Austin, Alvyn. 'Only connect: The China Inland Mission and transatlantic evangelicalism'. In *North American Foreign Missions, 1810–1914: Theology, theory, and policy*, Wilbert Shenk (ed.), 281–313. Grand Rapids, Michigan and Cambridge, UK: William B. Eerdmans, 2004

Austin, A., and J.S. Scott (eds). *Canadian Missionaries, Indigenous Peoples: Representing religion at home and abroad.* Toronto, Buffalo, London: University of Toronto Press, 2005

Ballantyne, Tony. *Entanglements of Empire: Missionaries, Māori, and the question of the body.* Auckland: Auckland University Press, 2015.

_____. *Webs of Empire: Locating New Zealand's colonial past.* Wellington: Bridget Williams Books, 2012

_____. 'Thinking Local: Knowledge, sociability and community in Gore's intellectual life, 1875–1914'. *New Zealand Journal of History* 44, no. 2 (2010): 138–56

_____. 'Review Essay: Religion, difference and the limits of British imperial history'. *Victorian Studies* 47, no. 3 (2005): 427–55

_____. *Orientalism and Race: Aryanism and the British Empire.* Houndmills, Basingstoke, and New York: Palgrave, 2002

Ballantyne, Tony and Brian Moloughney. 'Angles of vision'. In *Disputed Histories: Imagining New Zealand's past*, Tony Ballantyne and Brian Moloughney (eds), 9–24. Dunedin: Otago University Press, 2006

_____. 'Asia in Murihiku: Towards a transnational history of colonial culture'. In *Disputed Histories: Imagining New Zealand's past*, Tony Ballantyne and Brian Moloughney (eds), 65–92. Dunedin: Otago University Press, 2006

Bandyopadhyay, Sekhar (ed.) *India in New Zealand: Local identities, global relations.* Dunedin: Otago University Press, 2010

Barry, Amanda, Joanna Cruikshank, Andrew May and Patricia Grimshaw (eds). *Evangelists of Empire?: Missionaries in colonial history.* Melbourne: School of Historical Studies and the eScholarship Research Centre, University of Melbourne, 2011

Bays, D.H. and G. Wacker. 'Introduction: The many faces of the missionary enterprise at home'. In *The Foreign Missionary Enterprise at Home: Explorations in North American cultural history*, D.H. Bays and G. Wacker (eds), 1–9. Tuscaloosa and London: University of Alabama Press, 2003

Beaver, R. Pierce. *All Loves Excelling: American Protestant women in world mission.* Grand Rapids, Michigan: Eerdmans, 1968

_____. 'Missionary motivation through three centuries'. In *Reinterpretation in American Church History*, Essays in Divinity, vol. 5, Jerald C. Brauer (ed.),

113–51. Chicago and London: University of Chicago Press, 1968

Bebbington, David. 'Atonement, sin and empire, 1880–1914'. In *The Imperial Horizons of British Protestant Missions, 1880–1914*, Andrew Porter (ed.), 14–31. Grand Rapids and Cambridge: Eerdmans, 2003

Belich, James. *Replenishing the Earth: The settler revolution and the rise of the Angloworld*. Oxford: Oxford University Press, 2009

———. *Paradise Reforged: A history of the New Zealanders from the 1880s to the year 2000*. Auckland: Allen Lane The Penguin Press, 2001

———. *Making Peoples: From Polynesian settlement to the end of the nineteenth century*. Auckland: Allen Lane The Penguin Press, 1996

Bellenoit, Hayden, J. 'Missionary education, religion and knowledge in India, c. 1880–1915'. *Modern Asian Studies* 41, no. 2 (2007): 369–94

Belgrave, Michael. 'A subtle containment: Women in New Zealand medicine, 1893–1941'. *New Zealand Journal of History* 22, no. 1 (1988): 44–55

Bendroth, Margaret. 'Women and missions: conflict and changing roles in the Presbyterian Church in the United States of America, 1870–1935'. *Journal of Presbyterian History* 65, no. 1 (1987): 49–59

Beniston, Daphne. *The Call of the Solomons: The New Zealand Methodist women's response*. Auckland: Wesley Historical Society (NZ), 1994

Bennett, James. *'Rats and Revolutionaries': The Labour movement in Australia and New Zealand 1890–1940*. Dunedin: University of Otago Press, 2004

Berger, Stefan, and Chris Lorenz (eds). *The Contested Nation: Ethnicity, class, religion and gender in national histories*. Writing the Nation Series. Houndmills, Basingstoke: Palgrave Macmillan, 2008

Berry, Christine. *The New Zealand Student Christian Movement, 1896–1996: A centennial history*. Christchurch: The Student Christian Movement of Aotearoa, 1998

Bickers, R.A., and R. Seton (eds). *Missionary Encounters: Sources and issues*. Richmond, Surrey: Curzon Press, 1996

Binney, Judith. 'History and memory: The wood of the whau tree, 1766–2005'. In *The New Oxford History of New Zealand*, Giselle Byrnes (ed.), 73–98. Oxford and Melbourne: Oxford University Press, 2009

Black, Jeremy. *Maps and History: Constructing images of the past*. New Haven and London: Yale University Press, 2000

Blain, Michael. *Blain Biographical Directory of Anglican Clergy in the South Pacific*. http://anglicanhistory.org/nz/blain_directory/directory.pdf

Boone, Troy. 'Remaking "lawless lads and licentious girls": The Salvation Army and the regeneration of empire'. In *Christian Encounters with the Other*, John C. Hawley (ed.), 103–21. New York: New York University Press, 1998

Booth, Patricia. *In Heavenly Love Abiding: Memoirs of a missionary wife*. Wellington: Sarah Bennett Books, 2005

Bosch, David. *Transforming Mission: Paradigm shifts in theology of mission*. Maryknoll, New York: Orbis Books, 1991

Boyd, Mary. 'Racial attitudes of New Zealand officials in Western Samoa'. *New Zealand Journal of History* 21, no. 1 (1987): 139–55

Brash, Alan A. (ed.) *How Did the Church Get There? A study of the missionary activity of the churches and missionary societies belonging to the National Missionary Council of New Zealand.* Christchurch & Dunedin: Presbyterian Bookroom, 1948

Breitenbach, Esther. *Empire and Scottish Society: The impact of foreign missions at home, c. 1790 to c. 1914.* Edinburgh: Edinburgh University Press, 2009

_____. 'Religious literature and discourses of empire: The Scottish Presbyterian foreign mission movement'. In *Empires of Religion*, H.M. Carey (ed.), 84–110. Houndmills, Basingstoke, and New York: Palgrave Macmillan, 2008

Breward, Ian, 'Waddell, Rutherford 1850–1852? – 1932'. In *Dictionary of New Zealand Biography.* www.dnzb.govt.nz/

_____. *A History of the Churches in Australasia.* Oxford: Oxford University Press, 2001

_____. 'Religion and New Zealand society'. *New Zealand Journal of History* 13, no. 2 (1979): 138–48

Brewer, Sandy. 'From darkest England to the hope of the world: Protestant pedagogy and the visual culture of the London Missionary Society'. *Material Religion* 1, no. 1 (2005): 98–123

Bridge, Carl, and Kent Fedorowich. 'Mapping the British world'. *Journal of Imperial and Commonwealth History* 31, no. 2 (2003): 1–15

Brock, Peggy. 'Mission encounters in the colonial world: British Columbia and South-West Australia'. *Journal of Religious History* 24, no. 2 (2000): 159–79

Brookes, Barbara, Annabel Cooper, and Robyn Law. 'Situating gender'. In *Sites of Gender: Women, men and modernity in southern Dunedin, 1890–1939*, Barbara Brookes, Annabel Cooper and Robyn Law (eds), 1–14. Auckland: Auckland University Press, 2003

Brooking, Tom, and Roberto Rabel. 'Neither British nor Polynesian: A brief history of New Zealand's other immigrants'. In *Immigration and National Identity in New Zealand: One people, two peoples, many peoples?*, Stuart Grief (ed.), 23–49. Palmerston North: Dunmore Press, 1995

Brouwer, R.C. *New Women for God: Canadian Presbyterian women and India missions, 1876–1914.* Toronto, University of Toronto Press, 1990

Brown, Callum. *The Death of Christian Britain: Understanding secularisation 1800–2000.* London and New York: Routledge, 2001

Brown, Colin. 'The American connection: The United States of America and churches in New Zealand'. In *Religious Studies in Dialogue*, Maurice Andrew (ed.), 153–62. Dunedin: Faculty of Theology, University of Otago, 1991

Brumberg, Joan. 'Zenanas and girlless villages: The ethnology of American evangelical women'. *The Journal of American History* 69, no. 2 (1982): 347–71

Buettner, Elizabeth. *Empire Families: Britons and late imperial India.* Oxford: Oxford University Press, 2004

Bunge, Marcia J. (ed.) *The Child in Christian Thought.* Grand Rapids, Michigan: William B. Eerdmans, 2001

Burke, Peter. 'Strengths and weaknesses of the history of mentalities'. *History of European Ideas* 7, no. 5 (1986): 439–51

Burton, Antoinette. *Empire in Question: Reading, writing, and teaching British imperialism.* Durham and London: Duke University Press, 2011

———. 'Contesting the zenana: The mission to make "lady doctors for India", 1874–1885'. *Journal of British Studies* 35 (1996): 368–97

Burton, J.W. *The First Century of Missionary Adventure, 1855–1955.* Sydney: Methodist Overseas Missions, 1955

Bush, Henry, and Walter J.E. Kerrison (eds). *First Fifty Years: The story of Christian Endeavour under the Southern Cross.* Sydney: National Christian Endeavour Union of Australia and New Zealand, 1938

Byrnes, Giselle (ed.) *The New Oxford History of New Zealand.* Oxford and Melbourne: Oxford University Press, 2009

———. *Boundary Markers: Land surveying and the colonisation of New Zealand.* Wellington: Bridget Williams Books, 2001

Byrnes, Giselle, and Catharine Coleborne. 'Editorial introduction: The utility and futility of "the nation" in histories of Aotearoa New Zealand'. *New Zealand Journal of History* 45, no. 1 (2011): 1–14

Cannadine, David. *Ornamentalism: How the British saw their empire.* Oxford: Oxford University Press, 2001

Carey, Hilary M. *God's Empire: Religion and colonialism in the British world, c. 1801–1908.* Cambridge: Cambridge University Press, 2011

——— (ed.) *Empires of Religion,* Cambridge Imperial and Post-Colonial Studies. Houndmills, Basingstoke, and New York: Palgrave Macmillan, 2008

———. 'Companions in the wilderness? Missionary wives in colonial Australia, 1788–1900'. *Journal of Religious History* 19, no. 2 (1995): 227–48

Carpenter, Joel A. 'Propagating the faith once delivered: The fundamentalist missionary enterprise, 1920–1945'. In *Earthen Vessels: American evangelicals and foreign missions, 1880–1980,* Joel A. Carpenter and Wilbert R. Shenk (eds), 92–132. Grand Rapids, Michigan: Eerdmans, 1990

Carter, George C. *Valuable Beyond Price: The story of Sister Lina M. Jones, 1890–1979.* Auckland: Wesley Historical Society NZ, 1985

———. *A Family Affair: A brief survey of New Zealand Methodism's involvement in mission overseas.* Auckland: Wesley Historical Society NZ, 1973

Case, Jay Riley. *An Unpredictable Gospel: American evangelicals and world Christianity, 1812–1920.* Oxford: Oxford University Press, 2012

Castle, Kathryn. *Britannia's Children: Reading colonialism through children's books and magazines.* Studies in Imperialism. Manchester: Manchester University Press, 1996

Chambers, D. 'The Church of Scotland's nineteenth century foreign missions scheme: Evangelical or moderate revival?' *Journal of Religious History* 9, no. 2 (1976): 115–38

Chang, Kornel. 'Circulating race and empire: Transnational labor activism and the politics of anti-Asian agitation in the Anglo-American Pacific world, 1880–1910'. *The Journal of American History* (December 2009): 678–701

Christensen, T., and W.R. Hutchison (eds). *Missionary Ideologies in the Imperialist Era, 1880–1920*. Aarhus: Aros, 1982

Clapham, J.W. *John Olley, Pioneer Missionary to the Chad*. Rev. edn. London: Pickering & Inglis, 1966

Clarke, Alison. '"With one accord rejoice on this glad day": Celebrating the monarchy in nineteenth-century Otago'. *New Zealand Journal of History* 36, no. 2 (2002): 137–60

Colley, Linda. 'The difficulties of empire: Present, past and future'. *Historical Research* 79, no. 205 (2006): 367–82

Comaroff, John and Jean Comaroff. 'Through the looking-glass: Colonial encounters of the first kind'. *Journal of Historical Sociology* 1, no. 1 (1988): 6–32

Cox, Jeffrey. *The British Missionary Enterprise since 1700*. New York and London: Routledge, 2008

_____. *Imperial Fault-lines: Christianity and colonial power in India, 1818–1940*. Stanford, California: Stanford University Press, 2002

Craig, Jenni. *Servants Among the Poor*. Manila: OMF Literature Inc., 1998

Craig, Terence. *The Missionary Lives: A study in Canadian missionary biography and autobiography*. Leiden, New York and Cologne: Brill, 1997

Crawford, Janet. '"Christian wives for Christian lads": Aspects of women's work in the Melanesian Mission, 1849–1877'. In *With All Humility and Gentleness*, Allan K. Davidson and Godfrey Nicholson (eds), 51–66. Auckland: St John's College, 1991

Daley, Caroline. *Girls and Women, Men and Boys: Gender in Taradale, 1886–1930*. Auckland: Auckland University Press, 1999

Daley, Caroline and Melanie Nolan (eds). *Suffrage and Beyond: International feminist perspectives*. Auckland: Auckland University Press, 1994

Dalzell, Matthew. *New Zealanders in Republican China, 1912–1949*. Auckland: University of Auckland New Zealand Asia Institute, 1995

Daniel, Esther. '"Solving an empire problem": The Salvation Army and British juvenile migration to Australia'. *History of Education Review* 36, no. 1 (2007): 33–48

Davidson, Allan K. (ed.) *Living Legacy: A history of the Anglican diocese of Auckland*. Auckland: Anglican Diocese of Auckland, 2011

_____ (ed.) *A Controversial Churchman: Essays on George Selwyn, bishop of New Zealand and Lichfield, and Sarah Selwyn*. Wellington: Bridget Williams Books, 2011

_____. *Christianity in Aotearoa: A history of church and society in New Zealand*. Wellington: The New Zealand Education for Ministry Board, 2004

_____. '"An interesting experiment": The founding of the Melanesian Mission, 1849–1942'. In *The Church of Melanesia, 1849–1999*, Allan K Davidson (ed.), 13–48. Auckland: The College of St John the Evangelist, 2000

_____. '"Enlarging our hearts": The founding of the New Zealand Church Missionary Association'. *Stimulus* 7, no. 2 (1999): 23–27

_____. 'The interaction of missionary and colonial Christianity in nineteenth century New Zealand'. *Studies in World Christianity* 2, no. 2 (1996): 145–66

_____ (ed.) *Semisi Nau, the Story of my Life: The autobiography of a Tongan Methodist missionary who worked at Ontong Java in the Solomon Islands.* Suva: Institute of Pacific Studies, University of the South Pacific, 1996

_____. 'The New Zealand overseas missionary contribution: The need for further research'. In *'With All Humility and Gentleness': Essays on mission in honour of Francis Foulkes*, Allan K. Davidson and Godfrey Nicholson (eds), 41–50. Auckland: St John's College, 1991

Davidson, Allan K., Stuart M. Lange, Peter J. Lineham, and Adrienne Puckey (eds). *Te Rongopai 1814 'Takoto Te Pai!': Bicentenary reflections on Christian beginnings and developments in Aotearoa New Zealand.* Auckland: The General Synod Office, 'Tuia', of the Anglican Church in Aotearoa New Zealand and Polynesia, 2014

Davidson, Allan K., and Peter J. Lineham. *Transplanted Christianity: Documents illustrating aspects of New Zealand church history.* Palmerston North: Dunmore Press, 1989

Davin, Delia. 'British women missionaries in nineteenth-century China'. *Women's History Review* 1, no. 2 (1992): 257–71

Dench, Simon. 'Invading the Waikato: A postcolonial review', *New Zealand Journal of History* 45, no. 1 (2011): 33–49

Denoon, Donald. 'Re-Membering Australasia: A repressed memory'. *Australian Historical Studies* 34, no. 122 (2003): 290–304

Denoon, Donald, Philippa Mein Smith, and Marivic Wyndham. *A History of Australia, New Zealand and the Pacific.* Oxford: Blackwell Publishers, 2000

Dickey, Brian (ed.) *The Australian Dictionary of Evangelical Biography.* Sydney: Evangelical History Association, 1994

Douglas, Bronwen. 'Encounters with the enemy? Academic readings of missionary narratives on Melanesians'. *Comparative Studies on Society and History* 43, no. 1 (2001): 37–64

Dries, Angelyn, OSF. *The Missionary Movement in American Catholic History.* American Society of Missiology Series, no. 26. Maryknoll, New York: Orbis Books, 1998

Dunch, Ryan. 'Beyond cultural imperialism: Cultural theory, Christian missions, and global modernity'. *History and Theory* 41 (October 2002): 301–25

Edgar, Stan E., and M.J. Eade. *Towards the Sunrise: The centenary history of the New Zealand Baptist Missionary Society.* Auckland: NZBHS for the NZBMS, 1985

Edwards, Wendy J. Deichmann. 'Forging an ideology for American missions:

Josiah Strong and manifest destiny'. In *North American Foreign Missions, 1810-1914: Theology, theory, and policy*, Wilbert Shenk (ed.), 163–91. Grand Rapids, Michigan and Cambridge, UK: William B. Eerdmans, 2004

Elder, J.R. *The History of the Presbyterian Church*. Christchurch: Presbyterian Bookroom, 1940

Eldred-Grigg, Stevan, and Zeng Dazheng. *White Ghosts, Yellow Peril: China and New Zealand 1790–1950*. Dunedin: Otago University Press, 2014

Elleray, Michelle. 'Little builders: Coral insects, missionary culture, and the Victorian child'. *Victorian Literature & Culture* 39, no. 1 (2011): 223–38

Entwistle, Dorothy. 'Sunday-school book prizes for children: Rewards and socialization'. In *The Church and Childhood*, Diana Wood (ed.), 405–16. Oxford: Blackwell, 1994

Etherington, Norman (ed.) *Missions and Empire*. Oxford History of the British Empire Companion Series. Oxford: Oxford University Press, 2005

_____. 'Missions and empire'. In *Historiography*, Robin Winks (ed.) The Oxford History of the British Empire, 303–14. Oxford: Oxford University Press, 1999

_____. 'American errand into the South African wilderness'. *Church History* 39, no. 1 (1970): 62–71

Evans, Robert and Roy McKenzie. *Evangelical Revivals in New Zealand*. Paihia: ColCom, 1999

Fabian, Johannes. 'Religious and secular colonization: Common ground'. *History and Anthropology* 4 (1990): 339–55

Fairburn, Miles. 'Is there a good case for New Zealand exceptionalism?' In *Disputed Histories: Imagining New Zealand's past*, Tony Ballantyne and Brian Moloughney (eds), 143–67. Dunedin: University of Otago Press, 2006

Ferrall, Charles, Paul Millar, and Keren Smith (eds). *East by South: China in the Australasian Imagination*. Wellington: Victoria University Press, 2005

Flemming, Leslie A. 'A new humanity: American missionaries' ideals for women in North India, 1870–1930'. In *Western Women and Imperialism: Complicity and resistance*, N. Chaudhuri and M. Strobel (eds), 191–206. Bloomington: Indianna University Press, 1992

Flynt, Wayne J., and Gerald W. Berkley. *Taking Christianity to China: Alabama missionaries in the Middle Kingdom, 1850–1950*. Tuscaloosa: University of Alabama Press, 1997

Fowler, James. *Stages of Faith: The psychology of development and the quest for meaning*. Blackburn, Victoria: Dove Communications, 1981

Fox, C.E. *Lord of the Southern Isles: Being the story of the Anglican mission in Melanesia, 1849–1949*. London: A.R. Mowbray & Co., 1958

Fry, Ruth. *The Community of the Sacred Name: A centennial history*. Christchurch: Community of the Sacred Name, 1993

Gardner, Helen Bethea. *Gathering for God: George Brown in Oceania*. Dunedin: Otago University Press, 2006

Garrett, Shirley. 'Sisters all: Feminism and the American women's missionary movement'. In *Missionary Ideologies in the Imperialist Era*, T. Christensen and W.R. Hutchison (eds), 221–30. Aarhus: Aros, 1982

Gibbons, Peter. 'The far side of the search for identity: Reconsidering New Zealand history'. *New Zealand Journal of History* 37, no. 1 (2003): 38–49

———. 'Cultural colonization and national identity'. *New Zealand Journal of History* 36, no. 1 (2002): 5–17

Gilling, Bryan. 'Rescuing the perishing'. *Stimulus* 1, no. 2 (1993): 28–36

Glen, Robert (ed.) *Mission and Moko: The Church Missionary Society in New Zealand 1814–1882*. Christchurch: Latimer Fellowship of New Zealand, 1992

Godden, Judith. '"Containment and control": Presbyterian women and the missionary impulse in New South Wales, 1891–1914'. *Women's History Review* 6, no. 1 (1997): 75–93

Gooden, Ros. '"We trust them to establish the work": Significant roles for early Australian Baptist women in overseas mission, 1864–1913'. In *This Gospel Shall be Preached: Essays on the Australian contribution to world mission*, W.R. Hutchinson and G. Treloar (eds), 126–46. Sydney: Centre for the Study of Australian Christianity, 1998

Graham, Jeanine. 'Young New Zealanders and the Great War: Exploring the impact and legacy of the First World War, 1914–2014'. *Paedagogica Historica* 44, no. 4 (2008): 429–44

———. 'Editorial introduction'. *New Zealand Journal of History* 40, no. 1 (2006): 1–6

Gregory, Kenneth. *Stretching Out Continually: Whaatoro Tonu Atu: A history of the New Zealand Church Missionary Society, 1892–1972*. Christchurch: The author, 1972

Griffiths, Gordon. 'A home grown Australian mission: The formation of the Queensland Kanaka Mission/South Seas Evangelical Mission'. In *This Gospel Shall Be Preached: Essays on the Australian contribution to world mission*, W.R. Hutchinson and G. Treloar (eds), 86–97. Sydney: Centre for the Study of Australian Christianity, 1998

Grigg, Viv. *Companion to the Poor*. Australia: Albatross Books, 1984

Grimshaw, Patricia. '"Christian woman, pious wife, faithful mother, devoted missionary": Conflict in roles of American missionary women in nineteenth-century Hawaii'. *Feminist Studies* 9, no. 3 (1983): 489–521

Grimshaw, Patricia and Andrew May (eds). *Missionaries, Indigenous Peoples and Cultural Exchange*. Brighton, England, & Portland, Or.: Sussex Academic Press, 2010

Gunson, Niel. 'Victorian Christianity in the South Seas: A survey'. *Journal of Religious History* 8, no. 2 (1974): 183–97

Guy, Laurie (ed.) *Baptists in Twentieth Century New Zealand: Documents illustrating Baptist life and development*. Auckland: New Zealand Baptist

Research and Historical Society, 2005

Haggis, Jane. 'Ironies of emancipation: Changing configurations of "women's work" in the "mission of sisterhood" to Indian women'. *Feminist Review* 65 (Summer 2000): 108–26

———. '"A heart that has felt the love of God and longs for others to know it": Conventions of gender, tensions of self and constructions of difference in offering to be a lady missionary'. *Women's History Review* 7, no. 2 (1998): 171–92

Haggis, Jane, and Margaret Allen. 'Imperial emotions: Affective communities of mission in British Protestant women's missionary publications c. 1880–1920'. *Journal of Social History* (Spring 2008): 691–716

Hall, Catherine. '"From Greenland's icy mountains ... To Africa's golden sand": Ethnicity, race and nation in mid-nineteenth-century England'. *Gender and History* 5, no. 2 (1993): 212–30

Hall, Catherine, and Sonya Rose (eds). *At Home with the Empire: Metropolitan culture and the imperial world.* Cambridge: Cambridge University Press, 2006

Hansen, James L. (ed.) *A Heart to Serve: Ordinary people with an extraordinary God.* Cochabamba: Mision Andina Evangelica, 2007

Hanson, Frank. *The Sunday School in New Zealand Methodism.* Auckland: Wesley Historical Society, New Zealand, 1998

Hardesty, N.A. 'The scientific study of missions: Textbooks of the Central Committee on the United Study of Foreign Missions'. In *The Foreign Missionary Enterprise at Home: Explorations in North American cultural history*, D.H. Bays & G. Wacker (eds), 106–22. Tuscaloosa and London: University of Alabama Press, 2003

Harrison, Henrietta. '"A penny for the little Chinese": The French Holy Childhood Association in China, 1843–1951'. *American Historical Review* (February 2008): 72–92

Hastings, Adrian. 'The clash of nationalism and universalism in twentieth-century missionary Christianity'. In *Missions, Nationalism, and the End of Empire*, Brian Stanley (ed.), 15–33. Grand Rapids, Michigan: William B. Eerdmans, 2003

Hickford, Mark. *Lords of the Land: Indigenous property rights and the jurisprudence of empire*, Oxford Studies in Modern Legal History. Oxford: Oxford University Press, 2011

Hiner, N.R. and J.M. Hawes. 'History of childhood: United States'. In *Encyclopedia of Children and Childhood*, vol. 2, Paula Fass et al. (eds), 426–30. New York: Macmillan Reference, 2004

Henderson, Alice. *My Yesterdays in Sunshine and Shadow.* Christchurch: Presbyterian Church of New Zealand, 1947

Hercus, Ann. *From Orkney to Otago: 600 years of Hercus family history.* Christchurch: John and Anne Hercus, 2004

Hill, Myrtle. 'Gender, culture and "the spiritual empire": The Irish Protestant female missionary experience'. *Women's History Review* 16, no. 2 (2007): 203–26

_____. 'Women in the Irish Protestant foreign missions c. 1873–1914: Representations and motivations'. In *Missions and Missionaries*, Pieter N. Holtrop and Hugh McLeod (eds), 170–185. Woodbridge, UK: Boydell Press, 2000

Hilliard, Chris. 'Colonial culture and the province of cultural history'. *New Zealand Journal of History* 36, no. 1 (2002): 82–93

Hilliard, David. *God's Gentlemen: A history of the Melanesian Mission, 1849–1942.* St Lucia, Queensland: Queensland University Press, 1978

_____. 'The South Sea Evangelical Mission in the Solomon Islands: The foundation years'. *Journal of Pacific History* 4 (1969): 41–64

Howe, Renate. *A Century of Influence: The Australian Student Christian Movement 1896–1996.* Sydney: UNSW Press, 2009

_____. 'The Australian Student Christian Movement and women's activism in the Asia-Pacific region, 1890s–1920s'. *Australian Feminist Studies* 16, no. 6 (2001): 311–23

Hoyle, L.H. 'Nineteenth-century single women and motivation for mission'. *International Bulletin of Missionary Research* 20, no. 2 (1996): 58–64

Hudson, Pat. *History by Numbers: An introduction to quantitative approaches.* London: Arnold, 2000

Hudspith, Margarita Allan. *Ripening Fruit: A history of the Bolivian Indian Mission.* New Jersey: Harrington Press, 1958

Hunter, Jane. 'Women's mission in historical perspective: American identity and Christian internationalism'. In *Competing Kingdoms: Women, mission, nation, and the American Protestant empire, 1812–1960*, Barbara Reeves-Ellington, Kathryn Kish Sklar, and Connie A. Shemo (eds), 19–42. Durham & London: Duke University Press, 2010

_____. *The Gospel of Gentility: American women missionaries in turn-of-the-century China.* New Haven: Yale University Press, 1984

Hutchinson, M., and G. Treloar (eds). *This Gospel Shall Be Preached: Essays on the Australian contribution to world mission.* Sydney: Centre for the Study of Australian Christianity, 1998

Irwin, James. *An Introduction to Maori Religion: Its character before European contact and its survival in contemporary Maori and New Zealand culture.* South Australia: Australian Association for the Study of Religions, 1984

Jackson, Hugh. *Churches and People in Australia and New Zealand, 1860–1930.* Wellington: Unwin and Allen, 1987

Jenkins, Philip. *The Next Christendom: The coming of global Christianity*, rev. edn. Oxford: Oxford University Press, 2007

Jensz, Felicity. 'Origins of missionary periodicals: Form and function of three Moravian publications'. *Journal of Religious History* 36, no. 2 (2012): 234–55

Jensz, Felicity and Hanna Acke (eds). *Missions and Media: The politics of missionary periodicals in the long nineteenth century*. Stuttgart, Germany: Franz Steiner Verlag, 2013

_____. 'Forum: The form and function of nineteenth-century missionary periodicals'. *Church History* 82, no. 2 (2013): 368–73

Johnson, Henry, and Brian Moloughney (eds). *Asia in the Making of New Zealand*. Auckland: Auckland University Press, 2006

Johnston, Anna. 'British missionary publishing, missionary celebrity, and empire'. *Nineteenth-Century Prose* 32, no. 2 (2005): 20–47

_____. *Missionary Writing and Empire, 1800–1860*. Cambridge: Cambridge University Press, 2003

Jolly, Margaret. '"To save the girls for brighter and better lives": Presbyterian missions and women in the south of Vanuatu, 1848–1870'. *Journal of Pacific History* 26, no. 1 (1991): 27–48

Johnson, Todd M., and Kenneth R. Ross (eds). *Atlas of Global Christianity*. Edinburgh: Edinburgh University Press, 2009

Joseph, Robert. 'Intercultural exchange, matakite Māori and the Mormon Church'. In *Mana Māori and Christianity*, Hugh Morrison, Lachy Paterson, Brett Knowles and Murray Rae (eds), 45–68. Wellington: Huia Publishers, 2012

Jull, David. 'The Knapdale revival (1881): Social context and religious conviction in 19th century New Zealand'. *Australasian Pentecostal Studies* 7 (2003): http://webjournals.alphacrucis.edu.au/journals/aps/issue-7

Kidd, Colin. *The Forging of Races: Race and scripture in the Protestant Atlantic world, 1600–2000*. Cambridge: Cambridge University Press, 2006

King, Michael. *The Penguin History of New Zealand*. Auckland: Penguin Books, 2003

Lange, Raeburn. *Island Ministers: Indigenous leadership in nineteenth century Pacific Islands Christianity*. Canberra: Pandanus Books, 2005

_____. 'Indigenous agents of religious change in New Zealand, 1830–1860'. *Journal of Religious History* 24, no. 3 (2000): 279–95

Lange, Stuart M. *A Rising Tide: Evangelical Christianity in New Zealand 1930–1965*. Dunedin: Otago University Press, 2013

Langmore, Diane. *Missionary Lives: Papua, 1874–1914*. Honolulu: University of Hawaii Press, 1989

_____. 'Exchanging earth for heaven: Death in the Papuan missionfields'. *Journal of Religious History* 13, no. 3 (1985): 383–92

_____. 'A neglected force: White women missionaries in Papua, 1874–1914'. *Journal of Pacific History* 17, no. 3 (1982): 138–50

Latourette, Kenneth Scott. *A History of the Expansion of Christianity*. 7 vols. London: Eyre and Spottiswoode, 1938

Laurie, N., C. Dwyer, S.L. Holloway, and F.M. Smith. *Geographies of New Femininities*. Harlow UK: Longman, 1999

Leach, Fiona. 'African girls, nineteenth-century mission education and the patriarchal imperative'. *Gender and Education* 20, no. 4 (2008): 335–47

Leckie, Jacqueline. 'A long diaspora'. In *India in New Zealand: Local identities, global relations*, Sekhar Bandyopadhyay (ed.), 45–63. Dunedin: Otago University Press, 2010

Lee, Janet. 'Between subordination and she-tiger: Social constructions of white femininity in the lives of single, Protestant missionaries in China, 1905–1930'. *Women's Studies International Forum* 19, no. 6 (1996): 621–32

Levesque, Andree. 'Prescribers and rebels: Attitudes to European women's sexuality in New Zealand, 1860–1916'. In *Women in History: Essays on European women in New Zealand*, Barbara Brookes, Charlotte Macdonald and Margaret Tennant (eds), 1–12. Wellington: Allen & Unwin in New Zealand, 1986

Lewis, Donald M. (ed.) *Christianity Reborn: The global expansion of evangelicalism in the twentieth century*, Studies in the History of Christian Missions. Grand Rapids, Michigan, and Cambridge, UK: William B. Eerdmans, 2004

Lian, Xi. *The Conversion of Missionaries: Liberalism in American Protestant missions in China, 1907–1932*. University Park, Pennsylvania: University of Pennsylvania Press, 1997

Lineham, Peter J. 'Brethren childhood as a historical pattern'. In *Culture, Spirituality, and the Brethren*, Neil T.R. Dickson and T.J. Marinello (eds), 41–64. Troon, Ayrshire: Brethren Archivists and Historians Network, 2014

———. *Destiny: The life and times of a self-made apostle*. Auckland: Penguin Books, 2013

———. 'The rise and significance of the Destiny Church'. In *Mana Māori and Christianity*, Hugh Morrison, Lachy Paterson, Brett Knowles and Murray Rae (eds), 111–37. Wellington: Huia Publishers, 2012

———. 'The foundation of the Bible Training Institute'. In *Gospel, Truth and Interpretation: Evangelical identity in Aotearoa New Zealand*, Tim Meadowcroft and Myk Habets (eds), 49–67. Auckland, NZ: Archer Press, 2011

———. 'Missions in the consciousness of the New Zealand churches'. *Stimulus* 7, no. 2 (1999): 33–39

———. *Bible and Society: A sesquicentennial history of the Bible Society in New Zealand*. Wellington: Daphne Brasell Associates Press and the Bible Society in New Zealand (Inc.), 1996

———. '"When the roll is called up yonder, who'll be there?" An analysis of nineteenth century trans-Atlantic revivalism in New Zealand and Canada'. In *'Rescue the Perishing': Comparative perspectives on evangelism and revivalism*, Douglas Pratt (ed.), 1–17. Auckland: College Communications, 1989

———. 'Finding a space for evangelicalism: Evangelical youth movements in New Zealand'. In *Voluntary Religion*, Studies in Church History, vol. 23, W.J. Sheils and D. Woods (eds), 477–94. Oxford: Basil Blackwell, 1986

———. 'How institutionalised was Protestant piety in nineteenth century New Zealand?' *Journal of Religious History* 13, no. 4 (1985): 370–82

———. *There We Found Brethren: A history of assemblies of Brethren in New Zealand*. Palmerston North: GPH Society, 1977

Lissington, M.P. *New Zealand and the United States 1840–1944*. Wellington: Historical Publications Branch, Department of Internal Affairs, 1972

Loane, Marcus, L. *The Story of the China Inland Mission in Australia and New Zealand, 1890–1964*. Sydney: Overseas Missionary Fellowship, 1965

Lovell-Smith, Margaret. *No Turning Back: A history of the inter-church aid work of the National Council of Churches in New Zealand 1945–1983*. Christchurch: National Council of Churches, 1986

Lowenthal, David. *The Past is a Foreign Country*. Cambridge: Cambridge University Press, 1985

McClure, Margaret. *Saving the City: The history of the Order of the Good Shepherd and the Community of the Holy Name in Auckland, 1894–2000*. Auckland: David Ling, 2002

MacDiarmid, D.N. *Ship Ahoy and Hallelujah! Or from fo'c'sle to pulpit*. Kerikeri: The author, 1968

Macdonald, Lesley A. Orr. *A Unique and Glorious Mission: Women and Presbyterianism in Scotland, 1830–1930*. Edinburgh: John Donald Publishers, 2000

McLean, Rosalind. '"How we prepare them in India": British diasporic imaginings and migration to New Zealand'. *New Zealand Journal of History* 37, no. 2 (2003): 131–52

McDonald, Georgina. *The Flame Unquenched: Being the history of the Presbyterian Church of Southland, 1856–1956*. Christchurch: Presbyterian Bookroom, 1956

McEldowney, Dennis (ed.) *Presbyterians in Aotearoa 1840–1990*. Wellington: Presbyterian Church of New Zealand, 1990

McGeorge, Colin. 'Childhood's sole serious business: The long haul to full school attendance'. *New Zealand Journal of History* 40, no. 1 (2006): 25–38

_____. 'Race, empire and the Maori in the New Zealand primary school curriculum, 1880–1940'. In *The Imperial Curriculum: Racial images and education in the British colonial experience*, J.A. Mangan (ed.), 64–78. London and New York: Routledge, 1993

McGregor, Rae. *Shrewd Sanctity: The story of Kathleen Hall, missionary nurse in China, 1896–1970*. Auckland: Polygraphia, 2006

Malone, E.P. 'The *New Zealand School Journal* and the imperial ideology'. *New Zealand Journal of History* 7, no. 1 (1973): 12–27

Mangan, J.A. (ed.) *Making Imperial Mentalities: Socialisation and British imperialism*. Manchester: Manchester University Press, 1990

_____ (ed.) *Benefits Bestowed?: Education and British imperialism*. Manchester: Manchester University Press, 1988

Manktelow, Emily J. *Missionary Families: Race, gender and generation on the spiritual frontier*. Manchester: Manchester University Press, 2013

Marsh, Les. A. *In His Name: A record of Assembly missionary outreach from New Zealand*. 2nd edn. Palmerston North: GPH Society, 1974

Marsh Les, and Harry D. Erlam. *In His Name: A record of Brethren Assembly missionary outreach from New Zealand.* Palmerston North: GPH Society, 1987

Maslow, Abraham. *Motivation and Personality.* 2nd edn. New York: Harper & Row Publishers, 1970

Matthews, Nathan, 'Kaikatikīhama: "Our most precious resource"'. In *Mana Māori and Christianity*, Hugh Morrison, Lachy Paterson, Brett Knowles, and Murray Rae (eds), 141–58. Wellington: Huia Publishers, 2012

Maughan, Steven S. *Mighty England Do Good: Culture, faith, empire, and world in the foreign missions of the Church of England, 1850–1915.* Grand Rapids, Michigan, and Cambridge, UK: William B. Eerdmans, 2014

———. 'Imperial Christianity? Bishop Montgomery and the foreign missions of the Church of England, 1895–1915'. In *The Imperial Horizons of British Protestant Missions, 1880–1914*, Andrew Porter (ed.), 32–57. Grand Rapids, Michigan: William B. Eerdmans, 2003

———. '"Mighty England do good": The major English denominations and organisation for the support of foreign missions in the nineteenth century'. In *Missionary Encounters: Sources and issues*, Robert A. Bickers and Rosemary Seton (eds), 11–37. Richmond, Surrey: Curzon Press, 1996

May, Helen. 'Mapping some landscapes of colonial–global childhood'. *European Early Childhood Education Research Journal* 9, no. 2 (2001): 5–20

May, Helen, Baljit Kaur, and Larry Prochner. *Empire, Education, and Indigenous Childhoods: Nineteenth-century missionary infant schools in three British colonies.* Ashgate Studies in Childhood, 1700 to the Present. Farnham, Surrey, and Burlington, VT: Ashgate, 2014

Maynes, Mary Jo. 'Age as a category of historical analysis: History, agency, and narratives of childhood'. *Journal of the History of Childhood and Youth* 1, no. 1 (2008): 114–24

Mein Smith, Philippa. 'The Tasman World'. In *The New Oxford History of New Zealand*, Giselle Byrnes, (ed.), 297-319. Oxford and Melbourne: Oxford University Press, 2009

———. *A Concise History of New Zealand.* Cambridge: Cambridge University Press, 2005

———. 'The ties that bind (and divide) Australia and New Zealand'. *History Now* 9, no. 4 (Autumn 2004): 4–12

Mein Smith, Philippa, Peter Hempenstall and Shaun Goldfinch. *Remaking the Tasman World.* Christchurch: Canterbury University Press, 2008

Mintz, Stephen. *Huck's Raft: A history of American childhood.* Cambridge, Mass., and London: Harvard University Press, 2004

'Miss Eunice Preece, Missionary'. *Early New Zealand Families.* http://tortoise. orconhosting.net.nz/eunicepreece.html

Moloughney, Brian. 'Translating culture: Rethinking New Zealand's Chineseness'. In *East by South: China in the Australasian imagination*, Charles

Ferrall, Paul Millar and Keren Smith (eds), 389–404. Wellington: Victoria University Press, 2005

Moloughney, Brian and John Stenhouse. "'Drug-besotten, sin-begotten fiends of filth": New Zealanders and the oriental other, 1850–1920'. *New Zealand Journal of History* 33, no. 1 (1999): 43–64

Montgomerie, Deborah. *The Women's War: New Zealand women 1939–45.* Auckland: Auckland University Press, 2001

Moor, Mrs W. *Thirty-Seven Years with the Christchurch Methodist Women's Missionary Auxiliary: Remembering.* Christchurch: Christchurch Methodist Women's Missionary Auxiliary, 1994

Morris, Jeremy. 'Secularization and religious experience: Arguments in the historiography of modern British religion'. *The Historical Journal* 55, no. 1 (2012): 195–219

———. 'The strange death of Christian Britain: Another look at the secularization debate'. *The Historical Journal* 46, no. 4 (2003): 963–76.

Morrison, Hugh. "'As the sunshine dispels the darkness of the night": Settler Protestant children's missionary magazines in New Zealand c. 1840–1940'. *New Zealand Journal of History* 49, no. 2 (2015): 136–59

———. "'I feel that we belong to the one big family": Protestant childhoods, missions and emotions in British world settings, 1870s–1930s. In *Emotions and Christian Missions: Historical perspectives*, Claire McLisky, Daniel Midena and Karen A.A. Vallgårda (eds), Palgrave Studies in the History of Emotions Series, 218–39. Houndmills, UK and New York: Palgrave Macmillan, 2015

———. 'Theorising missionary education: The Bolivian Indian Mission 1908–1920'. *History of Education Review* 42, no. 1 (2013): 4–23

———. 'Empire, nation, and religion in Canadian and New Zealand Protestant juvenile missionary periodicals, c. 1890–1930s: "Men and women the King would wish you to be"'. In *Missions and Media: The politics of missionary periodicals in the long nineteenth century*, Felicity Jensz and Hanna Acke (eds), 19–38. Stuttgart, Germany: Franz Steiner Verlag, 2013

———. 'Representations of Māori in Presbyterian children's missionary literature, 1909–1939'. In *Mana Māori and Christianity*, Hugh Morrison, Lachy Paterson, Brett Knowles and Murray Rae (eds), 159–78. Wellington: Huia Publishers, 2012

———. 'Rew(r)i(gh)ting an "unfortunate neglect"?: John R. Mott and individual agency in New Zealand mission history'. *Colloquium* 44, no. 1 (2012): 59–77

———. 'Globally and locally positioned: New Zealand perspectives on the current practice of religious history'. *Journal of Religious History* 35, no. 2 (2011): 181–98

———. 'Maintaining the church in unsettled times, 1899–1918'. In *Living Legacy: A history of the Anglican diocese of Auckland*, Allan K. Davidson (ed.), 115–45. Auckland: Anglican Diocese of Auckland, 2011

———. 'Missionaries sent and received, Oceania, 1910–2010'. In *Atlas of*

Global Christianity, Todd M. Johnson and Kenneth R. Ross (eds), 284–85. Edinburgh: Edinburgh University Press, 2009

Morrison, Hugh, Lachy Paterson, Brett Knowles, and Murray Rae (eds). *Mana Māori and Christianity*. Wellington: Huia Publishers, 2012

Murray, Graeme A. 'John Takle'. In *Biographical Dictionary of Christian Missions*, Gerald H. Anderson (ed.), 656. New York: Macmillan Reference USA, 1998

Murray, J.S. *A Century of Growth: Presbyterian overseas mission work, 1869–1969*. Christchurch: Presbyterian Bookroom, 1969

Nair, Janaki. 'Uncovering the zenana: Visions of Indian womanhood in Englishwomen's writing, 1813–1940'. *Journal of Women's History* 2, no. 1 (1990): 8–34

Neill, Stephen. 'The history of missions: An academic discipline'. In *The Mission of the Church and the Propagation of the Faith*, G.J. Cuming (ed.), 149–70. Cambridge: Cambridge University Press, 1970

_____. *Colonialism and Christian Missions*. London: Lutterworth Press, 1966

Neville, R.J. Warwick, and C. James O'Neill (eds). *The Population of New Zealand: Interdisciplinary perspectives*. Auckland: Longman Paul, 1979

Newnham, Tom. *Kathleen Hall: Kiwi heroine in China*. Auckland: Graphic Publications, 2000

Ng, James. *Windows on a Chinese Past*. 3 vols. Dunedin: Heritage Books, 1993, 1995 and 1999

Noll, Mark. *The New Shape of Christianity: How American experience reflects global faith*. Downers Grove, Illinois: IVP Academic, 2009

Oddie, Geoffrey. '"Orientalism" and British Protestant missionary constructions of India in the nineteenth century'. *South Asia* 17, no. 2 (1994): 259–91

_____. 'India and missionary motives, c. 1850–1900'. *Journal of Ecclesiastical History* 25, no. 1 (1974): 61–74

Ogilvie, Gordon. *Little Feet in a Big Room: Frances Ogilvie of China*. Christchurch: Shoal Bay Press, 1994

Olssen, Erik. 'Where to from here? Reflections on the twentieth-century historiography of nineteenth-century New Zealand'. *New Zealand Journal of History* 26, no. 1 (1992): 54–77

_____. 'Towards a new society'. In *The Oxford History of New Zealand*, W.H. Oliver and Bridget Williams (eds), 250–78. Wellington: Oxford University Press, 1981

Olssen, E., and M. Hickey. *Class and Occupation: The New Zealand reality*. Dunedin: University of Otago Press, 2005

Openshaw, R. (ed.) *New Zealand Social Studies: Past, present and future*. Palmerston North: Dunmore Press, 1992

Page, Dorothy. 'The first lady graduates: Women with degrees from Otago University'. In *Women in History 2: Essays on women in New Zealand*, Barbara Brookes, Charlotte Macdonald and Margaret Tennant (eds), 98–128. Wellington: Bridget Williams Books, 1992

Paterson, Lachy. 'The rise and fall of women field workers within the Presbyterian Māori Mission, 1907–1970'. In *Mana Māori and Christianity*, Hugh Morrison, Lachy Paterson, Brett Knowles and Murray Rae (eds), 159–78. Wellington: Huia Publishers, 2012.

———. *Colonial Discourses: Niupepa Māori 1855–1863*. Dunedin: Otago University Press, 2006

Phillips, Clifton J. 'Changing attitudes in the Student Volunteer Movement of Great Britain and North America, 1886–1928'. In *Missionary Ideologies in the Imperialist Era, 1880–1920*, T. Christensen and W.R. Hutchison (eds), 131–45. Aarhus: Aros, 1982

Phillips, Jock and Terry Hearn. *Settlers: New Zealand immigrants from England, Ireland and Scotland, 1800–1945*. Auckland: Auckland University Press, 2008

Pickles, Katie. *Female Imperialism and National Identity: Imperial Order Daughters of the Empire*, Studies in Imperialism. Manchester: Manchester University Press, 2002

Piggin, Stuart. *Spirit of a Nation: The story of Australia's Christian heritage*. Sydney: Strand Publishing, 2004

———. 'Introduction: The reflex impact of missions on Australian Christianity'. In *This Gospel Shall Be Preached: Essays on the Australian contribution to world mission*, M. Hutchinson and G. Treloar (eds), 7–18. Sydney: Centre for the Study of Australian Christianity, 1998

———. *Making Evangelical Missionaries, 1789–1858: The social background, motives and training of British Protestant missionaries in India*. Abingdon: Sutton Courtenay Press, 1984

———. 'Assessing nineteenth century missionary motivation: Some considerations of theory and method'. In *Religious Motivation: Biographical and sociological problems for the church historian*, Studies in Church History, vol. 15. D. Baker (ed.), 327–37. Oxford: Basil Blackwell, 1978

———. 'Sectarianism versus ecumenism: The impact on British churches of the missionary movement to India, c. 1800–1860'. *Journal of Ecclesiastical History* 27, no. 4 (1976): 387–402

Pocock, J.G.A. *The Discovery of Islands: Essays on British history*. Cambridge: Cambridge University Press, 2005

———. 'Tangata whenua and enlightenment anthropology'. *New Zealand Journal of History* 26, no. 1 (1992): 28–53

Pollock, J.C. *Shadows Fall Apart: The story of the zenana Bible and medical mission*. London: Hodder and Stoughton, 1958

Porter, Andrew. 'Review essay: Evangelical visions and colonial realities'. *Journal of Imperial and Commonwealth History* 38, no. 1 (2010): 145–55

———. *Religion Versus Empire? British Protestant missionaries and overseas expansion, 1700–1914*. Manchester and New York: Manchester University Press, 2004

_____. 'Church history, history of Christianity, religious history: Some reflections on British missionary enterprise since the late eighteenth century'. *Church History* 71, no. 13 (2002): 555–84

_____ (ed.), *The Oxford History of the British Empire, Volume 3: The nineteenth century*. Oxford: Oxford University Press, 1999

_____. '"Cultural imperialism" and Protestant missionary enterprise, 1780–1914'. *Journal of Imperial and Commonwealth History* 25, no. 3 (1997): 367–91

_____. 'Religion and empire: British expansion in the long nineteenth century 1780–1914'. *Journal of Imperial and Commonwealth History* 20, no. 3 (1992): 370–90

_____. 'Evangelical enthusiasm, missionary motivation and West Africa in the late nineteenth century: The career of G.W. Brooke'. *Journal of Imperial and Commonwealth History* 6, no. 1 (1977): 23–46

_____. 'Cambridge, Keswick and late-nineteenth-century attitudes to Africa'. *Journal of Imperial and Commonwealth History* 5, no. 1 (1976): 5–34

Predelli, L.N. 'Sexual control and the remaking of gender: The attempt of nineteenth-century Protestant Norwegian women to export Western domesticity to Madagascar'. *Journal of Women's History* 12, no. 2 (2000): 81–103

Prentis, Malcolm. 'Guthrie Wilson and the trans-Tasman educational career'. *History of Education Review* 42, no. 1 (2013): 69–84

_____. 'Binding or loosing in Australasia: Some trans-Tasman Protestant connections'. *Journal of Religious History* 34, no. 3 (2010): 312–34

Prevost, Elizabeth E. *The Communion of Women: Missions and gender in colonial Africa and the British metropole*. Oxford: Oxford University Press, 2010

_____. 'From African missions to global sisterhood: The Mothers' Union and colonial Christianity, 1900–1930'. In *Empires of Religion*, Hilary M. Carey (ed.), 243–64. Houndmills, Basingstoke: Palgrave Macmillan, 2008

Prochaska, F.K. *Women and Philanthropy in Nineteenth-Century England*. Oxford: Oxford University Press, 1980

_____. 'Little vessels: Children in the late nineteenth century missionary movement'. *Journal of Imperial and Commonwealth History* 6, no. 2 (1978): 103–18

Prochner, Larry, Helen May, and Baljit Kaur. '"The blessings of civilisation": Nineteenth-century missionary schools for young native children in three colonial settings – India, Canada and New Zealand 1820s–1840s'. *Paedagogica Historica* 45, no. 1 (2009): 83–102

Proctor, J.H. 'Scottish missionaries in India: An inquiry into motivation'. *South Asia: Journal of South Asian Studies* 13, no. 1 (1990): 43–61

Puckey, Adrienne. 'Who you know: Māori, missionaries and the economy'. In *Spirit of the Past: Essays on Christianity in New Zealand history*, Geoffrey Troughton and Hugh Morrison (eds), 83–97. Wellington: Victoria University Press, 2011

Rabe, Valentin H. *The Home Base of American China Missions, 1880–1920*.

Cambridge, Massachusetts: Harvard University Press, 1978

Reid, Nicholas. 'A new world through a new youth: The life and death of the Catholic youth movement in New Zealand'. In *Spirit of the Past: Essays on Christianity in New Zealand history*, Geoffrey Troughton and Hugh Morrison (eds), 156–68. Wellington: Victoria University Press, 2011

Reeves-Ellington, Barbara. 'Women, Protestant missions, and American cultural expansion, 1800 to 1938: A historiographical sketch'. *Social Sciences and Missions/Sciences sociales et missions* 24, nos. 2–3 (2011): 190–206

Reeves-Ellington, Barbara, Kathryn Kish Sklar, and Connie A. Shemo (eds). *Competing Kingdoms: Women, mission, nation, and the American Protestant empire, 1812–1960*. Durham and London: Duke University Press, 2010

Robert, Dana. *Christian Mission: How Christianity became a world religion*. Chichester: Wiley-Blackwell, 2009

_____ (ed.) *Converting Colonialism: Visions and realities in mission history, 1706–1914*. Grand Rapids, Michigan, and Cambridge, UK: William B. Eerdmans, 2008

_____. *American Women in Mission: A social history of their thought and practice*. Macon, Georgia: Mercer University Press, 1997

_____. 'From missions to mission to beyond missions: The historiography of American Protestant foreign missions since World War II'. *International Bulletin of Missionary Research* 18, no. 4 (1994): 146–62

_____. '"The crisis of missions": Premillennial mission theory and the origins of independent evangelical missions'. In *Earthen Vessels: American evangelicals and foreign missions, 1880–1980*, J.A. Carpenter and Wilbert Shenk (eds), 29–46. Grand Rapids, Michigan: William Eerdmans, 1990

_____. 'The origin of the Student Volunteer watchword: "The evangelization of the world in this generation"'. *International Bulletin of Missionary Research* 10, no. 4 (1986): 146–49

Robertson, Yvonne. *Girdle Round the Earth: New Zealand Presbyterian women's ideal of universal sisterhood, 1878–1918*. Annual Lecture, Auckland 1993. Dunedin: Presbyterian Historical Society of New Zealand, 1994

Roke, Alf. *They Went Forth: Trials and triumphs of a pioneer SIM missionary in Ethiopia*. Auckland: Alf Roke, 2003

Rooke, Patricia T. 'The "new mechanic" in slave society: Socio-psychological motivations and evangelical missionaries in the British West Indies'. *Journal of Religious History* 11, no. 1 (1980): 77–94

Ross, Andrew. 'Scottish missionary concern 1874–1914: A golden era?' *Scottish Historical Review* 51 (1972): 52–72

Ross, Angus. *New Zealand Aspirations in the Pacific in the Nineteenth Century*. Oxford: Oxford University Press, 1964

Ross, Cathy. *Women with a Mission: Rediscovering missionary wives in early New Zealand*. Auckland: Penguin Books, 2006

Ross, Kenneth R., '"Blessed reflex": Mission as God's spiral of renewal'.

International Bulletin of Missionary Research 27, no. 4 (2003): 162–68

Rowbotham, Judith. '"Soldiers of Christ"? Images of female missionaries in late nineteenth-century Britain: Issues of heroism and martyrdom'. *Gender and History* 12, no. 1 (2000), 82–106

———. '"Hear an Indian sister's plea": Reporting the work of 19th-century British female missionaries'. *Women's Studies International Forum* 21, no. 3 (1998): 247–61.

Roxborogh, John. *Thomas Chalmers: Enthusiast for mission. The Christian good of Scotland and the rise of the missionary movement.* Carlisle, Cumbria: Paternoster Publishing, 1999

Rutherdale, Myra. *Women and the White Man's God: Gender and race in the Canadian mission field.* Vancouver and Toronto: UBC Press, 2002

Ryburn, W.M. *Through Shadow and Sunshine: The history of the Punjab Mission of the Presbyterian Church of New Zealand, 1909–1959.* Christchurch: Presbyterian Bookroom, 1961

Said, Edward. *Orientalism.* New York: Vintage Books, 1979

———. *Culture and Imperialism.* London: Vintage, 1994

Salesa, Damon. *Racial Crossings: Race, intermarriage, and the Victorian British Empire.* Oxford: Oxford University Press, 2011

———. 'New Zealand's Pacific'. In *The New Oxford History of New Zealand,* Giselle Byrnes (ed.), 149–72. Oxford and Melbourne: Oxford University Press, 2009

Salmond, J.A. 'New Zealand and the New Hebrides'. In *The Feel of Truth: Essays in New Zealand and Pacific history,* Peter Munz (ed.), 113–35. Wellington: A.H. & A.W. Reed, 1969

Salmond, J.D. *By Love Serve: The story of the Order of the Deaconesses of the Presbyterian Church of N.Z.* Christchurch: Presbyterian Bookroom, 1962

Samson, Jane. *Imperial Benevolence: Making British authority in the Pacific Islands.* Honolulu: University of Hawaii, 1998

Sanders, J. Oswald. *Expanding Horizons: The story of the New Zealand Bible Training Institute.* Auckland: Institute Press, 1971

Sanneh, Lamin and Grant Wacker, 'Christianity appropriated: Conversion and the intercultural process'. *Church History* 68, no. 4 (1999): 954–61

Savage, Murray J. *Forward into Freedom: Associated Churches of Christ in New Zealand missionary outreach, 1949–1979.* Nelson: Associated Churches of Christ Overseas Missionary Department, 1980

Schoepflin, Rennie B. 'Making doctors and nurses for Jesus: Medical missionary stories and American children'. *Church History* 74, no. 3 (2005): 557–90

Semple, Rhonda A. *Missionary Women: Gender, professionalism, and the Victorian idea of Christian mission.* Woodbridge, Suffolk, and Rochester, NY: Boydell Press, 2003

———. '"The conversion and highest welfare of each pupil": The work of the China Inland Mission at Chefoo'. *The Journal of Imperial and Commonwealth*

History 31, no. 1 (2003): 29–50

Seton, R. *Western Daughters in Eastern Lands: British missionary women in Asia.*
Santa Barbara: Praeger, 2013

_____. '"Open doors for female labourers": Women candidates of the London
Missionary Society, 1875–1914'. In *Missionary Encounters: Sources and issues,*
R.A. Bickers and R. Seton (eds), 50–69. Richmond, Surrey: Curzon Press,
1996

Sharkey, Heather J. *Cultural Conversions: Unexpected consequences of Christian
missionary encounters in the Middle East, Africa, and South Asia.* Syracuse, NY:
Syracuse University Press, 2013

Shenk, Wilbert (ed.) *North American Foreign Missions, 1810–1914: Theology,
theory, and policy.* Grand Rapids, Michigan, and Cambridge, UK: William B.
Eerdmans, 2004

Simpson, Jane, 'Women, religion and society in New Zealand: A literature
review'. *Journal of Religious History* 18, no. 2 (1994): 198–218

_____. 'Joseph W. Kemp: Prime interpreter of American fundamentalism in
New Zealand in the 1920s'. In *'Rescue The Perishing': Comparative perspectives
on evangelism and revivalism,* Douglas Pratt (ed.), 23–41. Auckland: College
Communications, 1989

Sivasundaram, Sujit. *Islanded: Britain, Sri Lanka & the bounds of an Indian Ocean
colony.* Chicago and London: University of Chicago Press, 2013

Stanley, Brian. 'From "the poor heathen" to "the glory and honour of all nations":
Vocabularies of race and custom in Protestant missions, 1844–1928'.
International Bulletin of Missionary Research , no. 1 (2010): 3–10

_____. *The World Missionary Conference, Edinburgh 1910.* Grand Rapids,
Michigan, and Cambridge, UK: William B. Eerdmans, 2009

_____. '"Missionary regiments for Immanuel's service": Juvenile missionary
organizations in English Sunday schools, 1841–1865'. In *The Church and
Childhood,* Diana Wood (ed.), 391–403. Oxford: Blackwell Publishers, 1994

_____. *The Bible and the Flag: Protestant missions and British imperialism in the
nineteenth and twentieth centuries.* Leicester: Apollos, 1990

Stearns, Peter N. 'Challenges in the history of childhood'. *Journal of the History of
Childhood and Youth* 1, no. 1 (2008): 35–42

_____. *Childhood in World History.* New York and London: Routledge, 2006

Stenhouse, John. 'The controversy over the recognition of religious factors in
New Zealand history: Some reflections'. In *The Spirit of the Past: Essays on
Christianity in New Zealand history,* Geoffrey Troughton and Hugh Morrison
(eds), 43–54. Wellington: Victoria University Press, 2011

_____. 'Religion and society'. In *The New Oxford History of New Zealand,*
Giselle Byrnes (ed.), 323–56. Oxford and Melbourne: Oxford University
Press, 2009

_____. 'Christianity, gender, and the working class in southern Dunedin,
1880–1940'. *Journal of Religious History* 30, no. 1 (2006): 18–44

———. 'God's own silence: Secular nationalism, Christianity and the writing of New Zealand history'. *New Zealand Journal of History* 38, no. 1 (2004): 52–71

———. 'God, the Devil, and gender'. In *Sites of Gender: Women, men and modernity in southern Dunedin, 1890–1939*, Barbara Brookes, Annabel Cooper and Robyn Law (eds), 313–47. Auckland: Auckland University Press, 2003

Stenhouse, John, and Jane Thomson (eds). *Building God's Own Country: Historical essays on religions in New Zealand.* Dunedin: University of Otago Press, 2004

Stoler, Ann Laurer. *Carnal Knowledge and Imperial Power: Race and the intimate in colonial rule.* Berkeley and Los Angeles: University of California Press, 2002

Strobel, Margaret. *European Women and the Second British Empire.* Bloomington: Indiana University Press, 1991

Stuart, John. 'Introduction: Mission and empire'. *Social Sciences and Missions/ Sciences sociales et missions* 21, no. 1 (2008): 1–5

Sutherland, Martin. *Conflict and Connection: Baptist identity in New Zealand.* Auckland: Archer Press, 2011

———. '"Better to Ignore the Past": New Zealand Baptists, scandal, and historical memory'. *Fides et Historia* 36, no. 1 (2004): 47–51

——— (ed.) *Baptists in Colonial New Zealand: Documents illustrating Baptist life and development.* Auckland: New Zealand Baptist Research and Historical Society, 2002

———, 'Seeking a turangawaewae: Constructing a Baptist identity in New Zealand'. *Baptist History and Heritage* 36 (Winter/Spring 2001): 232–50

Svelmoe, William. 'Faith Missions'. In *Encyclopedia of Mission and Missionaries*, Jonathan J. Bonk (ed.), 155–57. New York and London: Routledge, 2007.

Te Paa, J.P. 'Māori and the Melanesian Mission: Two "sees" or oceans apart?' In *The Church of Melanesia 1849–1999*, Allan K. Davidson (ed.), 143–59. Auckland: The College of St John the Evangelist, 2000

Tennant, Margaret, 'Sisterly ministrations. The social work of Protestant deaconesses in New Zealand 1890–1940'. *New Zealand Journal of History* 32, no. 1 (1998): 3–22

Thomas, Nicholas. *Colonialism's Culture: Anthropology, travel and government.* Cambridge, UK: Polity Press in association with Blackwell Publishers, 1994

———. 'Colonial conversions: Difference, hierarchy, and history in early twentieth-century evangelical propaganda'. *Comparative Studies in Society and History* 34, no. 2 (1992): 366–89

Thorne, Susan. 'Religion and empire at home'. In *At Home with the Empire: Metropolitan culture and the imperial world,* Catherine Hall and Sonya Rose (eds), 143–65. Cambridge: Cambridge University Press, 2006

———. *Congregational Missions and the Making of an Imperial Culture in*

Nineteenth-century England. Stanford, Ca.: Stanford University Press, 1999

Thorns, David and Charles Sedgewick. *Understanding Aotearoa/New Zealand: Historical statistics.* Palmerston North: Dunmore Press, 1997

Tonson, Paul. *A Handful of Grain: The centenary history of the Baptist Union of New Zealand, Volume 1 – 1851–1882.* Wellington: The New Zealand Baptist Historical Society, 1982

Trew, George (ed.) *Looking Back, Forging Ahead: A century of participation in overseas mission by New Zealand Brethren Assemblies.* 1st edn. Palmerston North: Missionary Services New Zealand, 1996

Troughton, Geoffrey. *New Zealand Jesus: Social and religious transformations of an image, 1890–1940.* Bern, Switzerland, and New York: Peter Lang, 2011

_____. 'Between the wars, 1919–1940'. In *Living Legacy: A history of the Anglican diocese of Auckland,* Allan K. Davidson (ed.), 178–206. Auckland: Anglican Diocese of Auckland, 2011

_____. 'Richard Booth and Gospel temperance revivalism'. In *Spirit of the Past: Essays on Christianity in New Zealand history,* Geoffrey Troughton and Hugh Morrison (eds), 112–25. Wellington: Victoria University Press, 2011

_____. 'Religion, churches and childhood in New Zealand, c. 1900–1940'. *New Zealand Journal of History* 40, no. 1 (2006): 39–56

Troughton, Geoffrey, and Hugh Morrison (eds). *Spirit of the Past: Essays on Christianity in New Zealand history.* Wellington: Victoria University Press, 2011

Tucker, Ruth. *From Jerusalem to Irian Jaya: A biographical history of Christian missions.* Grand Rapids, Michigan: Zondervan, 1983

Twells, Alison. *The Civilising Mission and the English Middle Class, 1792–1850: The 'heathen' at home and overseas.* New York: Palgrave Macmillan, 2008

Tyrrell, Ian. 'Making nations/making states: American historians in the context of empire'. *Journal of American History* 86, no. 3 (1999): 1015–44

_____. 'American exceptionalism in an age of international history'. *American Historical Review* 96, no. 4 (1991): 1031–55

Vallgårda , Karen A.A. *Imperial Childhoods and Christian Mission: Education and emotions in South India and Denmark.* Palgrave Studies in the History of Childhood. Houndmills, Basingstoke: Palgrave Macmillan, 2015

Van den Berg, Johannes. *Constrained by Jesus' Love: An inquiry into the motives of the missionary awakening in Great Britain in the period between 1698 and 1815.* Kampen: J.H. Kok, 1956

Van der Krogt, Christopher J. '"The evils of mixed marriages": Catholic teaching and practice'. In *Spirit of the Past: Essays on Christianity in New Zealand history,* Geoffrey Troughton and Hugh Morrison (eds), 142–55. Wellington: Victoria University Press, 2011

Vicinus, Martha. *Independent Women: Work and community for single women, 1850–1920.* London: Virago Press, 1980

Walls, Andrew. *The Cross-Cultural Process in Christian History.* Maryknoll, New York: Orbis Books, 2002

_____. *The Missionary Movement in Christian History: Studies in the transmission of faith*. Maryknoll, New York: Orbis Books, 1996

Walls, Andrew, and Cathy Ross (eds). *Mission in the 21st Century: Exploring the five marks of global mission*. Maryknoll, New York: Orbis Books, 2008

Ward, Kevin, and Brian Stanley (eds). *The Church Mission Society and World Christianity, 1799–1999*. Grand Rapids, Michigan, and Cambridge, UK: William B. Eerdmans, and Richmond, Surrey, UK: Curzon Press, 2000

Warren, Max. *The Missionary Movement from Britain in Modern History*. London: SCM Press, 1965

Welch, Pamela. 'Constructing colonial Christianities: With particular reference to Anglicanism in Australia, ca 1850–1940'. *Journal of Religious History* 32, no. 2 (2008): 234–55

White, Ann. 'Counting the cost of faith: America's early female missionaries'. *Church History* 57, no. 1 (1988): 19–30

Whitman, Darrell. 'Inglis, John. In *Biographical Dictionary of Christian Missions*, G.H. Anderson (ed.), 318. New York: MacMillan Reference USA, 1998

Williams, C.P. '"The missing link": The recruitment of women missionaries in some English evangelical missionary societies in the nineteenth century'. In *Women and Missions: Past and present, anthropological and historical perspectives*, F. Bowie, D. Kirkwood and S. Ardener (eds), 43–69. Providence & Oxford: Berg Publishers, 1993

_____. '"Not quite gentlemen": An examination of "middling class" Protestant missionaries from Britain, c. 1850–1900'. *Journal of Ecclesiastical History* 31, no. 3 (1980): 301–15.

Wood, Diana (ed.) *The Church and Childhood*. Vol. 31, Studies in Church History. Oxford: Blackwell, 1994

Yates, Timothy. *The Conversion of the Māori: Years of religious and social change, 1814–1842*. Studies in the History of Christian Missions. Grand Rapids, MI, and Cambridge, UK: William B. Eerdmans, 2013

_____. *Christian Mission in the Twentieth Century*. Cambridge: Cambridge University Press, 1994

Unpublished

Bateman, Grace. 'Signs and graces: Remembering religion in childhood in southern Dunedin, 1920–1950'. PhD thesis, University of Otago, 2014

Beniston, Daphne. 'New Zealand women of the Methodist Solomons Mission 1922–1992'. MA thesis, University of Auckland, 1992

Brooke, Jonathan. 'Providentialist nationalism and juvenile mission literature, 1840–1870'. Henry Martyn Centre Research Seminars, Westminster College, Cambridge, 2006: http://henrymartyn.dns-systems.net/media/documents/

Clark, Wendy. 'A truly Christian spirit? Christchurch and the Melanesian Mission, 1869–1875'. MA thesis, University of Otago, 1966

Coleman, Sarah C. '"Come over and help us": White women, reform and the missionary endeavour in India, 1876–1920'. MA thesis, University of Canterbury, 2002

Dow, Derek A. 'Domestic response and reaction to the foreign missionary enterprise of the principal Scottish Presbyterian churches, 1873–1929'. PhD thesis, University of Edinburgh, 1977

Early, Lisa. '"If we win the women": The lives and work of Methodist missionary women in the Solomon Islands, 1902–1942'. PhD thesis, University of Otago, 1998

Gillett, Rachel. 'Helpmeets and handmaidens: The role of women in mission discourse'. BA(Hons) dissertation, University of Otago, 1998

Gilling, Bryan. 'Retelling the old, old story: A study of the six mass evangelistic missions in twentieth century New Zealand'. PhD thesis, University of Waikato, 1990

Hitchen, John. '"Training tamate": Formation of the nineteenth century missionary worldview'. PhD Thesis, University of Aberdeen, 1984

Johnston, E. '"Cannibals for Christ": Oscar Michelsen Presbyterian missionary in the New Hebrides, 1878–1932'. MA thesis, University of Auckland, 1995

Kaa, Hirini. '"Te wiwi nati": The cultural economy of Ngāti Porou, 1926–1939'. MA thesis, University of Auckland, 2000

Keen, David. '"Feeding the lambs": The influence of Sunday schools on the socialization of children in Otago and Southland, 1848–1901'. PhD thesis, University of Otago, 1999

Lineham, Peter J. 'Missionary motivation in New Zealand'. In New Zealand Association of Mission Studies Conference 2000 (Collected Papers). Auckland, November 2000

McKay, Jolene. '"The tie that binds": Christianity in the New Zealand Women's Christian Temperance Union, 1895–1900'. BA(Hons) dissertation, University of Otago, 1995

Marshall, V.L. 'The policy of the foreign missions committee of the Synod of Otago and Southland in relation to the New Hebrides, 1867–1901'. MA thesis, University of Otago, 1967

Morrison, Hugh. '"It is our bounden duty": The emergence of the New Zealand Protestant missionary movement, 1868–1926'. PhD thesis, Massey University, 2004

———. 'The keeper of paradise: Quarantine as a measure of communicable disease control in late nineteenth-century New Zealand'. BA(Hons) dissertation, University of Otago, 1981

Parsonson, Gordon. 'Early Protestant missions in the New Hebrides, 1839–1861'. MA thesis, University of Otago, 1941

Potter, Sarah. 'The social origins and recruitment of English Protestant missionaries in the nineteenth century'. PhD thesis, University of London, 1974

Rixon, Diane. 'New Zealand mission and nationalism in the Punjab: The missionaries of the Presbyterian Church of New Zealand in the Punjab and their encounter with Indian nationalism between 1910 and 1932'. BA(Hons) dissertation, University of Otago, 1997

Roberts, R.L. 'The growth of the inter-denominational mission societies in New Zealand'. MA dissertation, University of Auckland, 1977

Ross, Catharine. 'More than wives? A study of four Church Missionary Society wives in nineteenth century New Zealand'. PhD thesis, University of Auckland, 2003

Stanton, G.N. 'The bishop of Dunedin, the Anglican Church and Polynesia'. BA(Hons) dissertation, University of Otago, 1961

Simpson, E.P.Y. 'A history of the New Zealand Baptist Missionary Society, 1885–1947'. MA thesis, University of Canterbury, 1948

Soutar, Monty. 'Ngāti Porou leadership : Rāpata Wahawaha and the politics of conflict : "Kei te ora nei hoki tātou, me tō tātou whenua"'. PhD thesis, Massey University, 2000.

Stanley, Brian. 'Home support for foreign missions in early Victorian England c. 1838–1873'. PhD thesis, Cambridge University, 1979

Sutton, P.E. 'The New Zealand Student Christian Movement, 1896–1936'. MA thesis, Victoria University College, 1946

Troughton, Geoffrey. 'Christianity and community: Aspects of religious life and attitudes in the Wanganui–Manawatu Region, 1870–1885'. MA thesis, Massey University, 1995

Voisey, Anita Renee. 'New Zealand women missionaries to China, 1891–1954'. MA thesis, Victoria University of Wellington, 2006

Welch, Christina. 'Educating the empire's wards: Training the children of colonized people'. Unpublished paper from Empires of Religion Conference. University College Dublin, June 2006 [used with permission]

Welch, Ian. 'Poona (Pune) and Indian Village Mission (PIVM)', Working Paper, August 2014: https://digitalcollections.anu.edu.au/bitstream/1885/13041/1/Welch%20Poona%202014.pdf

Whitelaw, Brooke. 'A message for the missahibs: New Zealand Presbyterian missionaries in the Punjab, 1910–1940'. MA thesis, University of Otago, 2001

Yuan, Sylvia Yang. '"Kiwis" in the Middle Kingdom: A sociological interpretation of the history of New Zealand missionaries in China from 1877 to 1952 and beyond'. PhD thesis, Massey University (Albany), 2013

INDEX